Dear Parents and Educators,

Welcome to Penguin Young Readers! As parents and educators, you know that each child develops at his or her own pace—in terms of speech, critical thinking, and, of course, reading. Penguin Young Readers recognizes this fact. As a result, each Penguin Young Readers book is assigned a traditional easy-to-read level (1–4) as well as a Guided Reading Level (A–P). Both of these systems will help you choose the right book for your child. Please refer to the back of each book for specific leveling information. Penguin Young Readers features esteemed authors and illustrators, stories about favorite characters, fascinating nonfiction, and more!

In the Forest

LEVEL 1
GUIDED READING LEVEL A

This book is perfect for an **Emergent Reader** who:
- can read in a left-to-right and top-to-bottom progression;
- can recognize some beginning and ending letter sounds;
- can use picture clues to help tell the story; and
- can understand the basic plot and sequence of simple stories.

Here are some **activities** you can do during and after reading this book:
- **Make Connections**: The three sections in this book name different plants, animals, and objects that are in the forest. Take a look at each section and brainstorm other things you might see there. For fun, have the child draw a picture of these objects or animals.
- **Word Repetition**: Reread the story and count how many times you come across the following words: *forest, in, grow, live, what*. On a separate sheet of paper, work with the child to write a new sentence for each word. Use the animals and objects brainstormed in the first activity in your new sentences!

Remember, sharing the love of reading with a child is the best gift you can give!

—Bonnie Bader, EdM
   Penguin Young Readers program

*Penguin Young Readers are leveled by independent reviewers applying the standards developed by Irene Fountas and Gay Su Pinnell in *Matching Books to Readers: Using Leveled Books in Guided Reading*, Heinemann, 1999.

To my dad, who showed me the beauty and serenity of being in the forest. And to the Black Hills National Forest, which never ceases to awe and inspire me—CK

Penguin Young Readers
Published by the Penguin Group
Penguin Group (USA) Inc., 375 Hudson Street, New York, New York 10014, USA
Penguin Group (Canada), 90 Eglinton Avenue East, Suite 700, Toronto, Ontario M4P 2Y3, Canada
(a division of Pearson Penguin Canada Inc.)

Penguin Books Ltd, Registered Offices: 80 Strand, London WC2R 0RL, England

Photo credits: cover: (sun) © Comstock/Thinkstock, (racoon, second tree) © iStockphoto/Thinkstock, (first tree, third tree, fourth tree, river) © Hemera/Thinkstock; cover, page 3: (fawn, flower) © iStockphoto/Thinkstock; page 5: (bears, grass) © iStockphoto/Thinkstock; pages 6–13,16–23, 26–32: (second tree) © iStockphoto/Thinkstock, (first tree, third tree, fourth tree) © Hemera/Thinkstock; page 6: (squirrels, stump) © iStockphoto/Thinkstock; page 7: (bears) © iStockphoto/Thinkstock; page 8: (moose, grass) © iStockphoto/Thinkstock; page 9: (blue jay, cardinal, robin, branches) © iStockphoto/Thinkstock; page 10: (doe, fawn) © iStockphoto/Thinkstock, (buck) © Hemera/Thinkstock; page 11: (top racoon) © iStockphoto/Thinkstock, (bottom racoon) © Hemera/Thinkstock; page 12: (monarch butterfly on left, monarch butterfly on pink flower) © Hemera/Thinkstock, (all other butterflies, orange flower) © iStockphoto/Thinkstock; page 13: (top skunk) © iStockphoto/Thinkstock, (bottom skunk) © Hemera/Thinkstock; page 15: (mushroom, pinecones, acorns) © iStockphoto/Thinkstock; page 16: (wildflowers) © iStockphoto/Thinkstock; page 17: (acorns) © iStockphoto/Thinkstock; page 18: (pinecones on branch) © Zoonar/Thinkstock, (all other pinecones) © iStockphoto/Thinkstock; page 19: (blueberries, strawberries) © iStockphoto/Thinkstock; page 20: (dark green leaves) © Brand X Pictures/Thinkstock, (light green leaves) © iStockphoto/Thinkstock; page 21: (mushrooms) © iStockphoto/Thinkstock; page 22: (nuts) © iStockphoto/Thinkstock; page 23: (top grass) © iStockphoto/Thinkstock, (bottom grass) © Hemera/Thinkstock; page 25: (nest with eggs) © iStockphoto/Thinkstock; page 26: (top beehive, bees) © iStockphoto/Thinkstock, (bottom beehive) © Hemera/Thinkstock; page 27: (rocks) © iStockphoto/Thinkstock; page 28: (roots) © Hemera/Thinkstock; page 29: (rivers) © Hemera/Thinkstock; page 30: (top nest) © iStockphoto/Thinkstock, (birds and nest) © Top Photo Group/Thinkstock; page 31: (logs) © iStockphoto/Thinkstock; page 32: (sun) © Comstock/Thinkstock.

Library of Congress Cataloging-in-Publication Data is available.

ISBN 978-0-448-46719-1 (pbk)   10 9 8 7
ISBN 978-0-448-46720-7 (hc)   10 9 8 7 6 5 4 3 2 1

ALWAYS LEARNING   PEARSON

PENGUIN YOUNG READERS

LEVEL

EMERGENT READER

1

In the Forest

by Alexa Andrews
illustrated by Candice Keimig
and with photographs

Penguin Young Readers
An Imprint of Penguin Group (USA) Inc.

See What Lives
in the Forest

Squirrels live in the forest.

Bears live in the forest.

Moose live in the forest.

Birds live in the forest.

Deer live in the forest.

Raccoons live in the forest.

Butterflies live in the forest.

Skunks live in the forest.

See What Grows
in the Forest

Flowers grow in the forest.

Acorns grow in the forest.

Pinecones grow in the forest.

Berries grow in the forest.

Leaves grow in the forest.

Mushrooms grow in the forest.

Nuts grow in the forest.

Grass grows in the forest.

See What Is
in the Forest

Beehives are in the forest.

Rocks are in the forest.

Roots are in the forest.

Rivers are in the forest.

Nests are in the forest.

Logs are in the forest.

Trees are in the forest.

Christian Vocations

marriage

religious life

priesthood

single life

Harcourt Religion Publishers

MICHELE McCARTY

Our Mission

The primary mission of Harcourt Religion Publishers
is to provide the Catholic and Christian educational
markets with the highest quality catechetical print and
media resources. The content of these resources
reflects the best insights of current theology,
methodology, and pedagogical research. The
resources are practical and easy to use, designed
to meet expressed market needs, and written
to reflect the teachings of the Catholic Church.

Nihil Obstat
Very Rev. Jerome A. Carosella, Chancellor

Imprimatur
✠ John J. Nevins D.D.
Bishop of Venice in Florida
July 7, 1999

The Imprimatur is an official declaration that a book or pamphlet is free of doctrinal or moral error. No
implication is contained therein that anyone who granted the Imprimatur agrees with the contents,
opinions, or statements expressed.

Theological Consultant—Rev. Charles Angell SA

Rev. Charles Angell SA, STD, is a Franciscan Friar of the Atonement of Graymoor, Garrison, NY, where
he is currently chaplain of St. Christopher's Inn, a shelter for homeless men. He is a former professor of
ecumenical theology at the Pontifical University of Saint Thomas Aquinas, Rome, where he also received
his Doctorate of Sacred Theology in 1983.

Printed in the United States of America
ISBN 0-15-950712-X

10   9   8   7

CONTENTS

CHAPTER 11

The Challenges of Married Life 238

CHAPTER 12

Family Life 272

PHOTO CREDITS

AP/ Wide World Photos—60; **Art Resource, NY**—218, Eric Lessing; **Comstock Stock Photography**—48, 95, 188, 203; **FPG, Int'l**—78, Tony Anderson; 65, Jeff Baker; 8, Josef Beck; 17, Burgess Blevins; 114, Jon Bradley; 14, 122, Ron Chapple; 10, 49, 82, 100, 323, Jim Cummins; 13, 68, Jean P. DeLa Forest; 93, Rob Gage; 29, Spencer Grant; 31, Mark Harmel; 51, 81, 148, Michael Krasowitz; 57, Richard Laird; 276, Kevin Laubacher; 66, 152, 317, Dick Luria; 62, Chris Michaels; 285, O'Brien & Mayor Photography; 110, Barbara Peacock; 204, Photomondo; 12, 151, 235, Stephanie Rousser; 75, Al Satterwhite; 220, Elizabeth Simpson; 56, 131, Stephen Simpson; 91, 101, 221, 255, 257, 315, 322, Telegraph Colour Library; 108, 207, Arthur Tilley; 39, 106, John Terence Turner; 32, 124, 146, 189, 265, 268, 296, VCG; **Jim France**—173; **Robert Fried**—116; Dianne Griffin—311; **Monkmeyer**—326, Grantpix; **Chip and Rosa Maria de la Cueva Peterson**—2, 117; **PhotoEdit**—213; **Gene Plaisted/The Crosiers**—163, 215, 216, 217; **Photo Researcher, Inc.**—314, Phillip Rayson; **Tony Stone Images**—141, 242, 292, 314, Bruce Ayres; 275, Elie Bernager; 114, Jon Bradley; 324, Peter Cade; 172, Myrleen Cate; 119, 224, Stewart Cohen; 290, Nicholas DeVore; 44, James Darell; 297, Patricia Doyle; 129, Laurence Dutton; 208, Fisher/Thatcher; 295, John Fortunato; 245, Charles Gupton; 187, David Hanover; 306, Chip Henderson; 205, 246, Walter Hodges; 144, Mark Harmel; 194, 232, Kaluzny/Thatcher; 147, Robert A. Mitchel; 251, Laurence Monneret; 240, Donald Nausbaum; 260, Ian O'Leary; 287, Peter Paulides; 46, 334, Lori Adamski Peek;113, Greg Pease; 300, Jake Rajs; 120, Rick Rusing; 277, Mark Segal; 153, 273, Timothy Shonnard; 143, Frank Siteman; 1, Jamey Stillings; 135, Tom Stock; 58, Charles Thatcher; 325, Bob Thomas; 139, 328, Penny Tweedie; 282, Nick Vedros/Vedros & Assoc.; 267, Susan Werner; 137, Ken Whitmore; 280, J.P. Williams; 27, David Young Wolff; **James L. Shaffer**—7, 18, 23, 28, 53, 67, 71, 125, 154, 155, 156, 170, 174, 176, 179, 180, 182, 183, 184, 191, 193, 196, 229, 234, 236, 250, 253, 262, 263, 298, 299, 311, 312, 332, 333; **SuperStock**—314; **Bob West**—227; **Whitmer Photography**—11, 150, 168, 239, 264, 302, 248; **Bill Wittman**—3, 20, 21, 24, 35, 54, 59, 87, 105, 118, 158, 165, 167, 178, 181, 198, 223, 228, 231, 252, 274, 278, 321, 331

Illustrations

Kirk Barron
Cathy Guisewite (CATHY)

CHAPTER 1

FINDING YOUR PATH IN LIFE

SCRIPTURE

Beloved, let us love one another, because love is from God;
everyone who loves is born of God and knows God.
Whoever does not love does not know God, for God is love.

1 JOHN 4:7–8

PRAYER

God of love,
As I get ready to begin life on my own,
   I must make so many major choices.
For a long time, I've wanted to be in charge of me.
I've looked forward to making my own decisions
   and taking responsibility for my life.
But pretty soon I'll have to live with those choices
   —and some of them will help shape my whole life!
You have created me out of love, and you call me to love.
Help me respond by making the best choices for my future.
Thank you for the talents you have given me.
Guide me to use them well in serving you and others.

Finding your way

As you prepare to finish high school, are you tired yet of hearing, "What are you going to do with your life?" Maybe you think, "If only I knew!" It's a challenging, exciting time—and somewhat scary.

Since so many important life choices lie ahead of you, wouldn't it help to have a road map of the best directions to go? A television ad series shows young adults listening to advice from their "older-wiser selves" about which future choices to make—and avoid:

FROM A TELEVISION ADVERTISEMENT FOR MUTUAL OF NEW YORK INSURANCE COMPANY

Activity

1. Write down insights you wish you'd had **before** you entered high school about
   - making friends, being a good friend
   - getting along with parents and teachers
   - growing closer to God
   - assuming responsibility
   - managing your time
   - doing well in your studies
   - coping with and solving problems
   - staying out of trouble
   - making the most of your high school years

2. Share your responses with the class. Compile the best ones into a booklet and obtain approval to distribute it to the younger students at your school. (Or perhaps sell it, giving the proceeds to a local charity.)

For discussion

1. What questions do you wish you could ask your older-wiser future self?

2. What value do you see in learning from others' wisdom about major life choices and relationships?

- What does your life mean?
- How can you determine what paths to take in life?
- How can you tell which vocation and occupation to choose?
- How can you discover the best type of education or training to pursue?
- Once you're on your own, how do you want to live?
- Haven't you wondered why so many relationships fail? Why so many marriages end in divorce?
- Wouldn't you like to know how to avoid such pitfalls in your future?

If your older-wiser future self could counsel you about your major life choices, it would certainly simplify your decision making! But life doesn't work that way. During this course, however, you will be able to consider what millions of others have learned about loving and living. You'll study the wisdom that, with God's guidance, has come to us through centuries of human experience and Christian tradition. This wisdom can guide you in discerning your paths in life and in making your most important relationships and commitments succeed.

Only love lasts forever.

POPE JOHN PAUL II

Life choices

Most of you will eventually marry; each of you will be single for at least a time. Many of you will raise children. All of you will experience special close relationships, choose an occupation, and adopt a certain style of living. To make such choices wisely and live them lovingly, you first need to understand what each life-choice means and involves.

The rest of this chapter will focus on discerning your purpose and direction in life and on practical aspects of your ministry and lifestyle. The next few chapters will explore love and communication, which are essential to every way of life. The remainder of this text will consider each main vocation choice—the single life, the consecrated and ordained lives, and, marriage and family life. Throughout the course, you will discuss what has helped others prepare for and live their vocations successfully. Only you, with God's help, can create your loving, happy, fulfilling future.

Meaning in life—your main purpose and mission: *why* you are here

Vocation—your *calling* and *commitment* to a specific way of life

Ministry—your *occupation* and *the other ways you regularly reach out* to help others

Lifestyle—how you *structure* your life according to your *values* and *priorities*

Activity

1. Read this book's contents pages.
2. Briefly list or describe what you hope to learn during this course.
3. Write down questions you would like to have addressed about the course topics.

For discussion

1. How do you feel when others ask what you're planning to do with your life? How do you respond?
2. What main choices and challenges do you face in preparing to live on your own? What are your biggest concerns and fears about this?

Why you are here

Where do you look for meaning in life? Those who've sought it in fame, money, or material goods have failed to find fulfillment. Your heart's deepest longings tell you that you're meant for much, much more.

God is your ultimate destination and fulfillment. Your life and the lives of all people begin and end in the mystery of God's love. God has given you life, sustains you in existence, and calls you to fulfill a purpose here. Your life has meaning only in relation to God. You and God can never become completely unattached: God is your beginning, your life's meaning, and your final goal. Your main purpose in life is to know, love, and forever be happy with God—and with others in God's love.

God's love makes human relationships and achievements possible: We can love because God has first loved us (see 1 John 4:19). Our material world reflects God's love, but does so imperfectly. Only God's heart can contain and return all your love completely and perfectly. Only God can help you realize your greatest potential and your deepest dreams. You'll find your purpose in life only in relationship to God.

Do you ever wonder, though, what God sees in you? As God's child you reflect God's own being. You are special and valuable: You alone can love God as you do, and you alone can make your unique contribution in others' lives. God has created you to live here and now for a special reason. You have a unique role in all of human history that only you can fulfill!

You won't always understand just where a specific path in life is taking you—or whether you're even on the right road! While muddling through daily trials and tangles, sometimes you'll feel lost and think your efforts are worthless, going nowhere. Especially at such times, don't lose sight of your overall purpose. Take things a step at a time and realize that whatever path you walk in life, God will always be walking with you. You're never, ever alone.

For what **person** is there who would wish to be surrounded by **unlimited** wealth and to **abound** in every material **blessing**, on condition that the person love—and be **loved** by—no one?

ADAPTED FROM MARCUS TULLIUS CICERO.

Journal entry

1. Describe how you are uniquely special to God and others.
2. Describe a time when you felt lost in life or as if your efforts were useless. Explain how you got back on track.
3. Write down one thing you will do to increase your everyday joy in living.

Activity

Give an example of a song that questions what life really means and an example of a song that proposes to answer that question. Explain whether the answer seems correct or incorrect in view of how you see your real purpose in life.

Project

Interview four adults, asking them how they discovered the real meaning of their lives. Write a two-page report describing and commenting on your findings.

For discussion

1. Describe someone you've met who seems truly happy. What do you think explains that person's happiness and fulfillment in life?
2. Describe a time when something prompted you to realize that there must be something more—an ultimate happiness, or a higher purpose.
3. Why does the question of what life means inevitably lead to God? How do you view your main purpose in life?
4. Why is who you are more important than what you do in life?
5. Why is joy one sign that someone is living his or her real meaning and purpose in life? Describe people you know—including other teenagers—who exhibit such joy in living. Do you feel this joy in your life now?

The power of love

Nothing is so important and powerful as love. It's the cornerstone and glue of human civilization. With love people build community and enemies are reconciled; people experience hope and happiness; people thrive and grow. Without love, little else has meaning; the human spirit dies.

Some abused children huddle in a corner when anyone approaches. Others try to tear the hair and eyes out of anyone who comes close. These children can't verbalize why they're so fearful or angry, but they may rip apart a doll to express their feelings. Though only a few years old, these children are severely emotionally damaged—because they've been denied love.

Love is a basic human need. Love is more important to your spirit than hamburgers, your room at home, and jeans are to your physical well-being. Loneliness is painful. We need love to survive spiritually, emotionally, and physically. We need love to live in peace and end hostilities. Refusing to love is deadly and destructive:

We know that we have passed from death to life because we love one another. Whoever does not love abides in death.

1 JOHN 3:14

Being loved energizes us to love. Have you met people who seem cold and indifferent, who lack warmth and vitality? When snubbed or put down, haven't you felt like not caring? But when someone compliments you or smiles at you—when you feel loved, aren't you friendlier and more generous? Feeling loved or unloved changes our outlook; it affects our behavior as well as our happiness.

Strengthened by love, a woman lifted an automobile to free her trapped children. Winning athletes acknowledge how God's love and other people's support have helped them surmount obstacles. Loving concern gives the firefighter courage to brave the flames and rescue stranded citizens. Such unselfish love always reflects God's tremendous love for us:

For God so loved the world that he gave his only Son, so that everyone who believes in him may not perish but may have eternal life.

JOHN 3:16

Love is the most powerful, creative force. Love touches and lifts the human spirit and brings unity, harmony, and peace. Out of love, starving concentration camp prisoners during World War II shared their food with others. Love explains why countless individuals have sacrificed their lives so that the rest of us might live in freedom. History's most influential figures haven't been the warriors and rulers, but the lovers: the prophets of Israel, Jesus, the Buddha, Francis of Assisi, Mahatma Gandhi, Martin Luther King Jr., Mother Teresa of Calcutta. Their love continues to inspire us:

Love is a gracious, radiating energy.

TEILHARD DE CHARDIN

Love is why we are here. We need to receive and give love. Studies have found that the peace—or fear—dying persons experience is directly related to whether they've experienced love, received and given, and tried to be of service to others. If so, they're at peace about dying. Otherwise, they feel unfulfilled and afraid.

God loves us totally and perfectly; we, in turn, must always try to love better—as Jesus taught us. The answer to the question, "What does it all mean?" is love—and the service to others that flows from love.

Journal entry

Briefly describe a relationship that made you feel better about yourself.

Journal activity

Imagine that you have only a short time to live. List the things that have **really** mattered. Share at least one of these with the group.

Activity

Write a one-page paper on one of history's great lovers of humanity, explaining how and why the person still inspires people toward greater goodness.

For discussion

1. Describe a time in your life when you felt unloved.
   - How did you feel?
   - What caused you to feel that way?
   - What helped you get over that feeling? Why?
2. How have you seen someone change for the better in a good love relationship?
3. Why does love give people physical strength, as well as emotional and psychological courage?
4. How does lack of love affect our society and world?

Vocation—our call to love

Love is God's essence: From the beginning, there was love. . . We've been created in God's image and likeness, in Love's image and likeness (see Genesis 1:27) in order to be lovers, too. God has given us our human nature so that we might be able to establish relationships with God and one another. God has created us to love. Love is what our religion and our lives are to mean. That's why, most of all, this book and this course are about loving.

Vocation is our calling in life. The essence of everyone's basic vocation is love. By Baptism, Christians are called to be more perfectly human as Jesus taught, and therefore closer to God. God calls all of us to realize our full potential by being loving persons. Because this root vocation involves our whole self, this course will address the role our mind, body, attitudes, and emotions play in living our vocations.

Our ultimate goal in loving is unity with God and others. As Jesus prayed,

"I ask . . . that they may all be one. As you, Father, are in me and I am in you, may they also be in us. . . ."
JOHN 17:20A AND 21A

Scripture speaks about working for this unity as building up the body of Christ, or God's reign on earth. This means bringing about human community through greater understanding, harmony, and acceptance among people and nations. In terms of our own vocations, it means trying to love others as God loves us.

God calls each of us to a particular vocation. All the baptized are called to ministry, which means "service." God invites you to love and help people through your temporary or permanent **commitment** to the single or married vocation. Within those two main ways of life, there are many possible vocational combinations. Some persons are called to specialized ministry, like ordained ministry (that is, bishops, priests, deacons) or to ordained or non-ordained ministry within a religious community whose members make the three vows.

Whether you stay single or you marry, what's important is how you love—in the everyday little ways. For true happiness and meaning in life don't occur suddenly, when one marries the right person or makes religious vows. It's unfair and unrealistic to expect anything or anyone else to fulfill in us what God alone can satisfy. Your real fulfillment, then, will result from your constantly drawing closer to God through your small daily choices to love.

Every day confronts us with moments when we must ask: Which choice leads to more goodness and love? Try always to choose love and goodness, for that's your main vocation. That's how you draw close to God and others. That's why you are here.

commitment
dedication to fulfilling a responsibility or obligation; a promise or pledge to do something

deacon
a person ordained to perform certain clerical functions

layperson
a member of the Church community who is not an ordained minister

Scripture insights

1. Read Genesis 1–2:4a. How does the story show God's selfless love for us?

2. Give examples of how Jesus' unselfish giving of himself revealed God's love and showed us how to love.

Activity

Write a two-page essay, a poem, or song on how loving is everybody's main vocation.

For discussion

1. Before discussing this chapter, what was your idea of vocation? What are your ideas now about vocation?

2. Do people usually realize their basic vocation in life? Explain.

3. In what specific ways have you tried to achieve the ultimate goal of your basic vocation?

4. Which particular vocation(s) are you inclined toward? Why?

5. List five instances in which you're faced with making an ordinary choice that will lead to more goodness and love. In which do you find it easiest, and hardest, to make the most loving choice? Explain.

6. Why is it unrealistic to expect another person to fulfill you or meet your deepest needs? How can you find such fulfillment?

Review

1. Where do we find our life's real meaning and purpose?

2. Why is love so important and powerful in people's lives? How do we learn how to love?

3. What is our basic vocation in life? To what are Christians called by virtue of Baptism?

4. What is the ultimate goal of our primary or basic vocation, and how can we best live this root vocation every day?

5. What are the two main vocations or ways of life? Can a person live more than one vocation at the same time?

The single or married life may also include other vocations, such as being a
priest   parent
religious brother or sister   **deacon**
                                        layperson, lay minister

It's time to choose

Below are typical daily choices teenagers face in living their basic vocation. Read them and then respond to the questions.

You're hungry, and standing in line in the school cafeteria. You see that someone else would like to move in front of you to be with a friend. **It's time to choose....**

You're busy doing your homework when you're asked to lend a hand in getting dinner on the table. **It's time to choose....**

You're talking to a friend on the phone when your mom asks you to help put away the groceries. **It's time to choose....**

You're looking forward to meeting your friends for a snack after school. On your way to your locker, you notice a classmate who seems extremely upset. You don't know the person very well. If you take time to talk, you'll be late in getting together with your friends. **It's time to choose....**

You're upset because you didn't get a good grade on a test. You know you should have studied harder for it. When you get home, you're asked what's bothering you. **It's time to choose....**

For discussion

1. What two main choices are before you in each instance?
2. Where would each choice lead you?
3. What would making each choice say about you as a person?
4. Which choice do you usually make or would you probably make in each case? Why?

To live in loving relationship with others is the fundamental vocation of every human being.
POPE JOHN PAUL II

Loving yourself

You bring who you are as a person to your relationships and to all you do in life. Jesus said: "You shall love your neighbor as yourself" (Matthew 22:39). Loving yourself is therefore essential: You can't love others unless you care about yourself. That's why Jesus used true love of self as the guideline for how we're to love others.

Research studies consistently confirm how right Jesus was: A main reason for relationship problems is that one or both partners don't love themselves properly. As we'll discuss more in the next chapter, lack of self-esteem blocks intimacy—especially in close, long-term relationships.

What does loving yourself mean? Unfortunately, people often misunderstand the "as you love yourself" part of what Jesus said. They think loving oneself is being selfish and conceited. (Selfishness and conceit can be misguided attempts to compensate for a lack of self-worth.) Loving yourself means caring responsibly about your physical, psychological, social, and spiritual welfare. That gives you the foundation to live your vocation successfully.

Love is a circle in which loving oneself and loving others is closely linked. If you're inwardly whole and healthy, then you're able to reach out to love and give to others. If your inner self is bruised or fractured, that is reflected in your relationships and your work. Most often the circle of love is first broken by neglect or abuse in childhood. But the circle can be joined again by receiving love from others or by learning to love oneself and then learning to share that love with others.

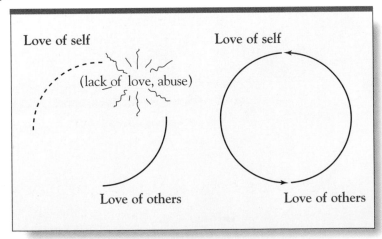

How to love yourself in a healthy way

Believe in yourself and your unique value as a person. If you know how valuable you are, then you can realize and respect how valuable everyone is. Maybe you're not rich, famous, good-looking, or extraordinarily gifted. But you have one thing no one else has: your uniqueness. No one else can think, say, or do things the same way you can because no one else is you. Nobody else can laugh or cry, experience joy or sorrow, or love as you do. Only you can be you!

Your individuality is God's gift to you and to the world. You are unique in all the universe. There's never been anyone just like you, and there never will be. You are special and of eternal value because God loves you: You are always important in God's eyes.

"Are not five sparrows sold for two pennies? Yet not one of them is forgotten in God's sight. But even the hairs of your head are all counted . . . you are of more value than many sparrows."
LUKE 12:6–7A AND C

Accept and respect yourself. To feel good about yourself, realize how God loves you unconditionally despite your imperfections. Adult faith means being convinced that God loves us and desires our happiness and fulfillment. Grow as a person by loving and helping others. Seek positive experiences and good relationships. And be honest with yourself and others, for self-respect demands **integrity**.

integrity
honesty and sincerity

Care about your total welfare but don't worry about it constantly. Don't obsess (as so many do today) over your health, appearance, fitness, or how long you're going to live. Being trim or beautiful isn't your goal in life, and none of us will live here forever! Keep things in proper perspective, and focus each day on what really matters. You won't be deeply happy if you live superficially. Care for your health responsibly but also live your life—don't just try to extend it.

Seek mainly to accomplish your mission in life and leave the rest in God's hands. Remember: God always cares far more about you than you do!

"So do not worry about tomorrow, for tomorrow will bring worries of its own. Today's trouble is enough for today."
MATTHEW 6:34

"Do not be afraid, little flock, for it is your Father's good pleasure to give you the kingdom."
LUKE 12:32

Where there is not love, put love, and you will find love.
ST. JOHN OF THE CROSS

Assignment
Research and write a two-page paper on teenagers and eating disorders or muscle dysmorphia (obsessively trying to enhance one's physique). Report to the class on your findings.

Activity
Bring to class examples of how advertisements
- encourage people to become too concerned about their health or appearance
- encourage people to judge one another superficially
- help inform and motivate people to care for themselves

Discuss how these types of ads affect young adults.

Scripture insights
1. Read Luke 12:13–31 and Matthew 6:24–34.
2. How is what Jesus said there relevant to us today?

Journal entry
Complete each statement in your journal:
- To accept myself more, I will. . .
- To be more honest, I will. . .
- To be less superficial, I will. . .

For discussion
1. What do you think it means to love oneself in a healthy way, as Jesus meant?
2. What is the difference between being conceited or selfish and loving yourself as Jesus meant for us to do?
3. Where does the "circle of loving" usually begin? Describe an "unloving circle." Explain how someone might break out of it and experience love.
4. What superficial things do you think teenagers worry too much about? What harm can that do? What nonessentials overly concern you?

much better than if you tell yourself "I'm going to flunk." And who ends up with the new friend or desired date, the one who thinks "I'm going to meet that person" and makes the effort or the one who does nothing because "I'm too shy"?

We've all experienced the truth of the great literary work *Don Quixote*: Love transforms what seems ugly in us and makes us feel beautiful. In his madness Don Quixote believed the prostitute Aldonza was a lady of virtue. So he treated her with respect although she ridiculed him for it. Don Quixote's constant belief in her as Dulcinea finally led her to believe in her own dignity and goodness. She then began to act like the lady Don Quixote believed she was.

When our attitude is positive, our behavior generally improves. Constant loving reinforcement enabled Aldonza to change her attitude about herself and thus to become her best self—Dulcinea. Here are some practical ways to build your self-esteem when you're down on yourself:

Building self-esteem

self-esteem
belief in oneself; self-respect

self-confidence
belief in one's abilities; self-assurance

When we lack **self-esteem** about who we are, we don't have **self-confidence** in what we do. Many people seem plagued with low self-esteem. That's why many successful employment agencies focus on enhancing their clients' self-esteem.

Belief in ourselves gives us energy and courage. When their self-esteem is low, people don't have the confidence to apply for the jobs they want—or to ask for the raises they deserve. But how do you gain self-esteem and self-confidence? Psychologists tell us this works: Make a habit of thinking positively about yourself and of acting as if you are self-confident. Changing your behavior will help you change your attitude.

Professional athletes use that technique effectively. They tell themselves before each game that they can win, and they visualize themselves performing well. Acting self-confident even when they're not boosts their achievement—and the score. If you approach a test with an "I can do well" attitude, you'll do

To boost your self-esteem

- Focus on your positive qualities and possibilities rather than on your shortcomings.
- Visualize yourself acting confidently and keep telling yourself that you are a capable person.
- Reach out. Make special efforts to be kind toward others and to recall how much God and others do love you.

narcissism

self-centeredness; conceit; a distorted or exaggerated sense of one's own importance, abilities, appearance, and such

At the opposite self-esteem extreme are **narcissistic** individuals who think way too highly of themselves. Narcissists have an inflated, distorted sense of themselves. They believe they're superior to others and act as though the world revolves around them. Sometimes narcissism results from lack of proper discipline in childhood—perhaps being praised no matter what one does, perhaps hardly ever being corrected. Narcissism represents an unhealthy, selfish, self-centered type of self-love.

Narcissists grow up believing that the world should serve them. They demand others' "respect" without earning it, but their greatly inflated self-opinion becomes their undoing. They can't handle it when others respond negatively to their conceited air of superiority. Because they've been undeservedly praised so often, they refuse to accept legitimate criticism. Whether gang leaders, abusive spouses, or brash executives, narcissists may explode angrily or erupt violently when others don't dance to their tune on cue.

Having a healthy self-esteem means being realistic about yourself and accepting your limitations. It involves having the humility to admit mistakes and accept just criticism. Not everyone can be a star athlete or an A student. The interesting gift of being limited and imperfect is that we can know we're loved for ourselves and not for our perfection. Perhaps that type of acceptance is the main thing the superior-seeming narcissist lacks.

Some day, after **mastering** the winds,

the **waves**, the tides, and gravity,

we shall **harness** for God

the energies of love,

and **then**, for the second time in

the history of the **world**,

[humanity] will have discovered **fire**.

TEILHARD DE CHARDIN

Activity

Bring to class examples of advertisements (print, TV, Internet) that appeal to people's insecurities and low self-esteem in order to sell products. Explain whether you think such ads foster even greater insecurity and lack of self-esteem.

For discussion

1. How does your attitude about yourself affect those around you? Give three examples.

2. Describe a time when you felt unloved and unlovable. What helped you get over that feeling, and why did it help?

3. Do most teenagers have enough self-esteem and self-confidence? Do you? Explain.

4. When you're feeling down on yourself, what helps boost your self-esteem and self-confidence? Which other suggestions given in your text do you think might also help?

5. Have you known individuals who seem narcissistic? Explain without mentioning names. How do you and others respond to persons who seem self-centered or conceited?

Review

1. What does it mean to love others as you love yourself?

2. Why is loving oneself an important part of living any vocation successfully?

3. What are self-esteem and self-confidence? How does lack of self-esteem affect relationships?

4. What is narcissism? What is the difference between narcissism and healthy self-esteem?

5. How can individuals learn to love themselves and build self-esteem in a healthy way?

Assessing your self-esteem

On the blanks, write the letter of the answer that best corresponds to how you see yourself. When you have finished, your instructor will guide you in interpreting your results. Be honest with yourself—you won't be expected to share your responses.

A — Yes, very much so, very strongly
B — Yes, pretty much so, somewhat strongly
C — Somewhat, but not very much, not very strongly
D — Not really, not very strongly
E — Hardly at all
F — No, not at all

_____ 1. Do you care responsibly enough about your physical well-being?

_____ 2. Do you feel accepted and loved by others for who you really are as a person—imperfections and all?

_____ 3. Do you constantly feel that your efforts are never quite good enough to match up to what others expect of you?

_____ 4. Do you believe that you were loved in your early childhood?

_____ 5. How much do you try to be like other teenagers in what you say, do, think, wear, and so on?

_____ 6. To what extent are you aware of and grateful for your unique gifts and abilities?

_____ 7. Do you realize the positive contribution you make to others' lives?

_____ 8. Do you respect yourself as being a good person?

_____ 9. Do you feel others respect you as a person?

_____ 10. Would you consider yourself a person of integrity—someone who is honest with yourself and others?

_____ 11. How much do you focus on your physical health, appearance, or fitness?

_____ 12. How much do you worry about what others think of you?

_____ 13. Do you often feel down on yourself?

_____ 14. Do you generally have a negative attitude about yourself or what you can do?

_____ 15. Have others told you that they think you're conceited or selfish?

_____ 16. Do you become upset when reasonably corrected or criticized?

_____ 17. Do you believe that you are superior to others?

_____ 18. Do you generally admit it when you make a mistake?

_____ 19. How much are you usually bothered by the small mistakes others make?

_____ 20. Are you aware of and realistic about your limitations?

_____ 21. Do you like yourself?

_____ 22. Do you feel that others like you?

Loving God and others

Loving God

God's love was revealed among us in this way: God sent his only Son into the world so that we might live through him.

In this is love, not that we loved God but that he loved us and sent his Son to be the atoning sacrifice for our sins. . . . .

God loved us so much. . .

> 1 JOHN 4:9–10, 11B

God loves us each completely—without condition. We learn human loving from the way God has first loved us. But how do we return God's love? How can we love someone we can't see? We love God within our hearts. But Scripture tells us that it's the love we show one another that gives meaning to our inner love for God:

"If you keep my commandments, you will abide in my love. . . ."

> JOHN 15:10A

The commandment we have from him is this: those who love God must love their brothers and sisters also.

> 1 JOHN 4:21

Loving God—or anyone—may be challenging and difficult at times, but it's also our deepest happiness. As Jesus made it clear, love is what brings true joy and fulfillment:

"I have said these things to you so that my joy may be in you, and that your joy may be complete. This is my commandment, that you love one another as I have loved you."

> JOHN 15:11–12

Love is sacred! It's how we participate in God's life and love. A key way we experience God's love for us is in being loved by others, and it is God's presence within us that makes it possible for us to love. Loving God means having the faith to meet and communicate directly with God in our hearts. It means letting God's love encompass and complete us by nourishing the deepest parts of our human spirit. Loving God also means having the faith to believe in loving others:

So we have known and believe the love that God has for us. God is love, and those who abide in love abide in God, and God abides in them.

> 1 JOHN 4:16

Love has many faces in your life: your own, those of others, and above all God's. For wherever you give and experience genuine love, you meet God.

For discussion

1. What things make you most aware that God loves you?
2. What do you feel is most challenging about experiencing or returning God's love?
3. Had you ever thought of being in love with someone as a way to experience and return God's love? Do you think people usually make that connection?

Loving others

We know love by this, that he laid down his life for us—and we ought to lay down our lives for one another. . . . Beloved, since God loved us so much, we also ought to love one another.
1 JOHN 3:16 AND 4:11

Joe is thoughtless toward his mother, uncaring about friends in trouble, aloof at school to kids he doesn't know, rude to customers where he works, and gruff to his teachers. Although Joe fancies himself a Romeo with the ladies, love doesn't work that way! It's no wonder that the young women Joe knows find him inconsiderate, boring, and selfish—concerned only about what interests him.

We bring to any intimate relationship who we are. And that largely depends on how we love ourselves and have learned to love others. The only way to become someone who will attract a special love relationship in the future is to be a loving person now—to family, friends, acquaintances, and even strangers. As Jesus urged and showed us how to do, particularly try to help those who are in greatest need.

Make a habit of being a loving person. Work on love's essentials, especially with those already close to you. If you're not loving in general, you won't be able to sustain any intimate long-term relationship. If you love and care now, you will be loving and caring in whatever path you walk in life. Jesus' Golden Rule is your best guide: "In everything do to others as you would have them do to you . . ." (Matthew 7:12).

> To **love** another person is to see the face of **God**.
>
> FROM *LES MISERABLES*

Activity

Based on what you've studied thus far in this chapter, write a one-page essay on the importance you want your love of God, of others, and of yourself to have in your life. Explain why.

For discussion

1. Why can't we separate being loving toward others in general from loving one particular person?
2. How could being a more loving person improve your special love relationships?
3. List five ways you think teenagers could be more loving at home and at school. Explain how this would also enhance their close personal relationships.

Review

1. How does God love us?
2. How do we best return God's love?
3. To truly love any one person, why must we be a loving person in general?

In summary

You have many important choices to make regarding your vocation, ministry, lifestyle, and what your future will mean. As you make those choices, consider others' wisdom. Never forget that God, who makes all love possible, is your ultimate destination, happiness, and fulfillment.

Your basic vocation is to return God's love by loving others as you love yourself. Loving yourself in a good way requires fulfilling your basic human needs and having a healthy self-esteem. God loves us each completely—without condition. By loving others, we participate in God's life and love.

Key concepts

basic human needs

finding your path in life

goal of human love

God's unconditional love

importance and power of love

Jesus' Golden Rule

love as a basic human need

love as sacred and a participation
  in God's life

loving God

loving others

loving yourself

meaning and purpose of life

narcissism

unhealthy self-love

self-acceptance

self-actualization

self-confidence

self-esteem

self-respect

CHAPTER 2

CHOICES AND COMMITMENTS

SCRIPTURE

"You did not choose me but I chose you.

And I appointed you to go and bear fruit,

fruit that will last. . . ."

JOHN 15:16A

PRAYER

Holy Spirit of God,

What should I do with the rest of my life?

How can I know what paths I should follow?

I don't want to make mistakes I'll regret.

I want to do good with my life. I want to find true happiness and help others be happy.

Give us the wisdom and courage to shape our lives in ways that always lead us closer to others and to you.

Thank you for the talents and abilities you've given us.

Help us choose the paths in life where we can use our gifts best.

In Jesus' name. Amen.

Ministry—commitment to serve

What is success? . . . To leave the world a bit better . . .

RALPH WALDO EMERSON

When you think of "minister," do you picture only a world diplomat or a member of the clergy? To minister actually means to serve or to help. Whether we're single or married, our primary vocation and mission in life is to love. Service (our ministry) is the active ways we commit ourselves to love. Love is empty—even on the most personal level—without a commitment to serve, to help another in whatever ways we can.

And if I have prophetic powers, and understand all mysteries and all knowledge, and if I have all faith, so as to remove mountains, but do not have love, I am nothing.
1 CORINTHIANS 13:2

When an elderly man died recently, his family discovered instructions saying that he wanted his tombstone to read, *Mission accomplished!*

At first his children and others thought that strange—even frivolous. Then they began to understand: This man had always been good and caring in his business and personal life. He was always willing to lend an ear or a hand to someone in need. He had had a successful marriage and raised a loving family. As a result, at the end of his life he was satisfied that he'd accomplished his God-given purpose here. Ministry is how we, too, actively fulfill our mission in life.

You may have several ministries.

Your occupation:
- being a good employee or employer
- serving clients or customers well
- being a caring co-worker

Other ways you regularly reach out to help:
- volunteering at your church and for other charitable causes
- caring for family members (preparing meals, cleaning house, disciplining children, fixing the family car)
- giving moral support to a hurting friend
- tending to needs of relatives who are sick or elderly

Attitude adjustment

"You are the light of the world. . . . let your light shine. . . ."
MATTHEW 5:14A AND 16B

Do you look at life as an obstacle course or as an opportunity? Do you your efforts seem like chores or chances to help? As with your vocational choice to stay single or to marry, your ministries will require a positive commitment every day. If you live only for the future, you'll miss life's most important aspects here and now.

So don't view your life as a series of hurdles to overcome in achieving some goal (to get a promotion, buy a new house, or keep the house orderly, for example). View whatever you do for others as your ministry. Appreciate the small things and enjoy the present moment.

You need to feel a sense of accomplishment—to feel that what you do, share, and give achieves something positive. If you do things only because you feel obligated to do them, you won't be as effective. If you do things selfishly, just for what you get out of it, you'll never be as happy.

So see your efforts as choices rather than chores, as ways to give instead of as burdens. View what you do as service to others, rather than in terms of deadlines, money, status, or being popular. In all your efforts, try to do good and to help achieve God's desire for human community. It was once said of Jesus' earliest followers: "See how these Christians love one another" (Tertullian, A.D.160–240). Let love for others be the hallmark of your life, too.

To each is given the manifestation of the Spirit for the common good.
1 CORINTHIANS 12:7

What is success?
To **laugh** often and much;
To win the respect of intelligent people
and the **affection** of children;
To earn the appreciation of honest critics
and **endure** the betrayal of false friends;
To appreciate beauty;
To find the **best** in others;
To leave the world a bit better,
whether by a **healthy** child, a garden patch
or a redeemed social condition;
To know even one life has breathed **easier** because you have lived;
This is to have succeeded.

RALPH WALDO EMERSON

Scripture insights

1. Read Matthew 5:14–16. What was Jesus saying here?

2. What's the difference between "letting your light shine" as Jesus meant and displaying your good deeds like the hypocrites referred to in Matthew 6:1–6?

3. Read Acts of the Apostles 2:42–47. How did the early Christians live what Jesus had taught them about community?

Activity

Explain whether you view each of the following mainly as a chore or mainly as an opportunity to help:

1. Doing the dishes or taking out the garbage at home

2. Running an errand for a family member

3. Giving a friend a ride home or helping a friend who's having trouble with schoolwork

4. Working on the clean-up committee for a school dance

5. Planning activities to boost school spirit before a big game

Being successful

Being successful in life isn't just your idea or something you can accomplish all by yourself. It's part of God's reason for putting you here.

Now there are varieties of gifts, but the same Spirit; and there are varieties of services, but the same Lord; and there are varieties of activities, but it is the same God who activates all of them in everyone.

1 CORINTHIANS 12:4–6

To be truly successful in life

- Enjoy what you do. Your daily attitude will make a world of difference to the happiness you and others experience— and to your productivity!

- Remember that who you are is as important as what you do. The kind of person you are directs and shapes your actions. The world's greatest persons are known for their character as much as their achievements. Be a good person. Only then can you become a great person.

"Bloom where you are planted."

- Establish and adhere to your priorities. God and people should come first, so put them first. Don't be a slave to your work or hobbies so that your personal and spiritual life and your relationships suffer.

Discerning life choices

- Are you trying to figure out where or whether to go to college?
- Have you wondered whether you'd be happiest staying single just temporarily or perhaps permanently?
- Have you thought about whether you want to live the single life as a lay person or as a priest or religious? Or whether you want to marry and raise a family?

Every vocation in life is a calling—an invitation from God that asks for our response. But how do you recognize what you're being called to do with your life? What say do you have in this matter?

discernment
the process of using one's reasoning ability and God's guidance, Scripture, Church teaching, and the wisdom of others to make wise and good choices

Don't expect to learn your vocation magically as in a dream, but look instead at your abilities, skills, activities, and relationships. For God motivates us from within and without in ordinary ways.

Self-discovery is a life-long process. You are entering the stage of vocation and career discovery in which you must examine your life options. Eventually, you will need to assume responsibility for your choices independently of your parents. You may think you know yourself pretty well by now. But you'll probably be surprised at how much more your ideas will change concerning the relationships, occupation, or way of life you prefer.

Give yourself enough time. Don't jump into a permanent vocation choice just because all your friends are. Making a commitment to marriage, the ordained ministry, the religious life, or the lay single life lightly or prematurely can lead to regret and unhappiness.

Live on your own for at least a few years after finishing your formal education or training. Even if you make a permanent commitment at age twenty-six, you'll be living it for the next fifty or sixty years! So don't rush things. Give yourself the best chance to achieve happiness. First learn enough about yourself, what you want of life, and what you've got to give. Then you'll be prepared to make the wisest permanent choices.

Use the valuable discernment process. Handed down through centuries of Christian tradition, this process can help you answer your life-choice questions. It's also useful in deciding whether to continue a serious relationship with someone. (In fact, this discernment process is an excellent method for making any big decision.)

Know yourself well enough to make a life choice:

1. Recognize your abilities—what you can give.

2. Understand your needs.

3. Know what makes you happy.

4. Know how you best relate with others.

To use the discernment process:[1]

1. Explore opportunities. Find information about the possibilities available to you. With the right motives, seek what is good and true.

2. Seek direction. (Look to Scripture, Church teaching and tradition, and to your convictions about what you want your life to mean. Get in the habit of praying for God's guidance.)

3. Ask advice. Talk the matter over with wise, knowledgeable persons of integrity. Seek a few people you can confide in and rely on for sound, honest insights.

4. Assess your needs, abilities, experiences, and relationships in terms of what this life choice requires and the possibilities and opportunities it offers.

Activity

Interview a single person, a married person, and a priest or a religious brother or sister about how they discovered their vocations. Write a two-page paper reporting their responses and describing what you learned from the interviews.

For discussion

1. What do you think is most difficult about figuring out your vocation in life? How often do you pray for guidance in discerning what to do with your life?

2. What do you need to know and want to learn about yourself before deciding permanently on a way of life? How much time do you plan to give yourself before making major vocational choices? Explain.

3. Which steps in the discernment process have you already found valuable in making decisions? Which one(s) haven't you tried yet? Explain.

4. When do you usually seek someone else's guidance? How have close friends and family members been helpful and not helpful, when you've needed advice?

5. Whose guidance could you rely on in discerning your paths in life? Why should you consider the insights of those who know you well? Explain.

Without realizing it, you've probably found this discernment process helpful already in dealing with personal problems and responsibilities at school and at home. That's why Catholic teaching recommends it so highly—especially in determining which vocation to follow and in living your vocation throughout your life.[2]

Choose your path in life freely and deliberately. Never make a vocational choice that you feel pressured into for personal, practical, or even religious reasons! You have the right to choose your own vocation and ministries and ways of living these. At the same time, don't ignore the wisdom of those who know you well—your parents, teachers, and perhaps your close friends. Listen to their insights. It will be an enlightening part of your discernment process. Seek God's guidance in being sure that the path you follow in life is ultimately your choice.[3]

Above all, discover how you can best love. Why was Mother Teresa of Calcutta's ministry so successful and inspiring? Because she tended to the physical needs of the poor and dying with contagious joy—loving as God does. How can you share yourself and your gifts with others most happily and enthusiastically? That's where you'll discover your greatest hope for fulfillment and meaning—and the vocation to which God and your heart are calling you.

The **place** God calls you to is the **place** where your deep **gladness** and the world's deep **hunger** meet.

FREDERICK BUECHENER

Life's values: What really counts?

Once you're living on your own, you'll confront many practical realities: Where and how do you want to live? What do you want, and not want, to own? What will you do with your leisure time? How you answer those questions will shape your **lifestyle**.

Your lifestyle is how you structure your life according to your values and priorities. It's the overall pattern of how you live your single or married vocation and your ministry. But how do you decide which type of lifestyle best suits you?

In today's fast-paced world, you will be pressured to feel you "must have this" or "gotta do that" just to keep up with "everybody else." You may be told you must ruthlessly "step on a few toes" and "stab a few backs" to get to the top in the business world. (One young woman's first boss told her his business philosophy: "You've got to do it to others before they do it to you.") Don't get suckered into a way of living that goes against your sound beliefs and ideals; such a life will eventually make you miserable.

To determine which type of lifestyle best suits you, first consider what's really important in life. Then base your practical priorities on those values. With so many influences pulling you in other directions, it won't always be easy to keep your priorities straight. You can keep your priorities straight only by keeping your main values in mind.

In some countries, because the annual rains wash away their shelter, people must rebuild their home every year! That may seem intolerable. But is it really worse than spending your working life unhappily pursuing money just so you won't lose a lovely home? People often become slaves to material things because they don't keep their true priorities straight. To earn more money or a bigger title, they make their job or career their whole life. When they lose sight of what counts most, their personal relationships, spiritual well-being, health, and other important things suffer.

Heed Jesus' warning—don't struggle just to get richer while you let life pass you by:

"Do not store up for yourselves treasures on earth, where moth and rust consume and where thieves break in and steal; but store up for yourselves treasures in heaven, where neither moth nor rust consumes and where thieves do not break in and steal."
MATTHEW 6:19–20

How we emphasize and value material things often reflects—and influences—our attitudes and relationships. One survey found that people prize certain objects not for their monetary value or practical uses but because they represent special ties with people. The survey distinguished two types of **materialism:**[4]

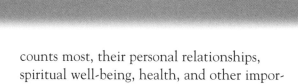

lifestyle
the way a person's life is structured according to that person's values and priorities

materialism
attitude or philosophy about the value and purpose of physical objects

terminal
final, extreme

instrumental
helpful or useful as a means to a goal

Terminal materialism—greedily seeking material goods for their own sake

Instrumental materialism—using material things to realize goals

One of the men in the survey responded that "there's something very close between the freedom to love and the freedom to go without."[5] Christianity tells us to cherish this world's goods, while using them for our benefit and that of others. It likewise tells us that we should also be able to let material things go when loving requires it.

Christians believe the world is good. It's been redeemed—made holy—and given into our care. We must take good care of Earth. We are to use the "things of this world" to bring greater love—not disharmony, greed, and destruction.

How does God's love abide in anyone who has the world's goods and sees a brother or sister in need and yet refuses help?
1 JOHN 3:17

Live simply. It's interesting how young adults start accumulating possessions and older adults begin getting rid of them! When you move out on your own, you'll certainly need to furnish the place where you live. But right from the start, tell yourself that you're not going to work just to get rich or to pile up possessions. Don't stretch your budget to the point that it's a struggle to pay for the new clothes, the more expensive car, or the bigger house.

And God is able to provide you with every blessing in abundance, so that by always having enough of everything, you may share abundantly in every good work . . . You will be enriched in every way for your great generosity. . . .
2 CORINTHIANS 9:8 AND 11A

Remember: Fewer possessions means fewer worries and responsibilities. As one young woman put it: "What I don't own, I don't have to dust!" Buy no more than you can afford. Keep what you need and a reasonable amount to enjoy and have a great time sharing with others! You'll be much happier if you live your true values and contribute positively to others' lives.

"For where your treasure is, there your heart will be also."
MATTHEW 6:21

Journal entry

1. Name three ways you can care for your material things and the environment.
2. Which talents do you have or desire that could help relieve others' physical, emotional, or spiritual poverty? Explain.

Activity

Choose one.

1. Find three good mottoes to help you keep your priorities straight. Make a poster or Web-page design using one motto.
2. Research the Internet for ideas on living simply. Write a two-page paper or design a computer graphic on the topic.
3. Find examples of how media promote "must have" and "must do" attitudes. Write a one-page paper or depict your findings in a collage. Explain terminal or instrumental materialism in these examples.
4. Write a two-page paper on the lifestyle you'd like to have. Explain the values and priorities of that lifestyle.
5. Make a collage or Web-page design on how media try to convince people that they must do this or have that and the values and priorities in these examples.

For discussion

1. How do "must have" and "must do" attitudes influence teenagers? How are teenagers influenced by terminal materialism?
2. How does your life become unbalanced with trying to obtain material things or get things done? How do you regain your perspective?
3. To which three charities would you contribute? Why?
4. What objects do you prize because of their special connection to people?
5. Would you like to live a simpler lifestyle in the future? Why? How could you live more simply now?

What do you need to be happy?

Read the list of basic human needs and what's required to satisfy them. Then respond to the questions.

Your four basic human needs

Physical needs

+ sufficient food and adequate clothing

+ clean, comfortable, healthy shelter

+ good health and proper healthcare; enough sleep and physical activity

+ reasonable physical comfort

+ reasonable access to necessary transportation

= physical comfort and security

Self-identity and self-esteem

+ self-acceptance, and belief that you're worthwhile and valuable

+ a sense of integrity, that you're a morally good person

+ recognition and confirmation by others of your value

= psychological health and balance

Companionship and intimacy

+ a close relationship with God and one or more other persons

+ good friends, closeness to family members or relatives

+ amiable relationships with peers, colleagues, co-workers

+ affectionate physical contact with others

= emotional and spiritual well-being

Self-actualization

+ service, giving of yourself, contributing to and helping others

+ development of your abilities, talents, skills

+ accomplishment or achievement

+ enough opportunity to express your imagination and creativity

+ enough relaxation and recreation

+ a well-rounded personality and life

= realization of your personal potential

For discussion

1. In your words, describe the four basic human needs and some specific ways people can satisfy each one.

2. What's the minimum you think you'd require in order to satisfy each of your basic needs?

3. How do your real needs sometimes differ from what you think you need?

4. What social influences affect your perceptions of what you need in order to be happy? How do the various media in our society affect your perceptions of this?

5. Why is it important to know what you actually do and don't need in order to be truly happy?

Remaining faithful

Hearts are crushed, marriages crumble, families are broken up, workers are fired, airplanes crash, and space shuttles explode—all because someone in some way wasn't faithful. Whether it's to the responsibilities of a relationship or a job commitment, fidelity is fundamental. Relationships and business deals often fall apart because people fail to keep their legitimate promises—or make promises they shouldn't have! You know how true that is if your heart's already been broken because someone wasn't faithful to you.

Centuries ago God made a covenant with the ancient Hebrews to continue loving humanity faithfully forever. Jesus' complete and unselfish giving of himself for our sake was the decisive revelation of God's faithful love for us. This lasting presence continues among us through the Holy Spirit, the Church's sacraments, and Jesus' promise to return at the end of time to bring love to its final fulfillment. God has remained faithful to us and asks that we remain faithful in love to one another and to God.

Being faithful requires **self-discipline**, self-control. That means having the perseverance to stick it out when the going is difficult. It means working to fix problems rather than making excuses for or trying to escape them. It means exercising self-control and resisting the temptation to lash out or to escape responsibilities and cover up with lies.

Years ago, researchers conducted an interesting study on self-discipline among a group of young children. Each child was left alone in a room, seated in front of two piles of candy, and told this: You may have the smaller pile of candy now. Or you may wait ten minutes and then have the bigger pile of candy. A hidden camera recorded how the children responded to their urge to seek immediate **gratification**. The candy was obviously very tempting!

Some of the children chose to not postpone satisfying their craving. They ate the small pile of candy immediately rather than wait for the greater reward. Years later, those who had exercised self-control were found to do better in school and have fewer serious problems as teenagers. Gained through practice, self-control is a very good habit to acquire for many reasons.

God has created us rational beings with free will to direct our thoughts and behavior. Those with little self-discipline simply give in to their anger, lash out, or just cave in when tempted to be unfaithful in a relationship. To learn how to love faithfully, one must learn how to exercise self-control.

One way to build self-discipline is to do little things well. Great achievements are built on small ones: You can do extraordinary things only if you first do small things well. It's in these small daily things that you'll find God and experience what life and love really mean.

"Whoever is faithful in a very little is faithful also in much. . . ."
LUKE 16:10

self-discipline
using one's will power to control one's thoughts, desires, emotions, or behavior; self-restraint

gratification
the satisfying of needs or desires, especially for what is pleasurable

Activity

Find in the Scriptures the passages that describe God's covenant and its renewals with humanity. Explain how the events revealed God's faithful love for us. (See Genesis 17 and Exodus 16, for instance.)

Journal entry

Write down one way you'll try to be more in control and exercise better self-discipline in your life.

For discussion

1. Why is it important to do small things well? What little things shouldn't be overlooked in relationships?

2. How would you hope to apply Jesus' teaching about being faithful in small things to your ministry in life? To your relationships?

3. If you fell in love with someone who demonstrated little self-discipline, would that affect your trust that the person would be faithful to you? Explain.

4. In what areas of your life do you find it easiest to exercise self-discipline? Hardest?

Review

1. How does God call each person to a particular vocation?

2. Why are self-knowledge and free choice important in selecting one's vocation(s)?

3. What is the discernment process and what steps does it involve?

4. What is the difference between terminal and instrumental materialism? How does each relate to what Jesus said about accumulating material things?

5. What attitudes does our society promote regarding material things?

6. How important is fidelity and how does one learn how to be faithful in a relationship? What did Jesus say about being faithful?

Facing reality

Every vocation involves certain practical challenges. These next sections can help you deal better with a few of the main ones you'll encounter soon.

Choosing your occupation

occupation
the type of work one does for a living

career
long-term employment in one occupation or line of work; profession

job
work done for pay or other compensation

Do you know what **occupation** you intend to pursue? Don't worry if you don't have a clue. Even if your **career** choice seems clear right now, your mind may change completely over the next several years. Many frustrated law students have ended up becoming happy carpenters, computer technicians, or sales people!

Discerning your occupation is a process. So be patient as you explore and rule out various options. Now is the time to begin focusing on areas that interest you and on which skills you will need to acquire for them.

On the other hand, you don't want to just drift into a **job** at which you'll be unhappy. Studies have shown that most people didn't deliberately choose their occupation; they initially considered it "temporary." Many stayed on because they were promoted or paid well, became experienced, or liked the people they worked with. Even if they were no longer happy after years at their job, they're now afraid to make a change.

Another common mistake is to keep griping about one's job without looking for something better—until **after** finally quitting in disgust (or being fired). Being unemployed is as hard on one's nerves as it is on one's finances! If you're unhappy at your job and can't improve the situation, look for a new position while you're still employed—and still young. Meanwhile try to adopt a positive attitude that will make your current job more bearable.

Start thinking seriously now about what you'd be successful at and enjoy doing. Once you get a home mortgage or begin a family, your financial responsibilities may limit your career choices. You don't want to end up feeling trapped in a job you hate—just to pay the rent or mortgage. So use your freedom to explore your career options in college and/or the business world before you make permanent commitments. Don't just look for the highest salary. Consider entry-level positions that will eventually lead to an occupation you'll truly enjoy.

Be flexible and eager to learn. From the assembly line to the hospital operating room, workers must constantly adapt to different needs and newer technologies. Life itself keeps changing and will continually present you with new challenges. So don't adopt a stuck-in-the-mud attitude that resists all change. Look forward to learning better ways to do things. In fact, a main purpose of education is to teach you how to keep learning on your own!

> To **God** there is nothing **small**.
>
> The moment we have **given** it to God
>
> it **becomes** infinite.
>
> MOTHER TERESA OF CALCUTTA

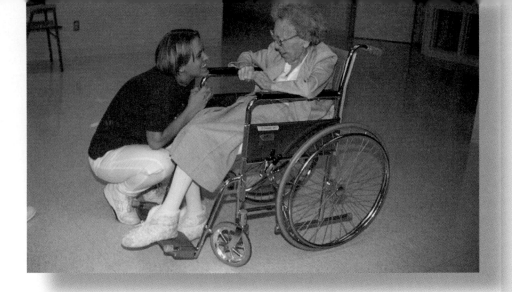

Scripture activities

Choose one.

1. Find five Gospel passages in which Jesus' teaching evidences his personal knowledge of human behavior, of nature, or of carpentry. Explain how this makes Jesus' teaching effective today.

2. Locate in the Gospels how Jesus prepared himself for his final ministry. Explain what you might learn from him about preparing for your future.

We make a living by what we get, but we make a life by what we give.
WINSTON CHURCHILL

Keep building on the knowledge and expertise you acquire. Some people work at one occupation all their lives. However, like most people, you'll probably change occupations once or several times—maybe under difficult circumstances. As one highly successful business executive recalled recently,

When I was young, I traveled many paths, not knowing which one would lead to my destination. Looking back, it now seems quite obvious how all the paths prepared me for the work I love today. Along the way, I always prayed for guidance and tried to do my best. Now I can see how losing a deal or getting laid off made me change direction and learn new skills. It's sure much clearer now than it was then how God must have been guiding me all along!

Jesus started out as a carpenter who served people by building things with his hands. He ended up doing something entirely different with his life—teaching, and helping people in other ways. But from his previous experiences with people, with nature, and with carpentry, Jesus drew examples that helped make his teaching effective. Jesus reached people because he followed his heart, while remaining in touch with everyday realities.

A successful college football coach realized while in college that he'd never have the physique to play football professionally. But he loved the game and also had a strong desire to teach. So he made it his goal to become a coach who would help his players develop the skills they'd need on the field and the values they'd need in life. In discerning his occupation, he established a worthy goal and was honest with himself in assessing his skills and his dreams.

Follow your heart in sharing your gifts with others. If you choose an occupation based mainly on the money you'll make, then going to work may end up being daily drudgery. You also won't be successful or happy at work for which you aren't qualified. So find and prepare for an occupation that engages you fully—heart, mind, and soul. Do what you love and prepare yourself well for it.

Discernment step one

Begin the process of discerning your occupation by doing the following:

1. Interview three adults who enjoy their occupation. Ask how they see it as a form of ministry—a way to help others—and what they find most fulfilling about it.

2. Interview someone in an occupation you might like to pursue. Ask what the occupation involves and what abilities, skills, and background it requires. Add your own questions.

3. Write a two-page report on the most helpful insights and information you've gathered in the interviews.

For discussion

1. Where are you now in the process of discerning your future occupation? Are you comfortable or somewhat anxious about that? Explain.

2. How can you avoid drifting from job to job or into an occupation you'll later hate?

3. Why does every occupation and job require flexibility? Is it easy or hard for you to be flexible? Explain.

4. How have you already found it valuable to keep building on the insights and expertise you've acquired?

Considering your options

Your occupation in life must be your choice. While you're deciding on your future plans, heated discussions may occur in your household about which alternative is best for you! Parents may have strong preferences or firm criteria about a choice of college, for instance. Once you're legally of adult age, you may make your own decisions independent of your parents. But your parents may choose which alternatives they will or won't support financially!

You shouldn't go to medical school just because someone wants a doctor in the family. On the other hand, don't just blindly resist a wonderful opportunity someone may be offering you. The first few years of college give all students the chance to explore possible fields of interest. That prepares them to make a wiser choice when they do declare a major field of study.

College isn't the best immediate choice for everyone, however. Some individuals are happier pursuing another type of job training. Some must work a year or two in order to afford college tuition or to become motivated enough to benefit from higher education. But don't make the mistake of postponing or deciding against college just to start raking in money in the business world. Lack of training and education will severely limit your future job opportunities. And that tempting salary might be just peanuts after you factor in taxes, living expenses, and low earnings potential!

So keep an open mind in considering your options—and consider your parents' advice. Respect their concern for you and enlist their support. If you share your ideas and dreams with them from your heart, they're more likely to see your viewpoint. Ultimately, though, it is your right to choose your occupation and career path. Pray for God's guidance to help you make the best choices.

Discernment step two

In a quiet place, reflect for a while on your favorite Scripture passages about what life really means. Think about what you have learned about the meaning of life from your religious beliefs and from other people. Consider the insights you gained from discernment step one, when you explored some of the occupational opportunities available to you. Write a one-page paper reflecting on what you want your life to mean.

For discussion

1. Why should you first discern and prepare for your occupation and then think about specific career plans? When people do the opposite, why do they often regret it later?

2. Do you feel any pressure to pursue a certain education or occupation after high school? How should a person handle such pressures?

3. Is it widely enough accepted that college isn't the best immediate choice for every high school graduate? When might another option be better? When do you think it's a mistake to not attend college?

4. What are your main plans for immediately after high school? Why are these best for you? What are your questions or uncertainties about them?

5. What do you think is the best way to handle differences with parents over which alternative to choose after high school? Explain.

What are you good at?

Which occupation do your abilities and preferences point you toward?
This activity may help you discern the answer more clearly.[6]

On the blank, write the number that best reflects your response.
In the **I'm good at** column, indicate to what extent you have the skill described.
In the **I enjoy** column, indicate how much you enjoy using that skill.

1 — Yes, very much so, very strongly   4 — Not really, not very strongly

2 — Yes, pretty much so, somewhat strongly   5 — Hardly at all

3 — Somewhat, but not very much, not very strongly   6 — No, not at all

I'm good at I enjoy

_____   _____ 1. Working with my hands or my fingers

_____   _____ 2. Activities requiring good physical coordination, strength, or energy

_____   _____ 3. Activities involving physical endurance or other special physical skills or abilities

_____   _____ 4. Physical activities that involve my whole body

_____   _____ 5. Making, creating, building, or assembling things with my hands, or taking things apart

_____   _____ 6. Working with small detailed tools or objects

_____   _____ 7. Repairing things, or cleaning or making them look new

_____   _____ 8. Working with medium or large objects or tools, or operating medium- or large-sized equipment

_____   _____ 9. Organizing or beautifying an indoor or outdoor environment

_____   _____ 10. Caring for plants or animals

_____   _____ 11. Helping or being of service to one person at a time

_____   _____ 12. Understanding and communicating well with individuals

_____   _____ 13. Advising, motivating, comforting, persuading, or reconciling others, or resolving conflicts between them

_____   _____ 14. Evaluating individuals' strengths and abilities

_____   _____ 15. Communicating well with small and large groups of people

_____   _____ 16. Entertaining, amusing, or inspiring groups of people

_____   _____ 17. Leading others

_____   _____ 18. Explaining things to a group of people

_____   _____ 19. Following through to get things done, or getting others to work together

_____   _____ 20. Initiating group activities

_____   _____ 21. Researching or compiling information

_____   _____ 22. Learning by observing people or things

_____   _____ 23. Being imaginative, inventive, or creative

_____   _____ 24. Analyzing ideas or information

_____   _____ 25. Logically organizing, prioritizing, or perceiving patterns in information

_____   _____ 26. Making decisions or solving problems

_____   _____ 27. Planning how to achieve a goal

_____   _____ 28. Dealing with numbers, or being involved in visual or dramatic concepts or in the arts

_____   _____ 29. Recording ideas or information, on paper, computers, film, or in other ways

_____   _____ 30. Remembering things, or keeping track of details

Making ends meet

QUOTED FROM TELEVISION ADVERTISEMENTS FOR
MUTUAL OF NEW YORK INSURANCE COMPANY.

How will you survive financially when you leave home? More than half a million people in our society file for bankruptcy each year. Many are young adults who have taken out loans they can't repay, overextended their credit, or failed to anticipate emergency medical expenses. Now they can't even meet their rent and utility payments. Even if declaring bankruptcy has erased all their bills, people often find themselves in financial trouble again within a few years!

Money is also a leading cause of problems in marriage. One reason is that couples don't cooperate in managing their finances. "What we can afford" can mean something very different to each person! The value of material goods depends on how we use them. Too frequently, though, individuals become so absorbed in money problems that they neglect life's more important things.

This is why we're discussing finances in a religion class: In order to live the values Jesus taught, we have to learn practical ways to keep material concerns in their proper perspective. It's hard to focus on being loving, happy, and generous if your finances are in shambles and you're struggling to pay your bills!

Material things should help you live your worthy values and attain your worthwhile goals—not control your life. That's why you must know how to manage your personal finances so that monetary concerns don't end up enslaving you. You can use money for its proper purposes if you learn to plan and manage your finances wisely.

Our Father, . . . Give us this day our daily bread.
Open the **way** for me to earn an **honest** living without anxiety;
but let me never forget the needs of others,
and make me **want** only that benefit for **myself**
which will also be their **gain**.

"A MEDITATION ON THE LORD'S PRAYER" BY WALTER RUSSELL BOWIE

Discernment step three

Choose three people you can confide in and rely on for sound, honest insights about yourself. Talk with each of them and ask their advice about your pursuing each of the occupations you are considering for your future.

For discussion

1. Why do you think people often get into debt again soon after bankruptcy has cleared their debts?

2. What does "what I can afford" mean to you? What might it mean to someone who:
   • is independently wealthy?
   • is considered poor in our society? in India?
   • has an upper-middle-class income in our society? a middle-class income? a lower-middle-class income?

3. How will you avoid buying more on credit than you can afford?

4. How can money affect your happiness and relationships in negative ways? In positive ways?

5. Why do you think money is a main source of marital problems? How can couples avoid those problems?

Surviving financially

To live on your own (even at college), you'll have to budget. That means projecting what your expenses will be and planning how you'll pay for them. You can get into debt quickly if you don't establish and follow a sensible budget! These young adults describe how they "graduated in debt" by not properly managing their finances as college students.

Daryl: Getting credit cards at college was so easy. They'd sign you up for them right at the bookstore—and everybody signed up. That little piece of plastic was like magic! It made us feel so adult: Somebody trusted us with lots of money. I could get whatever I wanted without having to work for it first.

When I'd go out with friends, I'd often say, "It's on me." I felt important, and I guess I just wanted to impress my friends. But owing twenty thousand dollars now doesn't feel so great. I'll have to keep working two jobs for three or four years just to get out of debt.

Cindy: I guess I wanted to have it all—now. What my parents had to work years for I thought I could have right away. So while I was in college, I bought great-looking clothes and a nice car. I didn't think twice about taking weekend trips with my friends.

I thought, "When I get a job after graduation, I'll be able to pay off my charge cards in a year—two at the max." I just didn't realize that, on a starting salary and with all the other living expenses, it wouldn't be that easy. Now I'm trying to avoid bankruptcy at age twenty-four, because I don't want a bad credit rating to hound me for years."

Jordan: I graduated on a Sunday; the following Monday I got the notice that the bank was going to repossess my car unless I could make the back payments. I had a great time in college living off of charge cards. But I never dreamed that pay-back time would be so tough.

*Now I'm on a **very** tight budget. I traded my classy new car for a cheap used one. I've worked out deals with all my creditors to pay what I owe and I've cut up the plastic cards that got me into so much trouble. If I don't have the cash or it's not in my budget, I don't buy it. It'll take a while, but I'm determined to live debt free: I don't ever want to sweat over money again! It's been a hard lesson, but at least I learned it early.*

To avoid similar financial problems, confront your personal attitudes about money. Know before you buy things how you'll pay for them and keep track of what you spend. (Tip: Buy a good money-management software program and use it faithfully.) Learn how to plan a budget—and stick to it!

What your budget should include

1. **Your take-home pay** (which will be less than your salary)
2. **Your main living expenses:**
   - Food
   - Rent
   - Utilities
   - Medical and dental
   - Laundry and household supplies
   - Phone
   - Transportation (car payment [when needed], gas, estimated auto maintenance, insurance, license, and so on)
   - Personal necessities (shoes, clothing, toiletries, and so on)
   - Church and charitable contributions, and gifts
3. **Occasional living expenses** (such as taxes and insurance payments)
4. **Regular savings for unexpected expenses**, emergencies, and for the future.
5. **A monthly allowance** for non-necessary items (recreation, eating out, computer games, music, and such.)
6. **Regular savings for items you want in the future** (a new car, a home)

Do you know how to

- write and endorse a check?
- balance a checkbook and a bank statement?
- keep accurate financial records?
- rent an apartment?
- be a wise, responsible, socially aware consumer?

Activity

Interview the one who oversees your family's budget. Ask what budgeting for a family involves and what are the hardest things about living within the budget. Add your questions. Write a two-page report on what you learned that will help you set up and live by a budget.

For discussion

1. What tempts you to spend money unwisely? How do you usually respond to such temptations?
2. What are your general attitudes about money—its importance, saving it, spending it? How have these attitudes been influenced by the ways you've been raised?
3. How would you advise someone who has trouble managing money? Where would you turn for help if you had financial problems?
4. What other practical questions do you have about living and surviving financially on your own?

Are you a tightwad or a spendthrift?

Early in life we all learn attitudes about money and managing it. This self-test can help you identify how sensible your attitudes about money are—or aren't. Your instructor will explain how to score your results.

On the blanks, write the letter that corresponds to the option you'd choose. Accept each question as-is; don't read other factors into it.

____ 1. If you had only $200 in savings and you received a $10,000 inheritance, what would you do?

    a. Put the money in a savings or retirement account.

    b. Invest it in a riskier stock market fund where I might make more money.

____ 2. Which would you be more inclined to believe?

    a. Children shouldn't have to work; they'll have to work long and hard enough as adults.

    b. To learn responsibility, children should earn all their spending money by working for it.

____ 3. Which attitude most corresponds with yours?

    a. Money is to be spent—life is short, and you should enjoy it while you can.

    b. It's important to save for a rainy day—you never know when something will come up that you need or want.

____ 4. When buying clothes, which do you consider more?

    a. How good the material is, how practical the item is, how well it will wear, or how long it will last.

    b. How much you like the style or color.

____ 5. If you and your spouse had full-time jobs, no children, and wanted to buy a home, how would you use your $5,000 Christmas bonus?

    a. To buy a life insurance policy in case something happened to one of you.

    b. To take a vacation to Europe, which you've both always wanted to do.

____ 6. What's your response when you see something you really like on sale?

    a. I usually buy it because it's such a bargain.

    b. I usually buy it only if I can afford it and would probably have bought it anyway.

____ 7. In general, how would you categorize most of the people you know?

    a. They're too tight with money.

    b. They spend their money too loosely.

____ 8. Do you usually wear brand-name clothes, shop in particular stores, or buy certain things because your friends do?

    a. Yes.   b. No.

____ 9. When you're given a gift of money or you earn more than you need for expenses, how do you most often respond?

    a. The extra cash burns a hole in my pocket. I usually spend it soon on something I want but don't need.

    b. I usually save the extra money for something I want to buy or do in the future.

____ 10. Have you ever risked getting into trouble over money (for example, borrowed more than you could easily pay back, stolen, lied about needing money or what you need it for)?

    a. Yes.   b. No.

____ 11. In the last few years, did you buy things you no longer like or have now lost interest in?

    a. Yes.   b. No.

____ 12. If a magazine ad offered you the chance to buy a genuine, one-carat emerald or a 14K gold chain for only $5.00 with "satisfaction guaranteed or your money back," would you be tempted to buy it for yourself or for someone else?

    a. Yes, I might send for it—at only $5.00 there's not much to lose with a "money-back guarantee."

    b. No, it sounds too good to be true—you get what you pay for, and I'd just be throwing money away on cheap junk.

____ 13. A "business advertising service" calls to tell you that you've won $1,000 worth of coupons at stores in your area. To claim your prize, you have to send $15.00 to cover the cost of postage and handling. Would you do it?

    a. Yes, it's a nice prize—$15 is cheap for $1,000 worth of merchandise coupons, even if I use only some of them.

    b. No, I'd just tell them I don't accept telephone solicitations and hang up.

____ 14. Do you often waste things you use (for example, food, notebook paper, paper towels, electricity)?

    a. Yes.   b. No.

____ 15. How much care do you usually take with your things (clothes, computer, car, books, sports equipment, and so on)?

    a. I'm very careful with my things.

    b. I really don't consider taking care of my things—I just enjoy them.

____ **Total score**

Managing your time

Does life sometimes pull you in so many directions that you feel overwhelmed? Leading a balanced life in our fast-paced world isn't easy! But not achieving that balance leads to job burnout and unhappiness at home. To stay in control of your life, always keep your most important priorities clearly in mind.

Be careful then how you live, not as unwise people but as wise, making the most of the time. . . .

Ephesians 5:15–16a

To renew your priorities, make time periodically to regain your sense of inner peace, stability, strength, hope, and direction. Set aside time each day to pray—to gather your thoughts and refresh your spirit alone with your Friend, God. Many people refocus on what really counts by reading a portion of the Scriptures every day. Christians find God's truest, fullest expression for us in Jesus' life and gospel teaching. It is truly amazing how helpful Jesus' basic guidelines are in coping with life's complexities!

Catholics find that the Sacraments of Eucharist and Reconciliation give us renewed strength, hope, healing, and forgiveness.[7] Celebrating the Lord's Supper together, Christians share in the Bread of Life and receive spiritual food for life's journey. In the Sacrament of Reconciliation, Catholics celebrate the mending of relationships our wrongdoing has damaged. Then we begin anew to live our main vocation of loving. Thus the sacraments Jesus gave us can help us experience God's living presence more tangibly in our busy lives.

Time management is a major problem in people's personal and professional lives. Life today is so busy and complex— especially for working parents! Despite today's technological advances and time-saving gadgets, all of us seem to have more to do and less time to do it. It can be hard to juggle your time to meet all your relationship and work obligations.

Time is the currency God gives you to spend on creating your life. Your time in this life is limited and precious—no moment will ever come again. So it's more important that you spend your time wisely than that you spend your money wisely. To lead a balanced life and live your priorities, learn to manage your time well. Don't be obsessively organized, though—always leave room for spontaneity! When you feel overwhelmed by all you've got to do, try following the suggestions on the next page.

Time management techniques

1. Make a *To Do* list for today or this week. (This organizes and calms your mind.)

2. Prioritize your list (1, 2, 3 or A, B, C), and plan when you'll do each task. (Tackle important things first—while you have most energy. The rest will then seem easier.)

3. Don't procrastinate. (Postponing tasks won't make them go away.)

4. Focus on one thing at a time. (One task is manageable; ten tasks seem overwhelming.)

5. Make tasks less tedious. (Play your favorite music, adjust your attitude, ask a friend to help, look forward to a treat afterward.)

6. Reward yourself when you're done!

A famous description of time and its importance is found in the Old Testament Book of Ecclesiastes.

For everything there is a season, and a time for every matter under heaven:

a time to be born, and a time to die;

a time to plant, and a time to pluck up what has been planted;

a time to kill, and a time to heal;

a time to break down, and a time to build up;

a time to weep, and a time to laugh;

a time to mourn, and a time to dance;

a time to throw away stones, and a time to gather stones together;

a time to embrace, and a time to refrain from embracing;

a time to seek, and a time to lose;

a time to keep, and a time to throw away;

a time to tear, and a time to sew;

a time to keep silence, and a time to speak;

a time to love, and a time to hate;

a time for war, and a time for peace.

ECCLESIATES 3:1–8

Discernment step four

Using the handout provided, assess what each of the future occupations you are thinking about would require of you. Consider what possibilities and opportunities each would offer you in terms of your needs, abilities, experiences, relationships, and priorities in life. Write a one-page paper summarizing what you have discovered during the four-step process of discerning your future occupation. Mention what you have found most enlightening or helpful about the process.

Activity

For this next week, follow these six steps for getting things done. Then report to the class on whether this process has helped you manage your time better. Suggest other time-management tips that have worked for you.

For discussion

1. Do you have trouble properly balancing the demands of school, work, and your personal relationships? Explain.

2. Do you spend enough time each day on your important relationships—with God, your family, and your friends? Explain.

3. What helps you periodically reset your priorities? How do your religious beliefs and practices help you do that?

4. What small moments have been the most precious in your life thus far? Did you touch a sense of God or the eternal in those moments? Explain.

5. When your room at home is an absolute mess, how do you usually tackle the clean-up?

6. How could you use your time better? What would you like to make more time for in your life?

Review

1. What is the difference between a job, an occupation, and a career?

2. Why must your future occupation be your choice? How is discerning it a process, and what does that process involve?

3. How can you best prepare for your future occupation(s), and what can you learn from Jesus about building on your previous experiences?

4. What role should material concerns play in your life? How can you avoid financial problems?

5. What is a budget, and why is budgeting important? Explain each step of planning a budget.

6. To live your priorities, why is it important that you manage your time wisely?

In summary

Every vocation is a calling from God which invites our response through the active ways we minister in service to others. To discern your vocation, know yourself well and give yourself time to make a wise choice. Use the discernment process to explore opportunities, seek direction, ask advice, and assess the possibilities in view of your needs and gifts. Then freely and deliberately choose the path in life that will best enable you to love. Consider simplifying your lifestyle to reflect your true values and priorities.

Practice self-discipline, keep your legitimate promises, and be faithful to your commitments. Identify which occupation(s) you'd be successful at and enjoy doing, and follow your heart in sharing your gifts with others. Let material things help you live your sworthy goals, and learn the practical aspects of responsibly living on your own. Above all, remember: You will achieve your mission and discover your meaning in life only by living your primary vocation to love.

Key concepts

being truly successful in life
career, career choice and flexibility, job
deacon
discernment, discernment process, discerning life
 choices freely
fidelity, being faithful, commitment
heartfelt work, sharing one's gifts with others
integrity
lay person
life choices, values and priorities
lifestyle: living simply

materialism, terminal and instrumental
minister, ministry, service
money management, attitudes about money
occupation: choosing, preparing for seeking immediate
 gratification
self-discipline, self-control
self-knowledge, self-discovery process
spiritual renewal
time management
vocation, calling to love, having more than one vocation

Endnotes

1. See *Human Sexuality: A Catholic Perspective for Education and Lifelong Learning,* (Washington, DC: United States Catholic Conference, 1991), 22.
2. See *Human Sexuality*, 22.
3. See *Human Sexuality*, 25–26.
4. Mihaly Csikszentmihalyi and Eugene Rochberg-Halton, "Object Lessons," *Psychology Today* (December 1981): 84–85.
5. Csikszentmihalyi and Rochberg-Halton: 85.
6. The items in this exercise are based on material in *What Color Is Your Parachute: A Practical Manual for Job Hunters & Career Changers* by Richard Nelson Bolles (Berkley, CA: Ten Speed Press).
7. See *Human Sexuality*, 21.

CHAPTER 3

LOVING ANOTHER

SCRIPTURE

I pray that you may have the power to comprehend, with all the saints, what is the breadth and length and height and depth, and to know the love of Christ that surpasses knowledge, so that you may be filled with all the fullness of God.

EPHESIANS 3:18–19

PRAYER

Loving God,

Thank you for the many ways your love touches our lives.

There's still too much coldness and loneliness in the world— and sometimes in our own souls.

We get so absorbed with our own concerns that we don't always see or care enough about others' problems.

Yet, your love intimately links us all.

Help us believe that and realize what that means.

Help us step out of our shyness, insecurities, and selfishness to reach out more to others.

Give us your hope and courage, so we don't give up on improving our world.

Let us understand how it's in loving one another— especially those in greatest need—that we love you.

What is love?

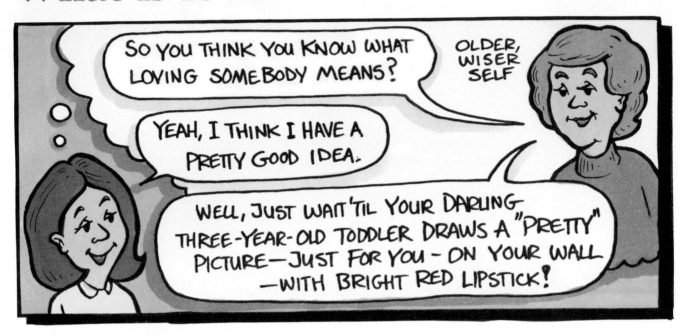

For centuries people have tried to describe and define love. They've written about "puppy love," "eternal love," "platonic love," "erotic love" and "romantic love." Ads constantly tell us we'll "love" this or that new product. Kids "love" their pets—and the latest movie or computer game. Parents "love" their kids—and the new house or car. There are different kinds of love and ways to love. But is everything that's called love really love?

Too many people have "fallen in love" and married without even knowing what love means. That may partly explain why, sadly, many young persons today have never witnessed a successful marriage in their families. No wonder young adults are often scared to make any kind of relationship commitment.

Being older doesn't always mean being wiser about what love means! Many adults have confused or distorted notions about love—for example, those who stay with an abusive partner because he or she "loves me." Or the TV journalist who explained that a man murdered his ex-wife "because he loved her so much he just couldn't stand to see her with someone else."

How can you know what love is and tell when it's truly present? What is love?

The core of all love is caring. Jesus' words and actions revealed how much God cares for us. They also showed us what it means for us to love someone: To truly love another is to care unselfishly about the other person's total welfare in the context of that person's real life circumstances.

This principle is fundamental to every love relationship: *Genuine love always desires good and not harm.* Without that foundation there can be no real love—pleasant or erotic feelings maybe but not love. If you care about someone, you're concerned that the person not be hurt unnecessarily. You desire only what's good for the one you love. For love is essentially an intention, an act of will, not an emotion. Emotions are certainly important in loving, but they're not love's essence!

Loving is a free decision to care—not because we have to, but because we want to care. That's why love doesn't stop while two people are disagreeing. (Sometimes people disagree because they care.) Although you might not feel cozy toward each other at the moment, you can still remain deeply concerned for each other's welfare. Loving is concern for the other— a concern that doesn't stop, even if warm feelings disappear.

When the firefighter risks death to save others, that's an act of love. The firefighter doesn't first size up the trapped victims' moral qualities to determine whether they're worth rescuing. The firefighter is unselfishly concerned about the welfare of people she or he doesn't even know. As Jesus explained, "no one can have greater love" than that (see John 15:13). It is from God's own Spirit of love that we receive the strength to love unselfishly, as Jesus did. Christian Baptism initiates and the Sacrament of Confirmation strengthens in Christians that kind of love which puts others' interests above one's own.

When Jesus said we must "love our neighbor," he didn't mean we must always like each other. He meant that we must always care about each other's total well-being. *Agape* (the word the original Greek Scriptures used for the love Jesus spoke about) doesn't mean falling in love, being friends, or even liking someone. Agape means "to wish well"—to desire the total good of others.

> *Love is patient; love is kind; love is not envious or boastful or arrogant or rude.*
>
> *It does not insist on its own way; it is not irritable or resentful; it does not rejoice in wrongdoing, but rejoices in the truth.*
>
> *It bears all things, believes all things, hopes all things, endures all things.*
>
> *Love never ends.*
>
> 1 CORINTHIANS 13:4–8A

We're to care that way for everybody—especially for people in greatest need, and certainly for individuals we feel special affection toward. In fact, to be able to love one special person, you must first be a loving person. One who claims to love one person while disdaining everyone else ends up treating the "loved" one shabbily, too. How you love is who you are.

Love one another, **recognizing** in the heart of each of you the same **God** who is being **born**.

TEILHARD DE CHARDIN

Journal entry

1. List the people you love–in Jesus' *agape* sense.
2. List the people you feel love you in that way.
3. List three things that reveal God's unselfish love for you.

Scripture insights

Give examples from the Gospels of how Jesus expressed who he was by the way he loved others in the agape sense.

For discussion

1. Do you agree that there can be no true love without basic concern for the other's total good? Explain.
2. What's the difference between what actually fosters someone's total good and what only seems good for someone or is good for someone only right now? Give examples.
3. How can emotions help or hinder us in loving? Why are emotions not the essence of love?
4. How do you think relationships would change if more people really understood and practiced what Jesus meant by loving others?

Who cares?

For discussion

1. How did each parent's response show genuine loving concern? How else might each parent have responded?

2. Do you think each parent's decision properly acknowledged the son's or daughter's real-life circumstances?

3. Describe a situation in which you felt unloved when someone wouldn't let you do something.

   • Do you now think that the person was right, or do you think you should have been allowed to decide the matter for yourself?

   • Did the person who refused you seem to understand your feelings and circumstances at the time?

Living love's essentials

Accept yourself and others.

- Understand that everyone is valuable, loved by God, and therefore worthy of your love.
- Love unconditionally, as God does. (Conditional "love" can be disguised selfishness.)
- Continue caring about someone—even if your special relationship ends.
- Don't put yourself or others down—or on a pedestal.
  - What does it mean to be accepted for who you are? To accept others for who they are? By whom do you feel most accepted as a person? Why?

Be responsible.

- Act in ways that foster the other person's total good.
- Never desire to hurt anyone. Think before you act about what will benefit or hurt someone.
- Behave in ways that reflect your sincere concern about the other person's well-being.
  - How do you think teenagers act responsibly in their relationships? Act irresponsibly? Explain.

Be honest and sincere.

- Be truthful. It's the only way to communicate yourself and your love.
- Respect another's dignity and integrity—and your own. Don't play deceitful games.
- Be yourself and accept others as they are—with their faults, flaws, and virtues.
- Be faithful and worthy of another's trust.
  - How much do you value honesty and sincerity in a relationship? Why? In what ways have others seemed dishonest or insincere in their relationships with you?

Be supportive.

- Care about who the other person is and can become—for his or her sake.
- Don't manipulate or be possessive.
- Want the best for someone. Help her or him grow as a person.
  - How do teenagers manipulate each other? Their parent or step-parent? Their teachers? (Give concrete examples.)
  - What is the difference between being supportive and being manipulative? How might you be more supportive toward your peers? Family members? Teachers? (Give examples.)

Give of yourself.

- Care more about what you can give to the relationship than what you can receive from it.
- Be there, sometimes without words, when someone needs you.
- Share your inner self—from the heart, even though you risk being rejected.
- Receive graciously from the other person.
  - What dishonest games do some people play in their romantic relationships? Do young women play different games than young men do? Explain and give examples.
  - Why do you think people don't share their inner selves honestly when they should? Explain.

Project *Love?* song

Analyze the words of a currently popular love song as follows. For #s 2 and 3, refer to specific words in the song to illustrate your point.

1. Write down the title and words to the song and hand them in with your assignment.

2. Describe the song's ideas or messages about love that support and/or contradict the essentials of love you discussed in this chapter.

3. Explain whether or not you think this song is about genuine love.

The Solomon choice

Read in 1 Kings 3:16–28 the biblical story of King Solomon's dilemma. Then read the following true account and respond to the questions.

Shortly after their birth, two baby girls were inadvertently switched at the hospital and given to the wrong parents. The mistake evidently occurred when the babies' ID bracelets fell off. One of the mothers, Paula, discovered the mix-up three years later when a DNA test was done on her daughter, Callie. At the time Paula discovered the mix-up, she could have kept it secret and done nothing. But she said she wanted to find out whether her biological child was safe and secure.

Subsequent DNA tests confirmed the biological parents' identity—and the fact that the two girls had been switched at birth. Kevin and Tamara, the parents who'd raised Paula's biological child, Rebecca, had recently been killed in an auto accident. They died not knowing Rebecca wasn't their biological daughter. Since then, Rebecca has been raised by both sets of her grandparents in a joint-custody arrangement. Kevin and Tamara's other child is also being raised by the grandparents.

On learning of the switch, one of Kevin's relatives suggested that the 3-year-old girls be given back to their biological relatives. She said that if it were she, she'd want to have her biological child, but continue to see the child she'd raised. (In another case a few years previously, a child was ordered returned to her biological mother and removed from the adoptive parents who had raised her.)

Paula's four other children have been extremely upset that they might lose their sister, Callie. They're concerned about how Callie will be told and whether she'll be able to understand what's happened. Both families, however, have said from the start that they want to do what's in the girls' best interests and settle the issue among themselves without going to court. Paula kept saying that she wants only what's best for both children—whether the families decide or a judge decides.

Paula said that at first the ordeal had tested her faith. She wondered why God had let the switch happen—and why she discovered it three years later. When she found out that Callie now had no other parents, she said she understood why—that both girls would need a mother. On finally meeting her biological daughter, Rebecca, Paula said that she tried to avoid scaring or pushing her. Sobbing, Paula said she loves Callie, the daughter she's raised as her own.

Some feel the girls should stay where they are and be told when they're older what happened. Then they could

meet their biological families if they wish. Others feel the girls should stay with their present families and also establish a relationship with their biological families. Still others feel Paula should be given custody of both the daughter she's raised and her biological child who's now without a mother.

For discussion

1. How did King Solomon know which woman was the child's real mother? On what value(s) do you think he based his decision?

2. Did Solomon's choice reflect or contradict what love really means? Do you think he made the right choice? Explain.

3. King Solomon's decision is often upheld as an example of how difficult decisions should be made. If Solomon were deciding who should be granted permanent custody of each girl in the "switched at birth" case, how do you think he would decide? Explain.

4. Whatever is decided, how should the situation be handled so as to respect love's essentials? Explain.

5. To whom would you grant custody of Rebecca? Of Callie? How would your decision reflect love's essentials and what love means? Explain.

How caring are you?

This exercise can help you assess how caring you are in practical, concrete ways. Nobody's perfect. So answer according to how you are, not how you think you should be. You won't be expected to share your responses or results.[1] On each blank, write the number from 0–5 that best reflects your response. Your instructor will then tell you how to tally and interpret your score.

0 — Never/Not at all
1 — Rarely/Hardly at all
2 — Seldom/Not very strongly
3 — Sometimes/Somewhat, but not strongly
4 — Often/Somewhat strongly
5 — Always/Very strongly

_____ 1. How often do you express concern for others (how they're feeling, did on a test, have been since you last saw them, and so on)?

_____ 2. How well do you remember the names and faces of people you meet?

_____ 3. Do you remember things people tell you about themselves and their families?

_____ 4. Do you make a note of birthdays and special days so that you remember in time?

_____ 5. Do you appropriately show appreciation, offer sympathy, or praise or congratulate someone?

_____ 6. Do you say good things about others more than you say negative things?

_____ 7. Do you go out of your way to help others (for example, picking up books they've dropped, letting their car go ahead of you, and so on)?

_____ 8. Do you go out of your way to welcome a new student?

_____ 9. At a party, do you try to see that someone who seems alone is included in the fun?

_____ 10. Do you do your fair share of the cleanup work at home, on a school project, in the school cafeteria, or in similar situations?

_____ 11. When you hear an ambulance siren or learn of some tragedy, do you hope or pray that things will turn out all right?

_____ 12. Do you try to relieve someone's trouble, unhappiness, or loneliness when you can do so rather easily?

_____ 13. Do you try to do the same even when it's inconvenient or difficult?

_____ 14. How quickly do you forgive and forget?

_____ 15. How often do you pitch in to help with what needs to be done—without being asked?

_____ 16. Do you try to be kind to everybody, not just those you want to impress?

_____ 17. How much can people rely on you to keep your word and your promises?

_____ 18. Can your family and friends count on you not to talk about their personal matters with others?

_____ 19. How quickly do you adapt to situations—for example, when someone wants to change the subject or to be quiet or left alone?

_____ 20. When you disagree with others, are you initially more inclined to suspect their motives than to credit them with good intentions?

Follow your instructor's directions to determine your total score.

_____ **Total score**

Project love

Complete one of these projects about what love means:

1. Make an abstract piece of sculpture, a drawing, or another symbolic creation showing what genuine love means to you. Be imaginative. Write a brief paper explaining what your creation expresses about love or be prepared to explain it orally in class.

2. Write a two-page paper on how the movies you've seen recently portrayed what love is and means. Explain how each movie succeeded and/or failed at depicting the essential elements of genuine love.

Review

1. What characteristics are fundamental to all love? What type of caring underlies all genuine love?

2. How is love essentially an intention rather than an emotion?

3. What did Jesus really mean by the kind of love he said we must have for one another?

4. To love one special person, why must one be a loving person?

Being in love

Caring is the most important part of love. Many other aspects of loving remain mysterious and confusing: What draws you to be friends with one person but not with someone else?

Why are you romantically attracted to one person and not to another? How can you tell whether your romantic attraction is or can become real love?

Understanding attraction

Strong, mutual attraction may occur the first time two people meet. Many researchers believe this is why: Based on how we experience love as children, we each seem to develop certain preferences in people. These characteristics form "love maps" of what most appeals to us in a friend or romantic partner. Our subconscious records those preferred nuances of speech, mannerisms, ways of thinking, physical characteristics, and so forth.

When we consciously or subconsciously recognize many of our preference traits in someone, we may then experience the electric delight of "**love at first sight**." (A comparable process may draw us to certain persons as friends.) Shakespeare described such love as a fever.

Infatuation certainly isn't an illness. But scientists have discovered that it does produce amphetamine-like substances in the body. That may account for the physical sensations that often accompany infatuation. As with other such drugs, however, the body builds

love at first sight

strong initial romantic or sexual attraction to someone

up a tolerance. It increasingly needs more of the substance than the body can continue supplying to sustain the same feelings. That may help explain why the initial passionate feelings inevitably fade after awhile.

If infatuation develops into a deeper loving attachment, another type of chemical is released in the body. Those endorphins produce the calming, contented, peaceful feeling that couples often experience in a solid love relationship.

As wonderful as it feels, love at first sight is only instant attraction. It isn't a deep love, because that type of love **can't** happen all at once. When the attraction is mutual, the emotional and sexual feelings can be extremely intense. (Some individuals love how the other person makes them feel more than they love the person himself or herself.) Mistaking the attraction for love, people often build unfounded hopes about their relationship's future. They may become sexually involved without even knowing each other well!

How current researchers view love's stages

Passion (lust and/or infatuation) ⇨ Intimacy and contented attachment ⇨ Commitment

infatuation
strong but superficial emotional attraction to someone

People get terribly hurt when they expect of a shallow emotional **infatuation** what only deep, enduring love can provide. They may do things they have reason to regret later—as did many women in the Roman Empire. To make themselves irresistible to a man, they would adorn their faces with a lead-based white powder. The resulting lead poisoning often proved fatal! Not long ago, authorities discovered that over twenty young women had been infected with the deadly HIV virus—by one young man! Why had they fallen for the man's charms? The young women said he'd often complimented them and made them feel loved.

Lasting love requires knowledge, growth, and effort to build. Deep caring involves knowing each other well and many opportunities for sharing. That always takes time!

Attraction certainly may lead to real love. If both persons' qualities remain as desirable over time as when they first met, the relationship can continue to grow. Be prepared, though, for the reality that infatuation often leads to disappointment. The qualities that attract us to someone aren't always the important things in a long-term relationship.

Also, people usually show their best side first and can end up being totally different from what they seemed initially. They might have long, deep conversations in which they really connect as if they were meant for each other. But it takes time for both persons to discover each other's flaws and learn whether they can accept them. The less desirable qualities always surface eventually. That's when romance typically fades, the road gets rocky, and, for some people, the relationship ends—often as quickly and intensely as it began!

Letting yourself develop big expectations of the relationship before you really know and love each other can be extremely hurtful. It's painfully disillusioning to have mistaken mere fleeting attraction for enduring love. So how should you handle intense romantic attraction? You'll never get burned if you don't get near the fire, but you will miss its beauty, light, and warmth.

It's probably wisest just to recognize infatuation for what it is—strong, emotional attraction. It's not undying love that requires an immediate, exclusive, eternal commitment! Keep reminding yourself of that before your hormones start to carry you away. Let your head counsel your heart. Even if you wish it were so, even if it feels like it, instant attraction is not love. So don't let yourself make an early emotional investment based on initial attraction. If necessary, help the other person understand what's really happening to both of you.

When torn between your heart and your head,

listen to the part of yourself that has the brains.

Many a **man** has fallen in **love** with a girl in a light so **dim** he would not have **chosen** a suit by it.

Maurice Chevalier

Journal entry

1. What do you hope to learn from the temporary romantic relationships you experience?

2. While you're single, what main truth do you hope to remember about love?

For discussion

1. Have you ever experienced instant romantic attraction or "love at first sight"? How would you describe those experiences?

2. Does it make sense to you that someone could truly love at first sight?

3. Have you ever "fallen out of infatuation"—or helped a friend do so? Explain what feelings resulted.

4. Why do you think most romantic relationships don't last?

5. Respond to this student's question: "I think you can get just as close to someone in a month or so as some people do in a year. Why do people believe you can be in love only if you're together for a year?"

6. Who do you think falls in love more quickly—men or women? Explain.

"It is only with the heart that one can see rightly; what is essential is invisible to the eye."

ANTOINE DE SAINT-EXUPERY

Rushing the relationship often backfires, scaring the other person away. Instead, take your time and enjoy the wonder of getting to know each other better. Your feelings may gradually develop into a deeper love. But remember that love isn't a ready-made package with "guaranteed lifetime satisfaction or your heart cheerfully refunded"! Being in love is a process that needs time and effort to grow.

Love is a wonderful mystery that each person experiences uniquely. People can gradually grow into love without being initially drawn to each other. As they come to know and love each other more deeply, they may feel the sparks of mutual attraction. Or their love may remain a quiet, reassuring friendship or contentment.

However you experience love, while you're single remember:

- Developing genuine love is worth the emotional risks and patient effort, even when the relationship doesn't last.

- Parting is painful. But how you've grown in loving will prepare you for more meaningful, lasting love and happiness.

- What's most important is not holding onto love, but letting it expand your heart.

Distinguishing love from infatuation

Students at three universities were asked, "What would you most like to know about love?" Many students responded with this question: "How can you tell the difference between infatuation and love?" Well, here's how:

Spare yourself heartache! Know how to tell whether it's

Infatuation	or	Love
1. ❏ happens quickly—in a few days, weeks, or months		❏ involves deep personal sharing that can develop only over time
2. ❏ doesn't know (or want to know) the other's faults, or hopes to change the other person		❏ knows the other's weaknesses and faults and still accepts and respects him or her as a person
3. ❏ is suspicious and jealous		❏ trusts in each other
4. ❏ is impatient or pushy; wants everything now		❏ doesn't rush things; considers where the relationship should go for the total good of both persons
5. ❏ concentrates on physical appearance, social or financial status, and/or immediate sexual gratification		❏ cares about the inner person
6. ❏ tempts one to compromise one's values and beliefs		❏ strengthens each other's innermost convictions
7. ❏ ends the relationship as suddenly and unexpectedly as it began		❏ lasts over time (even if the special relationship ends)
8. ❏ is a self-absorbed relationship that often causes problems and loss of interest in other areas of life		❏ increases energy, sensitivity, and the freedom to deepen all one's relationships
9. ❏ is overly anxious to please the other in order to keep the relationship going; restricts honesty		❏ is honest and lets you both be yourselves
10. ❏ leaves one constantly insecure or in emotional turmoil		❏ increases self-confidence, security, and peace
11. ❏ idealizes the other person and the relationship		❏ is practical and realistic, as well as optimistic
12. ❏ is possessive; allows the other person little freedom		❏ is a mutually supportive relationship

For discussion

1. In a relationship, how could you tell for sure if you were truly in love with each other?

2. What's your opinion about how one can best cope with infatuation? Explain.

3. When do you think a "relationship" is really just one person's or both persons' fantasy?

4. What do you hope to learn from the temporary love relationships you experience?

Love or Infatuation?

Read the typical love/infatuation examples below. On each blank, rate how much the relationship seems based on infatuation and how much it evidences the qualities of love. Be prepared to discuss your reasons for your ratings.

_____% Love   _____% Infatuation

_____% _____% 1. Jason has flipped over Ashley. He lies awake at night thinking about how gorgeous she is and how great she makes him feel.

_____% _____% 2. Carmen really likes being so important to her boyfriend, Matt. That he obviously wants her all to himself tells her how much he really loves her. She feels flattered that he gets so upset when he hears she's been talking to other guys.

_____% _____% 3. Ryan occasionally smokes marijuana at parties or on dates with his girlfriend Kate. She doesn't like it, but Ryan tells her it helps him feel better about himself and sexier toward her. He'd like her to smoke marijuana occasionally, too, so they'd both enjoy having stronger feelings toward each other.

_____% _____% 4. Tiffany spends three nights a week, including Fridays, doing volunteer work at a local hospital. She enjoys it and feels it helps her prepare for the medical career she plans. Her boyfriend, Darrin, wants her to stop working on Friday nights. He says she owes their relationship at least that much.

Tiffany explains that everybody else wants Friday evenings free, too, so that's when she's needed most. She refuses to quit working Fridays. Consequently, they've had to miss quite a few parties, concerts, and school dances this year.

_____% _____% 5. Evan feels down when his team loses a game. He feels it's partly his fault for not playing as well as he should have. His girlfriend, Sarah, trying to cheer him, tells him he's a great guy . . . and that "it's just a game."

_____% _____% 6. Bart gets very irritated sometimes at how his girlfriend nags him about his driving. He figures if she really loved him as much as she says she does, she'd get off his back and trust him to do the driving.

_____% _____% 7. The crowd Juan and Alanna hang around with were planning a big day at the beach. They were all going together in Carlos's van, leaving very early Sunday morning. When Alanna said she couldn't leave that early because she wanted to go to church first, Juan got really upset. He told Alanna she was being inconsiderate to him and their friends.

_____% _____% 8. Jan says, "I'm really in love with my boyfriend, but sometimes I don't quite trust him. Like, he'll say something to me, and I'll wonder if he really means it. Or I'll wonder if something he tells me is really true."

Project love

Complete **one** of these projects about what love means.

1. Make a collage or banner illustrating either "The myths of love" or "The reality of love." Write a two-page paper explaining your collage or banner, or be prepared to explain it orally in class.

2. Write a two-page paper on how love is positively and negatively portrayed on television:
   • Between children and their parents
   • Between siblings (brothers and sisters)
   • Among elderly persons
   • Between teenagers in love
   • Between single adults who have a romantic relationship
   • Between married adults
   • In documentaries or biographies of people who've significantly contributed to others' lives.

3. Write a two-page analysis of a romance story from a current magazine or TV show (such as a daytime or prime time soap opera). Explain how it portrays genuine love and/or infatuation—or confuses them. Cite specific examples that illustrate your point.

4. Based on what you've learned thus far in this course, write a two-page essay on
   • The importance I want my love of God, of others, and of myself to have in my life, and why.
   • What I want a special love relationship with someone to mean to me.

Review

1. What is instant attraction? Why does it occur?
2. What can be risky about being infatuated with someone? Can infatuation lead to genuine love?
3. How is love a process? Why may individuals experience it differently?
4. How can you tell whether a relationship is based mainly on infatuation or mainly on love?

Friendship

The best mirror is an old friend.
SANDY BATTIN

Why are we attracted to some people as friends, but not to others with equally good qualities? As with romantic love, friendship is part mystery. Something just clicks, drawing us to be friends. Or a friendship may come about more gradually, as a science-fiction android once put it: "As I experience certain sensory input patterns, my mental pathways become accustomed to them. Their inputs eventually are anticipated and even missed when absent."[2]

For us humans, there's certainly a lot more to friendship than just sensory pathway input! But whether friendship begins quickly or gradually, it develops only over time. Our friendships truly grow as we celebrate life's joys together and shore each other up through tragedy and discouragement.

Friendship multiplies joy and divides sorrow.

Friendship helps make our problems bearable. Friends respect, accept, understand, help, and confide in each other. Friendships often outlast many other kinds of relationships. Friends see each other through romantic break-ups, family squabbles, health problems, marriage breakdowns, and job stresses. A friend accepts you as a person—without having to agree with everything you say or do. Such friendship is often more stable and lasting than romantic or family relationships that don't have friendship as a solid basis.

A **friend** is one to whom you can pour out your **heart**—
the **useless** and the good grain together,
knowing that the **gentlest** of hands will sift it,
keep what's **worth** keeping, and
with a breath of **kindness**, blow the rest away.

PROVERB

Choosing friends

Friendship is a special gift—part of how God's love is shared with us. Jesus was willing to help everyone, but he chose certain persons to be his close friends. When choosing your friends, look for someone of a positive spirit and good character. You don't want to be friends with someone who's always getting you in trouble, tempting you to do wrong, or otherwise dragging you down.

Friendship must be a mutual relationship of equals—not one between a servant and a bossy superior. Real friendship must involve sharing. You don't want fair-weather friends who take everything you have to give but are never there when you need them. Nor do you want for a friend someone who's always unburdening problems to you but never listens to yours.

Our friends affect our lives profoundly. Parents are therefore obliged to see that their children don't hang around with friends who harm their character. But sometimes parents misjudge their child's friend because they don't have enough information about the individual. If a parent or another friend has questioned your involvement with a certain crowd, consider their concerns seriously and with an open mind. They might be seeing something you're missing. If you think your friends are being judged unfairly, help your parents get to know your friends better.

People want a friend who is honest and genuine, not a plastic people-pleaser who just says what they want to hear. Close friends can talk freely without embarrassment. They can kindly and appropriately tell each other the truth—even when it's uncomfortable. Friends help each other overcome faults, but they don't constantly criticize each other or poke fun at each other's shortcomings. With a good friend, you can comfortably be yourself.

If a wise person shows you your faults and what you should avoid,
follow that wise person as you would someone who reveals
*   hidden treasures.*
Do not have wrong-doers or hateful people for friends.
Instead, choose as friends those who are good and kind.

PARAPHRASED FROM THE SAYINGS OF THE BUDDHA.

While same-gender friendships are more common, many people are close friends with persons of the other gender. When one marries, however, one's main commitment is to one's spouse and the well-being of the marriage. Friendships with others should be encouraged without unreasonable jealousy. But they shouldn't be allowed to wrongly jeopardize the marriage relationship.

One of the nice things about friendship is that it isn't exclusive in the same way romantic relationships are. Friends should be glad and not jealous when their friends have other good friends. It's often through their friends that people make other good friends. Nevertheless, friends shouldn't take each other for granted. Whether in words or by a pat on the back or an arm around the shoulder, let your friends know how much you value them.

Scripture insights

1. What kind of friendship did Jesus have with his closest disciples?
2. How did Jesus show his love for his friends?

Journal entry

1. How have friends enriched your life?
2. How do you think you've enhanced theirs?
3. In what ways do you show your friends that you care about and appreciate them?
4. How could you do that better or more often?

For discussion

1. What attracts you to be friends with someone?
2. Why do you think close friendships are more likely to last than most romantic relationships?
3. Explain whether you think males or females are more
   • honest and open with a close friend
   • competitive or envious of their friends
4. Have you seen friendships outlast romantic relationships? Why do you think that is?
5. When do you think it would and wouldn't be right to continue a close friendship with someone else of the other gender after you marry?
6. How do you think friendships between men differ from those between women? Why do you think that is?

Being a good friend

There are different kinds of friends and degrees of friendship. Someone may like you more than you like them—or the other way around. But real friends always care about each other's total good. A true friend won't pressure you into something harmful—especially after you've clearly said you don't want to do it and don't believe it's right.

A common pressure young adults face today with their friends involves using alcohol irresponsibly. When you are of age, if you choose to drink alcohol, do so responsibly—and encourage your friends to do so. Insist that there be a non-drinking designated driver for your group. You don't want to attend the funeral of a friend whose death you could have helped prevent. Getting high on alcohol or other drugs often loosens the inhibitions that help us behave sensibly. It induces people to engage in high-risk sexual behavior they regret (or don't even remember!) the next morning.

Binge drinking is particularly dangerous; consuming too much alcohol too quickly can be lethal. Any pattern of alcohol misuse can lead to alcoholism—especially for those genetically predisposed to addiction, as so many people are. That's why trying certain illegal drugs even just once can rapidly lead to addiction for some people.

You can't know for sure whether you or your friends are predisposed to substance addictions. But any history of alcoholism or other drug addiction in your family means it's more likely that you are genetically predisposed to chemical dependency. Because of the widespread problem with alcohol on campus, many college students insist on living in alcohol-free (as well as smoke-free) dorms.

Jason, a college football player, can tell you the perils of driving while drunk. He was charged with second-degree manslaughter and drunken driving. Two of his friends (who were also drunk) were killed in the accident. At another university, a student died from consuming about fifteen shots of liquor in one hour. Not all college students binge drink. But despite the tragedies, surveys estimate that over 40 percent do engage in binge drinking.

Many college students are now countering their peers' binge drinking by having "no booze, no drugs" parties. They say they want to emphasize and enjoy their friendships, not see their friends get hurt. Help protect the friends you cherish. Encourage them to not abuse substances or drive irresponsibly. Discourage them from lighting up their first cigarette or taking their first dose of an illegal drug. And if your friends are experimenting with or addicted to such substances, support their efforts to stop.

The five rules of friendship

1. Be honest and sincere. Level with each other kindly, even though feelings sometimes get hurt.
2. Be supportive through good and bad times and aware of each other's needs.
3. Be unselfish, but not each other's doormat; don't take advantage of your friendship or each other.
4. Never harm or ridicule each other or put each other down.
5. Be loyal and keep legitimate confidences; never back-stab anyone, especially a friend.

For discussion

1. What quality do you think is most important in a friend?

2. How would you describe the difference between a casual and a close friend?

3. How have you felt pressured by your friends? Have you ever pressured a friend? Explain.

4. What do you think is the best way to handle being pressured by friends to do something you really don't want to do? Explain and be specific.

5. Why do you think some friends encourage one another to binge drink, use illegal drugs, speed on the highway, or engage in other irresponsible behavior?

6. What is your opinion of "The five rules of friendship"? What rules, if any, would you add?

Making and losing friends

Making new friends

One of the problems you may face for a while after you leave high school is the loneliness of being without your long-time friends. If you're lonely and don't know where to connect with others who share your values, try attending the young adult groups in your parish or the religious services at your college or a nearby college. Call the administration department and ask for information about the campus ministry program that your religious affiliation sponsors. One young woman says: "I went to college on Saturday, attended the campus Mass on Sunday, and by Monday felt like I was already making a bunch of new friends."

Even if you don't attend the college, you're still welcome to attend the regularly scheduled Catholic services there. Because the students usually help plan them, campus liturgies are often crowded with young adults who find the services extremely meaningful. Many campus ministry programs also sponsor retreats and social activities where you can deepen friendships and make new friends.

Do beware of the many cults whose adherents claim to befriend lonely young adults. Cults—religious or otherwise—are dangerous. Avoid **any** connection with them, even out of curiosity. Definitely don't attend "spiritual retreats" that aren't sponsored by authentic religious groups. College campus ministry offices are good resources for more specific information about the cults in the local area.

Ending a friendship

For understandable reasons, friends may grow apart. People can change and no longer share common interests. It's a shame, though, when good friendships end completely just because of inattention. A move to another city, a lifestyle change, or being busy with one's job or family shouldn't mean giving up good friendships. Some friends who get together only once a year are still able to pick up where they left off. As they fill each other in on the details of their lives during the past year, they know that each other's concern and understanding haven't changed.

Like some romantic relationships, some friendships should end. Friendship should boost the human spirit, not destroy it. If you find yourself in a one-sided or destructive friendship, how do you end the relationship? Sometimes the person's feelings will get hurt no matter how you handle it. Remember, though: Friendship can't be forced. You can't continue pretending to be friends or being a friend with someone with whom you can't be honest. (Honesty will help a person form and retain better friendships in the future.)

You might first try easing out of a friendship gradually by getting in touch with the person less and less often. Your friend might respond similarly until the relationship dissolves on its own. Or you might level with your friend, saying something like "I'll always value the good things we've shared, but I just feel we no longer have enough in common to continue being friends like we were." (Something similar may help you explain why you don't want to begin a friendship with someone.)

Staying in touch

As you leave home, keep in touch by phone and E-mail with the close friends you've already made. Write yourself reminders to connect with them on their birthdays and other special days. Also try to develop friendships with your brothers and sisters—including your much younger siblings as they grow older. Understand that not all family members are meant to be good friends, but you may find over time that that they may become your very best friends.

As with all friendships, don't let occasional family disagreements ruin the good relationship. For what you share with your family and the good friends of your youth is irreplaceable. You have a common background and precious memories that no one else will ever recall, appreciate, or understand in the same way. You will make wonderful new friends in the future, but continue to cherish your old ones.

. . . I can go to you without **dressing** up. . .
or having to give up any **part** of what is inside me.
When I am with you there is no need for me to be
[for]ever **defending** my ideas or my conduct . . .
no need to prove I am **right**. I find peace . . . .
You respect me . . .
What use to me is a friend who is forever
passing **judgment** on me?
If I **welcome** a friend into my house, I ask [my friend]
to sit down.
If [my friend] limps . . . I do not ask [him or her] to **dance**.
My **friend**, I need you like a hill-top
where I can **breathe** freely.

ANTOINE DE SAINT-EXUPERY

For discussion

1. If you get lonely after graduating from high school, where will you look to make new friends? What places will you deliberately avoid in seeking to make a new friend?

2. Have you witnessed or been involved in a one-sided or destructive relationship? Explain without mentioning names.

3. If you no longer want to be friends with someone, do you think it's fair to just distance yourself without explaining why?

4. What do you think is a good way to end a friendship with someone who wants to continue it?

5. Do you have any friends in your immediate family? With which of your relatives would you like to become friends or better friends? Explain.

6. How do you plan to stay in touch with your current friends after you leave high school?

Review

1. What attracts people to be friends, and how are good friends a sacred gift in each other's lives?

2. Why must friendship be a mutual relationship between equals?

3. What qualities do people generally want in a friend?

4. What does being good friends involve?

5. How can friends show that they care about each other's total welfare?

6. What are some ways young adults can make new friends?

7. When and how should a friendship end, and how can good friends stay connected?

Between friends

Respond to each of the following questions or problems teenagers have voiced regarding their friends.

Angela: "I've got this friend I don't feel I can depend on. She just 'forgets' things I rely on her to do or remember. How should I deal with this? I'd like us to stay friends."

Cody: "I loaned a friend some money, but he never paid me back. I really could use the money, and know he's got enough to repay me. But I feel awkward about bringing up the matter. I know he's aware of it, because the other day he referred to what he bought with the money. Is there a good way to get my friend to give my money back? In the future, how can I be a good friend without letting myself be taken advantage of?"

Nicole: "My good friend talks a blue streak—about herself. It's always 'me, me, me.' She hardly ever asks what I'm thinking or feeling, or what I've been doing. I'm beginning to feel our friendship is one-sided, with me doing all the giving. Is there any way I can help my friend see that?"

Pedro: My friend constantly criticizes and pokes fun of my shortcomings. I just laugh and try to ignore it, but it hurts inside. How can I get my friend to stop doing that?

Rob: I've got a fair-weather friend who's always dumping his problems on me and expecting me to help bail him out of trouble. But when I have a problem, he doesn't really seem to listen.

Pat: My main problem is that my parents don't like my friends. How can I get my folks to change their minds?

Jamie: I've got a friend who's kind of bossy. She gets miffed if you don't do things her way. I usually go along with her, but I'm tired of always letting her call the shots. Is there any way I can get her to stop being so bossy without losing her as a friend?

Darcy: My friend is so critical and negative—always emphasizing what's wrong with things. Everything's a problem, and nothing ever seems right. It's really dragging me down. Is there a way to get my friend to not be so pessimistic?

Rafael: My friend always agrees with me or goes overboard to try to please me. How can I get her to be more independent?

For discussion

1. How would you answer the teenagers' questions about friendship? Explain.
2. What things have bothered you the most about friends you've had? What things about you do you think sometimes bother your friends?
3. What further questions do you have about friendship?
4. What have friends meant in your life?

The special concerns of homosexual persons

homosexual persons
individuals whose primary or exclusive sexual attraction is toward persons of the same gender

gay
homosexual; pertaining to one or more homosexual males

lesbian
pertaining to female homosexuality or to one or more homosexual females

heterosexual
of or characterized by a primary or exclusive sexual attraction toward those of the other gender

gender identity
one's state or self-awareness of being male or female

sexual orientation
one's deeply rooted inborn tendency or ability to experience sexual attraction mainly or exclusively toward those of a certain gender or of both genders

THIS SECTION IS BASED ON CATHOLIC TEACHING FROM *ALWAYS OUR CHILDREN* (UNITED STATES CATHOLIC CONFERENCE) AND THE *CATECHISM OF THE CATHOLIC CHURCH*.

You no doubt attend school with gay students. In the future, some of your co-workers will probably be gay. Yet people often misunderstand homosexuality. Or they have questions about how the Catholic Church views **homosexual persons**. Because of the widespread—and unchristian—bias against **gay** and **lesbian** persons, it's important to understand their special concerns.

Our dignity as persons comes from this: We're *all* created in God's image. Our sexuality is God's gift to us. Our basic sexual orientation is part of how God wants us to share our love—and God's—with others. Every person is pricelessly precious. Nothing can ever separate any of us from God's love.

God loves each of us for the unique persons we are. That includes our male or female sexual identity and our inborn homosexual or **heterosexual** orientation. God loves people who are gay and lesbian just as much as God loves everyone else. Being homosexual in orientation is not sinful, for morality must involve being free to choose. To the extent that sexual orientation is a matter of choice, Catholic teaching states that one must choose heterosexuality. Most gay persons, however, don't experience their sexual orientation as something they've chosen but as part of who they are from birth.

The precise physical origin of our **gender identity** remains somewhat mysterious. We know that both genetics and the womb's environment play a role in whether we develop into a female or a male. Several factors may also help determine our **sexual orientation**. The exact role genetics or fetal environment may play remains open to discovery.

The scientific community widely agrees that the vast majority of homosexual persons are not gay because they've chosen to be gay. Their homosexuality is part of their deeply rooted personal identity from birth. Why, gay persons often ask, would they choose an orientation that causes them to endure so much rejection? Externals like early childhood environment, hormones, or perhaps individual choice may help determine sexual orientation for only a very few persons.

Temporary crushes are common among older children.

Gay persons have no obligation to attempt to change their homosexual orientation. They shouldn't be pressured into trying to do so. In addition, there's no guarantee that such therapy will be successful. While it may help some persons come to terms with their sexual orientation and gender identity, it can be very harmful for others psychologically.

About 2 percent of adults in our society identify themselves as homosexual. The actual percentage of gay and lesbian persons may be somewhat higher. Individuals become aware that they are homosexual after experiencing strong, persistent romantic and sexual attractions toward persons of their same gender. They also come to realize that they are not similarly attracted to persons of the other gender. Those realizations usually develop over an extended period of time.

Being gay doesn't mean that one therefore engages in homosexual activity. (Catholic teaching holds that homosexual persons have the same obligation to practice chastity as any other single adult. That will be discussed more in Chapter 6.)

Having had homosexual fantasies or experiences does *not* make one homosexual or necessarily mean that one is gay. Curious young children sometimes engage in innocent homosexual behavior as they become aware of their sexual identity and differences. Older children may have a temporary crush on a friend or teacher of the same gender. Such passing tendencies usually do not indicate that a child is gay. Individuals might not realize their homosexual orientation clearly until in their teens or twenties or even later.

For discussion

1. Which of the points discussed in this section do you agree with most strongly? Are there any with which you disagree? Explain.

2. What biases have you seen or heard teenagers express against gay persons? Did anyone speak out against those biases at the time? Explain.

3. How do you imagine you'd feel about—or how have you felt about—coming to the realization that you may be gay? Explain.

4. How would you advise a friend who wondered whether she or he might be gay?

5. What do you think would be hardest about being a gay teenager, if others knew you were gay? If no one knew you were gay?

6. What harm can be caused by spreading rumors that someone is gay without knowing the truth for sure? Explain.

"... for the **Lord** does not see as **mortals** see;
they look on the **outward** appearance, but the Lord **looks**
on the heart."

1 Samuel 16:7b

Responding in love

Put your faith completely in God.

ALWAYS OUR CHILDREN

Gay persons may initially find it hard to accept their homosexuality, understandably feeling terribly torn and confused. Strong peer pressures urge them to be heterosexual—or else. No wonder gay individuals often undergo a tormented inner struggle in confronting their homosexual identity. When they most need information and support, they must instead fear they'll be rejected. Teenage suicides have been epidemic in our society. It's estimated that as many as one third of those suicides are among gay teenagers.

Many gay persons conceal their sexual orientation for years from those they love. They're terrified of the disappointment, anger, and embarrassment they think they'll cause. They're afraid their friends, peers, and parents will reject them. Hiding who they really are often leads them to hate who they are and to feel guilty, ashamed, and profoundly lonely. It also leads to unhappy marriages when gay persons try to be what others expect of them. Sadly, many gay and lesbian persons don't come to terms with their sexual orientation until after they've married and started a family.

As Catholic teaching reminds us, we're to accept homosexual persons with "respect, compassion and sensitivity" (*Catechism of the Catholic Church,* #2358). We should focus on people as individuals rather than on their sexual orientation. We must view and treat one another as the equals we all are in God's eyes. To do that, we must realistically face and work to overcome our own fears and biases about homosexuality. Gay bashing in any form is wrong. Unkind jokes directed toward homosexual persons are not funny or harmless. They're extremely painful to gay persons and their loved ones.

We must all oppose the hostility and unjust discrimination that exist in our society toward gay persons. It's especially wrong to try to justify biases against homosexual persons by quoting out of context from the Bible! There is no way to defend such biases in the context of Jesus' message about loving our neighbor.

If someone you know is struggling with the issue of sexual identity—how should you respond? What if you're struggling with this yourself? It can help to apply the advice on the next page adapted from what Catholic teaching counsels parents.

For someone wondering about being gay—

- Seek appropriate advice and support from someone you trust to understand you and your situation—a parent, school counselor, local pastor, or close friend. Seek spiritual guidance. Catholic diocesan offices usually have special ministries designed to reach out to gay persons; call and ask for their advice and support.
- Remember that God loves and accepts you just the way God has created you. God will never reject you. Pray that you can accept yourself, too. Put your trust totally in God.
- Seek the truth. Don't try to hide, dodge, or repress it. Being homosexual is no cause for shame. Whatever your sexual orientation, you can live a happy, fulfilling life.
- Be well-informed. Ignorance and fear are most often at the root of intolerance. If you understand the situation accurately, you'll be better able to help others do so.
- Don't run from your fears or rebel in harmful ways against others' intolerance.
- Don't turn away from those who love you. Try to help them understand. Parents and friends will more likely be your allies if you accept them as persons and appreciate their concerns for you. If possible, enlist their help in your self-discovery process.
- If loved ones reject you, draw courage from Jesus whose friends turned their backs on him, too. Seek friends who will accept and understand you for who you are. Stay linked to or reconcile with your faith community. Catholics can draw strength from participating in the Eucharist and the Sacrament of Reconciliation.
- Never give up on yourself! Turn your discouragement into determination. The compassion and understanding you learn from your trials will deepen the love and happiness you can know in the future.

If someone tells you he or she is gay—

- Remember that the person is still the same. Let her or him know that your love and support will also remain the same.
- Respect the person's trust in sharing with you something so personal and important.
- Let the person know you appreciate his or her honesty and that you'd like to continue communicating with each other honestly and openly.
- Appropriately discuss with the person—maybe after thinking it over first—your thoughts and feelings about what she or he has told you.

Matthew Shepard, a first-year college student, didn't broadcast that he was gay. But he was honest with people about it. Because Matthew was homosexual, prosecutors say he was kidnapped one night, driven to the edge of town, and brutally beaten. Matthew's assailants tied him to a fence, bashed in his skull, and left him helpless in the below-freezing weather.

Many hours later another young man discovered Matthew and sought help. By then Matthew had lapsed into a coma. His face was covered with blood—except for where his tears had washed his cheeks clean. Matthew later died.

Matthew's parents described their son as loving, intelligent, and caring—a gentle young man. They said he had seen everybody as a possible friend. Matthew's parents had accepted their son's gay orientation. Tragically, his killers had not. Many gay teenagers die inwardly every day because of their classmates' sneers and snide remarks.

How you can help foster understanding and tolerance—

- Talk openly about how you think gay persons should be accepted as persons just like anyone else.
- Make it clear that you wouldn't reject a friend for being homosexual—and mean it.
- Clearly reject prejudice against gay persons, and voice your disapproval of bias against homosexual persons.
- Be well-informed so that you can counter the ignorance that breeds intolerance. Don't stereotype gay persons. Counter others' stereotyped viewpoints with accurate information.
- Don't presume that someone is gay unless the person reveals that to you or others.
- Help people understand that being a good friend of a gay person doesn't mean that one is also gay.
- If someone is confused about her or his sexual orientation identity, help the person obtain reliable information and moral guidance to discern the truth.

God gives each of us a special purpose in life that only we can fulfill. Gay persons have made incredible contributions to humanity, and their love and friendship can greatly enrich your life. Don't reject a friend or family member for being gay. Help those who are searching for or struggling to accept their sexual identity. Try to help gay friends who are rejected by their families. Remember Jesus' words: "Truly I tell you, just as you did it to one of . . . these who are members of my family, you did it to me" (Matthew 25:40b and d).

Research activity

Find three outstanding contributions persons with a homosexual orientation have made to humanity. Write a one-page paper briefly describing these contributions and what humanity would have lacked without them.

Journal entry

1. Do you have any biases against homosexual persons?
2. How could you be more understanding of persons with a homosexual orientation?

Project understanding

Develop and conduct a survey of students at your school about their attitudes regarding homosexual persons—particularly gay and lesbian teenagers. Discuss any areas of ignorance and intolerance the survey results reflect. As a class, implement a project that will help enlighten and increase your peers' understanding of persons with a homosexual orientation.

For discussion

1. Why do you think people often focus more on someone's homosexual orientation than on the person as an individual? Why is that hurtful and unfair?
2. Are there pressures at your school to "be heterosexual or else"? How do you think such pressures probably affect those who are gay or wondering whether they might be gay?
3. How might you help establish a more Christian climate of tolerance and acceptance for gay students at your school or among your friends?
4. How would you probably feel if you had to choose between hiding your sexual orientation identity or being rejected for it?
5. What would you say to someone who quoted the Bible in defending wrongful biases or behavior against persons with a homosexual orientation? Explain.
6. If a close friend revealed to you that he or she was gay, how would it probably affect your relationship? How would you respond to the person? Explain.

Review

1. Explain what Catholic teaching says about homosexuality and persons with a homosexual orientation and how we are to view and respond to them.
2. When and why is being homosexual in orientation not sinful?
3. What do we know—and what do we not yet know—about how sexual orientation originates?
4. How do individuals usually become aware that they are homosexual? Must they then try to change their homosexual orientation?
5. When might homosexual fantasies or experiences indicate—or not indicate—that one is gay?
6. What often makes it hard for gay persons initially to accept their homosexuality?
7. What obligations do we have regarding wrongful biases against and unjust treatment of homosexual persons?

On being a gay teenager

Read the following situations that are based on actual experiences. Then respond to the questions.

Ever since the kids in elementary school learned that their mother was lesbian, Robin and Mike have had to cope with anti-gay hostility at school. They had hoped things would be better when they got to high school, but they now encounter the same ugly remarks about them and their mother, whom they love.

Laura has hidden her homosexuality from her peers at school. She tries to fit in and be like everyone else, but she's tired of pretending she's someone she's not. She cares a lot about her friends, but thinks that they probably wouldn't want to associate with her if she told them she was gay. Secretly, she's worried that she'll go to hell for being lesbian. She hates her life and herself and has seriously thought about suicide.

Tom isn't gay, but his long-time buddy, Gavin, is. They've grown up together, and have been loyal friends for years. Tom otherwise doesn't see any problem with remaining friends with Gavin, but he says, "People presume things. If you have a close friend of the same sex who's gay, they wonder if you're gay. Or if you're gay and have a friend of the same sex, they presume you're having sex with the person. Mainly I try to ignore it. My true friends understand the situation. But others can be pretty cruel sometimes. I know it hurts Gavin even though he doesn't talk about it."

For discussion

1. What do you imagine it would be like to be a gay teenager at your school, or what has been your experience as a gay teenager?
2. Researchers find that males seem more intolerant of homosexual persons than do females. Why do you think that is?
3. What biases against homosexual persons are evidenced in the above teenagers' lives? What do you think it would be like to be in each of their situations? Explain.
4. How do you think you would respond in Robin and Mike's situation? If you were Laura or her friends? If you were Tom or Gavin? Explain.

In summary

The core of all love is caring unselfishly about the other person's total welfare, as Jesus taught us. Genuine love, which differs from liking someone, always intends to do others good and not harm. To love one person, one must become a loving person. Real love involves acceptance, responsibility, honesty and sincerity, being supportive, and giving generously of oneself.

Strong mutual attraction may signal infatuation or "love at first sight." But it's important to be able to recognize what characteristics distinguish infatuation from love. True love involves knowing someone well and takes time and effort to develop. Love is worth the risks of being hurt, for it expands our hearts to be more loving. Friendship is likewise a wonderful gift and mystery that must be a mutual relationship between equals. Our friends profoundly affect our lives. We should try to choose good people as friends, treasure them, and be a true friend.

We should also respond with respect, understanding, and sensitivity to persons with a homosexual orientation. Young gay and lesbian persons often undergo a tormented inner struggle in accepting their sexual identity. We must oppose all injustice and discrimination against them and learn to accept ourselves and others as the unique, precious individuals God has created.

Key concepts

agape

attraction

being in love

caring

Catholic teaching on homosexuality and responding to homosexual persons

distinguishing love from infatuation

essential qualities of love

friendship

gay, lesbian

homosexuality

homosexual persons

infatuation

love, nature and meaning of love

love at first sight

love of neighbor

pressures among friends

sexual identity and orientation

Endnotes

1. Test adapted from and reprinted by permission from *The Book of Tests* by Bruce M. Nash and Randolph B. Monchick, Ph.D. Copyright © 1980 by Bruce M. Nash and Randolph B. Monchick, Ph.D.

2. *Star Trek: The Next Generation*, "Time's Arrow" episode.

CHAPTER 4

GROWING IN LOVE

SCRIPTURE

O LORD, you have searched me and known me. . . .

Even before a word is on my tongue, O LORD, you
know it completely. . . .

Where can I go from your spirit? Or where can
I flee from your presence? . . .

If I take the wings of the morning and settle at the
farthest limits of the sea,

Even there your hand shall lead me, and your right
hand shall hold me fast. . . .

For it was you who formed my inward parts; you
knit me together in my mother's womb.

I praise you, for I am . . . wonderfully made . . .

In your book were written all the days that were
formed for me, when none of them as yet existed.

. . . I come to the end—I am still with you.

FROM PSALM 139

PRAYER

Merciful God,
You know our hearts and our deepest feelings
  and longings.
You have given us into each other's keeping.
It is your desire that we draw close to one another.
Help us cherish those we love,
  and overcome what blocks us from greater
  intimacy with you and others.
Let your Spirit nourish our relationships and revive
  our lost hopes.
When we need it, mend and strengthen our broken
  hearts with your gentle, understanding love.
We ask this in Jesus' name. Amen.

Intimacy in relationships

Let there be spaces in your togetherness.

KAHLIL GIBRAN

cherish
to hold dear, to love tenderly, to protect and take good care of

intimacy
deep loving closeness that usually involves sharing what is most personal and private

After a while, couples often begin noticing that "something's missing in our relationship—it's not the way it used to be." They lament how the romance has cooled. Even in good marriages couples may mistakenly presume that the love has disappeared along with the romantic feelings. In reality, they may have grown much more caring about and in love with each other. That's why Catholic teaching says it's so important for couples to realize more profoundly the difference between romance and love.[1] But is there a way to revive the romantic sparkle?

Romance may be hard to define, but couples in love know when it exists! Their initial attraction ignites the romantic feelings. They're eager to grow together because their relationship is new and each person is still mostly a mystery. Learning more about each other seems effortless and exciting. After two people come to know each other well, some of the initial electric feelings naturally decrease. It's unrealistic to expect that they'll always stay the same—partly, perhaps, because of the body's chemistry. But why do some couples feel closer than ever after a lifetime together, while others become strangers after a few years?

When infatuation begins developing into love, it enters the attachment phase. The couple begin to truly **cherish** each other. At that point lovers need to concentrate more on building **intimacy** than on preserving romantic feelings. For it's the genuine loving closeness that determines how deeply meaningful any love relationship is. It's the mutual cherishing and shared intimacy that keep both the relationship and the romance alive. The rest of this section will focus on what such intimacy means and involves.

66 Chapter 4

Assignment
Write a two-page paper (one-page typed) on what cherishing someone means to you.

For discussion

1. Who do you think is more romantic—adults or teenagers? What might account for any differences you find?

2. Which do you think is more important in a lasting relationship—romance, or intimacy? Are they mutually exclusive? Explain.

3. How might romantic feelings enhance, or inhibit, growing in intimacy?

4. What problems can occur when couples focus on romance instead of building intimacy—or when they confuse the two?

What intimacy means

Long ago, humanity reached a turning point in understanding love:

> . . . the LORD set his heart on you
> and chose you . . .
> because the LORD loved you.
> DEUTERONOMY 7:7B AND 8B

Those words describe the beginning of God's intimate relationship with us. Every other love relationship reflects and participates in the ways God loves us. We are loved and we are able to love others because God first loved us. It is God's Spirit living in us that helps us deepen our intimacy with God and others. Participating in Eucharistic Communion is one of the most powerful ways of sharing intimately in divine and human life and love.

In every human love relationship, two people must similarly decide how deeply close they wish to become. We do that through our many small choices to share or not share of ourselves as the relationship progresses. Those choices, made throughout the relationship, determine our continuing degree of personal intimacy.

Personal intimacy doesn't mean having strong feelings or being physically affectionate.

Love is the greatest of all risks . . . the giving of myself.

JEAN VANIER

In fact, physical intimacy may not involve any personal intimacy! A couple can fall in love, marry, live together, have sex, raise a family, and celebrate their fiftieth anniversary without ever being deeply intimate personally. Yet two good friends who live miles apart can share much intimacy without physical contact.

Intimacy is a spiritual connection—a shared inner closeness. Feelings and physical affection may enhance intimacy, but intimacy itself is much deeper. It includes what our affection means and the reasons behind our gestures and emotions. That's why, although there may be intimate physical contact, without personal intimacy there can be no real physical intimacy.

Through caring we come to love another, and through shared intimacy that love deepens. We can best begin to understand human intimacy by looking at God's loving intimacy with us:

> O LORD, you have searched me
> and known me.
> You know when I sit down and when I rise up;
> you discern my thoughts from far away.
> You search out my path and my lying down,
> and are acquainted with all my ways.
> PSALM 139:1–3

Activity

At the library or on the Internet, look up some of the correspondence written to dear friends by famous figures such as Beethoven, Chopin, Dorothy Day, Van Gogh, Michelangelo, Elizabeth Barrett Browning, or Einstein, or that between U.S. President John Adams and his wife Abigail. Or read an excerpt from Pope John XXIII's *Diary of a Soul*, or from the writings or conversations of Mother Teresa. Write a one-page paper describing what insights the writings reveal about the correspondents and their close relationships.

It is through and in Jesus, God's greatest gift of love, that we most fully experience how lovingly close God is to us.

He who did not withhold his own Son, but gave him up for all of us, will he not with him also give us everything else? . . . Who will separate us from the love of Christ? Will hardship, or distress, or persecution, or famine, or nakedness, or peril, or sword? . . .

For I am convinced that neither death, nor life, nor angels, nor rulers, nor things present, nor things to come, nor powers, nor height, nor depth, nor anything else in all creation, will be able to separate us from the love of God in Christ Jesus our Lord.

ROMANS 8:32, 35, 38–39

God's love for us makes intimacy possible. It also shows us the kind of intimacy God wants us to share with each other.

"I ask . . . that they may all be one. As you, Father, are in me and I am in you . . . The glory that you have given me I have given them, so that they may be one, as we are one, I in them and you in me, that they may become completely one . . .

"I made your love known to them, and I will make it known, so that the love with which you have loved me may be in them, and I in them."

JOHN 17:20–21A, 23A, 26

The loving intimacy between people is special and sacred. It's probably the closest we'll come in this life to the type of unity that awaits us in God's fullness of time. So it's sad when spouses look elsewhere to experience an intimacy they don't share with each other, or when valuable friendships are lost because people don't nourish what brings them closer.

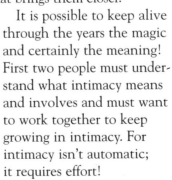

The moment we experience true love, we experience it as valid forever.

VICTOR FRANKL

It is possible to keep alive through the years the magic and certainly the meaning! First two people must understand what intimacy means and involves and must want to work together to keep growing in intimacy. For intimacy isn't automatic; it requires effort!

For discussion

1. Why do you think individuals so often become sexually involved without being intimate in a deeper personal sense? How common do you think that is among teenagers?

2. Which do you think is the more difficult decision in a romantic relationship—to become more intimate as friends are or to become sexually involved? Explain.

3. Do you think television shows and movies portray couples more superficially or as sharing a deeper personal intimacy? Explain and give examples.

4. What personal aspects of themselves are teenagers more likely to share with family members? With close friends? With someone with whom they're romantically involved? Explain.

Review

1. What keeps relationships and romance alive?

2. What does personal intimacy mean and involve?

3. What does God's relationship with us tell us about human intimacy?

What's your intimacy IQ?

This questionnaire can help you assess how much you possess the qualities essential for true personal intimacy. You won't be expected to share your answers or result.

Write A–F on each blank to indicate which response best describes you:

A — Never/Not at all
B — Rarely/Hardly at all
C — Seldom/Not very strongly
D — Sometimes/Somewhat, but not strongly
E — Often/Somewhat strongly
F — Always/Very strongly

_____ 1. Do you enjoy people with notably unique personalities very different from yours?

_____ 2. Do you find it hard to tell whether the person you're with is having a good time?

_____ 3. How sorry do you feel on hearing that someone is hurt, upset, in trouble, or worried?

_____ 4. How happy do you feel when told that something good or exciting has happened to someone?

_____ 5. Do you talk about your real feelings with people you care about?

_____ 6. Have you been told in some way that your behavior or reactions could be more mature?

_____ 7. Do you try to help someone feel less embarrassed, such as by sharing a similarly embarrassing experience of yours?

_____ 8. How much do you complain?

_____ 9. Would it bother you if someone you were romantically serious about continued a main hobby or interest that you considered a dumb waste of time?

_____ 10. While disagreeing, do you put the other person's needs before your preferences or consider how you might both get what you want?

_____ 11. How often have you unintentionally embarrassed someone or hurt someone's feelings?

_____ 12. When you're used to doing things a certain way, does it bother you to have to change and do them differently?

_____ 13. Should someone who deeply cares about you be able to understand your feelings and needs without you having to explain them?

_____ 14. When alone, do you spend your leisure time imaginatively or creatively, such as by making things or playing music?

_____ 15. Do you feel uncomfortable around other people?

_____ 16. Do you give others the impression that you're somewhat aloof, distant, or uninterested?

_____ 17. Have you felt younger students or children shouldn't have privileges you didn't have at that age?

_____ 18. When working with a group, do you usually volunteer to be responsible for a task?

_____ 19. Have others confided in you about their problems because they felt you'd understand?

_____ 20. Does it bother you that teachers differ in homework, grading, or classroom behavior policies?

_____ 21. When choosing a gift for someone you know well, do you usually know what the person likes?

_____ 22. When facing a difficult personal problem, do you ask others for advice?

_____ 23. Do you convert awkward or embarrassing situations into enjoyable ones?

_____ 24. Do you give in to others or let them have their way so they'll think better of you?

_____ 25. Do you think you're too assertive, aggressive, nosy, or abrupt with people?

_____ 26. Do you get upset when little things go wrong or don't turn out as you wanted?

_____ 27. Are others able to open up and share their real feelings with you?

_____ 28. If your spouse continued enjoying a certain sport once a week but you chose not to participate, would you feel left out?

_____ 29. When others feel uneasy or uptight, do you usually help them feel more at ease and relaxed?

_____ 30. How hard is it for you to talk about your deeper thoughts and feelings honestly and seriously with someone you trust?

_____ 31. On a scale of 0–150 (with 150 being the ideal), how would you rate your "IQ"— intimacy qualities?

_____ 32. On the same scale of 0–150, how would those who know you probably rate your intimacy qualities?

_____ **Intimacy Quotient**

Growing in intimacy

The intimacy vital to close relationships is often missing because people don't know how to cultivate it. So how can you keep your relationships alive over time?

Caring about each other's total good must be the foundation for all real intimacy. People in love may speak of becoming one or of giving their heart and soul to each other. But you can't be intimate with someone at all unless you truly care about each other's welfare. Deepening your love requires unselfish caring and generosity. That doesn't mean slavishly sacrificing your **individuality**!

Intimacy bonds two distinctly different people, but it doesn't merge two identities into one. Many lovers mistakenly think, though, that they must always try to please: If the other person says "Jump," you say "How high?" Real intimacy challenges us to remain ourselves—and become our best selves. As one young man recently put it, "I want to marry someone with whom I can be a better person than I ever could be without her." Intimacy helps us grow as individuals so that we have more to bring to our relationship. Intimacy involves sharing, not sameness or selfishness.

If you start wondering where the romance went in a relationship, it's time to begin renewing your sense of wonder about each other. When mutual discovery stops, people start taking each other for granted. Then their relationship stagnates. Like a river, we each change continually, never remaining exactly the same. There is always something new to learn about a person. So never lose your sense of mystery about someone. It's essential to intimacy and romance.

People often don't realize how much closer they could become by sharing their deeper thoughts and feelings with each other. Be realistic, though. Don't confide your most personal confidences to someone who won't respect your trust. Jesus warned against misplacing our trust: ". . . do not throw your pearls before swine, or they will trample them under foot and turn and maul you" (Matthew 7:6). Be willing to risk trusting someone, but not blindly, naively, or foolishly!

individuality
total combination of qualities that make each person unique

Activity

Discover two new insights about someone you've known for years. Explain how that helps you know the person even better.

Journal entry

1. What aspect of yourself do you wish your friends or classmates would see more than they do?

2. What aspect of yourself do you wish your family members would see more than they do?

3. In what ways have you stopped getting to know more about your friends, family members, or classmates?

Arise, my love, my fair one, and **come** away . . . let me see your face, let me hear your **voice** . . . You have **ravished** my heart . . . with a **glance** of your eyes. . . .

Song of Solomon 2:13–14 and 4:9

For discussion

1. How can couples be so "together" that they lose the individuality that intimacy requires? Give examples (without mentioning names).

2. Name five qualities, talents, or values that you consider integral to you as a person. Next presume that someone you're in love with asks or demands that you give up one of those qualities, talents, or values. How would you feel about that? How would you respond? Explain.

3. Suggest three ways to enhance individuality and therefore intimacy between
   • couples in love
   • close friends
   • spouses
   • family members

4. What is the difference between intimacy and romancing via Internet E-mail?

Sharing thoughts and feelings about God and praying together also helps people grow closer. Our religious beliefs are extremely personal. We pray about what means the most to us. A shared faith in God helps friends, couples, and family members bond more deeply. Sharing our religious faith with someone also deepens our intimacy with God. "For [as Jesus said] where two or three are gathered in my name, I am there among them" (Matthew 18:20).

Activity (refer to page 73)

Compare what tenderness means in loving with what it means regarding meat. Do this in an imaginative way—either with words (and perhaps music) or with a graphic presentation. Give as many comparisons as you can.

Scripture insights
(refer to page 73)

Find three passages in the Gospels that describe how, in his relationships with others, Jesus lived one or more of the key elements of intimacy.

Review (refer to page 74)

1. What is the basic requirement for all personal intimacy?

2. What role does individuality play in personal intimacy between two people?

3. What are some of the best ways to deepen personal intimacy in a relationship?

Build trust

- Take emotional risks—but do so sensibly!
- Be wise, not gullible.
- Allow time—be patient rather than pushy.
- Inspire confidence by being consistent.
- Be understanding and supportive.
- Be honest and trustworthy.
- Respect legitimate confidences.
- Never misuse sensitive personal information.
- Show that trust is appreciated.

For discussion

1. What's hardest about sharing your deepest thoughts and feelings with someone you love? Why?
2. What causes you to hesitate about trusting someone? When is trusting someone worth the risk? Explain.
3. In what ways do you think teenagers are sometimes pushy or foolishly trusting about their romantic relationships? Explain and give examples (without mentioning names).
4. Why do you think it takes time to build trust?
5. How can you encourage someone to trust you more? Respect someone's trust in you? Give examples.

Show empathy

- Understand how the other person feels and thinks.
- Imagine how you would feel in the other's place.
- Share in the other person's joy, success, and contentment.
- Show **compassion** when the other person suffers troubles and sorrows.

For discussion

1. What does empathy mean to you?
2. Why is our ability to empathize—to feel with someone—so important to being human?
3. How would you describe the difference between empathizing and feeling sorry for someone?
4. What role do you think empathy should play in intimacy? Explain, giving examples.

Be mature

- Be responsible.
- Keep your priorities straight.
- Stand by your principles. Don't back down or quit when the going gets rough.
- Admit when you're wrong and learn from your mistakes.
- Don't be childish, making a big deal out of small matters.
- Shoulder small pressures gracefully with good humor and bigger hardships with courage.
- Keep your word to follow through with what you begin.
- Be unselfish—put the other's needs before your desires.
- Overlook insignificant faults and irritations.
- Talk over the things that get on each other's nerves. Seek to improve yourself rather than the other person.
- Don't be unnecessarily apologetic—or never willing to give in.

For discussion

1. How would you define maturity? Explain.
2. Why should maturity increase with age? Why doesn't that always happen?
3. Give an example of a mature and of an immature attitude, response, or behavior you've encountered in each of the following: a young child, an adult, another teenager. Explain the similarities and differences among those age groups.
4. What are some ways of coping maturely with minor irritations? Of turning them into less unpleasant or even enjoyable experiences? Give examples.

empathy ability to share in another's thoughts or feelings so that one understands the person better

compassion feeling sorry about another's difficulties or suffering, and desiring to help the person; profound sympathy

Express tenderness

- Be kind and understanding.
- Be thoughtful and considerate; show your appreciation.
- Respond warmly, not mechanically.
- Know when and how to be gentle, accepting, and restrained.
- Know when and how to be firm, giving, and expressive.
- Tell and show others how special they are to you.
- When expressing affection emotionally or physically, be sensitive to what's too much, too little, or just right.

For discussion

1. What do you think men need to learn about expressing tenderness? What do you think women need to learn? Explain.
2. Give examples of thoughtful things others have said to you or done for you that you've appreciated.
3. Give examples of how this statement applies to tenderness: "It's the little things that count."
4. Why do people sometimes stop telling each other of their love and admiration?
5. Describe cold responses you've received from people. Describe responses that conveyed genuine warmth. How did each type of response make you feel?

Be aware

- Know yourself and what you have to give.
- Be sensitive to the other person's feelings, needs, and preferences.
- Be interested in the other's thoughts and opinions.
- Notice the other's attractive, pleasing, unique qualities and personality traits.
- Learn to anticipate without having to be told.
- Spend enough quality personal time together.
- Arrange for surroundings that encourage personal sharing.

For discussion

1. Why is each kind of awareness important for intimacy?
2. Why do you think some people are more aware and sensitive than others are? Are less so? Explain.
3. How might your awareness regarding your family members be improved? What would you like them to be more aware of about you?
4. How much quality personal time do you spend each week with those you love? How much would you ideally like to spend with them? Explain.
5. What encourages you to open up to someone about personal matters? What kinds of atmosphere help you do that? Explain.

Be imaginative

- Create special shared times, places, and experiences.
- Delight in discovering and enjoying your differences and similarities.
- Vary from the routine "same old things" that can dull relationships.
- Have fun together, enjoying each other's sense of humor. Experience joy and celebrate life!
- Perceive reality in unique ways.

For discussion

1. How can routines enhance intimacy? Dull intimacy?
2. What imaginative activities did you engage in as a child? Why were they so enjoyable?
3. From early childhood on, how are people usually discouraged from being imaginative? Be specific.
4. What's discouraged you from being more imaginative? How would you like to release your imagination more? Explain.
5. Why is shared humor so important in healthy relationships? How would you describe joy and it's importance to intimacy?

How romantic are you?

This questionnaire is based on things many people find important to romance. To assess how romantic you are in these ways, answer each question honestly. Note that even the similar questions contain subtle differences. You won't be expected to share your score or responses.

Write A–F on each blank to indicate which response best describes you:

A — Never/Not at all
B — Seldom/Hardly at all
C — Less than half the time
D — Sometimes/About half the time
E — More than half the time
F — Always/Almost always

_____ 1. When relaxing in any room (for example, a restaurant, your bedroom or other room at home), are you usually aware of enjoying the atmosphere?

_____ 2. How often do you give little gifts (including those that don't cost money) for no special reason except that you care for the person?

_____ 3. How often do you surprise others by doing something you know they'd appreciate?

_____ 4. How often do you tell family members or friends that you like or love them?

_____ 5. How comfortable do you feel about telling others why you like or love them?

_____ 6. Would it bother you if your boyfriend, girlfriend, or spouse continued friendships with individuals whose personalities he or she knew you didn't like?

_____ 7. While in the presence of someone you like, do you think about how much you enjoy the person?

_____ 8. Does or would it bother you to cry in front of someone to whom you feel very close?

_____ 9. How imaginative or creative are you in the positive things you say to or do for people?

_____ 10. How much pleasure do you feel when helping someone in a small way (letting a car squeeze in front of you in traffic, picking up an item someone's dropped, and so on)?

_____ 11. Do you look directly into someone's eyes when conversing?

_____ 12. How often has someone told you how thoughtful or considerate you are?

_____ 13. How often has someone told you that you have a warm smile, or friendly eyes, or otherwise communicate your feelings warmly?

_____ 14. If your girlfriend, boyfriend, or spouse were enjoying being flirted with at a party but wasn't returning the attention seriously, how much would you also enjoy the situation?

_____ 15. Do you help with planning and arranging for birthdays, holidays, and other celebrations involving your family or friends?

_____ 16. Do you enjoy hearing about someone's hobbies, experiences, or jobs?

_____ 17. Can you make dull situations into positive experiences (a boring class lecture, an everyday task, a weekend with "nothing to do," and so on)?

_____ 18. How embarrassed or awkward are you when someone cries in front of you, especially if the person doesn't usually show such emotion?

_____ 19. How easy would it be to share your thoughts and feelings about God, religion, and prayer with someone to whom you're close?

_____ 20. How uneasy or uncomfortable has it been for you to consider your responses to these questionnaire items?

_____ 21. How romantic are you?

_____ 22. How romantic do others probably think you are?

When finished, follow your instructor's directions to determine and interpret your score.

_____ **Total score**

Obstacles to love and intimacy

It's not love's going hurts my days But that it went in little ways.

Edna St. Vincent Millay

Starry-eyed new couples declare their love passionately and then wonder a year later why "you don't bring me flowers anymore." Why do relationships cool when people want to remain close? Why do distances develop even when people love each other deeply? How can people overcome the barriers that keep them from growing in intimacy?

After years in a relationship, couples can find it awkward to say to each other things they delighted in expressing when they were dating. Family members or long-time friends feel embarrassed to compliment one another. Greater intimacy seems threatening—they're afraid that the deeper parts of themselves won't be accepted. Lack of self-acceptance is a key obstacle to intimacy. Professional counselors agree that a poor self-image is often the root of the problem.

Sustained intimacy involves the risk of placing our deeper selves in another's hands. If we get close enough, as in contact sports, we can get hurt! Some people are too terrified to take that risk. They may let themselves fall in love and marry, but then the protective wall goes up: "That's close enough." Underlying the lack of openness is often the belief that, "if you really knew me for who I truly am, you wouldn't love me."

We're all somewhat afraid of being **vulnerable**—and we should be. Our instincts help protect us from being taken advantage of emotionally or physically. But they shouldn't be an unreasonable barrier to all personal intimacy. Those who've already been deeply hurt have more reason to be afraid. The roots of their fears may lie in childhood abuse, neglect, put-downs, shame, or guilt. Or their insecurities may stem from previous rejection.

vulnerable
unprotected, exposed to being hurt

Some people are so paralyzed by their unreasonable fear of intimacy that they won't take the initiative to become more intimate with someone. They won't let the other person know what they like, want, or feel because they might be laughed at, thought less of, loved less, rejected. Instead, they limit their relationships to the superficial level because that seems acceptable and safe. That's often why couples, friends, and families get into stale routines that avoid real communication and undermine relationships.

To experience heartfelt intimacy, you must be able to express your deeper feelings. Achieving the inner freedom necessary to do that takes conscious effort and mutual support. One young wife told her husband that she'd never felt so close to him as when she saw him cry for the first time. He responded that he'd always been afraid and embarrassed to cry in front of anybody, even her. We must all work to overcome our unreasonable reluctances that block intimacy. The depth of love that results is worth the risks!

Journal entry

1. How do you think your self-image affects your relationships?
2. In what ways might improving your self-image improve your relationships?
3. What mainly keeps you from getting closer to those you love?

For discussion

1. How do people protect themselves from greater intimacy? Give examples of ways you think teenagers do that.
2. What routines do friends adopt in order to feel accepted and avoid being rejected? Does that enhance or block further closeness between them? Explain.
3. For fear of being rejected, what don't people let others know about themselves? How might sharing those things bring people closer—or would it?
4. How much do you think a weak self-image affects teenagers in the following areas. Explain.
   • Awkwardness in relating with others
   • Ability to sustain intimacy

Intimacy killers

External factors such as stress and the hectic pace of daily living also affect intimacy. In new relationships, couples give each other priority. They focus on their relationship, rather than on their jobs, money, the house, the family, or similar concerns. Gradually, they begin letting outside factors interfere with intimacy and no longer spend time just being together. Parents and kids are "too busy" to spend time with each other. Friends can't rearrange schedules to meet for lunch. Even when people are with their loved ones, other things preoccupy their minds.

When people are too stressed with work, household tasks, chauffeuring the kids, or studying for exams, they stop concentrating on doing little things for each other. Life's practical necessities become so consuming that intimacy is no longer a priority. It's a luxury, enjoyed only if there's time and energy left over—which there rarely is! But loving intimacy is the air our spirits breathe, and life's pace and pressures can damage our personal relationships just as toxins do the environment. Who feels like being intimate when we're exhausted or have a tension headache?

How you handle and balance such stresses will greatly affect the quality of your work, your health, and your relationships. It's a matter of priorities—which people often misplace when they don't get enough sleep or relaxation. Feeling harried and being always on-the-go certainly interferes with intimacy!

To cope with the pressure, some people resort to artificial crutches. They rationalize that they "need" the beer or the wine in order to feel intimate with someone. A teenager may seek a drug-induced high to cope better at school or at home. A married couple may rely on having a cocktail or some marijuana before they can talk about their feelings or feel passionate about making love. It can be nice to share a glass of wine with a loved one occasionally, but that's not what brings about real intimacy.

Genuine intimacy can't be produced artificially! When any drug is **needed** to induce good feelings, it's a sign that something is wrong and deeper needs are going unmet. The drugs only mask the real problems that are preventing intimacy. It's much better to

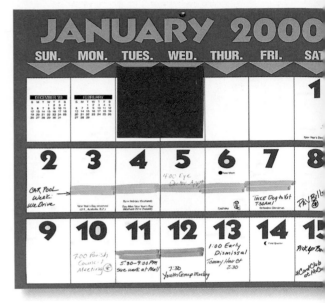

focus instead on what both persons inwardly need in order to share more of themselves in the relationship. Relying on alcohol or other drugs to feel happier, more sociable, or more romantic destroys rather than creates intimacy. Mind- or mood-altering drugs never resolve personal problems. They become the main problem. In our society, the abuse of drugs is a major relationship wrecker.

To be intimate with someone, each person needs

- to be listened to and heard
- to feel loved, appreciated, and supported
- to be depended on and to depend on
- to communicate their needs
- to feel secure about the relationship

For discussion

1. After a tough day with lots on your mind, what relaxes you enough to enjoy your loved ones? What helps you reduce your stress level?

2. What needs must be met before you can comfortably let someone get to know you more intimately? Explain.

3. Give and explain three examples that illustrate the difference between
   - satisfying your needs and being selfish
   - satisfying others' legitimate needs and giving in to their selfishness

4. What kinds of attention do you need when you're sick? How do you try to doctor yourself by meeting those needs? What types of attention do you prefer not having when you're sick?

5. Give three examples of how people may have the same basic intimacy needs, but need to have them met in very different ways.

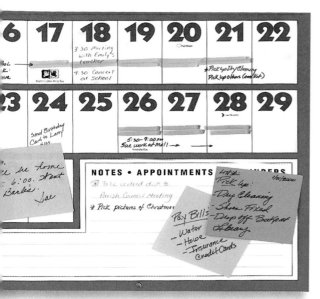

Other relationship killers

Other common relationship killers are possessiveness, jealousy, and suspicion. There's no way you cankeep someone's love if that person chooses not to love you. Giving up interests and friends not shared and always doing the same things together can actually destroy a couple's closeness. If a young woman doesn't want her boyfriend to go anywhere without her or a young man won't let his girlfriend have outside interests, the couple can lose their togetherness.

Being possessive and nourishing jealousy or suspicion merely alienates the other person and jeopardizes the relationship. Where there is reason for mistrust and suspicion, it's wiser to strengthen what love exists than tear it down by trying to force love. Love and trust are matters of the heart and therefore free choices. We really can't force someone to love us, or keep the person's heart from leaving us.

Being in love with someone, rather than simply being infatuated, must involve a mutual relationship. So never pressure someone who's unsure about continuing a relationship—or lead someone to expect more of the relationship than you think is true. Don't hang on for dear life to someone who, despite your efforts to grow closer, can no longer feel the same way about you.

Maturity doesn't come just by making it through life, but by learning from life.

Activities

Choose one.

1. Write a poem about why initial romantic feelings tend to fade after a while in a relationship and/or how to recapture the romance.

2. Interview three adults about their advice on how to keep relationships alive and growing over time. Write a two-page paper reporting and responding to their suggestions.

3. Make a collage or write a poem about one of the key elements of or obstacles to intimacy.

4. Interview an architect on how she or he designs space in homes or commercial buildings to enhance or inhibit human interaction. Write a two-page paper reporting your findings on how physical environment affects relationships.

5. Select a popular song that deals with a key quality of personal intimacy. Write a two-page paper explaining the insights the song provides—or lacks—about that quality.

Journal entry

1. How does stress or lack of sleep interfere with your relationships?

2. What other things interfere with your being truly present to someone?

3. What can you do to keep such influences from interfering with your relationships?

For discussion

1. What main stresses sometimes interfere with the closeness in your relationships? Why do you think we let such stresses interfere?

2. How do some teenagers use alcohol or other drugs to cope with stress or problems? What added problems does that cause? Explain.

3. Do you think teenagers are more likely to use drugs to avoid genuine intimacy or to try to achieve it? How do you think such drugs typically mask or magnify their real problems that prevent intimacy?

4. What do you think causes jealousy and suspicion in relationships?

5. What would you advise someone who is jealous or suspicious about the person he or she loves? Explain.

6. Why do you think people find it so hard to let go of a relationship that is no longer mutual?

Review

1. What is romance and why are romantic feelings usually more intense at the beginning of a relationship?

2. What is intimacy? What is the difference between romance and intimacy?

3. Why do people set up barriers to intimacy in their relationships?

4. Why is the fear of intimacy natural and sometimes beneficial? When does it become an unreasonable barrier to intimacy?

5. How can individuals overcome the barriers to intimacy?

6. Why can't intimacy be produced artificially? What is the problem with trying to do so?

7. Why can't love or trust be forced?

Through your eyes

Read the following summary of a movie that rather uniquely and impressively portrayed a way to enhance and renew intimacy. Then respond to the questions.

A young man and woman meet in the restaurant where she works and begin dating. He is strongly attracted to her spontaneous, imaginative qualities. He particularly enjoys making discoveries about life through her more carefree nature. The two fall in love and marry.

After a while, the husband begins taking for granted the very qualities that first attracted him to his wife. He insists that she quit her job—which she does, just to please him. But she feels bored and confined staying at home all day. So she begins going out every day to explore the city, and thoroughly enjoys her carefree excursions.

Since she's never home, her husband begins to suspect his wife of seeing another man. He hires a private detective to follow her. Every day the detective goes wherever the wife goes and does whatever she does. Without words or physical contact, the woman and the detective develop a silent relationship as they take turns leading each other about the city. Each comes to experience things through the other's eyes, imagination, and feelings—just as the wife and her husband used to do before they married.

The detective reports back to the husband that his wife hasn't been unfaithful. But the detective warns that he's losing her in another way. The husband loves his wife very much and doesn't want to lose her, so he asks the detective what he should do. The detective tells the husband this: Take my place tomorrow in following your wife. Do not speak to her, just be there. Follow her in whatever she beckons you to see and do.

In doing as the detective suggested, the husband begins to recapture his enjoyment of his wife's free-spirited nature. He realizes that he had lost this sense of wonder—and even tried to change the very quality he most cherished about his wife! As he follows her wordlessly about the city, the couple begins to resurrect their ability to share each other's perceptions and feelings.

For discussion

1. What aspects of intimacy are touched on in the above story? Be specific.
2. What obstacles to intimacy are portrayed—and overcome? Explain.
3. Why is this story a good parable for everybody who wishes to grow closer in his or her relationships? What lesson does it teach about intimacy in particular?
4. What did you learn from this "parable" that might help you grow closer to those you love?

Losing someone you love

More than likely, at some time you will face the ending of a love relationship. Perhaps you've been through this unhappiness already. As the songs say, breaking up is hard to do—sometimes very hard. The emotional pain of a break-up involves a grief process similar to that of facing death or coping with a loved one's death. Losing a loved one's affection does seem like dying inside.

With any loss, it's important to understand what you're going through and how to survive the hard times. How you handle the loss of relationships now will affect how you view and form future relationships. This chapter's insights may help you heal your emotional heartbreaks.

The grief process

Then he withdrew from them about a stone's throw, knelt down, and prayed, "Father, if you are willing, remove this cup from me; yet, not my will but yours be done." Then an angel from heaven appeared to him and gave him strength.

LUKE 22:41–43

Shock and denial

It's a shock when a serious love relationship ends or when someone close dies. Whether the end was expected or a surprise, at first there's disbelief.

- I just can't believe it's over.

- It's hard to really believe she's gone.

- I can't believe this is happening.

Bargaining

Then comes a kind of bargaining process. There's the struggle to keep the loss from happening, to hold onto or win back the person, to make things the way they were. Some enlist friends to try patching things up. Others attempt to get the person back by making her or him jealous. Most people pray.

- Please, oh please, God, don't let this happen.

- I'll do anything, if only . . .

- Please, God, get us back together.

- Just tell me what's wrong and what you want from me.

Anger and guilt

Gradually, the realization hits that the separation is for real. Then your anger surfaces—at the other for leaving, at yourself for "letting it happen." You may have hateful feelings for the other person or toward yourself or God.

The anger and guilt are merely symptoms of your emotional pain. What you really feel is deeply, terribly hurt.

- God, why did you let this happen to me? How could you possibly love me if you let this happen to me!

Mixed with the anger is guilt.
- If only I'd been . . .
    - If only I hadn't said . . .
- If only I'd done . . .
    - I shouldn't have . . .
- I should have . . .
    - Why didn't I . . . ?
- Why did I . . . ?

There's the anger at life in general.
- It's not fair.
- Why me?
- Maybe I deserve this.
- Maybe it's just me, the way I am.
- Why does this always happen to me?
- I don't deserve this.
- It's all my fault.

Depression

Once hope of reunion fades and the anger and guilt have been exhausted, you may begin feeling depressed. You may drag around in a lifeless, listless daze—trying not to care, tired of feeling unhappy but not wanting to be happy either. Because the emotional overload has been draining, even little things may get on your nerves and small problems may seem hard to bear.

Concerned friends and loved ones may advise you: "Put it behind you." "Let go." But your loss can still be very hard to endure. At this point, some people become emotionally unstable and feel as if they're losing control. If that happens to you, it's a sign that your grief has become too much to handle alone. Be smart enough to seek the professional help you need.

Acceptance

After successfully working through the other stages of grieving, one is finally ready to face reality—to admit that it's over. Now it's time to pick up the pieces and get on with your life. It's time to start living more in the present than in the past, time to think about future possibilities instead of dwelling on the pain. Gradually, it **does** become possible to enjoy life again. With God's help, this is when you should bury any bitterness and remember the love and the lessons you've learned.

Moving on

repressed
restrained or held back so as to prevent the natural expression of; kept from consciously focusing on painful ideas by forcing them into the unconscious part of one's mind

To reestablish a healthy emotional life, we must successfully pass through the stages of grieving—although not necessarily in the order given above. Those who never lived their childhood when they were young often childishly try to live it later. Like other important growth stages, the grief process must be completed before the next phase of living can begin. That's why not facing and expressing your feelings of personal loss will only hurt you rather than help you heal. Eventually you must deal with them. **Repressed** feelings will surface later in some way—in physical illness, emotional problems, or perhaps a fear of new relationships.

Losing a loved one involves a painful dying inside. To recover from losing a meaningful relationship, you must let yourself undergo the grieving process. It's much healthier to grieve than to avoid the pain. Death and resurrection are at the heart of how we Christians understand life and of how everyone can best cope with losing a loved one. Our love for someone is what causes us to feel the loss of that person's love so deeply. But that love is also the seed of greater love and understanding—and of this hope: With God's help, you will rise above your loss and know love again.

I hold it **true**, what e'er befall;

I feel it, when I **sorrow** most;

'Tis better to have **loved** and lost

Than never to have **loved** at all.

Tennyson, "In Memoriam," XXVII.

Very truly, I tell you, unless a grain of wheat falls into the earth and dies, it remains just a single grain; but if it dies, it bears much fruit.

John 12:24

Scripture insights

Read Matthew 26:36–56, Mark 14:32–53, and Luke 22:39–53.

1. How did Jesus respond to losing a loved one?

2. Did Jesus ever seem to experience any of the grief process stages as he faced his or a loved one's death?

3. How did Jesus' disciples cope with his death? Did their responses reflect any of the grief process stages?

For discussion

1. Have you or any of your friends ever suffered through a relationship break-up? If so, how did the resulting feelings and reactions compare with those described in the grief process? Explain.

2. What thoughts and feelings would be examples of repressing grief in coping with a relationship break-up?

3. Why and how do repressed feelings surface later to affect a person's relationships?

4. Which Bible passages do you find most meaningful or helpful in coping with the end of a relationship or the loss of a loved one? Explain.

After it's over

Be thankful for brief dreams, but let them go.

A broken heart hurts as much as a broken bone, but both can heal. Nobody hopes to experience them, but you probably will suffer some painful personal losses in your lifetime. Barricading yourself behind a protective, unbreakable heart of stone will bring you no joy. So when it does happen to you, how can you mend your broken heart and end up being a better, wiser person?

Let your feelings out. However true or false your lost love was, when it's over—

- Let yourself feel the hurt—at least for a while. Don't hide your feelings, but express them without harming anyone.

- Cry, but not constantly on everyone's shoulder for the next three years! Don't make things worse by playing the martyr.

- Sob yourself to sleep, but don't accuse your teacher, your mother, or your boss of picking on you when that's not really what's bothering you.

- Smash your pillow, not the first person that cuts in front of you on the road or in the lunch line.

- Swim, run, or otherwise physically work the anger and frustration out of your system. Don't drive like a maniac to let off steam.

- Talk over your feelings with an understanding friend or adult. Don't snipe at your mother or co-worker because you've just lost the love of your life.

- Take out your feelings by playing tennis or volleyball, not by starving yourself or eating like there's a famine tomorrow just to feel better.

- Don't harbor a "get even" grudge, start a fight, or spread nasty rumors about your "ex" or his or her "new love." (Others will regard that as pitiful.) Instead, dig into a project you want to finish or get caught up with your work.

- Let yourself feel in ways that heal rather than cause more pain.

Take it step by step. Broken bones don't mend in a day, nor do broken hearts. Deeper wounds take time to heal; be patient with yourself. Don't expect a miracle or believe you'll never get over this loss. Confront your loss, without dwelling on it. Gradually turn to positive thoughts and feelings.

Thinking about how things were, what we did, what she used to say, what he used to do, or how happy we were is probably necessary for a while. As when a loved one dies, it's common to focus for a time on past shared experiences. But the time comes to begin looking ahead, incorporating the good, but not living in the past. Eventually you must say goodbye and get on with life.

Accept help. Some people automatically turn to others for emotional support. Others shut themselves off, not letting their feelings show. At times you should let yourself lean a bit on others. It's as foolish not to accept needed emotional assistance as to try walking on a broken leg without support. Gradually you must become more self-reliant. But don't be afraid to seek support from others for a time. Always rely on your Friend, God.

Help yourself. While you're hurting, go easier on yourself. Think positively. Treat yourself to things you especially enjoy. Never turn to alcohol or other drugs to ease your pain—that always creates far worse problems! Your emotional heart is similar to your physical one in this way: It can't survive being permanently anesthetized. It must be exercised to remain alive. So don't just sit there waiting for someone to make you happy again. Begin taking steps yourself to rebuild your happiness.

*People fall
in love, but
they have to
climb out.*

JOHN CIARDI

Learn from your mistakes. Many relationships should end. You may both discover that you've just been infatuated rather than truly in love. Or that you can't get along even though you do care greatly for each other. But if you understand why things didn't work out, you can perhaps prevent that from happening in the future. Unfortunately, people often don't learn and just keep repeating their same unhappy relationship mistakes!

If you realize why someone was wrong for you, avoid picking the same wrong type of person over and over. Be more careful to not again mistake infatuation for love. Proceed more slowly. You can also ask the person why the feelings for you are no longer the same and why she or he wants to end the relationship. You could learn something valuable about yourself that will help you improve your relationships.

If the relationship just ends abruptly for no apparent reason, then you'll at least know it wasn't that deep anyway. Why mourn over an illusion? People sometimes grieve over an illusory lost love, when their pride and unrealistic hopes are really hurting more than their heart! Sadly, some people close their heart so they won't be hurt again. But others run right into the arms of their next mistake. Rebound romances and marriages usually fail because they're only temporary shelter from emotional pain. Lacking a solid foundation, they collapse—which only causes further anguish.

Don't presume that something's wrong with you just because the other person preferred someone else! But if you realize after a break-up with someone that you were partly at fault, turn that into an opportunity for self-improvement. Get beyond just blaming yourself. Take positive steps to overcome your faults so you become even more loving and lovable.

Often people *are* told that they're too possessive, bossy, aggressive, non-communicative, or nagging. *But they don't listen.* After it's too late, when the other person wants to end the relationship, *then* they say they want to change!

Be more aware of possible problems next time. Have you ever seen a romantic break-up coming, even though one of the partners had no idea the relationship was rocky? To prevent surprise relationship rifts, let the other person see your less-than-ideal side. If you're aware of what bothers someone about you, then you can change if you want to do so—before it's too late.

Be grateful for the love. There's always some heartache when a close relationship ends. To minimize the pain, don't expect a commitment where none has been made. Then you'll be more prepared to accept it if the relationship doesn't last. However the relationship ends, don't become bitter, disillusioned, and too scared to open your heart again. Instead, realize how much goodness you've shared, and how it has enriched you. Be grateful that love has so beautifully touched your life.

As you go through the various lessons and losses of loving throughout your life, this is a good prayer to remember:
*Your trees before winter
  give up their leaves to fall
and raise their arms empty to heaven.
  You alone give meaning
to our being together and our being apart.
  What is it that abides?
What is it that touches eternal?
We place our hope in Your love among us
  for You alone give meaning
to our being together and our being apart.
  Our life grows and fades
  as quickly as the flowers
and passes ever on to where we cannot see
  You alone give meaning
to our being together and our being apart.
  Our being human is pain and blessing,
  it is searching and not finding all we want.
  You alone give meaning
to our being together and our being apart.*[2]

After a break-up, keep telling yourself . . .

- I'm going through a very common human experience. Throughout history people have survived broken hearts to live happy futures. So will I. I'll let their experiences give me hope.

- I've suffered losses and hurts before when I felt I couldn't face tomorrow or ever again be happy. But I did go on to be happy, and I will again. In time, I will get over the pain.

- The person I loved had good qualities, but also had faults and wasn't perfect. There are many other wonderful people—some in this same situation, wishing they could meet someone like me.

- Chances are that the person I'll love most in life will have been through this same experience.

We'll appreciate each other more because we both grew from the loves we'd lost.

- Would I have wanted to continue this relationship anyway if someone even more wonderful had come along? When I meet someone I like better, how will I feel then about the fact that this relationship is over?

- What can I learn from this unhappy experience that will help me be happier in the future?

- I am a worthwhile, lovable person. I'm loved by God and by others. I will meet someone else to love, but only if I'm open to the possibility.

- After painfully losing love, I'll treasure it all the more when love touches my life again in a special way—and it will!

For discussion

1. Why do you think some people fail to see or correct their faults until it's too late in a relationship?

2. Suppose you sadly realize that you could have kept your relationship from breaking up if only you'd changed some things about yourself sooner. What, if anything, should you do about it?

3. When should love relationships end? How would you react if someone gave you no reasons for ending a relationship with you? Explain fully.

4. What's the difference between grieving the loss of a love that was real and mourning over a mirage?

Which do you think occurs more often when teenage relationships end? Explain!

5. Why do you think unhappy rebound relationships are so common? What is a better alternative?

6. What's your best advice for coping with a relationship break-up? Explain.

7. What can you learn from coping with broken relationships that can help you in the future? What have you or others you know already learned about that from experience? Explain.

1. Compare having a broken leg with having a broken heart. Be specific.

2. After suffering a personal loss, how can you confront the experience without rehashing the negative aspects? Explain.

3. When do you turn to others for emotional support? How do you rely on yourself to make it through difficulty?

4. When coping with a major loss or disappointment, how do you turn to positive thoughts and feelings? Explain.

5. What has helped you to get over personal hurts—especially from broken relationships? How did those things help?

6. Why do people repeat the same relationship mistakes? Have you seen that happen with people you know? Explain, without mentioning names.

7. Why do you think so many people turn to alcohol and drugs to cope with emotional pain? How common do you think that is among teenagers? Explain.

Review

1. What type of death and resurrection process do individuals go through in parting from a loved one? Explain each stage of this process.

2. How can one best deal with the painful ending of a love relationship?

3. What mistakes do people make in handling the loss of a love relationship?

4. Why are alcohol, drugs, and rebound relationships unwise ways to try healing a broken heart?

Picking up the pieces

Below are common reactions people have to relationship breakups. In the spaces, write and explain

a. your reactions about what each person is saying

b. your advice for each person in coping with his or her feelings

1. Everything was so perfect—how could it have ended? Somebody else comes along and suddenly it's over between us. It's so hard. I just can't understand it.

   a.

   b.

2. Can't I do something to bring back the love— to make it the same as before? I'd do anything. If only I knew what to do . . . .

   a.

   b.

3. We broke up a month ago, and I hardly feel like doing anything anymore. I still choke back the tears every time I hear our song. I can't bear to go to a party where I might see the one I loved so much dancing with somebody else. I just can't seem to get over it.

   a.

   b.

4. Why does somebody have to lie to you? How can somebody tell you they love you and are yours forever, and then turn right around and drop you?

   a.

   b.

5. All I feel inside is hate. Yesterday I loved somebody and today I hate the person. I know you're not supposed to hate anybody. Sometimes I hate myself for being so hateful, but I can't help it—that's how I feel. After everything you've shared together, how can somebody just not love you anymore?

   a.

   b.

6. Nobody understands. All I get at home and at school is hassled. I know I've been moody and haven't kept up with my schoolwork. But I really don't care about anything since we broke up. I've gotten in trouble for cutting a couple of classes. But some days I just can't handle being in the same room for an hour with somebody who dumped me only a few weeks ago. I can't help it.

   a.

   b.

7. My friends and my parents say that I should forget it—like I could just make it all disappear. Well, it's not that easy. Maybe we weren't really in love like I had thought, maybe it was only infatuation or "puppy love"—but it still hurts like hell!

   a.

   b.

8. It was so special. I'll never love anyone else like that again. Now that it's over I keep thinking it's all my fault and blaming myself. I know that won't bring us back together. But I still feel that if I could just figure out what I said and did that was wrong, I could fix things between us.

   a.

   b.

In summary

Relationships often begin with heightened attraction, mystery, and excitement that develop into genuine loving closeness and personal intimacy. True intimacy is a close spiritual connection that reflects and is made possible by God's love for us as fully expressed in Jesus. Growing in intimacy is a process that requires unselfish effort and respecting and fostering each other's individuality. The caring foundation of intimacy is distinguished by several characteristics: trust, empathy, maturity, tenderness, awareness, imagination. Common obstacles to intimacy are a poor self-image, lack of self-acceptance, fear of rejection or personal involvement, possessiveness, jealousy, suspicion, and other external stress factors.

Coping with the ending of a love relationship is often extremely painful and involves a grieving process. As part of that process, one may undergo shock and denial, bargaining, anger, guilt, and depression until finally arriving at acceptance. With God's help, there are steps that help the healing. It's good to express one's feelings, take things step by step, accept support, help oneself, learn from mistakes, and be grateful for the love.

Key concepts

artificial attempts to produce intimacy

awareness

being imaginative

being in love as a mutual relationship

being vulnerable

cherish

compassion

empathy

ending a love relationship

God's intimate relationship with us

grief process

growing in intimacy

healing a broken heart

individuality

intimacy

intimacy needs

jealousy

losing a loved one

maturity

obstacles to love and intimacy

personal intimacy

possessiveness

physical intimacy

repressing feelings

romance

suspicion

tenderness

trust

Endnotes

1. See *A Positive Vision for Family Life: A Resource Guide for Pope John Paul II's Apostolic Exhortation "Familiaris Consortio,"* Commission on Marriage and Family Life, Department of Education, United States Catholic Conference, Reverend Thomas Lynch, gen. ed., Valerie Dillon, ed. (Washington, DC: United States Catholic Conference, 1985), 89.

2. Messenger Corporation (Auburn, Indiana, 1975).

CHAPTER 5

COMMUNICATION: KEY TO INTIMACY

SCRIPTURE

If I speak in the tongues of mortals and of angels,
but do not have love,
I am a noisy gong or a clanging cymbal.

1 CORINTHIANS 13:1

PRAYER

Gracious God,
You've expressed your eternal Word to us fully
  in Jesus.
Through him, you've let us know who you are
and who we are to be for one another.
Thank you for giving us the ability to communicate
our thoughts and feelings through our words
  and gestures.
For without that gift, we would remain forever lonely—

imprisoned in the solitary confinement of our
  own minds.
Help us use our gifts of communication wisely—
so that we don't just talk, but communicate,
and don't just hear, but really listen.
Let our communications build bridges, not barriers,
  between us.
And keep our hearts always in touch with you.
We ask this in Jesus' name. Amen

Building communication skills

communication skills

specific techniques or abilities that enable people to communicate effectively

Communication now runs our world. Good communication prevents wars and makes peace. Businesses spend millions every year to improve management and employee communication skills. Good communication is certainly vital for healthy, fulfilling personal relationships.

Because communicating well is so important, Catholic teaching recommends that communication-skills training be part of Catholic education. Catholic teaching also encourages Catholics to actively help others communicate better. Communication links our minds and hearts, moving us toward our ultimate destiny of unity with God and one another. That unity is Jesus' main prayer:

". . . that they may be one, Father, as we are one."

JOHN 17:11B

Communication is far more than just saying words. It's understanding each other through words and gestures that let us share our thoughts and feelings. You can talk at a brick wall, but you can communicate only with someone who understands what you mean. Effective communication is a two-way street. If no one understands you, you might as well keep quiet. If words "full of sound and fury" reach no one, they "signify nothing."

Always remember that you're communicating with someone who's different from you. People often think they're communicating when they're really just expressing themselves. They're thinking of the message they're trying to get across rather than how

it's being understood by the other person. Or they're hearing but not really listening—concentrating more on their own thoughts than on what the speaker is saying.

A professional football player described learning that lesson the hard way. He said that in the huddle he'd be focusing on the next play rather than the snap count the quarterback was giving. When the snap count began the play, the player would then move too soon and draw a penalty—or too late and miss a tackle. When he started listening to the snap count more carefully, his performance on the field improved.

We learn to talk very early in life, but we can always learn to communicate better. Some of the greatest talkers are the worst communicators! Most relationship friction results from poor communication. If you want your relationships to grow and last, learn to communicate more effectively.

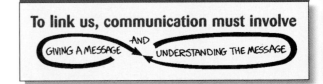

To link us, communication must involve GIVING A MESSAGE —AND— UNDERSTANDING THE MESSAGE

Journal entry

1. With what person do you feel you communicate well?
2. What person do you think understands you best?
3. With whom do you communicate poorly, or with whom you would like to communicate better?

For discussion

1. How can poor communication threaten humanity's welfare? How can good communication foster it? Give examples.
2. Without mentioning names, do you know people who talk at you but don't seem to be communicating to or with you? Do you ever talk at, rather than to or with, someone? Explain.

Talking it over

We communicate verbally with spoken words, and nonverbally (without words) using body language—gestures, facial expressions, and posture. This self-test can help you identify where your verbal communication needs improving. Your instructor will tell you how to determine and assess your score. You won't be expected to share your responses or results.

On each blank, write the letter from A–F that best reflects your response.

A — Never/Not at all
B — Rarely/Hardly at all
C — Seldom/Not very strongly
D — Sometimes/Somewhat, but not strongly
E — Often/Somewhat strongly
F — Always/Very strongly

_____ 1. Do you monopolize a conversation or talk too much?

_____ 2. Do you gossip?

_____ 3. Do you talk about happy or positive things more than about problems or negative ideas, feelings, or experiences?

_____ 4. How much do you complain?

_____ 5. Other than discussing problems, do you try to have serious or meaningful conversations—especially with family members?

_____ 6. Do you take too seriously—or not seriously enough—things other people say?

_____ 7. Rather than becoming angry or upset, do you take in stride or laugh about little things that go wrong?

_____ 8. Do the same problems or annoyances bother you over and over?

_____ 9. Do you value others' opinions—even though you don't agree with them?

_____ 10. In conversation, do you try to get others to agree with you?

_____ 11. Does it upset or frustrate you when others disagree with you?

_____ 12. When disagreeing with someone, do you focus on trying to win or get your way?

_____ 13. When you realize that you can't do or have something you really want, can you easily give it up without arguing or complaining?

_____ 14. In disagreements about who gets to have or do something, do you try to determine who needs it the most?

_____ 15. In serious, sensitive, or heated situations, do you think before you speak?

_____ 16. Have you regretted something you said—or didn't say?

_____ 17. Are you afraid or shy about expressing an opinion when you think others probably won't agree or will think it stupid?

_____ 18. When you should speak up, do you instead avoid tension or conflict by keeping quiet, or by agreeing with or letting others have their way?

_____ 19. Do you state your opinions as fact—for instance, saying "This is dumb" or "You should" instead of "I don't think this will work" or "I think you should"?

_____ 20. How often has someone become angry or upset unexpectedly by something you said?

_____ 21. When you think something should be said that hurts or criticizes another, how much thought do you give to the best way of saying it?

_____ 22. Do you usually put conversations with family members and friends before other less important concerns?

_____ 23. How often do you feel others misunderstand you?

_____ 24. How often have others told you that you didn't understand them?

_____ 25. How often do you take time by yourself to relax, think things through, or sort out your feelings?

_____ Total score

Improving communication

As the exercise you just completed probably reminded you, we can all improve our communication skills! To enhance the intimacy in your relationships, work on the fundamentals below.

Put people first

- Who you are speaking to is more important than what you are saying. Don't give the message that "I'm more important than you are" or "What I have to say means more to me than you do."
- Rather than promoting yourself, value the listener. Care about who's receiving your message and how that person is perceiving it.
- When you communicate well with someone, you've already grown closer.
- Don't be so busy that you neglect or reject opportunities to communicate with those you care about. Too many married couples bury themselves in newspapers, preparing dinner, doing dishes, and watching television, and rarely converse with each other meaningfully. Parents put off a child who wants to talk with "Not now, can't you see I'm busy?"
- Be sensitive to when conversations can and should be postponed until later, and when someone needs for you to stop what you're doing to listen or talk now. Other things can often wait. Most things aren't as important as a person's need to be heard. Don't put tasks and things before people. Take the time to listen and to be with one another.
- Make people your priority. People always come first!

For discussion

1. Give three examples of how "proving a point" can become more important than the person to whom one is communicating.

2. In each of those situations, how could and should the person be valued more than the points being made?

3. Give two examples of someone failing to listen to you when you really needed to talk. How did you feel as a result? Why?

4. How can you tell when someone really needs to have you stop and listen (especially if the person doesn't clearly say this)?

> ## If you do not **understand** my silence, you will not understand my **words**.
>
> SOURCE UNKNOWN

Don't push, pry, or pressure

- Don't hog the conversation; it's no way to draw closer to your listener.
- Don't give the impression that others must agree with you—allow for give and take.
- Don't arm-twist someone into revealing what she or he isn't ready to share. Encourage others to share things about themselves when they're ready.
- Remember that pushing, prying, and pressuring put people off!

For discussion

Give a common example of pressuring each other unfairly into sharing personal information by

- a parent and teenager
- a brother and a sister
- two friends
- a couple in love

Keep confidences

- Don't gossip! If you want others to trust you, then be trustworthy.
- Respect the thoughts and feelings others share with you, rather than spreading these around as the latest rumor.
- True intimacy requires that two people trust each other with their deeper thoughts and feelings. That means keeping each other's secrets safe.
- If you want to create credibility, keep confidences!

For discussion

1. Why is it hard to trust a gossip?
2. Why is gossip harmful?
3. Why do you think people gossip?

Praise, and phrase positively

- Be positive rather than constantly dwelling on the negative. This usually produces better results. Nobody can stand chronic complaining!
- Don't whine, bicker, or nag—a common grievance in families.
- Engage in thoughtful, serious conversations—and not just when there's a problem.
- Let your good sense of humor keep you from taking petty things too seriously.
- Focus on and let others know the good qualities you see in them.
- Try to follow St. Paul's advice to the Christians of Philippi:

   . . . whatever is true, whatever is honorable, whatever is just, whatever is pure, whatever is pleasing, whatever is commendable, if there is any excellence and if there is anything worthy of praise, think about these things . . . and the God of peace will be with you.

   PHILIPPIANS 4:8–9B

For discussion

1. How do you react to people who chronically gripe or whine? Why?
2. What is the difference between being a positive person and being someone who isn't realistic or candid enough to point out real problems?
3. In what ways do you think friends too often focus on the negative—on what's wrong with things, people, or situations?

Listen and learn

- Let others know what you really think, and listen to their responses.
- People's opinions may be wrong, but what they think and feel is just as important to a relationship as the facts are. Opinions tell us what people are like and what's important to them.
- Voice your opinions appropriately. Don't let others walk all over you just to avoid disagreement.
- Don't be opinionated. State your opinions as opinions, rather than as facts.
- Be willing to listen to ideas and information that can further enlighten you.

For discussion

1. How do people give the impression that others must agree with them—or else? How can that be avoided, and why should it be?
2. How do people state their opinions as if these were facts? Give three examples, and then reword each "factual" statement into an opinion statement.
3. What's the difference between having opinions and being or seeming opinionated? Give specific examples.

Notice needs now

- Don't get into power struggles over whose way wins.
- Address needs (what one must have to function well) as soon as possible. Wants (what one desires but can do without) can wait.
- Recognize that needs and wants differ with individuals and circumstances. One person's wants can be what someone else needs. What a person wanted last time might be needed this time. To help resolve a conflict, determine whose need is greater right now and how that need can be met first.
- Put needs before wants. Be able to postpone what you want for the sake of what you need.

Think things through

- Think before you speak, especially in sensitive situations or where potential conflict exists. Don't "put your mouth in motion before your brain goes into gear"!
- Be aware of how your words affect others. Careless remarks can be extremely damaging.
- Speak honestly but not unkindly or cruelly.
- Be thoughtful and considerate and respect the other person's feelings. That helps avoid unnecessary hurt or friction.

Pick the right time and place

- Be sensitive to how important timing and setting are in enhancing communication.
- When discussing personal or important matters, provide the necessary time and privacy. Don't blurt out questions about your boyfriend or girlfriend's former dates on a crowded bus just two streets before your stop!
- Find the right time to talk. Think in advance about where and when you can both relax and be honest without being overheard or interrupted. Asking someone, "How do you really feel about me?" while walking down the hallway to your next class isn't very wise.
- If necessary, create the right time and place to talk. One married couple has coffee on the patio each night so that they can relax together and talk about the day's concerns without interruption.

For discussion

1. Give an example of a typical disagreement that might be resolved by distinguishing between needs and wants between
   - two friends
   - a daughter or son and her or his parent
   - a married couple
2. In those disagreements, who do you think should postpone his or her wants in favor of the other person's needs? Explain why.

For discussion

1. What types of careless or cruel remarks do you hear most often at school?
2. What harm do those remarks do?
3. What do they reveal about those who make them?

For discussion

Give three examples of when someone's insensitivity to the time and place for serious communication has been a source of irritation or embarrassment to you or others. Explain why this was so.

There is no **difficulty** that enough love will not **conquer**.

EMMET FOX

Take time to pray and reflect

- Take time to look within yourself. Set aside quiet time each day just for you. Calmly strengthen your convictions and reestablish your priorities. Inner silence puts you in touch with your deeper thoughts and feelings and enables you to communicate more effectively with others.

- Don't let your life become so cluttered with the details of living that your thinking and communication become muddled. In the tide of minor problems and frustrations, don't lose track of what you really think and feel.

- Relax in God's presence, and daily recommit your life, concerns, and loving to the One who can help you make sense out of confusion, bring hope out of despair, and draw you closer to others.

For discussion

1. What types of things prompt you to seek some quiet time alone? What helps you the most in these moments of silent solitude?

2. Do you find that praying helps you connect better with other people, as well as with God? Explain.

> Think **twice** before you speak, **especially** if you **intend** to say what you think.

ANN LANDERS

Crossed wires

Read the following situation, which actually occurred. Then respond to the questions.

Natalie and Aaron had been married only a few months when they had their first serious misunderstanding. Natalie usually got home from her job before Aaron returned from his law-school classes. She looked forward to their time together. But after greeting Natalie each evening, Aaron would head straight for the den and spend half an hour or so playing computer games.

Natalie felt hurt and furious. She decided Aaron must not love her as much as she'd thought. He seemed to look forward to playing those "stupid games" more than to being with her. When Natalie couldn't hold her feelings back any longer, she exploded, telling Aaron just how little he cared for her. Aaron, in turn, blew up at Natalie, saying that she didn't understand him.

For discussion

1. How would you probably have felt and reacted in Natalie's situation? Why? In Aaron's situation? Why?

2. Based on the communication tips you discussed previously, how many things can you find wrong with how both parties responded here? What other factors could be part of the problem? Explain.

3. Which communication tip(s) might help Aaron and Natalie resolve their problem? Do you have any other suggestions for them? Explain.

Scripture insights

Read the story of Martha and Mary—Luke 10:38–42. Which of the suggestions for improving communication does Jesus support there? What lesson can we draw from that?

Scripture assignment

Search the Christian Scriptures for examples of Jesus' communication techniques. Write a two-page report describing them.

Activity

Write a poem, song, prayer, or meditation about the meaning and importance of silence in your life.

Review

1. Why does the Catholic Church promote good communication between people?

2. How is good communication a two-way street?

3. What is involved in communication that
   - puts people first
   - doesn't push, pry, or pressure
   - keeps confidences
   - praises and phrases positively
   - listens and learns
   - notices needs now
   - thinks things through
   - picks the right time and place
   - takes time for thought and prayer

Communication styles

Communication isn't always simple. People have different ways of communicating; different groups communicate differently; people who know each other well communicate in a different way than do strangers. Variety and uniqueness prevail.

How you say it

How we say something and how well we *listen* to someone are just as important as what we say to others. Sharing our *feelings* with someone is just as important as sharing our *thoughts*.

To some extent our voice is due to our genes and our hormones—things we can't change. On the other hand we can change habits that block closeness. We can be aware that our voice may at times grate on people's nerves. We can improve the way we speak. Volume is high on the list. Some people talk too loudly most of the time—unaware of how much that annoys or embarrasses others. People don't like to be shouted at or have their private conversations overheard all the time.

Some people have bothersome high-pitched voices. Others unintentionally sound monotonous, sing-songy, whiny, or sarcastic. With conscious effort people can improve those vocal characteristics—and do wonders for how others respond! A softer voice with

feeling behind it seems more intimate than harsh or monotonous tones.

So be aware of how your voice might convey your thoughts and feelings more meaningfully and pleasantly. Also note how your tone of voice may be contradicting your words. Your tone of voice can give an unfair, irritating double message that can result in many communication problems! It certainly won't improve your communication nor your relationships.

Communication experts also note how men and women communicate differently in the workplace—in ways that often mirror the roles they assumed as children. In the workplace, however, these two styles may conflict. Little girls more often engage in a cooperative style of play centered on feelings and relationships. The resulting skills they acquire help make them good negotiators at work. Women also more often say "thank you" and "I'm sorry" about the very smallest

> *While enormous strides have been made in communications in recent years, there's a lot to be said for the smile.*
>
> FRANKLIN P. JONES

communication style

a particular way of sharing information and feelings with another person based on the personality and experiences of the one sharing and the position of the one shared with

matters. Unfortunately, male co-workers who don't understand that communication style may think it weak instead of thoughtful—or irksome if the woman always seems to be apologizing.

At play, little boys more often challenge each other. They learn to be and follow a leader. At work, female co-workers may misunderstand the man's direct manner as curt or rude. Yet a woman who is equally direct may be unfairly viewed as bossy. Little boys' competitiveness may prepare them for dealing with the pressures of business competition. But learning to be "tough" and to hide emotion rather than to listen to and understand others can be a definite drawback in the business world and in relationships!

It's a shame all children aren't raised with broader communication skills and styles. But as males and females work to learn from each other, we must also understand each other as we are. It's dangerously unfair, though, to stereotype! Really, no one communicates in a "typical male" or "typical female" style. Because we are individuals, our **communication styles** are somewhat unique. For instance, some people need time alone to sort through a personal problem, while others do it better while discussing it with someone.

Students often look down on "apple polishers" who try to get on the teacher's good side. In the real world, though, you'll need to learn and work with your boss's and co-workers' ways of communicating and doing things. So instead of expecting everyone to communicate the same way you do, be aware of each person's individual communication style. Be flexible enough to work with and enjoy others' differences.

For discussion

1. Explain the meaning of this adage: "I can't hear what you're saying because how you're saying it is ringing so loudly in my ears."

2. Which voice qualities and tones of speaking do you find most appealing? Most unappealing or irritating? Explain.

3. Would you say that your childhood play style was more cooperative or more competitive—or that it was a good balance of both styles? How does it affect the way you communicate now?

4. Do you think male and female communication styles are more different from each other or more similar? Explain.

5. Which communication styles do you find more comfortable to deal with in someone else? Which do you find most difficult or uncomfortable? Why?

Making contact

This self-test can help you determine how well you make contact with others through the ways you communicate, listen, and express your feelings. Your instructor will tell you how to determine and interpret your score. You won't be expected to share your responses or results.

On each blank, write the letter from A–F that best reflects your response.

A — Never/Not at all

B — Rarely/Hardly at all

C — Seldom/Not very strongly

D — Sometimes/Somewhat, but not strongly

E — Often/Somewhat strongly

F — Always/Very strongly

_____ 1. When talking with someone, do you think about what you're going to say before the other person has finished speaking?

_____ 2. In class are you impatient for other students to finish talking so that you can contribute your answer or opinion?

_____ 3. While talking with others, are you aware of what they seem to be feeling as well as saying?

_____ 4. Do you sense when others are thinking or feeling something important that they're not expressing?

_____ 5. Do you respect others' wishes to not talk about something or not to talk about it now?

_____ 6. In class discussions do you really listen to what other students are saying?

_____ 7. In conversations with friends do you focus more on whether you agree with what's said than its importance to the person making the statement?

_____ 8. Do you judge or jump to conclusions about what someone is saying before the person has finished explaining?

_____ 9. Before you criticize or disagree with someone, do you make sure you've correctly understood what the person meant?

_____ 10. How aware are you usually of your own feelings?

_____ 11. Do you share with others how you feel as well as what you think?

_____ 12. Are you able to express your feelings to someone even when it makes you uncomfortable?

_____ 13. When nobody else is around, do you feel free to cry when you feel like it?

_____ 14. Do you think (or have others suggested) that your tone of voice is unpleasant (for instance, too loud or soft, sarcastic, whiny, too sweet or gruff or harsh, lacking in expression, or too emotional)?

_____ 15. Have others been worried, upset, bothered, or angered that your tone of voice expressed something different from your words?

_____ 16. Do you have any facial expressions that others might find irritating, distracting, or misleading?

_____ 17. Are you sensitive to what someone's posture, gestures, or other body language reveals about what the person really thinks or feels?

_____ 18. Do you have any body-language habits, other than facial expressions, that bother or distract people when you converse?

_____ 19. Does your posture convey a negative impression of you?

_____ 20. How relaxed are you when conversing with others?

_____ **Total score**

Body language

body language

posture, gestures, facial expressions, and other bodily mannerisms that communicate something about the person or the person's attitude

Much of our communication is nonverbal—through our posture, gestures, facial expressions, and other bodily mannerisms. It's much easier to lie with words than with one's **body language**. Crossed arms may reveal a distance or disagreement between people that their words don't express. Studies have found that, while talking, happy couples sit close together and touch each other much more often than those who have a less satisfying relationship. Even the positions people sleep in reveal things about them and their relationships. Our body language speaks volumes!

Some body language habits are appealing, while others seem rude, though unintentionally. One girl discovered that her nervous habit of playing with her hair while talking conveyed the impression that she didn't care about the conversation. A teenage boy drove everybody crazy by nervously and loudly (though unconsciously) cracking his thumb while giving presentations in class. Another girl found out why others thought her a snob—that the way she walked appeared "arrogant" to others.

How we stand, sit, walk, and shake hands can either tell a lot about us or be very misleading. It's a good idea to be aware of what our bodies as well as our words are communicating. If our nonverbal communication gives undesirable messages, we can change our body language. We should also be aware of what others' body language may be telling us that their words are not saying.

Couples have discovered that sitting close together while talking helps them *feel* closer. Many couples find that holding hands while disagreeing prevents many arguments! Their body language reminds them that they're more important to each other than what they're disagreeing over. The right body language sustains and increases intimacy.

Facial expressions

Facial expressions communicate feelings powerfully. They can support or contradict our words. A frown or biting the lip, for example, may convey worry or nervousness, suspicion or sternness, a lack of humor, or a profound concern. Instead of clearly reflecting inner thoughts and feelings, some people's habitual facial expressions mislead others.

More often, the saying "Your face reads like a book" is true. Facial expressions generally communicate emotions and thoughts quite accurately, even though the person's words give no clue to their true feelings. So be sensitive to what others' facial expressions may reveal about their feelings, and be aware of how your facial expressions affect your communication.

To grow closer, look into the eyes of those you love.

Eye contact

It's been said that "the eyes are the windows of the soul." Looking into someone's eyes is one of the best ways to reach the person. Yet it's amazing how reluctant people often are to look directly at the person to whom they're speaking. People's eyes reveal much about their thoughts and feelings. Eyes reflect happiness, contentment, uncertainty, anger, confusion, shame or guilt, pride, and countless other things.

The messy room

Read the following mother-daughter "dialogue." Then respond to the questions.

MOM (PLEASANTLY BUT FIRMLY)   JENNY (IN A WHINY, DISGUSTED TONE OF VOICE)

JENNY, YOUR ROOM'S A HEALTH HAZARD. PLEASE CLEAN IT UP THIS AFTERNOON.

(SIGH...) OH, ALL RIGHT!

MOM (BECOMING UPSET)   JENNY (UPSET AND IN THE SAME WHINY, DISGUSTED TONE OF VOICE AS BEFORE)

DON'T YOU TALK TO ME LIKE THAT, YOUNG LADY!

BUT ALL I SAID WAS "ALL RIGHT"!

For discussion

1. How does Jenny's mother ask her to clean up her room? Does she seem antagonistic?

2. How does Jenny respond to her mother's request? Why do you think she responds that way—is it because of the way she's asked, or for another reason?

3. Why does Jenny's mother reprimand her?

4. When Jenny tells her mother that all she'd said was "all right"—

   • What does Jenny's statement mean literally?

   • What underlying point is Jenny trying to make? Does she make it fairly or appropriately?

   • Is Jenny's statement true?

5. List the communication elements involved in the Mom–Jenny dialogue. Explain the role each element plays in the dialogue.

6. How could Jenny and her mother have responded to each other better at each point? How would that have helped them grow closer rather than upset each other?

For discussion

1. What body language have you found a barrier in getting to know someone better or growing closer to the person? Why?

2. What types of body language help you feel friendly or think positively about someone? Why?

3. Which facial expressions do you notice most? How do they help you understand the person? Explain.

4. Do you find it hard to look directly into someone's eyes while speaking with the person? Which makes you more uncomfortable—when someone, while speaking to you, looks into your eyes or does not look into your eyes? Explain.

5. Why is it harder to lie to someone while looking into his or her eyes?

Listening

The first duty of love—is to listen.
PAUL TILLICH

active listening
giving feedback to indicate that a message has been understood

When communication fails, so do marriages and so do relationships between family members and among friends. And most communication breaks down because people don't listen to each other. Parents take great pride in what their toddler says but often give little thought to teaching the child how to listen. It's presumed that whoever can hear can listen. But there's a vast difference between hearing words and really listening.

Many people complain that their spouse is a great talker but never listens. We can be poor listeners on two levels: We can fail to hear all of a person's words and therefore misunderstand. Or we can fail to listen to the *person* behind the words. (It's said that "the walls have ears," but more often it's true that the ears have walls! People often hear only what they want to hear.)

You may have heard of the trainers who "listen" to horses. They use a method of patiently "listening" to the horse's subtle ways of communicating apprehension, displeasure, trust, or receptivity. In that gentle manner, they get a wild horse to willingly accept a saddle, bridle, and rider in half an hour, instead of a month or more with the traditional painful pressure and domination tactics. People likewise respond better to a patient and gentle kindness that really listens and responds to them as an

individual! There's no need to painfully dominate either a horse or a person.

Listen to the message.

To become a better listener—

- **Concentrate on what the other person is saying** more than on what you plan to say as soon as you get the chance!

- **Be mentally quiet** while someone speaks, so you can thoughtfully understand.

- **Avoid making snap judgments** before someone finishes speaking. If you react too quickly, especially if you react negatively, the person won't feel that he or she has had the chance to be heard. And instant agreement or disagreement is meaningless. So hear someone out before you make a judgment.

- **Listen respectfully**, and then your opinion will more likely be respected.

- **Reflect back** what you think the person said and meant. Ask if you understood correctly. That tells the person that you're interested in what he or she has said. If you've misquoted or misinterpreted, you can then clarify your understanding instead of jumping to false conclusions. That will prevent many hurt and angry feelings, and it will increase your closeness.

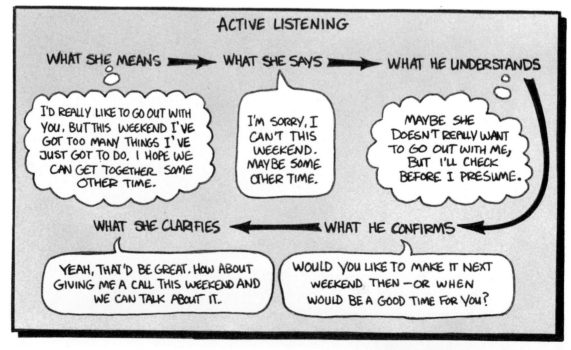

Listen to the person.

- **Understand the person** as well as the message. In personal conversation, people want themselves to be understood. More than just our message, we want our words to convey who we are. It's more important that the other person accepts us than just understands and agrees with our words. Listening to those close to us requires that we consider what they say to be important because they are important and they are saying it. Otherwise, we might as well be reading a book—just trying to understand ideas instead of relating to someone.

- **Give your undivided attention.** Don't pretend to listen. If you can't pay attention at the moment, then explain that rather than faking your attention.

- **Be honest** but not ruthless. You don't have to agree with someone, or acknowledge as important things you think are trivial. But you can express your opinion with kindness as well as candor.

- **Listen to the person** behind the spoken words. Remember that the person behind the ideas is always valuable. What others say is meaningful if only because it means something to them. People often fear that others will reject them if they reveal personal things about themselves. If we reject their less important communications, individuals will presume we'll dismiss the more intimate ones, too.

Listen to God through others.

Do not answer before you listen and do not interrupt when another is speaking.
SIRACH 11:8

There is another, a sacred, dimension of listening. People sometimes describe deep communication as a kind of prayer. When others reveal part of their soul in sharing their thoughts and feelings with us, we connect with the holy. God's Spirit is within us all, and we encounter God's presence through people's words and voices. In truly listening to others, we meet God.

Activity

Write a poem, song, prayer, or meditation about listening.

Journal entry

1. Write down one way you're a good listener.
2. Write down one way you're a poor listener.
3. Write down one way you will try to be a better listener, beginning today.

For discussion

1. What do you think usually causes people's failure to understand each other? Explain.
2. How can you tell whether someone really is—and isn't—listening to you? Explain and give examples.
3. How do you feel when someone really listens to you as well as to your words? When someone doesn't?
4. What does the sacred dimension of listening to someone mean to you?

Feelings

Feelings are where most of us really live. You're happy or unhappy now not because of what's happened lately but because of how you feel about it. Our feelings are such a part of us that we can't know each other intimately without sharing them. Without feeling, letters, conversations, and relationships are boring and lifeless.

Many people find it hard to disclose their feelings, even to someone they love very much. Unless you share your feelings with someone, you'll never become really close. To share your feelings you must first know your feelings. Sometimes we hide our feelings from ourselves because we're afraid to face them. They make us vulnerable and remind us of how scared we are to be hurt. But we must recognize and understand our feelings. For strong feelings don't just go away; they go deeper inside—where they may do more harm than good. It's said that sharing our feelings multiplies our joy and divides our grief. Letting our feelings out and sharing them does help us understand and cope with them. Yet so many of us are afraid to express feelings that we wish we could share. By blocking out feelings or locking them up inside, we lose out on real intimacy. While body language can give us clues, we can't know for sure what someone is feeling unless we're told.

We do need to know it's safe to express certain feelings to someone. Sharing your feelings can also reassure others that it's okay for them to share theirs. Without pressuring, you can gently let others know you're interested in how they feel. Simply ask how they feel about certain things. Even if someone hesitates at first, in time and in their own way they may let you know how they feel.

Journal entry

Complete these statements:

1. When I have trouble sharing my feelings, it's because . . .

2. One way I will try to share my feelings more with others is . . .

Activity

Write a poem, song, prayer, or meditation about feelings.

For discussion

1. What role do feelings play in communication and closeness between people?

2. Why do you think people are sometimes reluctant to share their feelings? Why are you?

3. Which feelings do you find easiest to express? Hardest to express? Explain.

4. Why do you think many couples gradually stop sharing their feelings after a while? Have you ever stopped sharing your feelings with someone close to you? Explain.

5. How would you encourage someone to share his or her feelings with you? What usually helps you share your feelings with someone?

Review

1. How important to effective communication are the way we say things and how we understand others' communication styles? Explain.

2. What is body language? What role does it play in communication and closeness between people?

3. What role do facial expressions and eye contact play in communicating with and understanding others?

4. What does it mean to really listen to someone, and how important is it to good communication? How can one become a better listener?

5. Why is sharing feelings so important in personal relationships? What can encourage people to share their feelings?

How do you feel about it?

Read the following reality-based situations and respond to the questions.

A teenager laments . . .

I wish my mom would treat me like a person instead of an object who happens to be her son. She tells me this and tells me that, but somehow I get the impression that I don't really count. I guess I do the same, though, with my friends. I get so caught up in talking about something that it probably wouldn't matter who's listening.

A young man says . . .

I know this may sound stupid, but I sometimes wonder how my parents really feel about me. I know I'm their son and they're supposed to love me—and I'm sure they do, in that way. But in other ways I'm not so sure, and I'd like to know.

A young woman wonders . . .

How can I find out how my boyfriend really feels about me? He's told me he loves me, and he acts like he really cares. But he hardly ever tells me his feelings about anything—including me. How can I get him to tell me?

A wife sadly explains . . .

When we were going together and after we first married, my husband shared his feelings with me often. Now he hardly ever does. I wonder why he doesn't seem to love me as much anymore. Is there anything I can do to help him open up to me more?

For discussion

1. How could the teenage son improve his communication with his mother and his friends? Explain.

2. How might the young man in the second situation find out what he wants to know? Do you think his question is a common one among teenagers? Explain.

3. How could the young woman find out how her boyfriend really feels about her? Why might he be reluctant to share his feelings with her?

4. How might the wife encourage her husband to resume sharing his feelings with her? Why do you think he might have stopped doing so?

Disagreements

Disagreements will occur in any relationship, however loving and close. When disagreeing with their parents, children often say and feel, "You don't love me anymore." They may grow up to react in the same childish way with their spouses. We shouldn't expect to always see eye-to-eye with others.

Lack of agreement doesn't mean lack of respect or love. As someone put it, "When two people always agree, that usually means that only one of them is doing the thinking!" So instead of being disillusioned by disagreements, learn to handle conflict creatively. To help their employees do so, many businesses give them formal training in conflict management.

Don't expect to be understood immediately—even by those closest to you. We each see and feel things differently, and words can have a different meaning for each of us. Misunderstandings don't usually indicate a lack of love, but rather a failure to communicate well. So when you have a misunderstanding with someone, don't conclude that your relationship is collapsing. Instead, work on improving communication. Also keep in mind that some people need some time alone to sort through a problem, while others do that better by talking with someone about it.

Constantly getting upset or bickering, however, damages relationships and harms one's health! It raises blood pressure and weakens the body's immune system. If you have a habit of flying off the handle at the slightest provocation, consider that you might be shortening your life. Ask yourself: Is it really worth it to get so upset over this? Is it something I can change anyway? If the answer is no, then stop making mountains out of molehills!

Also remember that anger is often a disguise for frustration, fear, or hurt feelings. So instead of reacting angrily to someone else's anger, calmly try to get to the root of the problem. In the 1800s, a noted French-man told his wife who was "prattling on" about matters, "Be quiet, woman, you talk non-sense." She never spoke another word to him for their remaining thirty years together! While her reaction was extreme, people often handle communication conflicts poorly. To see how well you do in communication conflicts, complete the following self-test.

How well do you handle communication conflicts?

On each blank, write the letter from A–F that best reflects your response. Your instructor will tell you how to determine and interpret your score. You won't be asked to share your responses or results.

A — Never/Not at all

B — Rarely/Hardly at all

C — Seldom/Not very strongly

D — Sometimes/Somewhat, but not strongly

E — Often/Somewhat strongly

F — Always/Very strongly

_____ 1. Does a disagreement with someone close to you make you feel the person doesn't care about you?

_____ 2. Do you believe you'll never have disagreements with someone you're really in love with?

_____ 3. When disagreeing with people, do you interrupt them while they're talking?

_____ 4. Do you let verbal disagreements become verbal or physical fights?

_____ 5. Do you give advice to others, even when they don't seem to want it?

_____ 6. In the middle of a disagreement, do you tell the person how she or he should think or feel?

_____ 7. When people tell you no and obviously mean it, do you nag until they reconsider or get angry?

_____ 8. During a serious personal disagreement with someone, do you point out the positive things you think and feel about the person?

_____ 9. When someone disagrees with you, do you take it personally—feeling as though you, not just your ideas, are being rejected?

_____ 10. Do you keep the bothersome things about others to yourself until you reach your tolerance limit and finally blow up?

_____ 11. Do you try to settle disagreements on the spot rather than waiting for a more appropriate time?

_____ 12. When things aren't going your way in a disagreement, do you react childishly?

_____ 13. When someone has hurt your feelings, do you keep the hurt inside rather than tell the person how you feel and why?

_____ 14. Do you blame others or seek to hurt them when something they said or did has hurt you?

_____ 15. When disagreeing with someone, do you bring up examples of past problems or conflicts to prove your present point?

_____ 16. Do you try to change the subject to prevent a disagreement or keep from losing an argument?

_____ 17. Would you use, or have you used, alcohol or another drug to help you feel more relaxed or confident in a disagreement?

_____ 18. When you're extremely upset with someone, do you say things that are mean or cruel?

_____ 19. Do you use threats when it seems the only way to get someone to agree with you?

_____ 20. When you need to criticize someone, do you point out only what's wrong rather than including positive qualities and ways of improving?

_____ 21. During a disagreement, do you try to make the other person feel inferior and yourself superior?

_____ 22. Do you become emotionally upset during or as a result of a disagreement?

_____ 23. When angry or emotionally upset, do you engage in violent or foolish behavior (hitting someone, driving recklessly, breaking or defacing things, and so on)?

_____ 24. Does not thinking things through before you speak ever cause you problems with others?

_____ 25. In a disagreement, do you adequately consider all sides of the issue before reaching your conclusions?

_____ 26. While heatedly disagreeing with others, do you take steps to avoid overreacting (for example, asking for time out to think or calm down)?

_____ 27. During a disagreement, do you look for nonverbal clues that might help you better understand and resolve your differences with the person?

_____ 28. When you can't resolve a serious personal difficulty with someone, do you seek unbiased guidance from someone qualified to help?

_____ 29. Are you willing to compromise only as a last resort or when you're losing the disagreement?

_____ 30. When disagreeing with someone, do you try to win?

_____ **Total score**

Disagreeing—DOs and DON'Ts

In a close relationship, disagreements and misunderstandings should be resolved intelligently and lovingly. Good will and clearer communication can prevent disagreements and misunderstandings from escalating into major conflicts. Here are some ways to avoid or resolve communication conflicts.

DOs

1. Respect each other's need for time to think —
- Take time to think rationally before you discuss serious matters.
- Respect others' need for time to reflect.
- When upset, calm down enough to respond sensibly.

2. Let each other know how to help —
- Let others know how to best approach you with problems.
- Avoid each other's most vulnerable areas when disagreeing.
- Discuss how to lovingly reach each other when either of you wants to pull away.
- Pick up on nonverbal clues to each other's needs.

3. Stick to the point —
- Address the present problem, without changing the subject or dragging up old grievances.
- Resolve one point of disagreement at a time.

4. Be positive and specific —
- Avoid exaggerated generalizations like "always" and "never." They're inaccurate, unenlightening, and antagonistic.
- Make positive, specific recommendations about what someone can do, or stop doing, to remedy a situation.
- Avoid purely negative criticism that is only a put-down.

5. Keep calm —
- Emotional overreactions muddy thinking and keep others from taking you seriously.
- Discuss issues with feeling, but don't let minor faults blow up into major frictions.
- Find a constructive way to deal with the root problem beneath a major conflict or continuing petty grievances.

6. Learn to agree to disagree —
- Disagreements don't mean you love each other less! As unique individuals, we should disagree now and then.
- Expect to differ with others—even those closest to you. Others can't always agree with you without being dishonest.
- When you can't resolve a difference, agree to disagree.

7. Address difficulties soon —
- Don't let small irritations pile up into major conflicts.
- Until you resolve the conflict, reassure each other of your love.
- Sleep on the problem to get a clearer, less biased perspective.

8. Seek help when necessary —
- Invest the time and effort to keep your valuable relationships alive and growing.
- Seek needed counseling before your relationship shatters. Focus on saving the relationship, not on your pride and ego.
- Make this pact as a couple: If either of us ever feels we need professional help, we'll get it together without delay.

DON'Ts

1. Don't interrupt —
- Interrupting is annoying, rude, and suggests that your thoughts are more important than someone else's.
- If you must interrupt, do it politely and explain why.
- If others habitually interrupt, tell them how you feel about it. Ask them to please wait until you've finished.

2. Don't give unwanted advice —
- Telling others what to think alienates them. People must solve their own problems and find their own answers. We resent someone's trying to run our life.

3. Don't threaten —
- Threats attempt to manipulate or gain control. They don't lead to mutual agreement, but replace affection with fear.

4. Don't seek revenge —
- Getting even is wrong, unchristian, and heals nothing. Seek what's good and fair rather than returning wrong for wrong. Two wrongs don't make anything right!
- If someone has hurt you, let the person know. It keeps anger from boiling over into hostility.

5. Don't react childishly —
- It's immature to respond with the silent treatment, slamming things, pouting, walking away, or turning on the tears.
- Don't emotionally browbeat someone into feeling guilty or fed up so that he or she gives in. That erases real communication and respect, and makes matters worse.

6. Don't nag —
- If your serious complaint or request falls on deaf ears, correct the situation yourself. Or accept it, letting others realize their behavior's consequences.
- Put up with minor irritations now and then. Constant negativity ruins intimacy!

7. Don't try to settle problems while influenced by alcohol or other drugs —
- Abusing alcohol or other drugs is a destructive, dangerous way to address problems. Many people become violent when angry or say things they don't mean. Such cruelty can damage a relationship beyond repair.
- Resolve problems rationally; don't compound them with consciousness-altering substances.

8. Don't fight —
- Shouting matches resolve nothing. There are much better ways to "clear the air"! Fist and verbal fights don't prove who's right.
- Verbal or physical abuse destroys love and relationships.

The listening key

In some Native American circles, whoever holds the ceremonial pipe has the right to speak. When the speaker is finished, he or she concludes with: "I have spoken." No one interrupts and everybody has a chance to be heard. Marriage counselors use a similar technique with couples having communication problems. Each spouse is given so many minutes to talk while the other spouse listens silently.

The correct approach to all communication, as St. Peter advises, is to

> . . . *have unity of spirit, sympathy, love for one another, a tender heart, and a humble mind. Do not repay evil for evil or abuse for abuse; but, on the contrary, repay with a blessing. It is for this that you were called—that you might inherit a blessing.*
>
> 1 PETER 3:8–9

Journal entry

Complete these statements:

1. One way I handle disagreements poorly is . . .
2. I will try to handle them better in the future by . . .

For discussion

1. How do you react when someone interrupts you? What's the best way to stop someone from habitually interrupting you? When is it okay to interrupt someone, and what is the best way to do it?

2. When is giving unwanted advice warranted? When is it out of place? How do you respond to unsolicited advice? Explain.

3. How are threats manipulative? Why aren't they usually effective? How do they undermine honesty and affection?

4. When hurt by something said, how do you usually respond? How might you respond better? Why is revenge unchristian; how does it compound the unfairness?

5. If someone unintentionally hurt your feelings, how would you let the person know? Explain.

6. What childish behaviors or overreactions have you seen people display while disagreeing? Which ones bother you the most? Of which ones are you most often guilty? Explain.

7. How do childish behaviors or overreactions increase the problem? What do you think is the best way to respond to such behaviors? Explain.

8. When have you felt nagged, and how do you usually react to that? How does your response affect the other person? What is a positive way to respond to someone's nagging and to avoid becoming a nag over things that chronically bother you?

9. Why do you think some people turn to alcohol or other drugs to cope with relationship problems? From your observation, how does that usually affect their relationships?

10. Why do you think some people who love each other resort to verbal fights instead of rationally resolving their disagreements? Give three ways you might stop that from happening between yourself and someone else.

Touchdown or fumble?

This activity will let you practice identifying common ways that communication connects people—or blocks them from reaching that goal.

1. Read the list of communication breakthroughs and blockers, patterned after those used in football. Then read the couple's dialogue.

2. On each blank in the dialogue, write the letter of the breakthrough or blocker that best corresponds to the dialogue segment. Be able to give good reasons for your choices.

Communication breakthroughs

A. Touchdown—arriving at a solution that respects and meets both persons' needs

B. Field goal—learning from the situation to better resolve similar conflicts in the future

C. Extra points—being supportive or acknowledging the other's good qualities

D. Safeties—agreeing to disagree

E. Pass completion—communicating clearly, effectively, and kindly

F. First down—listening; honestly trying to understand the other's viewpoint

G. Fumble recovery—admitting and correcting one's own mistakes

H. Interception—helping the other person avoid communication faults

I. Goal-line stand—not getting intimidated or overly upset by another's unfair remarks

J. Timeout—taking needed time to think or explore further possibilities before speaking/acting

K. Calling for a huddle—letting each other know how to help

Communication blockers

L. Clipping—nagging, using threats to get one's own way

M. Illegal block—interrupting to dispute what the other person is saying

N. Offsides—getting off the subject, putting words in the other person's mouth

O. Backfield in motion—not listening or paying attention

P. False start—aggravating or baiting the other person

Q. Ineligible receiver downfield—exaggerating or generalizing

R. Pass interference—interrupting to make a different point

S. Delay of game—refusing to communicate or listen at all

T. Unsportsmanlike conduct—fighting, shouting, reacting childishly or too emotionally

U. Roughing the passer/kicker—making hurtful or sarcastic remarks

V. Holding—inappropriately giving advice

communication breakthroughs
techniques that enhance verbal and non-verbal communication

communication blockers
techniques that interfere with communication

Honey, the game comes on in twenty minutes so, if you need to do anything noisy, I'd appreciate it if you'd do it now. (1) _____

Game! What game? I told my mother we'd come over for the day. (2) _____

How could you do that? (3) _____

You knew I was going to watch the game. (4) _____

No, I didn't; you never said anything to me about it. (5) _____

Well, you know I usually watch the games on weekends. (6) _____

Besides, this is an important one. (7) _____

Sometimes I think you do things like this just to annoy me. (8) _____

I'll bet you set this date up for us at your mother's today just because I forgot to pick up your suit at the cleaners. (9) _____

So this game is important, is it? Does that mean my mother isn't important? (10) _____

To you, football is more important than my mother, huh? (11) _____

Now that you mention it, on a scale of one to ten. . . (12) _____

How dare you equate a lousy football game with my mother! (13) _____

It's easy! The game is much more enjoyable, and it doesn't talk back! (14) _____

Now there's something I wish you wouldn't do. I wish you wouldn't talk back. (15) _____

At least while I'm in the room. (16) _____

Don't waste your time wishing; wishing never made anything happen in this place. I've been wishing for years that you could keep the house clean. (17) _____

But I know that chance doesn't even exist. (18) _____

Doesn't exist? Why, you ungrateful TV addict! (19) _____

I spend hours cleaning this house, and you never appreciate it! (20) _____

I'll show you!. . . (21) _____

Hey! Wait a minute! Shut off that vacuum cleaner! I can't hear the game! (22) _____

Then just turn up the volume on your hearing aid. (23) _____

You want a clean house. (24) _____

Turn up the volume, huh? You bet I will! (25) _____

Hey, turn down the sound on that TV! The walls are vibrating! (26) _____

So what, I don't care if the whole house falls in! I want to hear the game! (27) _____

Well, I'm not going to shut off the vacuum until you turn down the sound. (28) _____

Oh, yeah! Well, let's see you vacuum now! . . . (29) _____

Now you've really done it, you jerk! See what you've done? You just broke the plug, that's what! (30) _____

Now wait until you see what it costs to get it fixed. (31) _____

I don't care what it costs. Besides, you don't need a vacuum. With all your hot air, why don't you just open the door and blow all the dirt out? (32) _____

Hot air! I'll show you hot air! (33) _____

Hey! Turn that set back on! Turn it on right now! I'm warning you . . . I'll . . . (34) _____

Do you realize what we're doing? We're going at each other's throats over a lousy game. (35) _____

You're right, honey; I lost my perspective. (36) _____

I don't know what came over me. I'm really sorry. (37) _____

No football game is important enough to do this to us. (38) _____

If it means that much to you, call your mother and tell her we'll be over. (39) _____

Oh, honey, I'm sorry, too. I really overreacted to your wanting to watch the game instead of going to my mother's. I just don't know what happened. (40) _____

I'll tell you what—you finish watching the game, and I'll tell my mother that we'll be over later. (41) _____

Okay, honey—that sounds great. I really do love your mother. (42) _____

Thanks, honey. I needed to hear that . . . . (43) _____

By the way, while the commercial is on and before you get back to your game, can I ask you one question? (44) _____

Sure, go ahead. (45) _____

How did a sensitive, gentle woman like you ever get so interested in football! (46) _____

How and when to compromise

Compromising isn't necessarily a negative way to settle a problem. It doesn't have to mean giving up or giving in. Too often people don't even consider a compromise until the disagreement has become an all-out tug-of-war. Then they compromise reluctantly and only as a self-defense tactic, so they won't lose.

Having a win-lose attitude about disagreements engages people in a power struggle where each party resolves to win. But no one wins in a relationship unless both persons win. For what's really at stake ultimately is the relationship.

Compromise literally means "to promise with." Marriage is a compromise whereby two people promise to live life with each other—on the same side. Every relationship involves the basic compromise of learning to think in terms of "we" instead of just "me." Especially when disagreeing, each person should be on both sides.

So learn to confront disputes in terms of "How can we both win?" not "How can I convince the person to do what I want?" Approach the situation with the attitude "How can I help you get what you want in a way that also satisfies what I need and want?" Often that's all that's needed. Sometimes what someone really wants isn't to "win" but to feel understood, accepted, and loved.

> If you're **not** part of the **solution**,
> you're **part** of the problem.

Communication project

Choose one.

1. Reflect on your main strengths and weaknesses in communicating with others. Write a two-page paper on the specific ways you might improve your communication skills.

2. Interview a contract negotiator or someone else whose business is conflict management or mediating differences. Ask the person's advice on resolving differences between people. Write a two-page report on what you learn from the interview.

For discussion

1. Give an example of how compromising can be
   • giving up or giving in to the other person
   • merely a self-defense tactic
   • a good communication technique that respects both persons and viewpoints

2. Why don't two people who really care about each other think first about how they can both win in a disagreement?

3. Why do people turn differences into win-lose power struggles rather than seeking a mutually satisfying solution? What typically results?

Review

1. Why don't disagreements and misunderstandings necessarily indicate an absence or lessening of love?

2. In your own words,
   • What are the main DOs and DON'Ts of disagreeing?
   • What are some of the main communication "breakthroughs and blockers"?

3. How does every human relationship involve a basic compromise? How and why should people learn to compromise when disagreeing?

4. Why is good communication the key to intimacy in relationships?

Curfew conflict

Read the following dialogue about a common conflict that occurs between teenagers and parents over the matter of curfew. Then respond to the questions.

For discussion

1. How is this different from or similar to a "curfew conflict" you've experienced? Explain.

2. What rules of good communication does each party observe here? Violate here? Explain.

3. Do you think either party here seems to understand the other's viewpoint? Explain.

4. If it continued to proceed along the same lines as displayed above, how do you think the dialogue would end?

5. How in the future might mother and teenager communicate better with each other over this same issue?

The fallen domino

Read this account of a real situation that's unfortunately common in many marriages.[1] Then respond to the questions.

Cynthia and Joe had been happily married for four years. They didn't have much money and they had no children. Cynthia worked as a librarian, and Joe worked for a paper-manufacturing company. Very slowly, during the first four years, they furnished their own home, paying cash for everything.

After these four years, two things happened. A child was born—followed the next year by another—and Joe became assistant manager of the paper plant. Now Cynthia had . . . left her interesting job at the library and was home all day with two infants. Joe, as assistant manager, no longer was able to leave the office at five o'clock. He had to stay behind to check up on the day's production, or to see about personnel, and attend the executive meeting at six o'clock.

When Joe came home about seven thirty, he was really tired. Cynthia was also fatigued. With two young children, the small house was always untidy, and Cynthia didn't have time to prepare the kind of meals Joe was fond of. They no longer spent a pleasant hour . . . discussing the interesting things which happened during the day. . . . Joe had his drink at the executive meeting, and when he arrived home he was eager to eat quickly and go to bed.

Slowly, Cynthia began to believe that they no longer were companions or equals, that Joe had more interest in his business than in his family. Joe felt that Cynthia was being selfish when she wanted to go out after the children were asleep. He became irritable when she asked him to skip having drinks with the executives and, instead, go back to the old system of spending an hour before dinner with her in the evening.

. . . Slowly, Cynthia began to take less interest in preparing . . . meals for dinner. Joe gulped his food and no longer commented on her efforts. And when Joe was amorous in bed, Cynthia said she was too tired from looking after the children, feeling vaguely angry that Joe seemed to be interested only when he was in the mood, and was unresponsive to her needs when she showed the initiative.

Joe started eating out with other executives two or three times a week. Slowly, their needs became divergent in one area of their relationship after another, and Cynthia and Joe were about ready for a divorce.

Cynthia and Joe decided to consult a professional counselor before they saw a lawyer. . . .

For discussion

1. What was the root cause of Cynthia and Joe's problem? Explain.
2. List three things you think Cynthia and Joe should try in working through their problem.
3. If you were in Joe's or Cynthia's place, which of those alternatives would you try? Why?
4. If you were the counselor, how would you advise Joe and Cynthia? Why?
5. What "fallen domino" principle occurred in Joe and Cynthia's relationship? Why do you think couples so often let that happen in their relationships?

In summary

Good communication skills can be learned. To communicate better we should practice these fundamentals: putting people first, not pressuring, keeping confidences, being positive, listening, noticing needs, thinking things through, choosing the appropriate time and place, and taking time to pray and reflect. We must also learn to listen to the message, to the person, and to God. Our body language and how we say something are another important part of our communication. Because feelings come from the heart, people who love each other should share their feelings. It's likewise important to respond rationally to misunderstandings and disagreements. As the Church recognizes, good communication is a vital link in our global society and the key to intimacy in our relationships.

Key concepts

active listening

body language

Catholic teaching on human
  communication

communication breakthroughs
  and blockers

communication skills

communication styles

compromising

eye contact

facial expressions

feelings

handling and preventing disagreements

listening to God through others

listening to the message and to the
  person

needs and wants

Endnotes

1. The title and case are quoted from *The Mirages of Marriage* by William J. Lederer and Don D. Jackson, M.D. Copyright © 1968 by W. W. Norton & Company, Inc. Reprinted by permission of W. W. Norton & Company, Inc.

CHAPTER 6

THE SINGLE LIFE

SCRIPTURE

You did not choose me but I chose you.
And I appointed you to go and bear fruit,
fruit that will last . . . .
I am giving you these commands
so that you may love one another.

JOHN 15:16A, 17

PRAYER

Lord,

You were single in your life on earth.

Did you have the same questions we do about how to live as a single person?

Did you face the same sexual temptations we do?

Was it hard balancing your work with your relationships?

How did you choose your friends?

The Bible says that you were exactly like us, except that you did no wrong.

So you do understand.

In our relationships with others, help us be honest, generous, and responsible.

Help us to live our single life fully and richly, as you did.

We pray in your name. Amen.

Living the single vocation

Over the last twenty years, the number of single adults in our society has more than doubled.

Almost 40 percent of adults are single, and most of these have never married. More people are choosing to remain single permanently and, while most people do marry, they are waiting longer to do so. Over half of the households in our society are headed by a single person, and single persons living alone account for about one-fourth of our households. Even if you marry, you will first live the single adult lifestyle.

It's hard to define what *being single* means because it describes so many different lifestyles. Some people prefer to remain single, while others are single due to unfortunate circumstances—divorce or a spouse's death. Some remain single to devote themselves to caring for someone who's ill or severely disabled. Many view being single as a temporary vocation—until they find someone they want to marry.

Others choose being single as a permanent way of life. They're not attracted to marriage. They are happily absorbed fulltime in their careers and/or in service to others and wouldn't have time to meet the demands of marriage and family life. Living happily in this way might be an indication that one is called to remain single. For such persons have important responsibilities and do a great deal of good with their God-given talents. Whatever our vocation, what matters most of all is that we base our lives on loving God and others.

How single persons live their vocation differs greatly depending on age, interests, commitments, and so on. This chapter and the next will discuss some of the merits and challenges of the lay single lifestyle. Chapter 8 will focus on other single vocations such as the priesthood and religious life.

Ways of living the single life

As a **layperson**

Permanently   Transitionally

As an **ordained** minister (deacon, priest, or bishop)

As a **consecrated** religious or layperson

For discussion

1. How would you define the single vocation? In what different ways do adults you know live the single life?
2. Do you think you'd like living the single way of life temporarily (until you marry) or as your permanent vocation? Why?
3. Given how many single people there are in our society, do you think the single way of life is over- or under-emphasized? Explain.
4. Why do you think more people today are choosing to remain single—either for a longer time until they marry, or permanently?

A valuable vocation

The single life is a valuable vocation that reflects God's love in its own unique ways. Being single shouldn't be viewed negatively—as being unmarried, or just passing time until one marries. Yet an "I'm still not married—what's wrong with me?" attitude is sadly still too common among single persons. Whether temporary or permanent, being single is a worthwhile, desirable way of life! It has its own special blessings, relationships, advantages, opportunities, and challenges.

The single life is the most flexible vocation. Single persons may have more personal freedom to befriend or help people. Since single laypersons are not committed to a spouse, they may share a degree of romantic relationships with more than one person. They may change their relationship priorities and commitments as their needs and situations change. Single persons have greater liberty to relocate or adjust personal and work schedules without having to consider a spouse. Single persons may also decide to change their vocation at any time.

As Jesus acknowledged, not everyone is called to live the single life permanently. But for however long you are single, you can and should live your single vocation successfully.

Jesus was a single person. In his society, not many people chose to remain single. By choosing to not marry and raise children who would carry on his family's tradition, Jesus broke free of social expectations. He invited others to follow his way of serving others and encouraged them to pursue their futures according to their convictions. That is what the single Christian tries to do.

In the past, Churches and society in general emphasized marriage far more than the lay single life. We still don't ritually celebrate someone's permanently choosing the lay single life as we do other vocation choices. But we are finally beginning to recognize the great value of the single vocation. Communities still need to provide more programs for single persons, and all couples should make greater efforts to involve their "uncoupled" friends in social activities.

Today's Catholic Church is more aware of single persons' special needs and of their many valuable contributions. Its teaching affirms that **our main purpose in life doesn't depend on whether we marry, but on how well we love.** Whether temporary or permanent, the single life can be a happy, fulfilling way to live our basic human vocation of loving.

To be happy as a single person, you need to do the following:

- Be convinced that you are living a valuable, fulfilling way of life.
- See that your basic psychological, emotional, physical, and spiritual needs are met.
- Be self-confident, self-reliant, and motivated to live independently.
- Establish a support system of relationships with God and others that energizes you to reach out to love and help people.
- Be adaptable enough to live a flexible lifestyle, yet able to structure your life as needed.

Journal entry

1. Is my view of the single life a positive one?
2. How could I make it a more positive one?

For discussion

1. Do you think most people view being single as a vocation in its own right? Until now, have you viewed your being single that way?
2. How do you think your attitude about your single vocation will affect your happiness as a single person?
3. What blessings, advantages, and opportunities do you see in the single vocation? Which ones appeal to you the most? Why?
4. Which of the characteristics needed to live the single life successfully do you feel you have? Which ones do you most need to develop as you prepare to live the adult single life on your own?
5. Do you usually think of Jesus as a single person? How is he a model for single persons today? Explain.

Single ministries

Not married, or *not ordained* or *consecrated* doesn't mean not committed! Lay single persons minister to people in a wide variety of ways. Some are more readily available for friends, relatives, and acquaintances to turn to for advice and support. Some are gifted with a magnetic sociability that draws others together or out of their loneliness. Single friends often minister to each other. They meet after work or over lunch or dinner to discuss their problems, how to enhance their relationships, and how to be more effective in their work.

Their vocation's flexibility sometimes makes it easier for single persons to structure their personal schedules around others' concerns. Single and married persons serve others daily in the business world. By living their religious values in their decisions and dealings, they help raise society to a higher, more honest and decent level.

Laypersons often exercise leadership positions in the Church community. Lay ministers plan and lead various aspects of the parish liturgy, distribute Communion at the Eucharist, and welcome new members. They visit those who are sick, dying, bereaved, and lonely. They organize and instruct in youth programs and host prayer and Bible study groups. They help prepare candidates for Baptism and Confirmation and couples for marriage. Lay women and men help oversee and manage parish and diocesan programs and finances.

Where priests or deacons are unavailable and when appointed by the bishop to do so, laypersons may be pastoral administrators of parishes and preside at certain liturgical services. Single laypersons are actively involved in Church and secular ministries. Single persons bring their talents and dedication to their jobs or professions, to the Church, to community organizations, and to the wider society.

> As a candle shines only when that of which it is made is being **spent**, so **life** is real only when it is being spent for **others**.
>
> LEO TOLSTOY

In the evening of life, we will be judged by love.

ST. JOHN OF THE CROSS

What type of volunteer service suits you?

Could you do manual or clerical work?

Could you help refugees and the homeless poor?

Would you want to minister to people who are sick or dying, teach people to read, or help victims of domestic abuse?

Could you help organize and run programs?

Are you good at fixing, making, or building things?

Do you have computer skills?

Would you like to help run youth camps and other programs for children?

Would you prefer working in a city or in a rural area? By yourself or as part of a team?

Lay volunteers

Many single persons volunteer to help the needy. Some go wherever in the country or in the world they're most needed. Many high schools and colleges require their students to do community service. At some colleges there are waiting lists of students wanting to volunteer their time—and money—for spring-break trips to help the homeless or victims of abuse or AIDS patients. Students find that in such programs, they develop special friendships and receive as much as they give—if not more.

Whatever skills you have are greatly needed. As a lay volunteer, you would learn from real-life experiences, increase your skills, and meet different types of people. You'd learn and grow a great deal while adding valuable experience to your résumé. The insights you'd gain could help you determine which direction to choose for your future. Single volunteers who haven't started college or a job often find their future focus as a result of their volunteer experiences.

Most volunteer programs require some type of commitment—from a few days, weekends, or months during the summer to a year or more. Many provide lodging and transportation. Some would give you the opportunity to work with a secular organization. Or you might work, live, and pray with members of a religious community—whether or not you're interested in the consecrated way of life in your future.

Some single persons take a leave of absence from their jobs to do volunteer work at home or abroad. Some employers provide paid leave for employees who do volunteer work. Others volunteer on weekends, after hours, or during their vacation time. Some doctors and nurses fly on special medical missions to underdeveloped countries. Construction workers and college students donate their time and expertise to build houses for low-income families. While married individuals also volunteer in these ministries, single persons sometimes have more flexibility to be away from home.

Beware, though, of groups that are really cults or money-making scams. Such groups often promote themselves as caring or even religious organizations while preying on young adults' need for companionship, recognition, and support. They may smother you with attention and affection at an especially lonely time. (They target homesick college students.) They first offer you a free "psychological profile," or matchmaking opportunity, or invite you to attend a "retreat" weekend. Pretty soon they start taking over your life. Whether their approach is subtle or enthusiastic, it appeals especially to young persons interested in helping others or in developing their spiritual life or personal growth.

Project

Choose one.

1. Search the Internet for more information about how cults recruit members. Write a one-page paper on what you find. Report to the class.

2. Of the volunteer projects in your local area, draw up a list of ten that you'd be most interested in. Write a brief paragraph on what especially interests you about those projects. Share your interests with the class.

For discussion

1. In what negative and positive ways are single persons viewed as "available"? Explain.

2. Why does every vocation require flexibility? What type of flexibility does the single vocation require?

3. Describe how the lay single persons you know minister to others. How do you, as a single person, minister to others? Have you thought of that before in terms of ministry? Explain.

4. Have you given any thought to doing some type of volunteer service after you graduate from high school? What appeals to you most about the idea of being a lay volunteer? What type of volunteer ministry would you most like to participate in— and where? Explain.

5. Where would you go to find information about lay volunteer opportunities in your location or elsewhere in the country or the world? What should you beware of before you become involved with or make a commitment to any group?

Review

1. For what reasons are people single? What is the difference between lay and consecrated single vocations?

2. Why are both the temporary and permanent single ways of life valuable vocations?

3. How does the Catholic Church view the lay single vocation? How did the people of Jesus' day view it?

4. What support systems do single persons need? What's false about viewing single persons as "unattached" or "uncommitted"?

5. How does our purpose in life relate to being single or married? What is the special calling of laypersons in the world and Church community?

6. How do lay single persons minister to others? How can volunteer service especially suit and benefit single persons?

Those unprincipled groups often use other young members as their drawing card. Once the group finds your areas of emotional, psychological, and financial vulnerability, they will begin making demands. They will try to alienate you from your family and friends. Sooner or later they will demand your absolute commitment—and, of course, your money or material assets. If their demands aren't met, they'll make you feel guilty—or threaten you or your loved ones. They will manipulate, pressure, deceive, and cheat you until you're drawn into their world, rules, and structures.

These groups often target single people—especially lonely single people. So before making any volunteer commitment, check out the group with well-established Church or civic agencies. Colleges often post warnings on the Internet about which cults are known to be actively recruiting on campus. Before joining any group, ask individuals who are no longer involved with the group for their objective assessment. If the group is on the level, its operations and activities won't be a secret. So be especially wary of any group that's reluctant to answer your reasonable questions or that requires keeping secrets as a condition of membership!

Your local parish or diocesan office or your community social services agency can help you find a worthy group that matches your abilities and preferences to others' needs. Do think seriously about volunteering your services in some way. It's an enlightening way to learn how others view the world, and it's a wonderful opportunity for growing and giving. Your talents could really be used somewhere!

Single by choice

Read the following description of one single person's lifestyle. Then respond to the questions.

As a single man, Josh has many male and female friends and a few close friendships. Women are strongly attracted to him. He's an excellent conversationalist and a sought-out guest for dinner parties. Those who know him well, and those who meet him for the first time, are impressed by how Josh really listens to and genuinely cares about people. He likes and gets along well with children, and they clearly enjoy being around him. Josh goes out of his way to help people, and his friends know they can always count on him. Josh is an honest man who's always as good as his word.

Others have said that, given his background, Josh would never amount to anything. Indeed, as a member of a minority group, he has often been discriminated against. Motivated by prejudice, greed, or competitive rivalry, some individuals have even said they'd like to see Josh eliminated. Josh finds such attitudes painfully troublesome and speaks out strongly against them. Nevertheless, he prefers to combat such hateful attitudes by being kind and understanding.

Josh's early adult years spent working in the construction business taught him a great deal. But he prefers his present career, which enables him to work in a closer way with more people. Josh finds his career quite fulfilling, even though it requires traveling and being on the road a lot. He likes the opportunity that gives him to make new friends. Despite his busy schedule, Josh keeps his personal life balanced. He takes enough time for reflection and to nourish his close relationships with God and others.

Many of those in senior management positions, however, are jealous of Josh's success. They consider him a threat to their careers. At times Josh has openly criticized their management style and policies. But unless a directive goes against his conscience, Josh abides by corporate rules and obeys his bosses' legitimate authority. Josh has made it quite clear that he has no personal ambition or intention to advance to a higher management level. In fact, he's turned down several opportunities for advancement because he's perfectly content with his role in life at present.

Josh barely makes enough money to support himself, and his friends still encourage him to seek a higher position. Josh knows he could make much more money if he went back to his previous job or took a management position. But Josh is happy at what he's doing. He says he doesn't need any more out of life than what he has now—his relationship with God, loving parents and relatives, close friends, a place to sleep, enough food to eat, and doing what he enjoys most—helping and being of service to others.

Many of Josh's friends and acquaintances, however, just don't understand why Josh chooses to remain single.

For discussion

1. Describe the kind of person Josh seems to you to be.
2. How would you describe Josh's vocation as a single person? Josh's ministry? His lifestyle?
3. Why do you think Josh chooses to not marry?
4. What aspects of Josh's attitude or life would you hope to imitate as a single person? Why?

Loving in the single vocation

Single persons do have—and need—serious relationships and personal commitments! As a single teenager, you already experience that to some extent. But it will be even more important for you as a single adult living independently.

You will need a support system of close friends and relatives, colleagues at work, members of a group you belong to, and others who share your interests. It's those other stable close relationships that will help see you through your romantic turmoils! Don't forget, too, how important you are as part of your single friends' support system.

As a single person, you will need to build meaningful relationships and work at being part of a community of friends and of family. Don't make the mistake of becoming so busy with your schoolwork or career that you neglect to nourish your relationships with family, friends, and with God. For those relationships are what will bring you happiness. In your personal relationships, you'll encounter a dimension of God's presence that you can experience in no other way.

Journal entry

1. Who constitutes your personal support system now?
2. Do you ever take those persons for granted? Explain.
3. Whose support system are you a part of, and how?

Dating and romance

Single persons often say that it's hard to find someone they'd really like to date. Yet they frequently overlook the most obvious possibilities for meeting people with whom they'd be compatible. Later in the text we'll discuss in greater detail what compatibility involves. For now it's enough to note the three main areas—values, interests, and personality. You won't be happy having a romance, a friendship, or a marriage with someone who doesn't share your values. So know what your main values are and then figure out where you're most likely to meet others who share those values.

Many have found that Church groups, hobbies, co-ed sports leagues, volunteer work, and political campaigns offer good ways to meet those who share your values and interests. Personality compatibility can be assessed only as you go along. Another way to meet people is through family members and friends who know you well. Bars are not the best place to meet someone. Alcohol tends to alter people's personalities. So the half-tipsy "great conversationalist" you meet in a bar might normally be absolutely boring.

To attract people, show your best side. Be polite and have a good sense of humor.

You don't have to be good at cracking jokes, but you can let someone know that you enjoy life's funnier side. Never be pushy. If you're not interested in dating the person, say so up front and kindly. Don't make temporary excuses that string someone along. Focus on the other person rather than on yourself and how nervous or shy you're feeling. Be genuinely interested in the other person—not just in where the relationship might or might not lead.

Practice connecting with people you don't know and aren't interested in dating—like the person standing next to you in line at the store. That'll make it easier to strike up a conversation with the person sitting next to you in college English that you'd really like to meet. Don't try meeting people at uncomfortable or unsafe places you wouldn't want to frequent anyway. Look for quiet places rather than dance clubs where you have to shout to be heard by the person next to you.

Practice good communication skills (review the previous chapter) including good eye contact and active listening. Learn about the other person by asking questions that aren't prying or pushy. Be yourself, tell the truth, and show respect for yourself and the other person. (If you don't respect yourself, how can you expect the other person to respect you?) Enjoy meeting others. Adopt a positive and confident attitude, but without seeming arrogant, conceited, aloof, or like a know-it-all.

Dating co-workers isn't always a good idea. There's the office gossip to contend with, not to mention having to continue working with the person daily if the romantic relationship ends. A good question to ask yourself before engaging in an office romance is: If things don't work out between us, will I be sorry we dated? To preserve your job (and the other person's), know your employer's rules about dating co-workers. Also know the laws pertaining to sexual harassment in the workplace. With that in mind, business and legal experts advise workers to never date a superior or a subordinate from work. And don't presume your relationship can be kept strictly private. Surveys show that other employees almost always find out sooner or later.

To be physically attractive, you don't have to be Hugh the Hunk or Bambi the Babe. Save your hard-earned money and don't be duped into buying "miracle devices" that promise ("guarantee") to thin your thighs, blossom your bust, and multiply your muscle mass. Accentuate your positive physical attributes in common-sense ways that work, not in ways that cheapen who you are inside. Think about which of your features have drawn the most compliments and highlight those. If necessary, get professional advice about which hairstyles, cosmetics, colors, and clothing styles are most becoming for you. Don't compare yourself with professional models. (Their photos are altered by artists anyway to hide the subjects' blemishes and enhance their appearance). One famous movie star had six toes on one foot, but that's a little-known fact because no one focuses on it. If you pay more attention to who you are as a person, so will others.

Project

Interview an attorney or someone who works in a personnel office about the topic of sexual harassment on the job. Include what constitutes sexual harassment, how to avoid it, and how to respond if it happens to you. Write a one-page paper on your findings and discuss them with the class.

For discussion

1. Do you think teenagers tend to over-emphasize physical appearance in determining who they'd like to date? In assessing their own self-worth? Explain.

2. Aside from physical appearance, what attracts you to someone you'd like to meet and possibly date? What attracts you to want to continue dating someone?

3. If you needed to keep your job, how would you handle it if you discovered a mutual romantic attraction between you and each of the following people?
   • A single co-worker at the same job level as you
   • Your boss who is single
   • A single person who's subordinate to you on the job
   • Your boss who is married

4. In what ways do you think individuals could most often improve their appearance without physically altering themselves? Explain, without mentioning names.

What about on-line romances?

You might be able to enhance a current relationship through your on-line communications. But you can't really achieve personal intimacy on-line with someone you've never met. However detailed or heartfelt, on-line communications create only the illusion of personal intimacy. Like reading any detailed biography, diary, or letter, on-line correspondence can tell you many things about a person. But it can't substitute for face-to-face contact.

We mostly communicate by our body language. Unless you have a video connection, there's no way to assess someone's body language on-line. (The common on-line symbols for "I'm laughing" or "I'm frowning" are weak substitutes for the lifted eyebrow, the downward glance, and so on, that accompany someone's speech in person.) You can't read on-line the valuable clues body language conveys.

People commonly adopt on-line **personas** and nicknames that hide their true identity. Like wearing a mask, remaining anonymous on-line often loosens individuals' inhibitions. Someone's on-line personality is sometimes totally different from the real individual friends know in person. So not only does on-line communication fail to tell you what the person is really like,

persona
the external aspects of one's personality (whether genuine or faked) that one shows to others

it often gives a false or the opposite impression about who someone is.

Dating someone you've met only on-line can be downright dangerous—even aside from the very real threat of the molesters and murderers. Skillful con artists try to strike up relationships in order to swindle naive individuals out of their money. As with the rest of life, if it seems too good to be true, it probably is! Serial killer Ted Bundy was a real charmer. That's how he lured the many women he murdered. How should you proceed if you do encounter someone on-line whom you'd like to meet in person? Whether for an on-line friendship or for romance, heed these tips:

Safety tips for on-line relationships

1. Don't give on-line strangers any information that could identify you.

2. For some time, arrange to meet in busy, well-lit public places.

3. Do not let the person know where you live! Until you know much more about him or her, don't invite the person to your apartment or home, and don't go to theirs.

4. Tell someone else where you're going, with whom, and when you'll be home. (Let the person know you've told someone.)

5. Don't let the person drive you home or follow you home.

6. Trust your instincts and better judgment. If you feel at all uneasy, leave.

7. Never visit the person in another city.

8. Don't flood the person with E-mail, and do keep your E-mail short. Being pestered by E-mail is as annoying as too many phone calls.

9. Before seeing the individual on a more personal level, find out (and verify) where the person works and lives. Call the person at home. (Not wanting to give you a home phone number is usually a tip-off that the person is married.) Find a way to meet the person's family, friends, or co-workers. That can tell you much about the individual. Someone who wants to know you better should be delighted—not uncomfortable—that you want to meet the important people in her or his life.

10. If the person uses even subtle references to sex in the on-line communication, then you're being told that sex is what the person is really interested in. Don't be flattered; beware!

Finally, don't ignore these cautions, thinking that your relationship is the exception and that being someone's victim won't happen to you.

For discussion

1. What pros, cons, and cautions do you see concerning meeting people on-line? Concerning meeting in person someone you've met only on-line?

2. How can on-line communications enhance already-established relationships?

3. What do you think of the safety tips offered regarding on-line relationships? Are there any you'd add? Explain.

4. When would—and wouldn't—you be willing to exchange photos on-line with someone you've met only on-line?

5. What would you find—or have you found—unacceptable about people's on-line behavior?

6. Do you think that has anything to do with the anonymity of on-line personas? Explain.

Some people suggest exchanging photos before setting up a meeting with someone you've met only on-line. That may help ensure that both parties are genuinely interested in each other. It may also provide a bit of extra security (if the photos are accurate). But reveal no other identifying information about yourself until you've come to know the person well enough in person. Be aware, too, that most on-line romances don't work out. Don't pour your heart out to someone you've never met and automatically expect your feelings to be reciprocated. Many people find it easier to make on-line commitments than real ones.

On-line relationships

Explain exactly how you'd handle each of the following on-line situations.

1. Someone in an on-line chat room wants your phone number. The person seems friendly and polite on-line but thinks E-mail is too impersonal and wants to hear your voice.

2. You've been corresponding for a few months with someone on-line. It seems that you have a lot in common. Everything you're interested in seems also to interest the other person. You think you might have enough in common to establish a romantic connection in person. How could you confirm that first?

3. You find someone's behavior in an on-line chat room to be obscene and obnoxious. You'd like to continue to chat with the others from the group who regularly meet on-line.

Being realistic about relationships

As a single person, you will have many different types of friendship. Most may be purely social or professional. Others might involve more affection or romance. You will have to put time and effort into maintaining close relationships. You'll need to be mature enough to know how deeply involved to let yourself become. Above all, you must be honest with yourself and the other person about the relationship.

Share any uncertainty about what future you see for the relationship. Encourage the other person's honesty and openness with you. Respect each other's right to hesitate in making any commitments about the future. That avoids the hurtful unfairness of giving false impressions—and the unwanted pressures that push someone away. As Jesus taught us, our relationships should have our welfare and that of others at heart. In that spirit, discuss what concerns each of you about the relationship.

Respect each other and each other's needs. Keep the relationship on equal terms; don't let it become one-sided. Share your values and your dreams, your goals and discoveries—the positive aspects of your life, as well as your frustrations and disappointments. Don't just dump problems on those you love.

Single persons have the right to end a romantic relationship and begin a new one with someone else. People in love tend to forget that! It's fine to hope that a relation-ship might lead to marriage. It's fair to agree, if you both wish, that as long as you're romantically involved with each other, you won't be involved in a romantic relationship with anyone else. But if you expect a permanent romantic commitment outside of marriage, you may be painfully disappointed. That total and permanent commitment is the essence of marriage—not of the single life. It's unfair to expect a commitment that can't be kept. It's also harmful. For when the illusory "commit-ment" is broken, mistrust enters in and may block future personal intimacy.

If you do choose to end a relationship, don't just walk away and leave the other person wondering why. Have the decency to explain in person your reasons for breaking things off. You might say gently, "I still care about you a lot, but the feelings I thought would grow between us just haven't developed (or lasted) the way I thought they would." Sometimes people can then remain casual or close friends. Others need to make a clean break. People cope in different ways with the ending of a relationship they had hoped would continue. So don't expect that someone else will respond the way you do.

To maintain honest relationships —

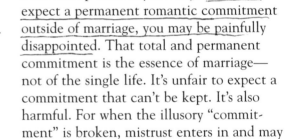

- Know what you want the relationship to mean and where you'd like to see it lead. Communicate that to the other person.
- Realize that you and other single persons are and should be free to end a romantic relationship.
- When you want to end a relationship, tell the person and explain why.
- Be realistic about the relationship's future.
- Enjoy living your present vocation as a single person.

Some people can maintain close relationships with more than one person at a time. They're comfortable with "no strings attached" relationships that may remain lifelong friendships or may end when one person relocates or marries, or as personal needs change. Other individuals are willing to become involved in a romance only if it is mutually exclusive. It's only fair to let each other know exactly what your expectations are.

If a romantic relationship seems to be going nowhere, don't hang on to it for dear life. Gambling everything on the unrealistic hope it will eventually lead to marriage cuts you off from other possibilities. If you want to marry, keep your options open until you find the right person who does want to marry you. In the meantime, be honest and realistic, not dumb and desperate!

To make any relationship work, two people must be honest with each other. But relationships often start off with one person saying that he or she is not ready for or interested in a serious commitment—or hasn't yet gotten over a previous heartthrob. The other person plays along, pretending to also feel casual about the relationship, but inwardly counts on things to change. Big mistake! When things don't change, the honest person is unfairly accused of being a two-timing rat—simply because the other person didn't want to listen!

Hopefully you'll continue to enjoy your single vocation as much as you probably do now. If and when single adults decide they want to marry, they sometimes begin convincing themselves that they're miserable being single. Remember that the single life is the one vocation you can always change. While you're single, you're called to live your single vocation, not just endure it.

On the other hand, don't remain single just because you've seen so many unhappy marriages and presume yours will be no different. It's healthy to not be too idealistic about married life, but don't take refuge in the single life just to escape marriage. Instead, take advantage of the opportunities the single life offers for learning how to establish beautiful relationships that do work.

For discussion

1. How are you realistic—and unrealistic—about your romantic relationships? As single persons, how might teenagers be more realistic about their relationships? Explain.

2. How would you try to handle your doubts about the future of your romance with someone? How would you handle the other person's being unsure even if you weren't? Explain.

3. As a single person, when and why should you feel free to end a romance or close friendship? Do you think teenagers usually understand and accept that? Explain.

4. What is the best way to end a romantic relationship? Why do people respond so differently to such breakups? How do you think you'd deal with the situation—or how have you?

5. What does a single person risk losing by unrealistically hanging on to a romantic relationship? What do you think the person should do instead?

6. What is your attitude now about being single? If you find in the future that you want to marry before you find someone to marry, do you think your attitude about being single might change? Explain.

Basic relationship patterns

There's a basic pattern—a *relationship cycle*—that occurs in almost all love relationships. People first notice each other's most appealing characteristics—that's what attracts them. To make a good impression, each person puts his or her best

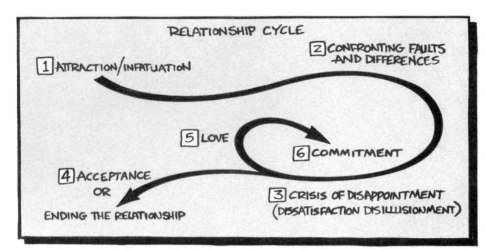

RELATIONSHIP CYCLE

1 ATTRACTION/INFATUATION
2 CONFRONTING FAULTS AND DIFFERENCES
5 LOVE
6 COMMITMENT
4 ACCEPTANCE OR ENDING THE RELATIONSHIP
3 CRISIS OF DISAPPOINTMENT (DISSATISFACTION DISILLUSIONMENT)

foot forward, letting the other person see the good side first. Nobody starts a relationship saying, "Well, I think you'd better know right from the start that I snore, have a lousy temper, am a tightwad, and can't stand onions, pizza, or people who disagree with me!" People try to make a positive first impression—that they're easy to get along with, generous, flexible, and an all-round nice person. There's usually no malice intended in that cover-up, just a sincere desire to please and win over the other person. The hope is that once the other person knows my strong points, he or she will then overlook my faults.

We can all be "perfect" for just so long, however, before our imperfections and idiosyncrasies start to surface. It takes time for that to happen naturally, especially in romantic relationships. After people spend enough time together, they start falling into their natural habits and roles. Then the imperfections begin revealing themselves.

Couples often let themselves get too serious about each other before that disclosure happens. (If recent polls on the subject are accurate, men tend to make an emotional commitment to a relationship sooner than women do.) People begin making emotional—or even marriage—commitments without knowing each other's flaws as well as virtues. Then—revelation! The unwelcome, unhappy discovery of faults and areas of conflict and incompatibility comes only afterward. Sometimes people discover that they've liked the idea of being in a relationship more than they've liked each other!

So it's wise to not make a major emotional investment in someone until you've had time to experience each other's faults as well as virtues. That's not always easy advice to follow, but it can spare you needless emotional pain.

For discussion

1. In what ways do people try to make a good first impression on someone to whom they're romantically attracted? Explain and be specific.

2. Before becoming seriously involved, how can two people discover each other's less-than-perfect qualities? How much time does it usually take for those to surface? Explain.

3. Explain why the concept "love conquers all"
   - represents an ideal Christian goal to strive for in relationships
   - can be a hurtfully naive notion when considering a serious relationship or marriage

4. Have you observed the relationship cycle in your own relationships or those of others? Explain, without mentioning names.

Review

1. What types of relationships do single persons have? What role do these play in their lives?

2. What are good ways for single persons to meet people they would enjoy dating?

3. What are the positive and negative aspects of on-line romances? What precautions should individuals take regarding on-line relationships?

4. How should single persons be honest and realistic about their relationships?

5. What is the relationship cycle? Why is it wise to consider that cycle when involved in a romantic relationship?

6. Why are single persons free—and why should they be free—to end a romantic relationship?

Cinderella and Prince Charming

Read the following and respond to the questions.

Myth can refer to a statement, story, or belief that is false or untrue. Or it can refer to a story whose details may be true or untrue, but whose underlying meaning contains important basic beliefs or truths by which people try to live.

In addition to being mythical in the first sense, some fairy tales also become myths in the second sense: They influence how people view themselves and their lives. The imaginary story of *Cinderella and Prince Charming* has come to represent these deeper beliefs and truths about life:

1. For every boy and every girl there's one and only one person out there somewhere just waiting to be found.

2. Finding that one perfect person for you is the only possible way you can be truly happy and fulfilled.

3. Looking for that one person is the purpose and focus of your existence as a single person.

4. Unless and until you marry your Cinderella or Prince Charming, you're doomed to be lonely, incomplete, and miserable.

5. Once you find your "one-and-only-true-love," you'll automatically live happily ever after together.

For discussion

1. Explain the two meanings of myth. How has the story of Cinderella and Prince Charming come to be a myth in both senses?

2. How do childhood fairy tales educate as well as entertain? As a myth in the second sense, how does the Cinderella and Prince Charming story convey each of the five beliefs listed above?

3. What is false about each of those five beliefs? Explain.

4. How have those beliefs negatively affected single persons' attitudes about their vocation? How do you think they negatively affect single teenagers' views and happiness?

5. Rewrite each of the five beliefs about life so that each makes a true, positive, and more realistic statement. Explain how you'd change the Cinderella and Prince Charming story to reflect the basic truths you've stated.

Sexual intimacy

copulation

uniting or linking together sexually

Our sexuality is given us by our Creator so that, in loving another person, we might share more fully in God's love. Having sex is the most intimate physical way two people can express their total love and permanent commitment. It's meant to be one of the most sacred ways of sharing our heart and human spirit.

We are sexual *persons*, but we are not *sex* objects. Casual sex is cheapening and demeaning. It reduces human sexuality to a purely physical level of **copulation**. Hooking up with someone—a common term for casual sex—sounds like hitching up a trailer or putting gas in the car at the pump! The damaged self-respect that results from casual sex was expressed by the tearful young woman who'd been sexually intimate with a high government official—when she wasn't sure he even knew her name!

Regarding the psychology of sex, researchers still find that men and women often view sexual experiences differently. More men than women are likely to view sex mainly as a means of physical release. More women than men view sexual involvement as expressing what the relationship means. It's easy to understand why the two views lead to misinterpreting both relationships and sexual experiences! The fact that young men are becoming increasingly concerned about how to respond to sexually assertive young women indicates that more than gender is at work here.

Sexuality is more than biology! It involves our whole person—how we relate to others as a woman or a man, as a person who is heterosexual or homosexual. We've already discussed that being homosexual in orientation is not wrong! There is a difference between the homosexual orientation that is God-given and homosexual actions that, according to Church teaching, are wrong. Like anyone else, homosexual persons can maintain close and loving relationships that are chaste and in keeping with the sexual responsibility all single persons should have.

Single individuals' sexual behavior poses serious concerns for single persons and for society. Catholic teaching emphasizes why it considers sexual intercourse outside of marriage to be wrong: **Sexual union is a total gift of oneself that can be properly realized only in the loving, committed relationship of marriage.**

Yet teenagers and single adults are too often dishonest with each other—and sometimes with themselves—about sex. If you've ever been the object of unwanted sexual advances, you've probably wondered, "What should I do when I don't want to have sex or be physically intimate with someone? How do I halt the amorous advances without hurting the person's feelings—or being rejected?"

When asked those questions, teenagers and young adults widely agree:

- Say clearly, and kindly—or firmly, if necessary—what you think and how you feel.
- Someone who respects you will accept your answer.
- Anyone who really cares about you won't stop dating you just because you refuse to be sexually intimate.

Because casual sex results in so much personal hurt and social harm, having sex outside of marriage concerns all of us. It's not true that everyone engages in premarital sex. Statistics show that most teenagers choose not to have sex. Increasing numbers of single adults are also choosing not to engage in sex.

For discussion

1. Give two examples of ways teenagers are dishonest with themselves or others regarding sexual behavior.
2. What is the best way to halt someone's advances without hurting the person's feelings—or being rejected? Explain.
3. In what ways are individuals viewed as sex objects by the media? By others? How is that damaging to personal dignity and self-respect?
4. How common is casual sex among teenagers? What negative consequences result for individuals and for society? Explain.
5. Why do teenagers choose to engage in premarital sex? Choose to not do so? Explain.
6. Comment on this saying: When it comes to sex, a woman needs a reason; a man needs a place.

The meaning of sexual union

To determine what you want your sexuality to mean, you must first determine what you want your life and intimate relationships to mean. We can be intimate with someone in many ways that needn't include romantic or sexual intimacy. Having a heterosexual or homosexual orientation doesn't necessarily lead to engaging in genital intimacy. All types of intimacy, however, must be based on personal intimacy.

For single persons, sexual intimacy often gets in the way of personal intimacy. After their sexual experiences, they often fear the possibility of pregnancy or disease. When a sexual relationship ends, they feel even more guilty, used, and betrayed. That mistrust carries over into other relationships and into marriage. If you don't believe that, consider this: A recent survey of parents-to-be found that the women wonder mainly whether the baby will be healthy, while the men wonder mainly whether the baby is theirs!

In addition, single persons often unrealistically expect complete, permanent fidelity from someone who hasn't pledged that to them. Fewer than half of the engaged couples who've formally promised to marry actually do end up marrying each other!

Without the complete commitment of marriage, sexual expression can't mean a total giving of oneself. Catholic teaching views sexual intercourse outside of marriage as wrong because it's dishonest; it tries to express something that doesn't exist—giving oneself in a complete, exclusive lifetime commitment. **You can't express a commitment you haven't made.**

That's why Catholic teaching points out that, except in marriage, sexual intercourse isn't a true sign of what the relationship means. It holds that God intends sexual intercourse to occur only within marriage between a man and a woman where it is open to possibly creating new human life. Since homosexual intercourse cannot fulfill that purpose, Catholic teaching also considers homogenital behavior wrong. It isn't that sex is wrong. It's that sex is sacred. Outside the complete marriage commitment, sexual intercourse can't express the full meaning God intended.

The positive Catholic view of human sexuality echoes what people generally want sexual lovemaking to mean. The Catholic view upholds those ideals and urges that you don't settle for less. People want a sexual experience to mean the most it can. Outside of marriage, however, sexual intimacy can't express what only committed love in marriage can mean. Too often single persons simply "fall into" having sex. So it means far less for them than what they ideally want it to mean.

For discussion

1. What does the gift of one's body in sexual intercourse symbolize? Why is that meaning lacking if one person withholds something or reserves the right to discontinue the relationship in the future?

2. What do you think most people ideally want sexual union to mean in their lives? What do you want it to mean in your life? How does Catholic teaching about human sexual union compare with those ideals?

3. How would you respond to someone who asks, "Why does the Catholic Church think sex is bad?" Explain, using examples of what the Church does teach.

4. Why do you think some teenagers "fall into" having sex, rather than upholding their ideals and personal dignity?

Chastity—expressing your sexuality in morally good and responsible ways that are appropriate to your vocation in life.

Celibacy—a gift, calling, and religious commitment to live the single way of life lovingly and chastely.

Sexual abstinence—choosing to not engage in sexual intercourse—either permanently or for a time.

Chastity (Married and single persons are called to live chastely.)

(Married persons must sometimes practice sexual abstinence, as during illness or for a time after childbirth.)

Sexual abstinence
(Single persons are called to practice complete sexual abstinence.)

Celibacy
is lived by single persons who make a special religious commitment.

Intimacy and chastity

genitally
having to do with the reproductive and sexual areas of the body

promiscuous
sexually loose, engaging in sex casually or with many different partners

AIDS
Acquired Immune Deficiency Syndrome, an often fatal illness

Single persons, whether heterosexual or homosexual, can certainly have warmly affectionate relationships without becoming **genitally** involved. In fact, having sex often spoils a good relationship. It's much easier to relax and enjoy intimate relationships when sex isn't the goal, focus, and source of anxiety and conflict. You can both focus more freely on each other as persons and on what your relationship means. Chastity doesn't deny or downplay your sexuality. It energizes and frees you to enhance and protect your love.

Many single young adults once believed it okay to be sexually intimate with "just one person." They felt "safe" because they weren't **promiscuous**. But after a series of "exclusive" relationships, they finally realize they have been sexually involved with many different partners. They've also assumed the same risks as if they'd had sex with everyone those partners had previously had sex with—and everyone they had previously had sex with, and so on!

By portraying single characters mainly in terms of their active sex life, the media reinforce the notion that casual sex is acceptable. That image distorts the single life. It leads single persons to believe falsely that sex is expected and okay because everyone is sexually active. The truth is that more single adults are choosing sexual abstinence until they marry. For one thing, they're sensibly scared to risk contracting sexually transmissible diseases, particularly **AIDS**.

YOU KNOW THAT ROMEO WHO WAS PRESSURING YOU TO HAVE SEX LAST WEEK?

SO? WHAT ABOUT HIM?

OLDER WISER SELF

NEXT MONTH HE TESTS POSITIVE FOR TWO NOT-SO-FRIENDLY SEXUALLY TRANSMITTED DISEASES.

Researchers have recently discovered "strikingly" high rates of the cervical abnormalities that can lead to cancer among teenage girls who are sexually active. Genital intimacy without intercourse will usually prevent pregnancy, but there is still a risk of contracting sexually transmitted diseases that way. "Safer sex" practices can help prevent disease, but only abstinence from genital or oral-genital intimacy is foolproof.

It's interesting, isn't it, that people speak of "losing" one's **virginity**. Even the vocabulary negatively reflects the experience. While the physical experience and the accompanying memories can't be erased, it is possible to redirect one's heart. What's past is done, but your future is in your hands—and it's the adult future you shape that counts from here on. It is possible to renew your heart and your resolve about what your sexuality will mean for you. If you need to do so, give yourself the chance to make a fresh start, beginning now.

To live by higher values and to avoid risking their health and their lives, more single persons are abstaining from further sexual involvement. They're realizing the positive benefits of chastity: They don't have to worry about possible pregnancy and diseases. Sex is no longer a key issue or pressure in their relationships. Greater inner freedom and assurance makes them feel more confident about refusing unwanted advances.

Being chaste means that your affectionate gestures express your relationships honestly and with respect. You're in control and responsible. You don't let your sexual urges and romantic feelings overwhelm your common sense and moral judgment. When your intimate relationships involve affectionate touches, be sure that you both understand what that means. That enhances the gesture's meaning and avoids misunderstanding kisses as commitments.

The ways Jesus related to others show us that close personal relationships are essential to being fully human. Chastity isn't meant to cramp our love life but to expand our hearts in deeper, less selfish friendship and caring. Given the powerful pull of natural sexual tendencies, being chaste isn't always easy.

virginity
the state of not having had sexual intercourse, or of being "untouched" or "unused"

But with God's help it is possible. Single Catholics often find that help in celebrating the Sacraments of the Eucharist and Reconciliation.

Jesus didn't condemn individuals for their sexual failings, but compassionately, lovingly forgave them when they repented. In doing so Jesus showed that it's not the technical aspect of virginity that's important. What counts most is loving others as Jesus loved—unselfishly and with honest respect and compassionate care.

As a single person, respect yourself and your sexuality. Don't let someone pressure you into a type of commitment you haven't chosen or haven't chosen yet. By choosing to not become sexually involved, you will feel less pressured into emotional commitments you don't want. You won't have to live with the guilt of going against your conscience by making immoral choices. You also won't have to worry about possible pregnancy and sexually transmissible diseases!

You must make your own decisions about your sexuality. No one else can make them for you. What your sexuality means will depend on the context in which you express it. Carefully weigh your choices and their possible harmful consequences. When your hormones are raging and your passions are flaming, stop and consider your responsibilities to yourself and others. Think about how your life and others' lives could be changed forever by your one irresponsible sexual choice. Listen to the wisdom of the Church and those who have loved you through the years. Pray to make the right decisions and stick by them.

As single persons, support one another's resolve to be chaste and sexually responsible. Focus on each other as persons, and discourage viewing people as sex objects. Be confident in yourself and respect your personal dignity. Love without compromising yourself and what you value most. Decide that, from here on, your sexuality will mean the utmost for you in view of what love, total giving, and commitment really are. Believe that it's possible to realize your sexuality's fullest meaning. You deserve to experience that. Don't settle for less.

Scripture insights

1. Read John 8:3–11. What does it show about Jesus' understanding of human nature?
2. What did Jesus' life as a single person show about what living relationships chastely means?

Journal entry

1. Ideally what do I want my sexuality to mean?
2. What could I do to achieve that meaning in my life?

Project

Interview two lay single adults, asking them these questions:

1. What do you experience as the greatest opportunities and benefits of being single?
2. How does the single life provide you with unique opportunities to help people?
3. How does your Church and civic communities view single persons and your vocation?
4. What role does your relationship with God play in your life as a single person?
5. Do you view your single vocation as temporary or as a permanent commitment?
6. Have you ever been stereotyped or misunderstood just because you're single? If so, how did that affect you?
7. What advice would you give single persons about establishing close relationships?

Write a two-page paper reporting your findings and giving your responses.

For discussion

1. Give examples of media portrayals that view the single life mainly in sexual terms. How do those images affect teenagers' perceptions of the single life?
2. Why do fewer teenagers and single adults engage in sexual intimacy?
3. What does it means to live chastely as a single person?

For single persons what are the positive benefits of sexual abstinence?

4. How are affectionate romantic gestures sometimes misunderstood? How common do you think that is among teenagers? What should single persons consider before expressing their romantic affection? Explain.
5. What are the typical results of teenage sexual experiences? Do you think the same is true for single adults? Explain.
6. How will your choices about expressing your sexuality affect your happiness and personal fulfillment and that of others?
7. What hurt and harm commonly result when teenagers engage in sexual activity without thinking about the possible consequences? Explain.

Review

1. Why does Catholic teaching regard sexual intercourse outside of marriage as not a true sign of what the relationship means? As wrong?
2. Why is the sexual behavior of single persons an important social concern?
3. What is meant by saying that we are sexual persons, not sex objects?
4. What kinds of intimate relationships should single women and men have?
5. In what sense is human sexuality far more than biological?
6. Explain the Catholic view of chastity, sexual abstinence, and celibacy, and who is called to live these. Where do people get the needed strength to love chastely and truly?
7. What two inseparable meanings does Catholic teaching say God has given to sexual intercourse?
8. Why doesn't sexual intercourse outside of marriage express what most people want their sexual experience to mean?

In summary

The single life is a positive, valuable vocation that people live in different ways and for various reasons. Being single allows greater flexibility in establishing relationship priorities and commitments. It also requires certain qualities, the meeting of basic needs, and a support system of meaningful relationships. There are many ways single persons can meet others who share their interests and values. As Jesus did, single persons need to establish a proper balance in their life. Church and society today are becoming more sensitive to single persons' concerns, needs, commitment, and contributions. Single persons minister to others in a wide variety of ways in both Church and society.

Misconceptions about the single life harmfully stereotype single persons.

Their intimate relationships needn't involve romance or sexual intimacy. Sexuality involves one's whole person and what one's life and relationships mean. Appropriately practicing chastity, sexual abstinence, or celibacy enhances the single person's vocation. As the increasing practice of chastity among single persons shows, sex isn't the focus of the single life. Catholic teaching holds that sexual intercourse outside of marriage is morally wrong because it can't mean what God has intended sexual lovemaking to mean. Single persons should be realistic about their relationships without unrealistically expecting permanent fidelity. As Jesus showed, warm human relationships are necessary to being a complete person.

Key concepts

abstinence

AIDS, basic relationship patterns

casual sex

Catholic view of human sexuality

chastity

celibacy

copulation,

cults

dating concerns

intimacy and chastity

Jesus and the single life

lay volunteers

maintaining honest relationships

on-line relationships

promiscuous sexual behavior

relationship cycle

relationships in the single life

risks of sexual involvement

sex as sacred expression of love and
    commitment

sexual intimacy

sexual responsibility

sexually transmissible diseases

single life

single ministries

single vocation

support system

transitional or permanent single life

CHAPTER 7

THE CHALLENGES OF BEING SINGLE

SCRIPTURE

. . . you were called to freedom, brothers and sisters; only do not use your freedom as an opportunity for self-indulgence. . . .

Live by the Spirit.

. . . the fruit of the Spirit is love, joy, peace, patience, kindness, generosity, faithfulness, gentleness, and self-control.

If we live by the Spirit, let us also be guided by the Spirit.

GALATIANS 5:13, 16A, 22–23A, 25

CHAPTER PREVIEW

PRAYER

God of joy,

We look forward to the freedom of adult life on our own.

Teach us to use our freedom to bring love and peace to
   ourselves and others.

Help us be kind and generous, true to our convictions,
   and faithful to our commitments.

Give us a gentle touch that's sensitive to
   others' needs and feelings.

Direct our impatience and our passions so that
they help us forge positive new roads in life
without overwhelming our better judgment.

As we face life's challenges, let us live and be
   guided by your Spirit.

Bless our lives with your joy.

We ask this in Jesus' name. Amen.

Misconceptions of the single life

cathy®

by Cathy Guisewite

In the past, being single wasn't considered a legitimate choice. People looked down on the single life and often on single persons. The single life is viewed much more positively today, but there are still misconceptions and subtle stereotypes about being single. Stereotypes of single persons sometimes still lead to discriminatory housing and employment practices, for example. We need to correct the misconceptions and eliminate the stereotypes; the following four views of the single life are especially common and need to be discussed.

"HE'S THIRTY AND NOT MARRIED? MUST BE IMMATURE AND AFRAID TO COMMIT."

In past generations people were expected to marry by their late teens or early twenties. Society pitied or was suspicious of those who didn't. Our language still reflects that bias against being single: Single persons are called "unmarried," but have you ever heard a married person referred to as "unsingle"? Unmarried describes single persons negatively—in terms of what they aren't instead of who they are!

Today most individuals in our society don't marry until their mid- or late twenties. More people wisely want to remain single for several years after they finish high school and college and start a career. Men and women want the opportunity to be independent, to develop their potential, and explore the interesting possibilities in careers, travel, and meaningful relationships. Young adults want to stay single longer, and more are choosing to remain single permanently as a happy, loving way of life. A significant number realize only after experiencing an unhappy marriage and divorce that they prefer being single. Widows and widowers often choose to not marry again.

People used to marry because they were afraid to remain single. Today there are people who stay single because they're afraid of commitment or marriage. They've never witnessed a happy marriage in their family and are afraid their marriage too will fail. While some lack the confidence or opportunity to marry, many remain single because it's what they prefer. These single adults aren't lonely or unhappy and certainly don't want to be pitied.

Fifty years ago a study found that most people thought something was morally or psychologically wrong with those who remained single well into adulthood. People were suspicious of those who never married. Permanently single persons were thought selfish—too concerned about themselves to marry. Or they were considered losers who probably had such serious personal faults or problems that no one would want to marry them.

It used to be more commonly presumed that men who don't marry might be homosexual. Even today it's sometimes assumed that an attractive, permanently single person is probably gay. Catholic teaching points out that gay persons are called to the single vocation. But social attitudes cause great harm when they lead gay or heterosexual individuals to believe they can be socially accepted only by marrying. When such pressures influence people to marry for the wrong reasons, hurt and heartache follow. The discovery that they weren't called to the married vocation causes them and their families great pain.

Yet single adults are still asked, "When are you going to get married?" or "Have you met anybody you're serious about yet?" (How many married persons are asked, "How come you're not still single?") Suspicion remains toward those who choose to not marry until later than average or who choose to not marry at all. Even those who become single as the result of divorce can be the object of talk—"Why couldn't she (or he) 'keep a mate'?"

At your age you're expected to be single. So you may not have encountered any of the typical stereotypes that are still directed toward many single persons. By their sheer number single persons have done much to correct misconceptions. There are many positive reasons for remaining single, as our society has finally begun to realize. The single lifestyle is not a vocation by default!

For discussion

- Do you think you have the same views of the single life that your parents have had? If not, how do your views differ from theirs?
- How do you think society's views or stereotypes about single persons affect your perception of the single vocation?
- Have you ever thought of staying single because you're afraid marriage might not work out? Explain.

Single adults can benefit from opportunities to share their experiences and their dreams.

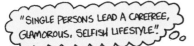

"I CAN'T BE FULFILLED AS A WOMAN UNLESS I BEAR A CHILD."

In the past, young adults—especially women—who didn't marry shortly after adolescence were considered "unmarriageable." Young women in that "predicament" were called spinsters or old maids. Those derogatory terms suggested that the young lady was a failure—she couldn't find a man willing to marry her. For today's single women, sometimes the pressures are self-imposed. A woman may feel pressured to marry before her "biological clock" runs out and she can no longer bear children. Or she may feel that, married or not, she must have children to be fulfilled as a woman. (Over one-third of single women in their thirties who've never married have had a child.) And some women still do view their personal worth in terms of their marriage prospects.

For discussion

- What pressures do you think single women and men today feel to marry or to have a family?
- What social attitudes do you think contribute to such pressures? What could help to change them?

"SINGLE PERSONS LEAD A CAREFREE, GLAMOROUS, SELFISH LIFESTYLE."

Some people view single adults as irresponsible fun seekers who spend their spare time in singles' bars looking for pleasure and self-satisfaction. Because single persons aren't married and usually don't have children, many people presume they're free of cares and have nothing but time on their hands. That simply isn't true! Single persons have their own problems, concerns, obligations, and responsibilities that aren't always so visible.

One person can't live half as cheaply as two. Expenses like rent or property taxes are the same no matter how many people live in the house. It often takes two incomes to support a household or buy a home. So single persons must work twice as hard or long to achieve the same economic stability as two working spouses. On top of that, they sometimes find it harder to get a loan. They may be passed over for a job or promotion in favor of someone who's considered more "stable" because she or he is married and has a family. Elderly single persons must live on one pension or government check, while elderly couples can pool their resources.

The single life, as such, is not a selfish lifestyle. (There are self-centered, self-seeking individuals in every way of life.) Most single adults lead moral and responsible lives. They care about and honor their relationships with God and others. Single parents manage jobs and care for their children at great personal sacrifice. An increasing number of single persons are adopting and raising children—something they wouldn't have been allowed to do in the past. Some single persons, on the other hand, don't see beyond immediate experiences to life's lasting, eternal dimension. They use others for their own pleasure.

It's naive to think that being single involves no commitments. Single persons aren't exclusively committed to one person, but they do have important relationships that involve responsibilities and obligations. It takes extra time and effort for single people to develop and maintain those relationships with persons they don't live with and see every day. That single persons do have important commitments isn't always recognized or respected.

For discussion

- Do you think our laws and social policies treat single persons fairly or unfairly? Explain.
- Do you see a double standard in how society views and treats single men versus single women? Explain.

"BEING SINGLE CAN'T BE A VERY HAPPY, FULFILLING WAY TO LIVE."

This misconception stems from the erroneous belief that man and woman were each created "incomplete." In that view people are meant to have a mate, to be a twosome—like a pair of socks! To become "whole" and "complete," one must link up with one's "other half." But not everybody is called to the married life. Finding love, happiness, and fulfillment is a matter of calling, choice, and commitment.

You can be happy and whole as a single person. In fact, unless you are, you won't be ready to make any other type of commitment—whether to marriage, the consecrated life, or parenthood. Each vocation requires its special gifts. Your happiness will depend on whether the life you choose suits your needs for growing and your talents for giving.

As more people live the realities of the single life, the misconceptions and stereotypes are disappearing. But those that remain still affect how single persons view themselves and their lifestyle, and how others view them. The misconceptions surrounding the single life should be recognized, confronted, and eliminated. It still isn't easy being single in a couple-oriented world. Single persons are often annoyed that they're presumed to be part of a twosome—or are not included in social gatherings because they're not a twosome!

It's not fair to take advantage of single persons by expecting them to bear more than their fair share of family and work obligations. Single

people are entitled to have privacy, independence, and a personal life. They don't have lots of extra time and money just because they're single. Sometimes the opposite is true. And it shouldn't always be the single person without children who has to fill in for colleagues who leave work early to take the kids to a doctor's appointment or a basketball game. (Volunteering to help out, however, can be a positive part of anyone's ministry to help others.) Single persons who must care for an elderly or ill relative should be eligible for the same family benefits at work as their married colleagues.

For discussion

1. Do you think our society is oriented more toward single persons, or toward couples?

2. Are social attitudes among your peers at school more positive toward couples than toward individuals? Explain.

3. One teenager thinks single adults should receive less pay than married adults for doing the same type and amount of work. What's your response?

4. How do you think businesses can and should fairly accommodate the personal needs of both single and married persons?

Activity

Draw up a list of the ways single persons and their lifestyle are portrayed on television and in the movies. Explain how realistic or unrealistic you think the portrayals are and point out any misconceptions, biases, or stereotypes you note.

Review

1. What is a stereotype? Why are stereotypes harmful?

2. What are some of the main misconceptions about the single life? How can single persons best respond to those?

The hidden message

Read each of the remarks pertaining to single persons.[1]
Then respond to the questions.

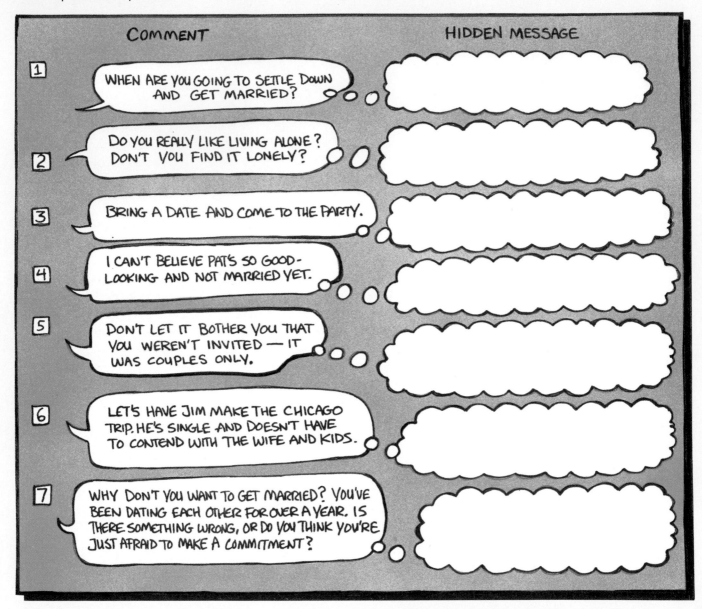

For discussion

1. What hidden message does each remark imply about the single person or the single life? Are there any similarities between these hidden messages and the attitudes mentioned previously regarding single persons?

2. Under similar circumstances would each remark have been made to or about a married person? If it had been, what kind of response do you think it would have gotten? Why?

3. How would you feel and respond if each remark were said to or about you as a single person? Explain.

4. Could each remark or question have been worded in a fairer, more enlightened and considerate way? If so, how? If not, why not?

5. What's the difference between having a misconception about the single vocation and having a bias against single persons? Give an example of what you mean.

6. How else do people reveal their biases and misconceptions about the single life or single persons? Give examples and explain.

Unhealthy relationships

Emotional and physical abuse occur so often that they are an urgent social problem. A woman is raped every minute in our society—over half of the time by someone she knows. One out of four women say that, despite their protests, a man she dated has tried to force her to have sex. One in seven college women say they've been raped at least once, and many more have been the victims of attempted rape—most often by men they knew or dated. Female students are most likely to be raped during their first semester at college.

Many men have also been rape victims. More often, they are physically assaulted by women they know. Men, however, are less likely to admit having been assaulted by a woman or to consider it physical abuse.

Whether it involves single persons or a married couple, nonconsensual sex is always rape, and it's always wrong. Being pushed hard, slapped or hit with objects, having one's hair pulled, or being kicked, choked, beaten, or threatened with violence is abusive. Such abuse is wrong and has tragic effects. The emotional and psychological aftermaths of physical and emotional abuse affect victims for years.

In an unhealthy relationship, you may experience feelings of worthlessness from being controlled and manipulated.

To address the widespread problem of physical abuse

1. **Let your peers know** that you consider rape, forced "affection," and other types of abuse to be wrong. Clearly voice your views against such behavior when others try to brag about, make light of, or otherwise condone it.

2. **Be prudent**, without being overly fearful, and take reasonable precautions to protect yourself from being a victim of rape or other forms of abuse. Help your friends do the same.

3. **When dating someone you've just met**, arrange to meet at public places or double date until you feel comfortable about the person. Provide your own transportation.

4. **Alcohol and other drugs may impair your judgment** and lower your resistance to unwanted advances. Beware of being slipped "date rape" drugs such as rohypnol. Always keep an eye on your drink. At a party, if you didn't open it, don't drink it.

5. **If you feel pressured, say so.** Clearly and firmly say that you want the person to stop—and say it without being timid or apologetic. Anyone who disregards that and violates you anyway is clearly using and abusing you, not loving you.

6. **If someone is threatening to physically abuse you**, get away immediately if possible. If necessary, scream and draw attention.

7. **If you've been physically assaulted**, realize that that's not your fault! Even if you exercised poor judgment in some way, you were not responsible for the attack. Seek medical help and report the crime immediately. Get in touch with a rape crisis or counseling center for assistance, advice, and support.

8. **Do not resume a close relationship with the person.** Don't believe that the abuse won't happen again. If you choose to maintain close contact with the person, it will happen again.

No one "owes" another person sexual favors! Never feel guilty for refusing emotional or sexual favors just because someone spent money on you, showered you with gifts, or showed you a good time. No one owns another person. If you're in a relationship where the person continually makes you feel worthless, controlled, or manipulated, then you are in an unhealthy relationship. If the other person won't seek professional help or won't change, then your only choice may be to leave the relationship. As a single person or as a married person, don't become so dependent on someone that you let yourself be used as an emotional punching bag. You will not be happy being miserable!

Journal entry

Complete these statements.

1. I have felt obligated to someone else, even though I shouldn't, when . . .
2. I try to exercise too much control over someone by . . .
3. I can make sure my close relationship with someone is healthy by . . .

Question box

On a blank sheet of paper, write down what other questions you'd like to have discussed about dating. Do not write your name on the paper.

For discussion

1. What is the best way to refuse someone's sexual advances without being rejected by the person? How would you respond if the other person became more persistent? How would you respond if that person refused to date you again? Explain.
2. Some women feel obligated to someone who spends a lot of money on them on a date. They feel guilty if they don't give in to their date's sexual aggressiveness. What is your response to that? Why?
3. Why do you think acquaintance rape and abuse are so common in our society?
4. What additional things do you think should be done to address the problems of date rape and abuse? Explain why you think these things would help.
5. Give three examples of how individuals may think they're loving someone, but are really being emotionally abusive toward that person.
6. Give three examples of how individuals may think they're being loved by someone, but are really being manipulated or emotionally abused.

Review

1. What are some of the signs that a relationship is unhealthy?
2. What is rape? What is physical abuse? Emotional abuse?
3. What are some positive ways to address the widespread problem of abuse in relationships?

Come back

Read about the following incident that recently occurred, and respond to the questions.

Kim had been dating Tim for over a year before she broke off their relationship. Kim had plans for college and a career and felt that Tim was getting too serious about a future together that she just couldn't foresee right now.

About a month later, Kim began dating Victor. She felt more comfortable with this relationship because Vic seemed to feel the same way she did about keeping things less serious for now. In the meantime Kim stayed friends with Tim, sometimes going to a movie with him or inviting him over just to talk.

Then one weekend Tim called and begged Kim to come back to him and stop dating Vic. He promised things would be different—that there would be no pressure. He just wanted them to be together again as a couple. Kim gently but firmly told Tim that she didn't think that was a good idea. By the end of the conversation, both Kim and Tim were in tears.

Tim said he couldn't live without Kim. He told her he thought of committing suicide unless she resumed their relationship as it had been. Kim was upset and didn't know what to do. She really did care for Tim, but otherwise her feelings hadn't changed about the situation.

Kim's mother asked her what was wrong, but Kim refused to say. She was afraid if she told her parents, they'd also get upset and overreact.

So Kim decided to tell no one and to be "just friends" with both Tim and Vic. That has seemed to appease Tim—for now. Vic is bewildered and senses that something's wrong. But he accepts Kim's decision that they just remain friends, if that's what she wants.

For discussion

1. Would you say that Kim is in or has been involved in an abusive or unhealthy relationship with either Tim or Victor? Explain.

2. Do you think that Kim's fears about telling her parents are probably well-founded? Should she tell her parents or a counselor about the situation? Explain.

3. How do you think your parents would react if you told them you were involved in a situation similar to Kim's?

4. Do you think Kim did the right thing or made a mistake in her responses to Tim? In deciding to be just friends with both Tim and Vic? Explain.

5. What do you think Kim should do if Tim pressures her further into resuming a romantic relationship with him or into not pursuing such a relationship with anyone else? Explain.

Challenges of being single

In addition to sexual and other relationship pressures, single adults experience other challenges: How do you cope with being lonely? What's the best way to meet other single persons? What about living together with someone?

Coping with loneliness

Solitude is the pleasurable, preferable experience of being alone. *Loneliness* is the painful, undesired experience of aloneness. We all need some solitude—the chance to quietly relax, think, pursue a hobby, work, pray, commune with nature, or enjoy the other positive benefits solitude affords.

Single people, like most people, are alone from time to time. Being single makes it easier to seek needed solitude. But even though single means "one," it doesn't have to mean lonely. Everyone experiences some loneliness, but single persons needn't be lonelier than anyone else. Maybe we need a better word for this way of life than single!

Some single persons move every few years or so and live away from relatives. Being so mobile can either be refreshing or cause single persons to feel rootless—like they don't belong. (That need for love and community is what sometimes draws lonely individuals into cults.) You've already discussed it, but it's important to repeat: As a single adult, you'll definitely need a personal support system! If you live far from your relatives your friends will be a big part of that support system. Establish and maintain close ties with people. Stay in touch with relatives and friends and seek new friendships.

It's easier to make new friends when you can bump up against one almost every day in the hallways on the school campus. It's different when you're a single adult on your own. Single adults commonly complain that they don't know how to meet people. Yet they may prejudge going to a party or striking up a conversation as a "waste of time"—unless a serious relationship might result. Or they let shyness keep them from meeting people.

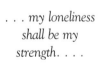

. . . my loneliness shall be my strength. . . .

GEORGE BERNARD SHAW

Some have internalized society's negative attitudes about the single life. They view being single as a "holding pattern" until they can find someone to marry. They let themselves become lonely and neglect the many ways they could add love and meaning to their lives.

A few weeks before her wedding, a woman was away on a business trip. As she waited to board her plane home, she began talking with the gentleman next to her. Ordinarily she wouldn't have bothered, since she was somewhat shy and he was several years older than she. But now that she wasn't looking for someone to marry, she struck up a lively, interesting conversation with the man. She discovered that he wrote biographies of famous people and was an artist whose paintings hung in museums around the world. As she flew home, the woman realized how much she'd missed during her single years—because she'd lacked self-confidence.

As a single adult, don't make that woman's mistake. Make an effort to meet people. Don't ignore or avoid non-romantic friendships; cultivate them. Don't deprive yourself of wonderful experiences by being either too independent or too preoccupied with the search for your "one and only."

Some single persons have too narrow a view of the gatherings designed to help single persons meet people. They think they'll be declaring themselves losers if they attend. But there's nothing wrong with trying to meet people. Singles' social gatherings don't have to be matchmaking meetings. They can just be good opportunities to get to know others with similar interests and concerns.

If you're lonely and have time on your hands, get more involved in activities you like. Enjoy more fully the things you do by yourself. Many single people feel lonely when eating out alone, so they eat out only with a companion. Instead, look on such excursions as interesting adventures. Adjust your attitude and use your imagination. Take the initiative to meet people. When you're feeling lonely, tell someone. Make contact! Others have much to share, and so do you. So much loneliness is unnecessary.

You may be by yourself, but you're never truly alone. Each vocation is an aspect of God's love. Married persons witness to the faithfulness of God's love. Your single vocation witnesses to God loves for each of us as unique individuals. As a single person, walk with God and count on God's love.

Shakespeare, Leonardo da Vinci, Benjamin Franklin, and Lincoln . . . were not **afraid** of being **lonely** because they knew that was when the **creative mood** in them could **work**.

CARL SANDBURG

Project

Interview two lay single adults, asking them these questions. Write a two-page paper on your findings and giving your responses.

- What are the greatest challenges of the single life?
- How do you cope with loneliness as a single person?

For discussion

1. What difficulties and disadvantages do you see in being single? Which ones have you experienced? Which do you think you'll find most challenging? Explain.

2. Suggest a good alternative to the term *single* for the single life. Explain your reasons.

3. As a *single* adult, how will you try to cope with lonely times? What types of solitude do you enjoy most now? Explain.

4. Describe your experiences of loneliness. What positive possibilities do they offer?

5. What typical opportunities do single adults have for meeting people? Do single adults and teenagers have the same attitude about that? Explain.

6. How would you advise a single adult who finds it "hard to meet anybody"?

7. Has your relationship with God ever helped you get through lonely times? Explain.

Review

1. What's the difference between loneliness and solitude? How can one turn a lonely experience into pleasant solitude?

2. How can single persons best deal with the loneliness they sometimes experience?

3. Why is living the single life only with a view toward getting married an unfair approach?

4. To what different aspects of God's love do married and single persons each witness?

Journal entry

1. At what times do you feel most lonely?

2. What steps can you take to help yourself break out of your loneliness? (What has helped you do that in the past?)

Living together

Although it's again become popular in recent decades, the idea of couples' living together before marriage isn't a new practice. It's actually an old idea Western civilization discarded long ago because of the widespread personal and social problems it caused and because of a developing understanding about what marriage is and means.

In past centuries, Church leaders like Saint Augustine had condemned as wrong the idea of unmarried couples living together. (Augustine himself had lived in such a situation before his conversion and learned the hard way.) The Church disapproved of such arrangements. Nevertheless, during medieval times, *concubinage*—living together with an exclusive partner—was rather widely practiced by both **laity** and clergy. Some viewed concubinage relationships as a form of marriage. We might compare those relationships to the common-law marriages civil law still recognizes in some places. A man and woman who live together as husband and wife for a certain period of time may be legally recognized as common-law spouses even though they've never officially married.

Eventually, however, both Church and society became less tolerant of people living together without formally being married. The practice often left women and children abandoned and without legal recourse for financial support when the live-in father abandoned the family. Then, as now, the rest of society had to help shoulder the burden of helping such families survive. Such arrangements also didn't witness to the sacred, permanent commitment of marriage in the Christian sense. Couples themselves began to realize that living together was no substitute for the formally declared permanent commitment they truly wanted.

Today couples who live together should—but most often don't—consider possible practical problems: What would happen if your partner leaves, dies, or becomes severely ill or incapacitated? If you've made no other legal provisions, you might have no recourse if your partner moves out with all the furniture and electronic equipment you've helped pay for! If your partner dies or if you die, assets could go to the next of kin. Neither of you would have any legal say in how the other partner should be medically treated in an emergency. Those decisions would be made by family members, not by the person's partner. And when children are involved, the practical problems are greatly multiplied!

laity
persons who are not members of the clergy (such as priests or ministers)

cohabiting

living together as a couple without being married

One **cohabiting** couple put their savings in a joint account toward the home they planned to buy together. A few years later the man met someone else and withdrew all the money from the account. His previous partner was left without enough money to hire an attorney to try to reclaim her share of the money! Another cohabiting couple bought a home jointly, but had no legal documents drawn up designating right of survivorship. When the woman was killed in an auto accident, her partner had to sell the home immediately because the woman's share of the house automatically went to her closest relatives. In another situation a man's live-in partner became severely ill. But he was denied visitation at the hospital, and the doctors would consult only with the "family" members.

Young couples who cohabit often don't think anything bad will happen to or between them. But when it does, they can be financially just as wiped out because what little they had together is all they have. If either partner is unwilling to make provisions for the other, then how much love is there? Is there really any commitment? If you are willing to make the other types of legally binding commitments to each other, are you really willing to accept a live-in relationship that means only sexual pleasure and convenience? Otherwise, why aren't you willing to formalize your personal commitment by marrying? Behind avoiding the practical matters often lie such deeper issues that live-in couples are afraid to discuss and face honestly.

For discussion

1. Why is the issue of cohabiting a concern of society and not just the couple's private business?

2. If someone with whom you were in love wanted to cohabit with you but wouldn't address the practical issues, what questions and concerns would you have? Explain.

3. Why do you think many couples aren't willing to consider the practical aspects of living together without the benefit of marriage?

4. What advice would you give a friend who was thinking about cohabiting?

Individuals in a live-in relationship are more likely to suffer from depression than persons who are married.

lonely and away from home, college life can seem overwhelming. It's interesting, though, that men and women give different reasons for living together as a couple. Men often say (to the researchers—not their live-in partner!) that they began a living-together arrangement more for the sex and convenience than with possible marriage in mind. For women, living together usually involves an emotional commitment that they definitely (though often secretly) hope will lead to marriage.

Single women from unhappy family backgrounds more often choose the living-together arrangement to have someone to depend on, to feel secure. Yet, ironically, more women than men support their live-in partners financially—often quitting school to do so! Women more often become jealous over their live-in partners and feel they've been used by their live-in lover. Violence occurs more often in live-in relationships than in marriages. In fact, physical abuse happens in almost one third of living-together relationships! Clearly, one person usually expects—or endures—far more than the other in a living-together relationship. Is it any wonder that individuals who cohabit with someone are far more likely to be unhappy and depressed than are married persons?

Why couples live together

Today couples enter living-together arrangements for various reasons. Some hope for more financial or emotional security. Others mainly do it for convenience or as a means to have "safe sex." Some single persons view sex and living together as necessary steps toward marriage, which they fear will otherwise elude them. Some couples become sexually involved and spend so much time together that they figure they're "practically living together anyway." One day they decide they "might as well" live together. (Later they may decide for a similarly poor reason that they "might as well" get married!) Today, living together seems inevitable, but not because it's right or the couple is right for each other.

College couples are sometimes pressured into living together by their couple friends who cohabit. Or they may enter a live-in relationship for companionship. When

For discussion

1. What do you think of the typical reasons single couples have for living together?

2. Why do you think couples often "happen into" a living-together arrangement?

3. Why do you think men's and women's reasons for living together tend to differ? Why do you think they're generally not aware of each other's real reasons for wanting to live together?

4. How would you explain the ironic finding that many single women live with a man for dependence and security, yet end up financially supporting him through college or graduate school?

5. Why do you think jealousy and physical abuse are more often part of live-in relationships than they are a part of marriage?

The effect on personal happiness

To make sure couples are compatible before marrying, wouldn't it be a good idea to test that by living together first? Social researchers once thought so, but what they've discovered since has surprised them. The Catholic Church and other religious groups have long held that living together first isn't good preparation for marriage. Now social researchers are agreeing.

Social research has consistently found this: Living together before marriage does not insure compatibility or increase success or happiness in marriage. More married couples who've first cohabited with each other have unresolved conflicts after marriage. That's especially true in the important areas of sex, money, recreational interests, showing affection, household management and roles, and friends. Of married couples, those who first lived together are less well-adjusted and less happy. They more often daydream about separating or getting a divorce. They tend to respect their spouse less than do married couples who didn't live together before their marriage.

The vast majority of live-in relationships don't last. Couples who live together before marrying break up more often than do engaged couples who don't cohabit. More couples who had cohabited separated before ten years of marriage than those who didn't live together before marrying. The divorce rate is significantly higher among couples who lived together before marriage than among those who didn't. In some young adult-age groups, it's almost twice as high!

Researchers find individuals who cohabit tend to emphasize self-fulfillment and self-interest more. They believe less in traditional social structures like marriage. Those who disregard the religious, family, and social traditions that disapprove of living together are more likely to lack the beliefs and attitudes that make a relationship last. They may lack belief in marriage as a permanent commitment or belief in fidelity. Put simply: If marriage isn't that important to someone to begin with, it's unlikely that it will become more important to the person after marriage. As researchers point out, the high incidence of living together certainly hasn't lowered the high divorce rate.

That begs these questions: Are people more likely to divorce because they cohabit? Or are those who cohabit less likely to be persons capable of making a commitment like marriage work? Either way, cohabiting is statistically riskier for someone who's looking for a permanent commitment!

Often individuals go from one live-in relationship to another, experiencing a series of broken hearts and shattered expectations. When single persons choose to cohabit, they often ignore their moral responsibilities and deeper values. Even strongly committed married couples know it takes strength and determination to stick together through life's challenges. When a couple's commitment has shallow roots to begin with, it's more likely to topple when a problem comes.

For discussion

1. Why do you think living together doesn't ensure a couple's compatibility, personal happiness, or marital success? Seems to lessen couples' chances for, rather than prepare them to achieve, a happy and lasting marriage?

2. Why do you think couples who've lived together before marrying seem less well-adjusted and happy after marriage?

3. Why do you think that after marriage those couples have more areas of unresolved conflict over the following areas?
   - Sex
   - Money
   - Recreational interests
   - Showing affection
   - Household management and roles
   - Friends

4. Why do you think couples who cohabit break up more often than engaged couples who don't live together? Why do you think the divorce rate is so much higher among couples who cohabited with each other before they married each other?

5. What do you think about a person when the person is willing to go against social wisdom, family wishes, and religious teaching in order to cohabit?

A man's dilemma

Read the following reality-based situation and respond to the questions. Then your instructor will tell you the actual outcome.

John was twenty-eight and single. He dated different women and was quite happy with his single life. Then he met Kay. They dated for about nine months, and Kay "fell very much in love" with John. She hoped they'd marry someday. Since Kay had a roommate and John didn't, the couple spent more of their time together at John's apartment. They became sexually involved, and Kay began staying overnight with John.

Finally, Kay brought some of her clothes to John's place so that she could go to work from there. Gradually, she was spending all her spare time at John's—and was doing most of the cooking and cleaning for him. John had never said he loved Kay,

but he did fly her back East with him one time so she could meet his parents. Finally, after two years of living together and presuming that some day John would ask her to marry him, Kay confronted him about the future.

John told Kay that he liked her very much but couldn't say for sure that he really loved her. As for marriage John said he didn't want to think about it right now. He told Kay he'd be happy for things to remain just as they had been. But he said he couldn't promise Kay a future commitment and would understand if she should decide to leave. Broken-hearted about what John had said, Kay ended their relationship.

About five months later, John met Susan. For the first time in his life, he really felt he was in love. They saw each other every day for almost a year. Finally, John asked Susan to live with him. He explained to her that he was considering the possibility of their marrying, but needed more time to make sure. In the meantime he saw no reason why they shouldn't live together, since "two can live more cheaply than one."

Susan, however, told John that living together was against what she believed in morally and that it would deeply hurt her parents. She said she saw no reason why they had to live together. At this point John wasn't sure if Susan really loved him, but he didn't want to lose her. So he asked a good friend for advice—should he try to persuade Susan to live with him or should he accept her desire to leave things as they were?

For discussion

1. If you were in Susan's place, what thoughts and questions would be going through your mind about the relationship? Why?

2. If Susan refused to live with John, should he continue the relationship with her? Explain.

3. If John continued pressuring Susan to live with him, should she continue the relationship? Explain.

4. If you were John's friend, what advice would you give him? Why?

5. What mistakes do you think were made by Kay, John, and Susan? What, if anything, should each person have done differently? Explain.

Why are live-in relationships less likely to last?

Those who think living together is a "trial marriage"—without the commitments or complications, generally discover that it's more trial than marriage! Sometimes it's the small things that interfere with the relationship. The couple usually lives at "his place" or "her place," not "our place," so one person never feels quite at home. They neatly divide expenses into "yours," "mine," and "ours"—rather than jointly and realistically coping with each other's spending habits and underlying values. They may each spend holidays with their own families, not dealing with the delicate, difficult matter of whose relatives to visit this Christmas. And they often feel guilty and nervous about concealing, or revealing, their living-together arrangement, especially with regard to their parents.

The woman in a living-together arrangement is usually less satisfied than the man with the relationship's sexual aspect. Sexual dissatisfaction is a leading reason why live-in relationships break up. Real differences are glossed over and personal complaints withheld. For those desiring marriage, there's the mistaken belief that "once we're married, things will be better." Sex becomes a substitute for meaningful, honest communication about problems. Live-in couples avoid confronting critical compatibility issues. They aren't permanently committed, so they can escape dealing with the practical matters that challenge good will and provoke resentment.

Underlying those difficulties researchers also find that there's often a lack of deep peace and joy. Individuals in live-in relationships are uncomfortable that their religion, and often their parents, don't approve of their living together. They're bothered by the deceit of hiding their live-

Decisions that are difficult for married couples are often more difficult for unmarried couples who are living together.

in arrangement from their families or their Church. And they're bothered by society's disapproval. By denying the relationship legal status and protection, society too refuses to condone the relationship.

Often, unmarried couples who live together don't share their problems and anxieties with their friends. So they lack the support they need for coping with their relationship problems. Their friends may even find it awkward to relate to (or even refer to) them as a couple. Cohabiting couples often present the social image that they're happy with their arrangement, while inwardly it seems like an inferior compromise. They realize it's not the permanent commitment that at least one of them usually would prefer.

Living together can have more problems than benefits.

For discussion

1. Can there be a "trial marriage" without permanent commit- ment. Is the term trial marriage self-contradictory? Explain.

2. If couples realize that their living together arrangement isn't permanent, why are their break-ups so traumatic?

3. Why does living together actually keep single couples from knowing each other better? Explain.

4. Which findings about living- together relationships surprised you most? Least? Why?

5. If your best friend were begin- ning to "fall into" a living- together situation and asked your thoughts about it, what would you advise him or her to consider seriously? Why?

6. If someone you were romantically serious about suggested that you live together, what would your main fears and concerns be? How would you respond? Why?

7. How would you respond to the teenager's statement that "If you know and love someone enough to want to marry the person, what's the point of just living together?" Explain.

A great many live-in arrangements don't last more than a few months! Some continue several months or years, even though one or both persons become increasingly unsure and uneasy about it. Will it continue? Should it continue? How can it end without hurt? When the couple breaks up, their emotional trauma is similar to divorcing. (Even the legal complications can be similar.) If, despite their unresolved uncertainties, the couple finally decides they "might as well" get married, they often experience marriage as a rude awakening and a bitter disappointment.

There are many ways couples can get to know each other well enough without living together. In serious relationships, couples generally spend most of their spare time together anyway! If couples don't honestly discuss and confront the important areas of compatibility, they're more likely to have an unhappy ending whether or not they first live together. Ironically, though, couples who cohabit usually don't even discuss those things in depth—because they're afraid it will disrupt their relationship!

The weight of social research and personal experience is stacked against living together. Couples may learn some things about each other through living together. But it doesn't improve their odds of compatibility, stability, or personal happiness. Living together seems to produce far more problems than benefits.

false to myself. Intercourse was my way of reiterating, "The relationship is still on"; of asking, "Is the relationship still on?" It was my way of saying, "Keep me, I'm good!" (even when sex wasn't always that good), and of reassuring myself, "See, he still loves me."

Important questions were never settled, things such as: "What if I get offered a good job in another state?" or "What if he decides to go back to school?" or "The Pill is making me depressed—should I stop taking it?" We'd just end up in bed again, without resolving things. I got to the point where I felt like yelling, "Sex, schmex! I just want you to talk to me!"

I told Tom I wanted to move out and think things over. I wanted him to really see me and hear me as a person—something our sexual involvement made it hard for him to do. I wanted perspective—and friendship.[2]

A woman's dilemma

Read the young woman's description of living together with her boyfriend and respond to the questions. Then your instructor will tell you the situation's outcome.

My own parents divorced fifteen years ago, so I was determined not to jump into marriage. That's why I moved in with Tom—so we could develop our relationship and get to know each other first.

It went from beautiful to miserable in about four months. I was knocking myself out to please him, feeling insecure whenever the arrangement seemed the least bit shaky. And I was using sex in a way that was

For discussion

1. Why did the young woman choose to live together with her boyfriend? Do you get the impression Tom probably had a similar reason for wanting to live together? Viewed the relationship the same way his live-in partner did? Explain.

2. What problems did the woman begin experiencing in the relationship? Might there have been a connection between her family background and some of those problems? Explain.

3. What part did sex come to play in the couple's relationship? How did the woman feel about this? Why do you think she felt that way?

4. How did a pattern of avoidance occur in the relationship? Why do you think that's so common in live-in relationships?

5. If Tom proposed marriage at this point instead of agreeing to live apart for a time first, do you think it would be wise for the woman to agree to marry him? If the couple married without living apart again first, what chance would you give their marriage of succeeding? Explain.

6. How do you think the woman should respond if Tom threatened to end the relationship unless she agreed to continue living with him? Explain.

7. How would you respond to each of the following situations?

   • The young woman asked you as a friend whether she was right to tell Tom she wanted to move out and think about their relationship more objectively for awhile.

   • Tom asked you, as his friend, what he should do about his girlfriend's proposal to live apart and try to get a new focus on their relationship.

8. How do you think Tom probably responded to what his girlfriend told him? Why do you think he would respond this way?

Catholic teaching regarding cohabiting

For the reasons already discussed and more, Catholic teaching opposes the idea of single couples living together. You know Catholic teaching considers having sexual intercourse outside of marriage to be morally wrong. But even if a living-together arrangement doesn't involve sex—and it might not—it still sets up a serious sexual temptation. It's not that the Church is "anti-everything" regarding sex. That charge is unfortunate and unfair. One practical reason Catholic teaching opposes cohabiting is that it actually weakens good relationships! The Church is on your side in wanting you to achieve the happiness in love that you deserve and deeply desire.

Married couples rely on the spiritual strength they receive from God and what the Sacrament of Marriage means to them. That's lacking in living-together relationships because the permanent commitment is missing. Couples who are not faithful to their religious beliefs are less likely to be faithful to each other—whether or not they're married. Couples who remain faithful to their religious values are more likely to also remain faithful to each other.

Many people strongly disapprove of single couples' living together. They've seen how it weakens social values and diminishes the sacredness of marriage. Those aren't small matters. You've undoubtedly been touched by the tragedy of divorce—either in your friends' lives or in your own family. The children born to single couples who live together are even more likely to suffer abuse or the instability of their parents' lack of a permanent relationship.

When couples' personal decisions become part of a social trend, as with the practice of living together, their relationship affects us all. The family is at the heart of our society. We're all part of the glue that bonds families together—especially in difficult times. Families need our support rather than our approval of behaviors that make the commitment to marriage and family life seem trivial, optional, or unnecessary.

Some couples have needed to marry privately in the Church, without society knowing. They have done so for practical reasons. Some employers, for instance, haven't permitted husbands and wives to work together in the same company or office. To keep both of their jobs, they've had to keep their marriage secret and live together discreetly. So it's important not to disapprove of particular situations without knowing all the circumstances.

Catholic teaching emphasizes that no one should be pressured into marrying. Marriage should be a person's free choice. Living together beforehand can jeopardize the ability to make a truly free choice of who and when to marry. Unfortunately, the partner who feels quite uncertain about the couple's future together often can be talked into getting married. The person can feel too emotionally or socially pressured to back out.

One shouldn't marry because one is expected to or feels obligated to do so. To be a marriage at all, marriage must be a truly free choice. Living together doesn't allow either person the emotional distance and objectivity to make that life decision. While living separately and independently, a couple can assess more freely and realistically their needs, relationship, and future together.

Can couples who live together marry in the Church?

For discussion

1. What is your response to the Church's reasons for opposing cohabitation? Which reason makes the most sense to you?

2. Does choosing to live together outside of marriage indicate that someone is less likely to be faithful to the relationship?

3. Why should we be careful not to judge couples who appear to be cohabiting?

4. What part do pressures play in cohabiting couples' decision about whether or not to marry?

5. How can living together keep couples from making a truly free and wise decision about marrying? How often do you think that happens? Explain.

6. If Catholic and non-Catholic friends of yours were thinking about living together before getting married, what would you advise them to consider first? Explain.

Just as strongly as it opposes cohabitation before marriage, so Catholic teaching supports a couple's right to marry. Single couples who've lived together can marry in the Church, and pastors are encouraged to consider each couple's circumstances. In fact, Pope John Paul II cautioned against making the rules too strict about who may marry in the Church.[3] He urged pastors to help couples rediscover and grow in their faith. But cohabiting does present a dilemma for Church officials. They want to support the couple and their relationship—and the religious values the couple seem to dismiss by choosing to live together before they marry.

Policies for dealing with that situation vary from place to place. Cohabiting couples may be asked or required to live apart for a few or several months before being married in a full Church ceremony. (Many other Christian Churches and some Jewish communities have the same policy.) The couple may be offered the alternative of having a private ceremony with just their immediate families present, rather than a large and public formal wedding in church.

Individual circumstances may be such that the couple is permitted to proceed with the church wedding they had planned. Diocesan and parish policies may vary, just as couples' circumstances do. But Catholics who want to marry in a wedding that is a full, public Church celebration (and non-Catholics who want to marry a Catholic) should consider those things before agreeing (or asking the one they love to agree) to live together before marriage.

Review

1. Why do many couples choose to live together before marriage?

2. Why does Catholic teaching oppose cohabiting before marriage? Why do social researchers agree that it's a bad idea for couples?

3. In what ways does one partner in a living-together relationship usually expect more than the other partner does? Endure more? Be specific.

4. Regarding living together, what practical matters should couples consider, but most often don't?

5. Why do couples cohabit, and how satisfying is the relationship for them usually?

6. How does cohabiting affect one's personal happiness and the success of the relationship before and during marriage?

A priest's dilemma

Read the letter one pastor wrote to cohabiting couples in his parish. Try to understand both his concerns and those of the couples he's addressing. Then respond to the questions.

Dear Friends,

You have asked me to witness your marriage and I am pleased that you wish to be married in the Church. Before I give you my answer about witnessing your marriage I want to share a few thoughts with you.

I am sure that you know that the Church does not approve of your living together before marriage, and I hope you are not surprised that I also disapprove of it. By asking me to witness your marriage with the usual kind of wedding celebration, you are putting me in an awkward position. I feel that if I do witness the vows in a big celebration I am giving tacit approval to your present behavior. I would be treating you in the same way as I would treat a couple who has not been living together. I am uncomfortable with that because I want to encourage young people to live up to Catholic Christian standards before marriage.

Let me try to explain why I think that what you are doing is wrong. I don't want to talk just in terms of the commandments, though I believe what you are doing is contrary to them. I would rather talk about your relationship to the community—both the civil community and the Church community. Both these communities disapprove of couples living together prior to marriage.

By your living arrangements, you are saying quite publicly that you don't care very much what these communities think. And yet, now you come to me, an official in the Church community, and ask me to treat you in the same way I would treat a couple who had respected the community's customs and rules.

Putting it another way, you have been living as if married, in effect saying to the community, to your friends and your families, that you wish to be treated as if married—at least you want to live that way. But now, you come and say you want to be treated as unmarried and have a big celebration of the fact that you are now marrying. There is some kind of contradiction here, and it puts me in a difficult spot. If I say

yes, I seem to be saying that what you are doing is okay. If I say no, I am refusing to help you get back into the community.

I think that living together and sexual relations prior to marriage are wrong. Sexual relations are a sign and symbol of a total gift of one person to another. That total gift is made in the marriage vows in which two people give themselves publicly and irrevocably to each other for life. To engage in sexual relations before making that formal, public, permanent gift and commitment in marriage is to falsify the sacred symbol that sexual intercourse is. It is to give yourself in this act that symbolizes total giving, but which in this case can be reversed because you haven't given yourself to each other in marriage. We don't like people who give gifts and then take them back. Even children see the error in that; but premarital sex can too easily become such a gift, which can be taken back.

God's laws regarding sexual behavior are not whimsical nor arbitrary. They are guidelines to the deep significance of sexuality in our lives. They recognize the profound sacredness of our sexuality and are directly opposed to the cheap, selfish and shallow view of sexuality that is found in so much of our culture.

I think I can understand the social and economic pressures and your own feelings that have led you to live together. I would like to hear your reasons, but I am convinced that another solution could have been found—and even still can be—that will permit me to witness your marriage.

I would be happy to witness your marriage in a simple, quiet ceremony with two witnesses and perhaps your immediate families. That is what I would do if you had been married in a civil ceremony and now wished to have the marriage validated in the Church.

By your living together you seem to be saying, "We want to be like married people." I would be very happy to treat you like married people, and witness your vows simply and quietly.

But I have serious difficulties with treating you like any other couple wishing to be married, who has not been living together.

Another possible solution might be for you to live separately from now until marriage. That would be a public statement to your family, your friends and to me that you are trying to live your courtship in a Catholic way.

I hope you will think about these things. I also hope you will come to see me again and that we can work out some way that will allow me to witness your marriage.

I am happy that you love each other, and that you wish to marry. I hope that we can work out the difficulties that I have had with your present living arrangements.

I hope to hear from you soon.[4]

For discussion

1. Why does this pastor feel that he has been placed in an awkward position? What contradictions concern him? Explain fully.

2. What difficulties does the pastor have with treating cohabiting couples the same as couples who haven't been living together?

3. Why does the pastor say that engaging in sexual relations before marriage falsifies the sacred meaning of sexual intercourse?

4. Pastors sometimes feel used when they get the impression that a couple just wants to be married in the church so that they can have a beautiful setting for their wedding, but have no real commitment to the Church. Couples may feel unwelcome or angry if they're told the wedding can't be celebrated as they wanted.

   • How do you sense the pastor above feels when couples who are cohabiting ask to be married?

   • How do you imagine you'd probably feel in the pastor's position? In the couples' position? Explain.

5. Most couples who ask to marry in the Church are not living together. Do you think it's unfair for cohabiting couples to expect the Church to celebrate their weddings in the same way? Explain.

6. How do you think you'd handle the situation in this pastor's place? Why?

You and the single life

Most single persons are truly happy. Whether temporarily or permanently single, they are finding fulfillment. While you are single, look positively on your single vocation. If you wish to marry, whether earlier or later in life, be happy in the meantime! But to be happy, whether you're single or married, you'll first need to discover a meaning to life that encompasses all vocations. You will find that meaning in loving and giving to others in the ordinary opportunities of your everyday life.

As a single adult living on your own for the first time, you'll have a chance to discover important insights into yourself and your relationships. As you live the single life, you might find that you prefer remaining single. In learning more about yourself, you may find that being single suits you better than would being married. You might find that a more independent way of life lets you be and give more of who you are. Or you may discover that your personality and temperament aren't suited for marriage or perhaps for parenthood.

Some people realize only after their divorce that they married because they felt it was what everybody expected of them. But they found that they "weren't very good at being married" and hadn't been called to the married vocation at all. Many single persons are committed to a job or profession that enables them to serve a great many people. But the job or profession demands so much time and energy that they couldn't handle both career and marriage—at least not at this time.

More individuals are discovering that it's wise to postpone marrying until both persons have completed their formal education,

Life is what happens while we're making other plans.

begun to establish their careers, and are economically stable. These are wise, not selfish, reasons for remaining single. On the other hand, if you definitely know that you want to marry and have a family someday, you should factor that into your career plans as a single person.

The "perfect" time usually never comes! You'll always face the challenge of balancing your plans with unforeseen circumstances. To stay afloat and headed in the right direction, keep your values and priorities straight. Stay close to God and to those you love. At the end of your life, it won't be the company you've founded or the money you've made that will have made you happy. It will be how well you've loved.

Even if you do want to marry eventually, don't forget that, while you're still single, your vocation is to be single! Don't put your life and happiness on hold (as so many single persons do) until you find someone to marry. Live the present rather than putting all your hopes in the future. Whether or not there's a romantic relationship in your life, focus on the positive aspects and possibilities of loving as a single person. Develop your career, but also lead a well-rounded life. Make enough time for friends, relatives, spiritual growth, volunteer work, and leisure.

The single life involves a special vocation of loving. Whether you choose to live it permanently or temporarily until you marry, live your single life in a happy, loving way.

Journal entry

List the top three challenges you think you'll face during the next few years as a single person. Briefly explain how you'll try to handle each one. Be prepared to share one of your challenges and explanations with the group.

For discussion

1. What do you hope to learn and experience in your vocation as a single adult? What are your greatest fears about living the single life?

2. What do you think would be selfish or negative reasons for choosing to remain single? What would be wise reasons for choosing to remain single temporarily or permanently?

3. How do you hope to find happiness and fulfillment as a single adult? How do you find it in your life now?

4. How has living your single vocation changed over the past few years? How do you think it will probably change further over the next several years?

Review

1. What is a good way to think about single life at present?

2. What attitude do you hope to have about the single life as an adult living on your own? Explain.

3. What are good ways to live one's single life right now?

4. How is living your vocation a journey?

When you **love** you are no longer at the mercy of **forces** greater than yourself, for **you**, yourself, become the powerful **force**.

PARAPHRASED FROM LEO BUSCAGLIA, LOVE

Views of the single life

Read each of the quotes from or about single persons. Then respond to the questions.[5]

1. There are two kinds of people who can live alone successfully . . . One is the thinker or tinkerer, content with solitary arts. The other is a "people person," someone who has no trouble making social contacts.

2. Women are finding that their . . . career goals put them in a situation of being alone. Many men still want their women in the old roles, and so men are alone because women have outgrown them.

3. I have made a conscious decision to remain single, although it's not a vow. The motivation to marry is not there. I'm too involved in my career . . . I approach . . . relationships the same way as I do my career, giving all of myself. But I found that I couldn't make a 100-percent commitment to both . . . I'm not sure anyone can.

4. People don't live alone and like it. They live alone as a compromise. It's miserable being alone . . . What happens then? You end up sitting at home waiting for the phone to ring, but it won't because no one knows you're there . . . Loving and being loved are what it's all about.

5. I've decided that I would rather be miserable alone than be miserable with someone else. That way, I'm responsible only for my own feelings.

6. Living with someone would be a trial with many irritations. I couldn't do things the way I wanted. Our taste in furniture might differ, and I would even have to compromise on the things I like to eat . . . The question is whether you get back more from a relationship than what you give up. I don't think you do . . . Day-to-day living takes the spice off any relationship. Things get dull, and you run out of things to talk about.

7. I'm very independent. I would need a very special person, one who also was independent and self-assured . . . and [would] allow me the same opportunity . . . I'm a good cook, and doing the laundry and housework by myself doesn't bother me. So the only reason to get married is stability, and I don't want to rush into it.

8. It's nice to go home to be alone, and it's nice to go home to somebody. I'm not out looking for the right person, but maybe someday I'll meet that person.

9. If I were to marry, I would have to make some compromises on my ideal . . . The trouble is that I'm very particular . . . I'm a perfectionist, looking for perfection in someone, and that's hard to find.

10. I've worked hard on developing my own sense of security. Now I feel quite comfortable with myself. I don't need a relationship for survival.

11. I go to a lot of parties, and sometimes I take an escort. But I think nothing of going alone. That way, I can be comfortable, and dance with whomever I want . . . I'm not that anxious to go out . . . just to go out.

12. Doesn't everybody get lonely, even when they're living with someone?

For discussion

1. What attitude does each person have about being single? Which attitudes do you think are positive, and which do you view as negative?

2. How do you think these persons' attitudes about being single probably affect their relationships? Their ministries? Their happiness and fulfillment as single persons?

3. What do you think you'll find most difficult or challenging about being a single adult? Why?

4. What do you think will be harder about being a single adult than being a single teenager? Explain.

5. What do you think the most positive aspects of your adult single lifestyle will be? Why?

6. What do you hope will be better about your life as a single adult than as a single teenager? Explain.

In summary

The single life isn't always viewed as positively as it should be, and misconceptions about it still affect single persons' happiness in their vocation. The single life is not a selfish lifestyle. And as more people live the realities of the single life, the misconceptions and negative perceptions of it are gradually lessening. Single persons should meet the challenge of loneliness by actively seeking to meet others and building a good support system. They also need to recognize and avoid unhealthy relationships, and realize that rape and abuse are always wrong.

Although single persons have various reasons for cohabiting, Church and society agree that it's a bad idea. Cohabiting decreases the chances for achieving happiness and success in one's live-in relationship and future marriage. The practice also has widespread social effects that undermine the stability of relationships, marriages, and families. It's often an unhappy and uncomfortable situation for the couples and for pastors when those couples seek to marry in the Church.

To be happy as a single person, look positively on your life and live it in a happy, loving way. Whether you live it permanently or until you marry, witness to and rely on God's love in how you live your single vocation.

Key concepts

Catholic teaching about cohabiting and about marrying in the Church

challenges of being single

cohabitation

common-law marriages

concubinage

emotional and physical abuse in relationships

establishing new friendships and relationships

happiness and fulfillment in the single life

effects of cohabiting

living together

loneliness and the single life

misconceptions and stereotypes about being single

moral responsibility and the single life

rape, nonconsensual sex

reasons couples cohabit

selfishness and the single life

social research and live-in relationships

trial marriage

unhealthy relationships

Endnotes

1. The idea for this activity, and some of the quotations, were taken from *Teaching About Family Relationships* by Richard H. Klemer and Rebecca M. Smith (Minneapolis, MN: Burgess Publishing Co., 1975), 279.

2. Juli Loesch, "Unmarried Couples Shouldn't Live Together," *U.S. Catholic* (July 1985): 16–17.

3. See Pope John Paul II's *Apostolic Exhortation on the Family*, 1981.

4. Rev. Thomas Kramer, "Living Together: What's a Pastor to Do?" (Bismarck, N.D.: Cathedral of the Holy Spirit), as reprinted in *Faithful to Each Other Forever: A Catholic Handbook of Pastoral Help for Marriage Preparation* (Washington, DC: USCC, 1989), 74–75.

5. Quotations in this activity are adapted from these sources: 1–3, 5–12 from *Cal Today: San Jose Mercury News* (24 January 1982), number 4, from Suzanne Douglas, Publisher/Editor-in-Chief INTRO Magazine.

CHAPTER 8

ORDAINED AND CONSECRATED VOCATIONS

SCRIPTURE

"As you have sent me into the world, so I have sent them into the world."

JOHN 17:18

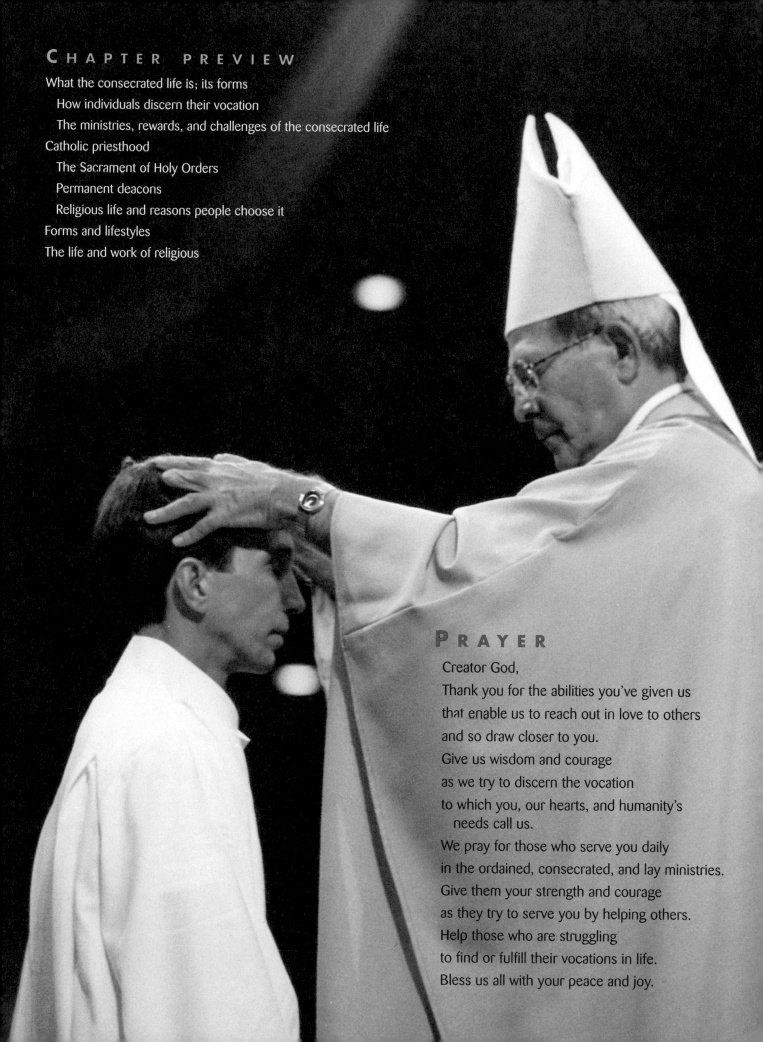

PRAYER

Creator God,

Thank you for the abilities you've given us

that enable us to reach out in love to others

and so draw closer to you.

Give us wisdom and courage

as we try to discern the vocation

to which you, our hearts, and humanity's
    needs call us.

We pray for those who serve you daily

in the ordained, consecrated, and lay ministries.

Give them your strength and courage

as they try to serve you by helping others.

Help those who are struggling

to find or fulfill their vocations in life.

Bless us all with your peace and joy.

The ordained and the consecrated life

lay
pertaining to laypersons (*laity*)—those who are not ordained

clergy
those specially ordained to preside at religious rites

evangelical
pertaining to the good news of the gospel

counsels
recommendations or advice

Every vocation is a sacred opportunity to witness to God's love and goodness. We should all try to grow closer to God by caring about others. Jesus recognized how **lay** single and married persons do that. He also called certain individuals to represent him and advance his mission in other ways through a particular way of life. This chapter will discuss the main ways Catholics live the ordained vocation and the consecrated life.

Jesus called some individuals to preach his message and continue his sacred actions through the signs that we today as Catholics celebrate in the seven sacraments. In the Catholic community, the **clergy**—bishops, priests, and permanent deacons—do that today. Jesus also invited some individuals to witness to his teaching by living in a special way, by living what Catholics call the **evangelical counsels**. Those dedicated to the religious life do that in today's Church community.

Those who live the ordained and consecrated vocations have contributed enormously to our society and world. Yet their way of life isn't always understood. You may have thought of becoming a priest, nun, religious brother, or deacon. Or maybe you're pretty sure for now that the ordained or consecrated life isn't your calling. But as you discuss your questions about it, try to understand better those men and women who live the ordained vocation and the consecrated life so generously. Consider, too, how you can support them in living their calling.

Catholic religious and clergy are among the most well-prepared people in any vocation. They receive extensive background training in theology, in the practical aspects of their ministry, and in the spiritual life. Their professional education and spiritual growth continues throughout their lives. Clergy and religious strive to be people of vision who understand current needs and ideas while helping to guide humanity wisely into the future. They've initiated educational, healthcare, and social programs that have become models for others and instruments of social change. It's no wonder that those in the priesthood and the consecrated life are personally and professionally among the most respected in the world.

States of life in the Catholic community

Clergy—bishops, priests, and deacons (some of whom are also members of the religious life)
- preach Jesus' message and continue his sacred actions
- attend to the Church's spiritual and liturgical needs

Laity—married laypersons and single laypersons
- assist the clergy, and serve God and help people in many other ways

Laypersons and clergy who live the religious life.

Ordained and consecrated lifestyles

Priesthood
- secular/diocesan priests
- religious order priests

Permanent diaconate
- unmarried deacons
- married deacons

Religious life
- active apostolate (sister, brother, or priest)
- contemplative (monk, priest, or nun)

For discussion

1. Describe contributions those who live the ordained vocation and the consecrated life have made and make
   - in our society
   - in the Church community
   - in the world
2. How have their contributions touched your life?
3. With which types of consecrated life are you most familiar? The least familiar? Explain.
4. What questions do you have about the ordained vocation and the consecrated life—for instance, about being a priest, permanent deacon, or religious sister or brother?

Discerning a vocation

Then I heard the voice of the Lord saying, "Whom shall I send? . . ." And I said, "Send me!"

ISAIAH 6:8

Vocation means one's calling; we believe our calling is from God. The experience of God's call is uniquely personal. Usually someone is attracted to a certain vocation. The person then assesses what that vocation is about and how well he or she can live it. For example, individuals who want to dedicate themselves to the consecrated life within the context of a community support system may choose the religious life.

All of us are called to be fully human and alive.

"I came that they may have life, and have it abundantly."

JOHN 10:10B

No one should undertake any vocational commitment unhappily or against his or her will. You shouldn't marry, remain single, have children, or become a priest or religious only because you feel you should do so or because it would please your parents. You shouldn't even choose a particular vocation just because you have a notion that "it's what God wants"— when you'd be much happier and better at being something else.

Candidates for the ordained vocation and the consecrated life must likewise choose it freely, rather than feeling pressured into it. The consecrated life certainly doesn't need cheerless candidates who can't get along with people. It needs psychologically healthy individuals who relate well with others. It was Mother Teresa of Calcutta's great joy in what she did that inspired her to accomplish so much—and to also inspire the world.

People have followed many amazing paths in discovering which way of life they're called to! Sometimes they discover their married, single, or consecrated vocation in quite unexpected ways. Generally, though, it's through a process that usually unfolds this way:

You meet someone you really connect with, either because of who the person is or how she or he lives a certain way of life. This may be someone you might want to marry or someone in the lay or consecrated single life whom you admire. You find that you're more and more attracted to this particular way of life. As you think and learn more about this way of life, you explore whether you'd be happy living it for a lifetime. You consider other alternatives but don't think they'd satisfy your heart as this way of life would.

Gradually you become satisfied that you'll be happier in *this* way of life than in any other. When you're convinced you can grow and give of who you are in this way of life, you're ready to think seriously about making a commitment to it.

Steps in discerning your vocation

Introduction ➪ Attraction ➪ Exploration ➪ Education ➪ Reflection ➪ Decision and commitment

Rather than being apart from others or the world's realities, those who live the consecrated life must be among those most in touch. Unhappy, lonely people aren't ready to make any vocational decision. All people bring who they are to the path they choose—whether marriage or the lay single, or the ordained or consecrated way of life. No one should make any lifetime commitment expecting it to undo his or her unhappiness or for other such reasons. Each way of life has enough challenges already! You should choose your vocation as a way to share your happiness and joy, not escape from an unhappy past.

One shouldn't choose the consecrated life to seek security, or to be looked up to, or because one is lonely or has failed in romantic relationships. One shouldn't even choose it mainly because one likes and admires certain men or women religious and the work they do.

Any way of life requires adjustments and giving up other possible options and pleasures. But never undertake a way of life with a "grin and bear it" attitude! You should be happy with your way of life, not view it as a terrible strain. Otherwise the other difficulties you're bound to face periodically in your life and work will become overwhelming burdens. In addition, you must have the personal qualities and gifts needed to live successfully the way of life you choose.

Many people are attracted to, but not suited for, the ordained or consecrated life. They might make good priests, nuns, brothers, or deacons if that were their calling. But it isn't. On the other hand, if your heart keeps nudging you to consider the ordained or consecrated life, it's possible that it might be your vocation.

Years ago, most men and women entered religious life or the priesthood right after high school, or even during high school. They didn't first have the opportunity to become self-sufficient and psychologically independent of their parents. Some felt pressured into choosing the priesthood or a consecrated lifestyle because they thought it would please God or their parents. They didn't make the decision with enough self-knowledge, maturity, or personal freedom. Sometimes they realized that only years later.

Today, men and women usually enter the seminary or the consecrated life in their mid-twenties or later, after they've gained adult work and life experience and have made decisions on their own. They're much clearer and more realistic about their available options and what they want to do with their lives. They've experienced adult relationships and are more prepared to make a decision for celibacy.

The reasons one *should* have for choosing *any* way of life:

- This is how I can best extend God's love to others.
- This is how I can best share with others my talents and my deepest values, beliefs, and hopes.
- I'm convinced I'll be happiest in this way of life, and most able to give to others generously and joyfully.

Scripture insights

Read these Gospel passages on how Jesus called others to live as he did—and the kinds of people he invited: Matthew 4:18–22 and 19:21, Mark 1:16–20 and 10:21, Luke 5:1–11 and 18:22. Pretending you're one of those individuals, write a one-page letter telling Jesus how you've decided to respond and why.

Journal entry

1. Toward what vocation (being single, married, ordained, or in the consecrated life) do you currently feel drawn?
2. What could you do over the next several years to discern whether that is the right vocation for you?

Biography

Read a biography of Mother Teresa of Calcutta, Albert Schweitzer, or another person whose life changed or inspired others. Write a two-page paper on how the person lived his or her vocation to made a difference in others' lives.

For discussion

1. Explain how you'd advise a friend who's considering the priesthood or consecrated life
   - but fears what others will think
   - out of fear of otherwise not making it to heaven
   - to please his parents
   - because she's just broken up with someone—there'll never be another love like that
   - because of a belief in Jesus' values and a desire to serve others the way he did
   - because of the good men and women religious do, and because she likes the religious she knows personally
2. How would you apply the steps in discerning your vocation to discovering whether you'd be happiest being married? Remaining single? Being ordained? Living the consecrated life? Explain.

The challenges and rewards

A young child once asked a nun who was wearing a habit if she had ears! Because the sister's veil always covered her ears, the child presumed she had none. That incident illustrates how men and women who live a consecrated or ordained lifestyle don't stop being human! Do nuns, priests, or brothers ever think about what it might have been like if they had married and raised a family instead? Sure they do. They experience all the normal human responses from time to time. Sometimes they have sexual feelings, and sometimes they get lonely. Far from being less than human, those who live the ordained or consecrated life are dedicated to becoming more fully human.

It's a mistake to think that because individuals live the ordained or consecrated life they're sheltered and out of touch. On the contrary, they are specifically devoted to loving, serving, and praying for others as Jesus did. Their ministry often makes them more aware than most people of real human conditions and needs. Their focus on and faith in Jesus' teaching helps them deal more wisely and effectively with social and global problems. Clergy and religious have made and continue to make tremendous practical and spiritual contributions. Whether in parishes, cloisters or monasteries, schools or hospitals, missionary endeavors, or a variety

of other ministries, they generously give of their time, talents, and energies.

In many cases, the dedicated service of those in the consecrated life and the ordained ministry has helped raise society's consciousness to a higher level of concern for others. When society refused to do so, religious and clergy were among the first to educate women and minorities, feed those who were hungry, shelter those who were homeless, and care for those who were poor, sick, and dying. Many religious congregations started with just a handful of members. They eventually expanded to include thousands. Today, however, their overall number is decreasing; so is the number of clergy in many countries.

Why are fewer people in our society entering the consecrated life and the priesthood? Clergy and consecrated women and men have accomplished their ministries so effectively that others now often do those tasks that once no one else would touch! Today married and other single lay persons in the Church take a much more active role in those ministries that were once considered exclusively the work of clergy and religious. And perhaps social influences, like the overemphasis on sex and material goods, also distract or discourage people from responding to a call to the consecrated life or ordained ministry.

Sometimes it's necessary to go a long distance out of the way in order to come back a short distance correctly.

EDWARD ALBEE,
THE ZOO STORY

Scripture insights

Read Matthew 6:20, 6:25, 8:20, 10:28, 19:21; Luke 9:58, 10:39, 10:42; Philippians 2:8; Romans 5:5; 1 Corinthians 7:32–35, 7:42; 2 Corinthians 8:9; and Colossians 1:24. Write a two-page paper explaining some of the ways those who are ordained or consecrated today try to follow Jesus' example, as illustrated in those passages.

For discussion

1. Why is it unfair to have unrealistic expectations of or to stereotype those who live the consecrated life? In what ways do you think people do that today?

2. Do you think that the media portray those consecrated persons and their way of life fairly or unfairly? Realistically? Explain and give examples.

3. Why will there probably always be people willing to join the consecrated ways of life? What new forms and ministries do you think the consecrated life may or should involve in the future? Why?

Review

1. Why is every vocation sacred?

2. How did Jesus call some persons to continue his mission by living the ordained or consecrated life?

3. Who lives the consecrated life in today's Catholic community, and in what ways?

4. How can one discern one's vocation?

5. What are the right and wrong reasons for choosing any way of life?

6. In general, what are some of the main challenges and rewards of the consecrated life?

A noted medical researcher needed volunteers willing, like himself, to be injected with a serum containing inactive strains of a deadly virus. The serum might possibly help treat those dying from the disease or become a vaccine against it. The risks from the experimental serum were considered low, but real. When the call went out for volunteers, more than enough priests and sisters above retirement age responded. It seemed to everyone that there's no true retirement for those dedicated to God in unselfish service of others.

The religious community Mother Teresa of Calcutta founded to serve those who were destitute and dying has gained members worldwide. There will always be people willing to forego other commitments in order to more freely love all persons unconditionally—especially those who are most neglected or rejected. They, too, will set aside material gain and self-focused ambitions for the sake of what's eternally important—serving others as Jesus did. And they, too, will experience both the earthly and eternal fulfillment of a life lived in love and generous service.

Once upon a time, the story goes, a preacher ran through the streets of the city shouting, "We must put God into our lives. We must put God into our lives." And hearing him, an old monastic rose up in the city plaza to say, "No, sir, you are wrong. You see, God is already in our lives. Our task is simply to recognize that."[1]

By their commitment and their lifestyles, those in the ordained vocations and the consecrated life help us all recognize more often and more clearly how God lives among us.

Might you be happy in an ordained vocation or in the consecrated life?

On each blank, write the letter from A–F that best reflects your response.

A — Never/Not at all
B — Rarely/Hardly at all
C — Seldom/Not very strongly
D — Sometimes/Somewhat, but not strongly
E — Often/Somewhat strongly
F — Always/Very strongly

_____ 1. Would you like to help lead people in prayer and worship and to connect Jesus' teaching with their lives?

_____ 2. Are you good at drawing people together in understanding and in becoming involved in projects?

_____ 3. Would you like to be actively involved in helping the poor, the hungry, and the homeless?

_____ 4. Do others seem able to talk to you freely about personal problems or turn to you for help with those problems?

_____ 5. Do you pray regularly?

_____ 6. Do you feel your relationship with God is most important in your life?

_____ 7. Are you good at assuming and exercising responsibility?

_____ 8. Are you able to cooperate well with persons in authority?

_____ 9. Are you a dedicated and self-disciplined person?

_____ 10. Do you usually complete tasks even when they seem difficult?

_____ 11. Do you like helping others?

_____ 12. Are you committed to Catholic beliefs and living them in your everyday life?

_____ 13. Do you have a strong desire to help people— especially those in greatest need?

_____ 14. Do you usually get along well with your family members and others you work with closely?

_____ 15. Is celebrating the Eucharist important in your life?

_____ 16. Are you attracted to the priesthood or religious life?

_____ 17. Would you like to help others by doing what priests or religious do in their ministries?

_____ 18. Is prayer important in your life?

_____ 19. Do you feel you are a happy, secure person?

_____ 20. Do others consider you a good leader?

_____ 21. Do you have an enthusiasm or zest for living that others seem to find contagious?

_____ 22. Do you often go out of your way to help someone?

_____ 23. Are you more of a team- or group-oriented person than a loner?

_____ 24. Do you have a way of bringing others together, whether in understanding or for play or work?

_____ 25. Do you have a knack for making others feel at ease?

_____ 26. How important in your life is your relationship with God?

_____ 27. Does dedicating yourself to love many people, rather than one person exclusively, appeal to you?

_____ 28. Do you enjoy material things but find other things more important in life?

_____ 29. Would you be content with not achieving wealth, recognition, or status in your life?

_____ 30. Are you in good physical health?

_____ 31. Do you feel you are an emotionally well-balanced person?

_____ 32. Do you like working with others, including those who are very different from you?

_____ 33. Do you like to reflect or pray alone at times?

_____ 34. Are you sensitive to others' feelings and needs?

_____ 35. Are you a sincere, truthful person?

_____ 36. Do you usually accept and learn from honest criticism?

_____ 37. Do others find that you're a good communicator and a good listener?

_____ 38. Do you have a strong desire to develop your personal relationship with God and to share God's love with others?

_____ 39. Do you like and find that you get along well with persons of both genders?

_____ 40. Do you view religion as a matter of loving God by helping and loving other people?

Being a priest

priests
those specially appointed or anointed to perform religious rites and to help people communicate with and grow closer to God

Since ancient times, **priests** have been a bridge between people and God. But by Jesus' day, the priesthood had come to be, for many, a way to exercise power over others. These priests considered themselves superior, distanced themselves from others, and demanded special privileges. Jesus, however, taught his followers to serve others humbly. He showed clearly how priests shouldn't just preside at rituals, but should be leaders by their example and service. Serving people lovingly while bringing them closer to God and one another is what the Catholic priesthood means today.[2]

The Sacrament of Holy Orders

In the Catholic community

Laypersons	Priests
• try to become perfect, as God is	• are especially obliged to seek perfection
• try to live by God's word	• understand and teach God's message to others
• celebrate and live the sacraments	• draw the Christian community together in prayer and worship—especially by presiding at the sacraments
• set an example for others	• inspire and set an example for laypersons
• care about and help those who are poor and needy	• make helping those who are poor and needy a main priority

Sacrament of Holy Orders
the Catholic rites by which deacons, priests, and bishops are ordained to perform the rituals and functions of their ministry

grace of Holy Orders
God's special spiritual assistance that helps deacons, priests, and bishops fulfill their ministry

All Christians are to minister to others as Jesus did. In that sense, by our Baptism we're all called to be priests. So what's the difference between priests and laypersons?

The priest is ordained to represent Jesus-among-us in a special way. In the **Sacrament of Holy Orders**, priests are formally consecrated and given God's special **grace** to continue Jesus' mission. As with the sacraments of Baptism and Confirmation, the ordained priesthood is a permanent gift. It too involves a lifetime commitment. In certain circumstances, a priest may be given special permission to leave the active ministry and live as a layperson. But that priest always remains a priest, though no longer allowed to preside at the sacraments except in certain extreme emergencies. Unlike the single vocation, the priesthood is never a temporary vocation. A priest is a priest forever.

bishop
the third of the Holy Orders; a priest who is given the mission to guide a diocese and the power to ordain

diocese
territory under a bishop's jurisdiction

archdiocese
district under an archbishop's jurisdiction, usually larger than a diocese

vestment
special ceremonial clothing worn when presiding at religious services

anoints
touches or smears with oil as a sign of sacred office or service

chrism
oil specially blessed for use in celebrating the sacraments

chalice
cup which contains the Eucharistic wine used at Mass; special cup used for religious rituals

sign of peace
prayerful greeting, such as a kiss or handshake, shared at Christian services

Bishops, priests, and deacons represent different degrees of consecration to the priesthood. The bishop is most fully consecrated to Jesus' priestly mission, while deacons and priests share in certain aspects of that ministry. (The pope as the bishop of Rome is known as the "first among equals." All bishops are as fully consecrated to the priesthood as the pope is.) Only the bishop can anoint others to the priesthood.

Representing Jesus' role as Good Shepherd, the bishop teaches and guides us, and oversees the care of our spiritual needs. But the bishop can't do all that alone. By their ordination priests and deacons share in the bishop's priesthood and help the bishop serve the people. The bishop oversees the workings of a **diocese** or **archdiocese** and usually presides at the Sacrament of Confirmation. Priests and deacons assist the bishop in their individual parishes and ministries.

The priest presides at the Eucharist and other sacramental celebrations in the name of the entire Church community.[3] All Catholics' ministries are centered on the Eucharist (the Mass). Priests try to celebrate the Eucharist daily, for it is our Church's heartbeat. It celebrates God's living presence among us in Jesus and the loving union we all hope to share with God and one another.

Priests welcome us into the Church in Baptism. They bring us God's forgiveness and reunion with God and the Church community in sacramental Reconciliation. They preside as we celebrate marriage, and give us strength and hope when we're seriously ill through the Anointing of the Sick. The bishop confirms our dedication to our Christian faith and ordains new priests to continue Jesus' sacramental priestly ministry.

The Rite of Ordination to the priesthood

✠ In the name of Jesus and the local church community, the bishop lays hands on the heads of those being ordained priests. The bishop asks that God give these candidates the gift of priesthood so they may bring people closer to God and one another.

✠ The gathered community confirms that prayer and their support for the newly ordained priests by responding *Amen*.

✠ Next, the new priests are given the **vestment** they'll wear while presiding at the Eucharist, the center of their priestly life.

✠ The bishop **anoints** the new priests' hands with **chrism**, and they each receive a **chalice** containing water and wine.

✠ Then the newly ordained priests are greeted with the **sign of peace** and, together with the bishop, preside at the Eucharistic liturgy.

Scripture insights

1. Read 1 Peter 2:9. What does the verse say about the role of all Christians?

2. Give examples of how Christians can fulfill that role in everyday life.

For discussion

1. What main questions do you have about the priesthood?

2. How do most people view priests and their role in the Catholic Church? How do you view them? Explain.

Among the people

diocesan (secular) priest
a priest who represents and works directly for the local bishop

order priest
an ordained man who takes vows in a religious community

rectories
dwellings, usually next to the church, where parish priests live

Priests do much more than preside at the sacraments. They represent Jesus and continue his mission in everyday life as well as at the altar. Priests encourage Catholics to participate in and live the sacraments. Priests pray and read the Bible every day and show others how to pray and understand the Scriptures. Priests are to share Jesus' message with us in practical ways we can apply to everyday life. They are to minister to others humbly as Jesus did.

We're often obliged to put our families and personal relationships first. But priests are committed to serve all persons of all ages as Jesus would. To do that, clergy need to be kind-hearted and sincere. They need to be spiritually strong of character and must act with the dignity of their calling. Priests should be unselfish and unbiased, putting Christ's gospel and people's spiritual growth above any group or idea. They must be deeply committed to the common good, to religious truth, and to social justice. Priests also promote understanding and cooperation with people of other Christian denominations and with non-Christians.

Bishop and priests should be a team devoted to truth and charity rather than to their own interests. They help form us into a community where everyone feels at home and reaches out to help others in their city,

the nation, and the world. In some denominations, each congregation is self-governing. But Catholic clergy pool their talents in the larger Church of the diocese.

Priests devote special attention to those in need or difficulty. They imitate the Good Shepherd's compassion toward sinners and those who have lost faith in God or the Church. Ready and willing to be inconvenienced, priests are constantly on call to help. But that requires more time, energy, and creativity than priests can manage alone! Priests need our help in aiding those who are poor, visiting those who are sick and dying, counseling those who are troubled and rejected, sheltering those who are homeless, consoling those who are grieving, preparing liturgies, and maintaining a suitable place for community worship.

Instead of being a **diocesan (secular) priest**, an individual may become a priest within a religious order. Although that person works under the local bishop's authority, his main allegiance is to his religious community. **Order priests** often live with members of their religious order. Still, not all priests work in parishes and live in **rectories** or work and live in religious communities. Some teach in high schools, colleges, or universities, do scientific research, work in the administration of a diocese, or have other jobs.

Why can't women become Catholic priests? people often ask. Catholic teaching gives these main reasons: Jesus and his first apostles were men, and all priests since then have been males. The Church believes it doesn't have the authority to depart from Jesus' example and the tradition he established.

The priest's bishop or religious community generally determines where the priest works, taking into account each priest's gifts and situation. No priest is perfect, and parishes have occasionally been shocked and disheartened by a priest's scandalous behavior. But if national polls are any indication, most priests are good persons who live their calling well; priests consistently rank in the top ten of those most trusted and admired for what they do!

For discussion

1. Which qualities do you think a good priest should have?

2. Why do you think priests are generally trusted and admired?

3. What are your thoughts or questions about the Church's reasons for not ordaining women? Explain your thinking.

The challenges and rewards of being a priest

Because of the widespread Catholic priest shortage in many countries, the majority of priests are overworked. But they find stability in staying close to Christ and in their friendships with others. Like other single persons, priests need a personal support system and rely on one another for help, advice, and encouragement.

Priests should live simply and moderately. But they don't have to take a **vow of poverty** unless they belong to a religious community or a secular institute. Their focus on spiritual things frees them to hear God's voice in people's needs and concerns. Diocesan priests are paid a small salary that they may spend as they wish. Other money they are given is used for the Church and its charitable works.

Just as Jesus did, priests today face many challenges. They're sometimes expected to be superhuman and sometimes blamed for whatever goes wrong in a parish. But they're not always praised enough for a good homily, a meaningful liturgy, or a successful parish program.

vow of poverty
vow taken by religious to live simply, unattached to material things

Christ has no body now but yours.

ST. TERESA OF ÁVILA

Why can't priests marry? Celibacy is not essential to the priesthood. In the early Church, bishops, priests, and popes were often married—a tradition that continued for over a thousand years. In the Eastern Catholic Church, married men may still become priests (but not bishops), but priests may not marry after being ordained. In the Western, or Latin, part of the Catholic Church, the celibacy requirement for clergy was gradually enforced, but it is now the general rule. Exceptions are made for married Protestant clergy to be ordained as Catholic priests after becoming Catholic.

When they are ordained, diocesan priests promise obedience to their bishop. They also promise to remain celibate—to not marry. It isn't appropriate for celibate priests to date or become romantically involved. But they can still show affection and have close friends, just as married persons can have appropriate friendships with persons other than their spouse.

Celibate priests are totally dedicated to serving all humanity—particularly those who are poor and suffering. Their hearts and energies aren't split between their own family and the needs of those they serve. Their choice of celibacy lets everyone know they're wholeheartedly committed to loving and serving everybody.

Jesus lived a celibate way of life. The Catholic Church in the West, with some exceptions for married clergy in other denominations who become Catholic, requires celibacy on the part of its diocesan priests. Those in religious orders, of course, also make a vow of chastity, which includes celibacy. Though some people think it's impossible to remain celibate all one's life, the many consecrated persons in the Church bear witness that, with God's help, it is possible. These dedicated people find that their vocations are deeply fulfilling.

One priest describes his challenges and rewards in the celibate life:

I admit that celibacy has grown on me over the years. Dealing with sexual attractions was difficult in my younger days. Attractions are still there, but they are less urgent. I have learned to take the time necessary to enjoy good friendships with married and single people. I know I would not be able to cultivate all the friendships I enjoy if I were married. With many people in my life through ministry and friendship, I look forward to quiet times alone for prayer, reading, and reflection.[4]

How could you know if the **priesthood is the right vocation for you?** You might feel attracted to that way of life or be drawn to work with people in your area as a diocesan priest. The priesthood is a calling from the Church community as well as from God. Being told by others that you'd make a good priest might mean you have the qualities and perhaps the calling. Those interested can always contact any priest or the diocesan vocation office for more information.

How does someone become a priest? The person must first have the health, motivation, and other qualities needed to live the priesthood successfully. Once accepted, candidates enroll in a **seminary** program to study more about religion and the practical aspects of **pastoral ministry.** They pray, reflect, celebrate the Eucharist daily, do charitable work, and participate in recreational activities.

Confidential surveys find that priests are generally very happy and satisfied in their vocation. They find deep joy in helping people and bringing them closer to God.

seminary
a program of study in preparation for ordination to the priesthood; also the campus or institution in which the study takes place

pastoral ministry
work of overseeing and serving the local church community

Activity

One Catholic diocese has hired an advertising agency to encourage interest in becoming a priest. Two of their billboards advertise, for instance, "Enjoy the ultimate benefits package—become a priest," and "Become a doctor of souls."

Design a creative ad of your own for radio, television, or billboards that might attract individuals to consider becoming a priest.

Journal entry

Complete these sentences.

1. My view of what being a priest means is . . .

2. One way I am someone through whom God reaches others is . . .

3. One way I could be more loving and compassionate is by . . .

Scripture insights

1. Read Matthew 19:12. What does the passage say about Jesus' view of celibacy?

2. How do you think being celibate affected Jesus' life and ministry? How do you think it affects a priest's ministry today? Explain.

For discussion

1. What stereotypes do you think people have about priests and their vocation? Are those stereotypes unfair to priests? Why?

2. Why do you think priests are generally happy in their way of life?

3. Which of the challenges priests face do you think you'd find most difficult? Why?

4. What do you think you'd find most fulfilling about being a priest? Why?

Review

1. What does a Catholic priest's vocation, ministry, and lifestyle involve?

2. What's the difference between a diocesan (secular) priest and a religious order priest?

3. What challenges and rewards do priests find in living their vocation?

4. Must priests vow poverty? May Catholic priests be married?

5. Is being celibate essential to being a priest? How does it affect a priest's ministry?

6. How does someone recognize a vocation to the priesthood? Prepare to become a priest?

Are priests happy and fulfilled?

One priest responds:

I do believe that God is right here with us. I believe I encounter God in people and situations, even and especially in those which seem, at first sight, to be terrible and distorted. To enable myself and others to get beneath the sin and distortion in order to respond to the beautiful and good reality of redeemed creation is why I am a priest. Sometimes people welcome these insights, and for a time, the priesthood is glorious. At other times they reject the insight and attack me, and, for a different moment, the priesthood is a cross. But, then, glory and the cross were close together in the life of Jesus long before I came on the scene.[5]

Being a permanent deacon

"... *come, follow me.*"

MARK 10:21

[handwritten: outline / leave blanks]

permanent deacons
in the Catholic Church, those ordained to perform certain ministries, while not moving on to ordination to the priesthood; in other Churches, one who assists the minister

diaconate
state of being a deacon

deaconesses
women deacons who assisted the apostles and their successors in the early Church in service

clerics
ordained men: deacons, priests, bishops

Many Catholic parishes now have one or more **permanent deacons**. The **diaconate** ministry actually dates back to when deacons and **deaconesses** helped the apostles and their successors among the early Christians. They proclaimed God's word, assisted at liturgical celebrations, and did many works of charity, just as deacons do today. In those ways, today's ordained deacons continue the work of Jesus Christ "who was known among his disciples as the one who served others."[6]

Study is still underway regarding the diaconate in the early Church. Some scholars feel that the description of women deacons and their work as found in Scripture and other writings is different from what we understand today as the ordained diaconate. They believe women were not ordained to this ministry. Other scholars believe the issue is unclear, leaving open the possibility of ordained women deacons in the future. Many Catholics would like to see the ministry of deaconess restored, either ordained or not. It is clear that service was the key ministry of deaconesses in the early Church, as it is for many women today.

After the early Christian centuries, the permanent diaconate for men and women disappeared as the priesthood became more emphasized. But women have played an enormous and vital role in the Church community since its beginning. In early Christian centuries, society often considered women second-class citizens and second-rate humans. In the Church, however, women were respected and given responsible positions. Deaconesses carried out important ministries.

All candidates for the priesthood are first ordained deacons. For those persons, being a deacon is a transition step in becoming a priest. Others choose to remain a deacon permanently. All deacons are **clerics**— ordained clergy who are strengthened in their service by a special sacramental grace.

Deacons aren't ordained to celebrate the Eucharist or preside as minister of the Sacraments of Reconciliation or Anointing the Sick. But they assist the priest who presides at the Eucharist and other sacraments. The deacon leads the gathered community in prayer and may give the homily. Where priests aren't available, deacons may preside at the Liturgy of the Word, the Communion Rite, and other liturgical rites, such as Baptism, Marriage, and Christian burial. All deacons participate in the Sacrament of Holy Orders, and their ordination as deacon is for life.

When ordained a deacon, single men must promise permanent celibacy. A single or widowed permanent deacon may not later marry without a dispensation, but a married

The ministry of deacons

proclaim God's word   do works of charity

assist at liturgical celebrations

person may be ordained a permanent deacon. A permanent deacon who is not married may later become a priest if he wishes.

Permanent deacons must be at least thirty-five years old and transitional deacons twenty. Married candidates and their spouses must realize how the commitment will affect their family life, and the candidates' spouses are asked for their consent. Candidates are officially accepted in a special rite of admission. After at least three years of preparation, they are sacramentally ordained a deacon by the bishop. They are told:

Receive the Gospel of Christ,
whose herald you are.
Believe what you read,
teach what you believe,
and practice what you teach.

THE RITE OF PRESENTATION OF
THE RITE OF ORDINATION
TO THE DIACONATE.

Some individuals feel called to be married, pursue a secular job or profession, and serve the Church as an ordained minister. As a permanent deacon, they can do that. (Permanent deacons who serve the Church full-time are paid a wage to support themselves and their families.) Permanent deacons wear special clothing only at liturgical functions. Unmarried deacons may live in community or in a parish rectory; married deacons usually live with their family. More information about the permanent diaconate can be obtained from a permanent deacon, priest, or the diocesan vocation office.

. . . it is no **longer** I who live, but it is **Christ** who **lives** in me.

GALATIANS 2:20b

Scripture insights

1. Read 1 Timothy 3:8–12.
2. Which qualities did Paul say deacons and deaconesses needed? Which qualities do you think would be needed in those ministries today?

For discussion

1. Do you know any single or married person you think would make a good deacon— or deaconess, if that ministry were revived? Explain.
2. What rewards and challenges do you think would be involved in
   • being a permanent deacon?
   • being married to a permanent deacon?
   • being the son or daughter of a permanent deacon?
3. Why do you think one's spouse must consent to one's entering the permanent diaconate? If your spouse wanted to enter the diaconate, how do you think you'd respond? Explain.
4. Why do you think individuals choose to become permanent deacons? What do you find most and least appealing about that way of life?
5. Do you think you'd ever consider entering the permanent diaconate? Do you have any further questions about it? Explain.
6. Would you like to see the ministry of deaconess revived in the Catholic Church? Explain.

Review

1. What is a permanent deacon, and what main responsibilities does this ministry include?
2. What roles did deacons and deaconesses play in the early Church community? Could women ever again be deaconesses?
3. What's the difference between a transitional and a permanent deacon? Can a deacon ever stop being a deacon?
4. What liturgical functions may deacons perform and not perform?
5. Can a permanent deacon be married, or later become a priest? How may a permanent deacon's life differ from that of a priest?
6. How does a person become a permanent deacon?

One path to the priesthood

Individuals experience the call to their vocation in highly individual ways. Inner thoughts and feelings combine with outside experiences to draw the person to a particular way of life. Read how one priest discovered his vocation.[7] Then respond to the questions.

When I was in second grade, I had pneumonia a couple times. I was kind of a sickly little kid. But when I was in the hospital this guy in a funny brown dress would come up to see me every day, and he'd always make me laugh, no matter how bad I felt. When I got out of the hospital, people told me that the man in the funny brown dress was a priest from the parish. He was a Franciscan.

One day soon in school the teacher asked us to draw a picture of what we would like to be when we got older. I remember thinking how I'd love to be like that person and make people happy, so that's what I drew. That's really when the idea of becoming a priest got into my brain.

I kept up with it just a little, almost like an after-thought. Then when I was only in fifth grade I wrote a letter to the bishop and told him, "I think I'd like to be a priest." Well, the bishop thought that the letter came from a [student] in high school. So he sent the vocations director . . . to come out and talk to me. He came looking for a high school kid and instead found this little fifth grader! And that's how I first got in touch with the diocese.

Off and on over the years I kept in touch with [the vocations director], who was one of my best influences. During my [eleventh] year of high school I was on crutches awhile, which was dangerous because it gave me too much time to think! So I thought about it a lot and figured this was really what I was going to do. But I had this image of priests based on [old] movies. I thought priests were like that, and I was just me, so it would never work.

I had to try it, though, so I went to college seminary. There I got involved in soup kitchens and things like that. The best thing about college was finding out that the [movies' idea of the] robot-priest just didn't exist. There were all kinds of people from all kinds of backgrounds interested in all different things, but we all felt the same pull toward something greater.

I grew up in a Franciscan parish, and the Franciscan life of service to the poor and mission work still influences me a great deal. But I chose the diocesan priesthood because it stands for work in the parish. There are so many wonderful ministries in the Church, and in a way I'd like to experience all of them. But somehow for me it all comes back to the parish, and that's what I'm drawn to.

The joy is inexpressible. To work with people one-on-one and then bring them together to worship—it's what I feel the Lord would do.

For discussion

1. How would you describe the way this man discovered his call to be a priest?

2. How did he respond at each stage during his youth to the idea of becoming a priest?

3. As a high school student, what image of the priesthood did he have? How did that affect his thoughts about possibly becoming a priest?

4. How did this priest find out more about the priest-hood? What did he discover about it?

5. Why did he choose to be a diocesan rather than a religious order priest?

6. What happiness does this priest seem to experience in his vocation? Explain.

7. Are there any negative or stereotyped images of the priesthood that would stand in your way of thinking about becoming a priest? Explain.

What is religious life?

religious congregation, religious community
group of persons, formally recognized by the Catholic Church, who share a vowed communal form of religious life based on the evangelical counsels and their founder's guidelines

religious
a layperson, priest, or deacon who is consecrated to serve Jesus and the Catholic Church community by living a sacred commitment to poverty, celibacy, and obedience

hermit
one who lives a solitary life, usually for spiritual or religious reasons

Jesus didn't found a **religious congregation**, but he did invite some persons to follow him, join his work, and live as he lived. Since then, women and men **religious** have dedicated themselves to imitate Jesus by living the evangelical counsels of poverty, celibacy, and obedience. Some have done this by living a prayerful life alone as **hermits**. Others, led by someone whose Christian love and example inspired them, have formed **religious communities** as a means of living the consecrated life.

Each religious order has a unique spirit and guidelines based on the aspects of Jesus' teaching that its founder emphasized. For instance, some religious congregations help those who are sick or poor, while others concentrate on teaching the gospel message. The community's formal guidelines help its members discern how they should live, pray, work, and dress to accomplish their ministry effectively. Those guidelines change to adapt to changing needs and times. All religious communities are centered around prayer, community life, and service to others.

The vowed commitment to religious life is sacred, but not a permanent sacrament as is Marriage or Holy Orders. So those who do leave religious life for one good reason or another may receive special Church permission to be released from their vows. They are then free to pursue the vocation of a lay single or married person.

Occasionally, harmful religious fanatics, cults, and crooks try to portray themselves as legitimate religious groups. That's one reason the Catholic Church must formally approve a group's way of life as representing what Jesus taught and Catholics believe. Catholic religious communities generally work with and are subject to the authority of the local bishops.

Overall, membership in religious communities has been declining. Many religious communities struggle with how to support their elderly members without the financial input of sufficient working members. A collection is held each year to assist retired religious who often taught or did other works of service for only enough money to survive on at the time. In their time of need, they deserve our help; they have generously contributed so much to the Church and its members.

Who lives the religious life?

Clergy   Laity

Some religious communities have both clerical and lay members.

Some religious communities have all lay members (sisters and brothers).

Interview

Choose one.

1. Choose a religious community that has members in your area. By personal interviews and/or researching the Internet, find out about the community's spirit, goals, lifestyle, ministries, and so on. Write a one-page paper and report to the class on your findings.

2. Interview a priest, permanent deacon, or religious sister or brother about what his or her vocation means and what is most rewarding and challenging about that way of life.

3. Interview one or more elderly priests or members of a religious community about their experiences in ministry. Then write a one-page paper or a song or poem on what it means to be "Father," "Sister," or "Brother" to others.

For discussion

1. Why do religious communities need to keep changing with the times? How can they best adapt now and in the future?

2. With which religious communities are you most familiar? What do you know about them?

"Come and see."

JOHN 1:39

Some religious communities are phasing out, and others are combining in federations. Where there's no reasonable hope that a religious community will continue to grow, it is directed by the Church to accept no new members. Interestingly, religious communities have actually seen a revival in some Protestant Churches. And Catholic communities are still increasing in many less-developed countries.

Religious life will continue to change and assume new forms and ministries to adapt to the needs of the times. Some religious communities may become large again. Others will die out, and new ones will arise to meet special needs. But there will always be those who consecrate themselves to God in the unselfish service of others. Wherever human needs would otherwise go unmet, God will call people to respond. No way of life is always easy, and no one lives his or her vocation perfectly. But religious men and women generally experience deep happiness and fulfillment in their vocation.

Steps in becoming a religious

Final profession of vows—for life

Temporary profession of vows (usually 3 to 6 years, or more)—being fully involved in the community's life and ministry and further evaluating one's ability to be happy and effective in the religious life

Novitiate (1 to 2 years)—praying, studying, and examining religious life more deeply and assessing whether one is suited to live this vocation

Candidacy (1 to 2 years or more)—studying about religious life and participating in the community's lifestyle and works to be sure one fully understands and is ready for such a commitment

Contact programs of initial inquiry into religious life—meeting informally with members to learn about their community's lifestyle, spirit, and work

Living the religious life

God has loved us first (see 1 John 4:10). By Baptism, all Christians are specially consecrated to God. No Christian vocation is holier or higher than another. **All vocations are valuable blessings and equally holy paths to God and eternal life.** Consecrated religious follow Jesus' teaching and example by being unattached to material goods. They also remain single for the sake of God's kingdom. They devote their lives to serving those in need.

In a special ceremony, men and women religious **vow** to live the three **evangelical counsels** of poverty, chastity (in this case, celibacy), and obedience in imitation of Jesus. (Some religious take an additional vow, generally stability, meaning remaining in one place, as in a monastery.) Religious pray and reflect daily on the Scriptures, and try to participate in the Eucharist frequently. Their efforts to become more like Christ inspire us to live our vocations more generously and completely. Like all vocations, the religious life is a special gift and calling from God, a calling to which not everyone is suited. Within a religious community, clergy (priests or deacons) and lay religious have different roles but equal status.

vow
make a sacred promise to God

evangelical counsels
vows made in imitation of Jesus as a means of living his gospel message

Journal entry
1. Do you view your vocation right now as a valuable blessing?
2. Do you view it as an equally holy path to God and eternal life?
3. In your present vocation, how might you be more attentive to those in need?
4. How might being less attached to material goods give you greater freedom in your life now?

Living the vows

habit
distinctive, often uniform clothing worn by members of a religious community

In vowing poverty, consecrated religious detach themselves from the desire to own material things. Jesus identified with those who were poor; consecrated religious seek to do likewise. Being poor can be humiliating, degrading, and depressing. Choosing religious poverty proclaims that all persons are valuable—not for what they have, but for who they are.

Vowing poverty means sharing and living simply, with one's heart unattached to material things. Religious use what they need and share the rest of their resources with others, especially those who are poor. Yet they consider themselves among the richest people in the world. Their lifestyle reminds us that love is the only lasting treasure.

Members of religious communities originally dressed in the ordinary clothing styles of the times. When their attire didn't change with the times, it became a

distinguishing **habit** and a sign of their consecration to God and service of others. When laws prohibited priests from dressing distinctively, they began wearing business suits with simple Roman-style collars. Those, too, eventually became their habitual dress. Today, religious and clergy dress simply, modestly, and according to the needs of their ministries. In our style-conscious society, their clothing makes a religious rather than a fashion statement.

Even while greeting world leaders, Mother Teresa inspired others by dressing in the simple sari of the poor she served.

Scripture insights

1. Search the Gospels for examples of how Jesus' lifestyle and teaching about material goods helped others and challenged the people of his day.

2. Read 1 Corinthians 7:32–35. How do Paul's words pertain to the ways people live their vocations today? Do you think what he said still applies? Explain.

For discussion

1. Suppose that you want to found a religious community based on responding as Jesus would to the needs in your local area. To what particular ministry would it be dedicated? Why?

2. If you were interested in becoming a consecrated religious, which type of religious community would interest you most? Explain why.

3. How do the media usually portray consecrated religious and their way of life? Do you think any of those portrayals unfairly stereotype religious men or women? Explain.

4. What's your response to this student's question: "Why just be a brother instead of going all the way and becoming a priest?"

5. Might religious sisters or brothers one day be allowed to marry? Explain.

6. What do you think you'd find most rewarding about the religious way of life? Most difficult or challenging? Explain.

. . . as having nothing, and yet possessing everything.

2 CORINTHIANS 6:10

Why can't religious brothers or sisters marry? By giving up marriage and romantic involvements, consecrated religious free their heart and energies to focus more on loving God in all humanity. They can go where they're most needed and can share their unselfish, unconditional love with many persons. Living a celibate life isn't always easy. Celibate persons do get lonely and they do have sexual feelings. But they appropriately express affection in non-romantic ways. Their faith in God, their companions in religious life, and other close friends together form their personal support system.

One important difference between religious life and the priesthood is that the vow of celibacy is essential to religious life. It's integral to the commitment religious brothers or sisters choose. For religious to marry would be like saying one could choose to be single and married at the same time! One may, however, be a priest or deacon and live the religious life. If women are ever again permitted to be deaconesses, some religious women might be among the most qualified and willing to serve in that liturgical ministry.

Every vocation involves some self-sacrifice. By vowing obedience, men and women religious give themselves for others unselfishly, as Jesus did. Men and women religious try to discern God's will in the needs of others and to be open to where God's Spirit is leading them. Sometimes that means sacrificing their preferences for the greater good of the community and those it serves. But individual religious also have the whole community's strength and support behind them in their work.

Living in community

Most consecrated religious live a community lifestyle, or one centered on a religious community. It's a way of life with others who together strive to be of service to others. Like the earliest Christians, religious seek to be of one heart and purpose and share a common faith vision, common goals, values, and ideals. They become as sisters and brothers to one another, as well as to those they serve. The Church is a community of believers, and the world must become a human community. In seeking to form a truly Christian community, religious hope to show how human harmony is possible by living Christian ideals.

While diocesan clergy usually minister within one territory, consecrated religious may serve God's people throughout the country or the world. To choose a religious community, one should look for a community whose spirit, lifestyle, and ministries are compatible with one's own needs, interests, and abilities. There are lots of choices!

Religious life isn't an escape from the world, from other people, or from personal problems. It's not just a "me and Jesus" relationship. Religious devote their lives to helping the Church and the human community through their prayer and work of bringing Jesus' message and love to others. One person doing good can make a difference. A community devoted to the same work is an even more powerful spiritual force for good. Together, religious women and men can accomplish what one person could never do alone.

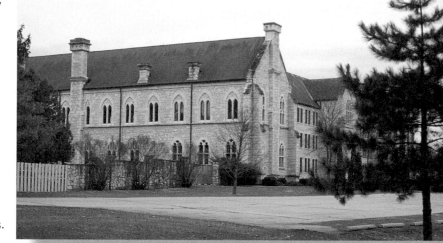

Types of religious communities

Active communities (sisters or "nuns," brothers)
- Members live a more active life.
- Members pray, but spend most time working at various ministries in the world.
- Members take vows of poverty, celibacy, obedience.

Contemplative communities (nuns, monks)
- Members live a more cloistered life that emphasizes formal prayer, silence, and solitude more than active service.
- Members take vows of poverty, celibacy, obedience.

Monastic communities
- Members may combine formal prayer with service to others that is usually performed within or near the monastery.

Other options

Societies of common life
- Members live a community lifestyle dedicated to similar objectives and values as consecrated religious. But they are not members of religious life, since they do not make formal vows.

Secular institutes
- Members are groups of men and women laypersons and clergy who vow privately to live by the evangelical counsels.
- Priest members live and usually work in priestly ministry. Most lay members work at regular jobs.
- Members seek to enlighten and enrich society's secular institutions and structures with Christian values.
- Members do not belong to religious life, since they do not make public vows or live the common life.

Some of the works consecrated religious do

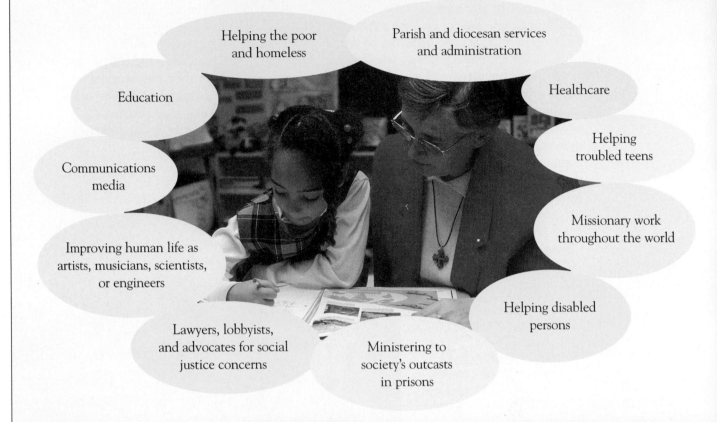

- Helping the poor and homeless
- Parish and diocesan services and administration
- Education
- Healthcare
- Helping troubled teens
- Communications media
- Missionary work throughout the world
- Improving human life as artists, musicians, scientists, or engineers
- Helping disabled persons
- Lawyers, lobbyists, and advocates for social justice concerns
- Ministering to society's outcasts in prisons

For discussion

1. What do you think would be most difficult about living with a community of adults as religious do? What do you think would be most beneficial about it?

2. What are the differences between a religious order priest and a diocesan priest? Do you know priests who live each of those lifestyles? Explain.

3. How would you advise a friend who wanted to join religious life but didn't know how to figure out which religious community to join?

4. Which of the ministries religious women and men do would you find most appealing? Least appealing? Explain.

5. What are missionaries? What do you think would be most rewarding about being a missionary? What do you think you'd find most challenging about it? Explain.

Review

1. Did Jesus found religious life? What is a consecrated religious?

2. What types of religious life and religious communities are there in the Catholic Church? In what ministries are their members involved?

3. How did today's religious orders begin and what is unique about each of them?

4. What are the stages in becoming a religious, and what is the purpose of each one?

5. Is any vocation holier or higher than another? Explain.

6. What are the evangelical counsels? How do those in religious life try to live each of them?

7. Why and how do in religious life live a community lifestyle?

In summary

Jesus confirmed that all vocations are holy. Clergy preach Jesus' message and continue his sacred actions in the sacraments and humble service to others. The Sacrament of Holy Orders is a permanent gift and commitment that empowers priests for their ministry. Bishops teach, guide, and meet the spiritual needs of the people and ordain priests and deacons. Priests may be diocesan (secular), or belong to a religious congregation. Some Catholic priests are married, but most must promise lifelong celibacy. Candidates prepare to become priests in a seminary program of religious study and pastoral ministry.

Deacons and deaconesses contributed greatly in the early Church. Today permanent deacons are sacramentally ordained to share in certain priestly ministries. The diaconate can be a transitional step to the priesthood, or it can be a permanent vocation. Single or married men can become permanent deacons, but single deacons must remain celibate. Permanent deacons may dress, live, and hold secular jobs as do other laypersons.

Those in religious life serve Jesus and the Church by vowing to live the evangelical counsels. Religious generally live in communities based on their founder's spirit and on changing needs. Some religious communities include both laypersons and clergy, and becoming a religious involves a several-stage process. All religious pray and work—some in active ministries, and others in a more cloistered life of prayer and work. Religious have greatly contributed to humanity through their unselfish service to others. A way to discern your vocation is to assess your ability to live the way of life happily and generously.

Key concepts

anointed
archdiocese
becoming a priest
becoming a religious
bishop
celibacy
chrism
clergy
consecrated life
deacon—permanent or transitional
deaconesses

diaconate
diocese
diocesan (secular) priest
evangelical counsels
grace
laypersons
living religious life
married clergy
men and women religious
pastoral ministry
priests, priesthood

religious communities, orders, congregations
religious life
religious order priest
Rite of Ordination
Sacrament of Holy Orders
seminary
vestment
vocation
vows
women and the Catholic priesthood

Endnotes

1. Joan Chittister OSB, "Seven Surprising Ways to Find Holiness in Your Daily Life," in *Vision '91: The Annual Religious Vocation Discernment Handbook* (Evanston, IL: Berry Publishing Services, Inc., 1991), 96.

2. See the teachings contained in the "Decree on the Ministry and Life of Priests," The Documents of Vatican II.

3. See *The Documents of Vatican II*, "Decree on the Ministry and Life of Priests," Chapter 2, section 1, #5, and Chapter 1, section 1, #4.

4. Rev. Joseph Gagnon, Archdiocese of Detroit, in "What Does a Diocesan Priest Do All Day?" in *Vision '91: The Annual Religious Vocation Discernment Handbook* (Berry Publishing Services, Inc., 701 Main Street; Evanston, IL 60202, 708/869-1573 - FAX-869-4825, 1991), 44.

5. *Vision '91*, 44.

6. *The Roman Pontifical* (Washington, DC: USCC 1978), Chapter 8, Ordination of Deacons, #14.

7. *Vision '91*.

CHAPTER 9

The Meaning of Marriage

SCRIPTURE

O LORD, you have searched me and known me.
You know when I sit down and when I rise up;
  you discern my thoughts from far away.
You search out my path and my lying down,
  and are acquainted with all my ways.
Even before a word is on my tongue,
  O LORD, you know it completely.
You hem me in, behind and before,
  and lay your hand upon me. . .
For it was you who formed my inward parts;
  you knit me together in my mother's womb.
I praise you, for I am fearfully and wonderfully made.
  Wonderful are your works;
that I know very well.
  My frame was not hidden from you,
when I was being made in secret,
  intricately woven in the depths of the earth.
Your eyes beheld my unformed substance.
In your book were written
  all the days that were formed for me,
  when none of them as yet existed. . .
Search me, O God, and know my heart . . .
  and lead me in the way everlasting.

PSALM 139:1–5, 13–16, 23A, 24B

CHAPTER PREVIEW

What marriage is and means

   The right and wrong reasons for marrying

   How the institution of marriage has developed and changed

   Marriage as a sacred covenant

How individuals can help ensure the success of their marriage

   Civil and religious requirements for marrying

   How couples can assess their compatibility before marrying

   The engagement period and being ready to marry

PRAYER

Loving God,

We thank you for the gift of love in our lives.

Help us appreciate those we love

   and not take each other for granted.

You know our hearts and what we need to satisfy our deepest
   longings.

Give us the courage and determination to not abandon our
   high ideals,

   but to live and achieve them in our relationships with one
     another.

Enlighten and strengthen all those who are preparing to marry,

that they may make wise decisions about their future together.

This we pray in Christ's name. Amen.

What marriage means

Like most people you will probably marry eventually. How can you make your marriage lasting and happy? How can you avoid becoming a divorce statistic? Marriage is unique for each couple. Nevertheless, the valuable insights others have learned from their joys and mistakes can help prepare you to build a loving, lifelong marriage.

Why marry?

Even if you think you won't marry, you should know enough about marriage to make that choice intelligently. Many insights about compatibility and making a marriage work also apply to other relationships. So let's start at the beginning—with why people do and don't want to marry.

It's good that people are now able to remain single longer or permanently without feeling apologetic about it. But there is increasing concern worldwide that too many people are viewing marriage as optional and unnecessary—even if they intend to have children. Although the number of teenage single mothers has decreased, more older women are deliberately choosing to be mothers apart from marriage. In fact, many women in our society are conceiving or bearing their first child when they are older.

Many sociologists believe that marriage as a social institution is in transition. This change may be partly due to the increased independence of both men and women. Anyone can pop a frozen dinner into the microwave. Men do their share of laundry and other chores. Women are better prepared for the workplace, have more job opportunities, and no longer must depend on a man for financial survival.

But those observations don't address the real reason so many individuals downplay the idea of marrying: **fear**. They've experienced the trauma of their parents' divorce and have seen their friends and other family members go through painful divorces. Or they've lived in a home where their parents' marriage was unhappy or abusive. They don't want that to happen to them! They may have been through unsuccessful, hurtful relationships themselves and are scared that marriage wouldn't succeed for them either.

Some people do buy into the social attitude that makes single parenting seem more ideal than it is in reality. Hollywood stars may boast about having their children out of wedlock. But ask other single parents—and their children—if it wouldn't be much better to having a loving marriage and a happy family life that includes both parents. Their answer is almost always "yes." Yet more and more people are viewing their personal ideal of a life-long happy marriage (which is also the Church's, by the way) as unattainable.

If you want to marry in the future, what can you do to overcome such fears and realize your dream of a happy, lasting marriage? These things are key:

- Understand what marriage is and means.
- Know how to find a suitable marriage partner.
- Know how to make your marriage work.
- Be determined to do all you can to build a happy, lasting marriage.

This chapter and the next two chapters will focus on those four essentials. As you read about and discuss the topics, do examine the ideas, attitudes, and fears you have regarding marriage. Don't give up on your ideals. Learn how to achieve them.

Journal entry

1. What is your personal ideal of a happy marriage?

2. What are your main fears about marrying?

3. What do you think is the reason for those fears?

4. If you marry in the future, what is one thing you could do to help overcome your fears and achieve your ideal

For discussion

1. What conflicting views, attitudes, or feelings do you think people have about marriage? Explain.

2. Do you think you might want to marry in the future? What are your negative thoughts, feelings, and fears about marrying? Explain.

3. What is your reaction to the number of deliberate out-of-wedlock births among adult single women? Why?

4. How has divorce and its frequency affected your perception of marriage? Why?

5. Do you think marriage as an institution is in trouble? Explain.

Marriage in the Jewish-Christian tradition

Judeo-Christian tradition
The heritage of beliefs and practices dating from the ancient Hebrews to modern-day Jews and Christians

dowry
money, goods, or animals paid to compensate for the loss of the woman's labor from her father's household

egalitarian
characterized by equal rights for every person

To better understand current ideals, practices, and attitudes about marriage, we need to look at how they began and developed historically. No one knows just when or how the institution of marriage itself first started. Anthropologists propose that to primitive humans it may have amounted to little more than physical mating.

The Bible's story of the first humans was probably written hundreds of thousands of years after the first people inhabited our planet! The story wasn't intended to present facts about how human relationships started. It was meant to present important religious beliefs and truths about what relationships mean. Many of our society's marriage customs and ideas do derive from the **Judeo-Christian tradition** and how its religious beliefs developed in history. As we'll see, your personal ideals of marriage are probably rooted in what Jesus taught.

Even ancient cultures recognized marriage and family as important social units. But their perceptions and practices about marriage certainly differed from ours! Throughout Western civilization, women had few rights of their own until modern times. Marriages were generally arranged by parents. Women were considered their fathers' property until given to a husband in exchange for a **dowry**.

In the early Roman Empire, a groom would carry his new bride over the threshold of his home to show that she was now part of his household and that he, not her father, was now her master. He gave her a piece of cake to symbolize that she now shared in the responsibility of worshiping his household gods.

With occasional exceptions, the couples of ancient times didn't marry out of love. Marriage was (and still is in some cultures) a contract a man makes to obtain a woman who could bear children and help with the work. In most ancient cultures men could divorce their wives at will. (Women generally couldn't initiate the divorce.) Some cultures still practice polygamy or view marriage as a convenience arrangement of mutual help in physical and financial survival.

Just as some of our wedding customs reflect ancient traditions, so present attitudes about marriage are influenced by the past. Our society is still trying to more equally apply marriage and family laws to men and women. Spouses are working to overcome traditional patriarchal influences and attitudes and treat each other as equal partners. History has indeed influenced our perceptions of marriage. Only recently has humanity come to view marriage in the ideal way Jesus taught—as an exclusive lifetime commitment between two equals who share a sacred bond of love. But we must continue to grow in understanding and applying what that means.

Humanity's understanding of marriage

In ancient times (such as in Abraham's biblical clan)

- Marriage was a **patriarchal** (headed by men) property arrangement.
- **Polygamy** (having more than one wife) was the norm.
- Few practiced **polyandry** (having more than one husband).

Today in our society

- **Egalitarian** (equal partnership) marriages based on love become more common.
- Many marriages are still **somewhat patriarchal**.
- **Monogamy** (having one spouse) is the norm and the only acceptable practice.
- **Bigamy** (knowingly marrying again while one is already legally married) is a criminal offense.

Scripture insights

Read the story of Jacob and Rachel—Genesis 29:1-28.

1. How does that story portray ancient practices regarding marriage?
2. How does it reflect the new ideal of marriage God was beginning to reveal? How does that new ideal compare with your view of love and marriage?

For discussion

1. How have society's present attitudes about marriage been influenced by the past? Why is it important to understand how history has influenced your perceptions of marriage?
2. How did Jesus view marriage? When did humanity come to share that view of marriage—or do you think it has? Explain.
3. How does Jesus' view of marriage compare with what most couples today ideally want for their marriage? How does it compare with your ideal about marriage? Explain.

Covenant—Promise of lasting love

People usually hope their marriage will be a loving, faithful, permanent relationship. Yet some brides and grooms enter marriage thinking secretly, "If things don't work out, I can always get a divorce." Given that attitude, it's no wonder so many marriages fail. Two people can't be wholeheartedly dedicated to making their marriage work if one of them is ready to head for the door when major problems arise!

Marriage isn't just a hope. **Marriage is a sacred, solemn promise—a covenant, like the one God has made with us.** The Old Testament tells how God covenanted with the ancient Hebrews—and through them with all humanity. In that covenant God promises to be present with us always—never to leave us. God, who loves us faithfully and unconditionally, invites us into a lasting relationship.

> "... and I will be your God, and you shall be my people ...."
> JEREMIAH 7:23B

In the sacred vocation of marriage, one plus one always equals more than just the two people in love. Marriage is a primary way people love God and share God's life and love with each other, their family, and the world. Marriage is a way God's love reaches the couple and everyone their married lives lovingly touch. God doesn't love us just a little, or sometimes, or only when we're good—but completely and always. The fidelity and permanence of marriage are to reflect that lasting, faithful, complete way God loves each of us and wants us to love one another. In marriage, the partners' mutual promise to love each other faithfully for life symbolizes and reflects God's complete, lasting love for each of us.

So when people say marriage isn't the wedding license or the ceremony, they're absolutely right.

Marriage is the couple's mutual promise of a lifetime of faithful love. Marriage is a commitment that "we'll be there for each other—for richer or for poorer, in sickness and in health, in good times and in bad, as long as we both shall live."

For a marriage to work, both spouses must be completely determined to make it work! They must both believe "This is for better or for worse, until death do us part." In fact, maybe it would be better to talk about determination than commitment regarding marriage. Commitment can sometimes seem more like a burdensome obligation that, once made, a person is chained to and must see through, like it or not. But determination in the commitment is the ongoing attitude needed to achieve your desired goal. That mutual determination is what enables couples to build a marriage that does succeed.

What's the difference between marriage as a civil contract and marriage as a sacred covenant? A civil contract is originated by and can be ended by people. A sacred covenant is far more. The authors of the U.S. Declaration of Independence recognized that when they wrote the document that sparked the beginning of freedom and democracy in the Western Hemisphere. They emphatically made it clear that freedom and human rights aren't the products of brilliant human minds, but are given to us by our Creator! That's precisely why the permanent and sacred gifts of freedom, human rights, and equality are so valuable and must never be taken away by anyone. Marriage is likewise a sacred bond of intimate mutual love whose meaning and permanence originate with God.

The Catholic Church holds that **every true marriage is a freely chosen, permanent, sacred covenant** whereby two people choose each other over all others. That's why the Church recognizes all true marriages as valid and sacred, whether or not the parties are Catholic. It's also why the Church doesn't recognize as valid those "marriages" into which people were pressured or coerced against their will, or in which either party couldn't make a free and permanent commitment. Words, ceremonies, and licenses don't create a marriage. Only a couple's free and mutual promise to faithfully accept, understand, and love each other for a lifetime together constitutes a marriage. The community of love that marriage initiates doesn't just benefit the married couple. It provides stability and a future for their children, for society, and for the world.

Just as a couple's marriage originates with God, so the couple needs God's help to keep the marriage alive through the years. Those who see their marriage as rooted in God experience deeper strength, comfort, and joy in knowing that their love is in Love's hands. They realize that they're more than just two married people—that their love flows from something much larger than themselves. Through their loving commitment to—their covenant with—each other, they share in God's infinite, everlasting love. By their loving determination, they build together a happy marriage that does reflect the Love that lasts.

Scripture insights

Read the second creation story in Genesis 2–3. What does the story show about human loneliness and God's response to it?

For discussion

1. Share your positive thoughts and feelings about marrying.

2. What is the problem with entering into marriage with the attitude that if things don't work out, you can always get divorced? Would you want the person you marry to have that attitude? Explain.

3. If you chose to marry, what would you want your marriage vows to mean to you and to your spouse? Why?

4. How would you respond to someone who feels marriage is "just a piece of paper"?

5. In what sense does building a successful marriage require determination and commitment? What kind of determination would you want you and your spouse to have? Explain.

6. What "crazy risks" are involved in religious faith? In marrying in the Catholic sense? What are the alternatives to accepting those risks, and why are Catholics and many others convinced that it is so worthwhile to accept the risks?

7. What part would you want your beliefs about God and religion to play in your marriage? Why?

Review

1. How have social attitudes about the institution of marriage changed? What are some of the reasons for the changes? How have they affected society?

2. What is the origin of the institution of marriage and our society's ideas and customs about it?

3. Why is marriage a sacred covenant? Why is viewing marriage as a sacred covenant different from viewing marriage as a purely civil contract?

4. What kind of pledge are marriage vows meant to be?

5. Why does the Church hold that to enter into a true marriage, the couple must freely and deliberately choose to marry each other? What relationships does the Church therefore not recognize as valid marriages?

6. How can and should a couple's belief in God enrich their marriage?

The covenant choice

Read the following about another decision many couples must make before they marry. Then respond to the questions.

In some places, a new "covenant marriage" law is making it harder for married couples to break up. Before a couple can marry legally, the new law requires them to see a counselor. In addition, they must decide what kind of legal relationship they intend to enter—a standard marriage or a more legally binding covenant marriage. The standard marriage would enable the couple to obtain a quick and easy "no-fault" divorce, should they ever want one. To divorce under the covenant marriage option, one of the partners would have to prove in court that the other party was abusive or alcoholic, committed adultery, abandoned the spouse, or was in prison for a felony. Divorcing for less important reasons would require waiting and living apart for two years.

The lawmakers say the purpose of the new marriage law is to prevent couples from entering into bad marriages and to help them do all they can to save a marriage that's in trouble. Critics say that task should be up to the couples, their families, and their religion—not the government. The lawmakers counter that marriage is important to our social fabric. When marriages fail—especially when children are involved—it affects all of society. Ultimately, they say, keeping marriages together is society's business. They claim that the new law is designed to support the institution of marriage. In many places, ending a marriage legally certainly is much easier than breaking an auto lease or a contract to paint the house!

Some couples say the covenant marriage law makes them stop and think about what they really want in marriage and about how serious the commitment is. They say they like the added support the law gives to marriage. Others are afraid the law will trap people in unhappy, loveless marriages. They maintain that divorce is painful and costly enough without added legal fees to try proving that one's spouse is blameworthy. Furthermore, not all individuals can prove that their spouse has been abusive. Above all, the law's critics claim, children will be caught in the middle.

Some Christian Churches are requiring their members to choose the covenant marriage option. (While supporting the permanence of marriage and requiring some pre-marital preparation, Catholic officials prefer to leave reasonable legal requirements up to the state.) The law does support some of the values about marriage that religion has long upheld. Other religious leaders are concerned that the covenant marriage option will unfairly brand divorced persons. They think the covenant marriage option may pressure couples into making an even bigger mistake by entering a type of commitment for which they're not ready. Whatever the merits and drawbacks, more places are considering adopting such a covenant marriage law. The covenant marriage option is certainly provoking interesting discussions among engaged couples!

For discussion

1. What do you think of the reasons given above for and against the covenant marriage law? What do you think are the pros and cons of such laws? Explain.

2. If you lived where covenant marriage laws were in effect, would you want to choose that option for your marriage? How would you feel and respond if your intended spouse absolutely refused to even consider the option? Explain fully.

3. Would you, or do you, support the idea of a covenant marriage law? What position do you think the Catholic Church should take regarding such laws? Explain.

Preparing to marry

In just one community, six couples obtained a license to marry, while 219 couples were granted a divorce! No doubt the divorcing couples had thought they were ready to marry when they applied for their marriage license. But the statistics sadly announced that they were wrong.

The high divorce rate in our society shows that couples often marry without being ready for a permanent commitment. Some suggest it should be harder for couples to marry than to divorce! Marriage is sacred and important. The Catholic Church—and many other Christian Churches—have established guidelines to help couples prepare more meaningfully for marriage.

When couples are ill-suited for each other, marry for the wrong reasons, or aren't adequately prepared for married life, their marriages are bound to have serious problems. The rest of this chapter will explore some of the main compatibility areas couples should examine before they marry. It will also consider some of the sound and unsound reasons for getting married and ways couples can better prepare

themselves for marriage. But first let's consider the main reasons people have for marrying and why some of these reasons lead to a happy married life, while others are almost always disastrous.

Love does not consist in gazing at each **other** but in **looking** together in the same **direction**.

ANTOINE DE SAINT-EXUPERY

The reasons people marry

Unhappily

We're deeply in love.
Love, strong attraction, and good intentions aren't enough! We could each fall in love with or be sexually and romantically attracted to many people—but we might not be compatible. Marrying such a person could be a nightmare.

I feel secure and accepted only when I'm with her. Without him, I don't feel loved or happy.
Marriages must be based on free choice—not need—or the couple won't be happy and won't survive. Unhappy, insecure people bring their unhappiness and insecurities with them.

I'm pregnant and he's willing to marry me.
Marriages entered into mainly because of pregnancy are among the least likely to be happy and the most likely to fail.

My friends are all married and starting families. My biological clock is ticking and I want to have a child before I'm much older.
The responsibilities involved in raising children are too much of a strain on a marriage that lacks a strong, mature love.

It would make my folks happy. I'm tired of getting bugged about when I'm going to "settle down and marry."
Those who marry to satisfy others become dissatisfied when their own needs aren't met.

As least I'd be on my own and not under my parents' control anymore.
Age is critical: Couples who marry while either partner is a teenager are over three times as likely to divorce—and about three times as fast! Marriage shouldn't be an attempt to escape parents or grow up. Thankfully, most people in our society don't marry until their mid- or late-twenties. By then, they've entered a career, been independent of their parents, and gained important self-knowledge and life experience.

I'm tired of playing the dating game.
No way of life should be chosen as a means of escaping problems or unhappiness.

It would be great to have a spouse to help take care of the house. Besides, I've been issued an ultimatum that our relationship will end unless we marry.

Happily

I could be happy on my own or find someone else to love. But this is the person with whom I want to share the rest of my life.

AND

I'm happy and secure, and I want to share my happiness and contentment with this person.

AND

We seem compatible enough to enjoy spending our lives together.

AND

This is the person with whom I want to have and raise children.

AND

We respect and genuinely care about each other.

AND

More than just in love, we're also best friends.

AND

We communicate really well with each other.

For discussion

1. What is dangerous about the myth that there is only one person in the world with whom you could fall in love and live happily? What is the reality?

2. What part do you think love, romance, and sexual attraction should and shouldn't play in deciding whether to marry someone? Explain.

3. Give five examples of marriages based on need. Why don't need-based marriages work?

4. What is your response to each of the above good reasons to marry? Explain.

5. What are some other poor reasons for marrying? Why are they poor reasons?

6. Why is one's age at the time of marriage such a significant factor in marital happiness?

Requirements for marrying

lawfully
according to officially required procedure

validly
truly, genuinely

There is a crucial difference between marrying **lawfully** and marrying **validly**. If a couple isn't married validly, they aren't considered married at all. A valid marriage must correspond to what the Church or the State views as essential to marriage. Marrying lawfully means that the marriage is both contracted validly and according to officially correct procedure. Some Church and State requirements for validity and lawfulness are similar, while others differ.

Before civil law or the Church will recognized a couple's marriage as valid, certain basic requirements must be met. That's because marrying is a social act, not just a private decision. A couple's marriage affects relatives and friends, religious communities, society, and even the world. Marriage also has legal implications, as newlyweds notice when they find themselves jointly responsible for their wedding bills!

Requirements for marrying validly

✚ Church   ✔ State   ★ both Church and State

★ Free, mutual consent

★ Minimum age (✚ nineteen, in our society; ✔ Civil age requirements usually range from 14 to 21, depending on parental consent.)

✚ Intent that the marriage is permanent—will last until the death of either partner

✚ Unconditional pledge to love and remain faithful to each other for life

✚ Intent to remain open to having and lovingly raising children, if that is God's will (✔ Married couples assume legal responsibilities to raise and responsibly care for any children they may have; intending to do that is not required to marry validly.)

★ Not close relatives (definitely may not be immediate relatives, such as parent-child and sister-brother; laws regarding other relatives vary in different places and cultures)

★ Freedom to marry (must not already be married—bigamy is prohibited)

★ Must be free from other impediments that would prevent a true marriage (being forced or pressured into marriage, too young to understand what marriage is and means, and so on)

Certain marriage requirements differ from state to state.

Requirements for marrying lawfully

✚ Church ✔ State ★ both Church and State

★ Minimum age

✚ Marriage preparation (instruction in the meaning of marriage for Catholics, communication, sexuality, handling finances, and other important areas of married living)

★ Public notified of the forthcoming marriage (✚ **banns** of marriage announced in church)

✔ Pre-marriage waiting period (✚ completion of the marriage preparation program)

✔ License to marry

✔ Certification of being free of certain transmissible diseases

✔ Certification of fulfilling previous marital obligations (such as child support, for those who are divorced)

★ Duly authorized official witnesses (✚ Proper permission must be obtained to marry without an official Catholic minister—usually the pastor or pastor's delegate—and two witnesses present.)

★ Proper documentation (✚ such as certificates of Baptism and Confirmation; ✔ birth certificate, and so on)

✚ Baptism and, if possible, Confirmation of the Catholic party (participating in the Sacraments of Reconciliation and the Eucharist is strongly urged)

✚ Proper permission from Catholic Church officials if a Catholic is marrying a non-Catholic or if the ceremony will be somewhere other than the Catholic's parish church

---

Every person has a natural right to marry. Providing that they meet the basic requirements, it's up to the couple, not the Church, to determine whether they're ready to marry. To help engaged couples assess that wisely, Catholic parishes offer preparation programs for those planning to marry in the Catholic Church. Couples must participate in such a program for several months to a year before marrying and should allow for that when setting their wedding date. They usually find it a meaningful, enlightening experience. Such Church requirements aren't meant to make things harder, but to help the couple make a marriage commitment that will be more meaningful, happy, and successful.

Research assignment

Write a two-page paper addressing these questions:

1. What legal documents must a couple formally complete before marrying? Why?

2. What must Catholics know and affirm before getting married in the Catholic Church community? Why?

3. Why do the civil laws and Church policies regarding the celebration of marriage vary from place to place? How could you find out which laws and policies would apply to you in marrying?

4. Why should Catholics be sacramentally confirmed before they marry? How does the Sacrament of Confirmation relate to the marriage commitment they are making?

For discussion

1. If you were in charge of planning a marriage preparation program for engaged couples, what would you include? Why?

2. Which of the civil and the Church requirements for marrying make the most sense to you? What would happen if those things weren't required? Explain.

3. Why do you think special permission is needed

   • For a citizen of this country to marry a non-citizen?

   • For the Catholic community to celebrate a Catholic's marriage to a non-Catholic?

4. Is there anything else you think civil law or the Church should require of couples before they marry? Explain.

What about the law?

Read these comments people sometimes have about marriage requirements. Then respond to the discussion questions.

1. Everybody has a right to marry if they want to. So why should you have to get a license for it?

2. What business does the priest have asking couples all sorts of personal questions before they get married—like about whether they were married before? It's nobody else's business.

3. Why do you have to present your birth certificate before you get married? You're here—doesn't that prove you were born? And why do you need your baptismal certificate? If you've been going to the same parish church for the last fifteen years, doesn't everybody know you're a Christian? Doesn't the pastor trust you?

4. Is it true that the priest makes you swear a secret oath on the Bible before you get married in the Catholic Church? What does this oath really contain?

5. Why does the non-Catholic partner have to satisfy Catholic requirements before marrying a Catholic in the Catholic Church? Why can't each party just fulfill his or her own Church's or religion's requirements?

6. If the couple marries each other, then why does the Catholic Church say a priest has to marry them?

7. If you don't follow all the rules in getting married, does that mean you're not really married in the eyes of Church or State?

8. Why do you have to be a certain age to get married? Some teenagers are more mature than some adults in their forties!

9. Why can't you marry your uncle or your first cousin? What right does anybody have to tell you whom you can or can't marry?

10. People have to learn how to drive before they get a driver's license. So why don't they have to learn anything about being married in order to get a marriage license?

Review

1. What serious challenges is the institution of marriage now facing?

2. What reasons should individuals have—and not have—for marrying each other?

3. What is the difference between the civil and Catholic views of marriage? Between requirements for marrying validly and for marrying lawfully?

4. What does the Church consider essential in order for a couple to enter into a true marriage?

For discussion

1. What is your response to each of the previous questions and comments? Explain.

2. What do you think the minimum age required by civil law should be for couples to marry with their parents' consent? Without parental approval? Why?

3. Do you think getting married should be made more difficult than getting legally divorced? Explain.

4. What functions do civil laws perform regarding marriage and divorce? What is the purpose of Church law regarding marrying in the Catholic Church community?

5. How are the roles of Church and State different here? How are their concerns similar?

Being ready to marry

There are many things couples should discuss honestly and agree on before becoming engaged or announcing their marriage plans. Not doing that only increases their problems later. So before you pop the question or accept the engagement ring, seriously and carefully address these questions together:

Communication

- How well do we communicate with each other?
- What communication problems do we have, and how do we address them now?
- What patterns keep us from communicating better now?
- Throughout our marriage, how can we best resolve communication problems and keep improving communication between us?

Goals and plans

- What career (or other) goals and plans do we each have? Are they compatible?
- What problems could they present in the future, and how will we address those?

Religion

- What are our individual religious beliefs and practices?
- What do those mean to us each now, and what do we want them to mean to our children?
- How can our religious faith enrich our lives together?
- What problems might our religious differences create, and how will we resolve them?

Money

- What roles and responsibilities will we each have in managing our finances?
- What are our short- and long-term financial needs and goals, and how can we achieve them?

Sexuality

- How do we each feel about our sexual needs as a married couple?
- What makes each of us uncomfortable about sex?
- How will we communicate and resolve our sexual needs, anxieties, and problems?

Lifestyle

- What kind of lifestyle are we each used to living based on our family backgrounds?
- How do we each envision our lifestyle together? What lifestyle do we each desire and need?
- What tensions will likely arise from our differences in background and preferences? How will we cope with those?

Roles

- What idea do we each have about what being a wife and a husband means and involves?
- Are our views about husband-wife roles compatible? How will we address possible problems?

Household management

- What household tasks and responsibilities will we each assume?
- Which ones do we each like and dislike?
- What will probably irritate each of us about that, and how will we deal with it?

Children and family life

- How much do we each want to have children? How many children would we like to have?
- How were we each raised as children? How will that probably affect how we raise our children?
- How soon would we each like to begin having children? How will we raise and discipline them?
- What roles and responsibilities will we each assume about having and raising children?
- What tensions are likely to arise from our differences about that? How will we resolve them?

Leisure time

- How do we each enjoy spending our leisure time now?
- How do we each envision spending it together— and independently—in the future?
- What friction can we anticipate given our preferences? How will we deal with that friction?

Handling conflicts

- Are we each realistic enough to expect occasional conflicts between us? How will we resolve them?
- How do we handle—and feel about how we handle—conflicts between us now?

Decision making

- Who will have the final say about major and minor decisions—like buying new furniture, where to live or vacation, what kind of car to buy, what movie to see or TV program to watch, what to have for dinner, and so on?
- What process will we follow when faced with tension-filled or difficult decisions?

Handling relationship problems

- How can we best let each other know when we feel there's a problem in our marriage?
- How will we each respond when the other person feels that our marriage has a problem?

Family background and relatives

- What kind of family background do we each have?
- What major joys and difficulties did we each experience in our family? How will those likely affect our life together?
- How do we feel about our family members and our future in-laws?
- What relationship do we envision maintaining with them individually and as a couple?
- What practical concerns and strains will our family relationships likely bring to our marriage? How will we deal with that?

Being faithful

- What does marital fidelity mean to each of us? How important do we each think it is?
- What anxieties do we have about each other's possible lack of fidelity?
- What would sexual infidelity do to our relationship? How can we help each other remain faithful?
- What could tempt us each to be unfaithful? How can we avoid and resist such temptations?

Friendships

- What do we each feel and believe about friendships with others—including other male-female relationships?
- What makes us each feel jealous or worried about that, and how will we handle our feelings and fears after we marry?
- How do we feel about each other's friends? About spending time with them individually or as a couple?

Intimacy

- How will we each probably feel when our romantic feelings begin to fade?
- How can we encourage daily intimacy between us? To maintain it, what do we each need?
- How will we respond when either of us feels intimacy is lacking in our relationship?

Ideals and expectations

- What ideals and expectations do we each have of marriage? Are they realistic?
- How have our family backgrounds influenced our ideas of marriage positively and negatively?
- How will our ideals and expectations about marriage probably affect our marriage?

Personal priorities and standards

- What personal priorities do we each have in life?
- What are our individual goals, values, and ethical standards?
- How will those things likely affect our marriage relationship?
- Which ones might strain our marriage, and how would we deal with that?

Each person is something of a mystery. You can't know everything about someone before you marry the person. But each of these questions certainly should be discussed before becoming engaged. It may seem unromantic to answer a marriage proposal with, "Let's talk about it first." But it's just too risky to agree to marry when too many unknowns remain.

Some individuals aren't ready to answer "yes" to a marriage proposal, but also feel uncomfortable about waiting. They're afraid the other person might misunderstand and back away or change his or her mind. So they accept the proposal, but wait several months for a holiday or family gathering to announce their engagement. In the meantime, they can talk more seriously about practical marital concerns. And they can still change their minds—without causing the public disappointment and embarrassment.

Some believe there should be a socially recognized pre-engagement period—an "engaged-to-be-engaged" time for couples to test and assess their relationship. However you manage it if you're considering marriage, be sure to take all the time you need to make the right decision!

Journal entry

Complete this statement: Five things I'd definitely want to know about someone before marrying the person are . . .

For discussion

1. What serious marital problems could you see arising if a couple marries before discussing the issues raised in this section of your text? Be specific.
2. What do you think about an "engaged-to-be-engaged" period for assessing a couple's compatibility? Explain.
3. If someone you wanted to marry proposed to you before you had discussed what spending the rest of your lives together would involve, how would you respond? Why?
4. Explain your response to this statement: Before getting married, couples don't need sexual experience. What they need is enough experience with their relationship and with keeping promises.
5. How do you think couples can get to know each other well enough before marriage without living together? How might they actually get to know each other better by not living together first?

Assessing compatibility

Based on a concept in the television advertisements for Mutual of New York Insurance Company.

In our society, people usually select a marriage partner through the dating process. But why is our divorce rate so high—almost 50 percent? The most commonly given reason for divorcing is "irreconcilable differences." While love should be the basis for marrying, romantic love obviously isn't enough to make a marriage work. Couples must be compatible!

How can two people tell whether they're compatible before agreeing to spend their lives together?

What do you look for to determine how compatible you are with someone? How compatible do you have to be to live together happily with a college roommate? To get along well in a long-term romantic relationship or friendship? To live together harmoniously with a spouse for life?

Our differences as well as our similarities attract us to each other. So being compatible doesn't mean being exactly alike. It means being able to get along, to appreciate and enjoy each other's similarities and differences. Compatibility means sharing enough yet being different enough in the ways necessary to make our relationship successful and happy. *Compatibility depends not only on what each of us is like, but also on what we need from each other.*

Like different yet complementary colors, people can have quite different personalities and still be compatible. If one loves to tell jokes and the other has a good sense of humor but can't remember a punch line,

they can be compatible. But if one person is athletic and the other thinks athletic pursuits are a total waste of time, the two won't be compatible in that area. Compatibility depends on needs as well as on similarities and differences—and needs definitely vary.

Do "opposites attract"? Can opposite personalities be compatible? Individuals who are very different often do attract each other initially. But the strong attraction is much more likely to last between those who have much in common. We're fascinated by people who are completely different from us, but in close long-term relationships, we need to have more in common. In marriage, people need to be more alike than different in values, interests, and personality traits. Of those key compatibility areas, values and interests are the most important to being happy.

Another big compatibility mistake couples commonly make is to presume that they can change each other. Instead, they should approach marriage "as-is"—no refunds or exchanges. But, sadly, people are often as ignorant about love as about how they spend money: They don't read the labels, and they ignore the fine print. They don't first determine whether this emotional investment suits their needs, desires, lifestyles, and budgets—or whether they're willing and able to repair what breaks down. Yet the problems of an unhappy, broken marriage are far worse than a computer that crashes or a car that leaks oil!

People in love commonly idealize each other. Love too often is blind when selecting a marriage partner. Studies have shown that people become romantically involved based on feelings, but they then remain ignorant of what each other is really like. (Interestingly, they seem unaware of each other's true positive qualities as well as the negative ones!) So we engage in wishful thinking about each other—perceiving what we want to see rather than what's really there!

Couples in love often magnify the good, idealizing the one they love and want to marry. Then they must daily confront the reality of the disappointing, disillusioning truth! As marriage counselors report:

> After several years of marriage, people often say, "If I had known as much before I got married as I know now, I'd still be [single]." Hogwash! One can learn as much about a possible husband or wife before marriage as ten years after. The unpleasant fact is that the people concerned frequently do not wish to do so.[1]

So before you consider marrying (or getting back together with) someone, confront your idealism—about yourself, the other person, and being together "happily ever after." See the real picture and think about whether you can accept it if changes don't occur. To succeed, marriage and long-term relationships must be based on reality, not just on romance.

Throughout life we all need to keep changing for the better. In adjusting to married life, partners must make certain lifestyle and behavior pattern changes. Adapting to life's unexpected events and problems requires additional flexibility. To grow as a person, we'll always have to change. But we can change only ourselves—we can't change someone else. So don't base any long-term relationship commitment on empty promises and hopes that someone will change. Don't expect yourself to make unrealistic or unhealthy compromises to please someone else. If you can accept each other "as-is," you'll more likely be able to enjoy life together.

COMMON FALSE ASSUMPTIONS

HE'LL CHANGE. I JUST KNOW HE WILL—BECAUSE HE LOVES ME.

SHE'S SO PERFECT. I DON'T WANT HER TO EVER CHANGE.

I CAN CHANGE HIM. I JUST KNOW I CAN.

Journal entry

1. Do you accept a person as is or immediately size up the person's flaws?

2. How could you be more accepting of others?

As-is activity

Make an "as-is" collage or advertisement featuring the shortcomings someone would have to know about and accept in you before you'd marry the person. Write a brief paper explaining your collage—or be prepared to explain it in class.

Compatibility interview

Survey several married couples, asking them what areas of compatibility (or incompatibility) they've found most important in their marriage. Write a two-page paper describing your findings and what you've learned.

For discussion

1. Why isn't love alone enough to make a marriage work? Of the people you love, with whom are you most—and least—compatible? Explain.

2. If couples should be more alike than different, why do so many not have enough in common when they marry?

3. To what extent do couples "in love" idealize each other? Why are good friends more likely than couples "in love" to realize each other's faults and good qualities? Explain.

4. Do you ever feel your close friends and family members don't appreciate your good qualities? Do you appreciate theirs and let them know that?

5. Why do you think couples often remain unaware of each other's main positive qualities?

6. What fine print or warning signs would you look for before deciding to marry someone? Explain why.

Values

Our fundamental values are the ideals by which we live, make decisions, and find meaning and happiness in life. It's very hard to change or compromise one's deeply rooted values. For values aren't just likes or dislikes—they determine what's viewed as important or trivial, right or wrong, necessary or unnecessary in life.

Couples newly in love tend to see each other as the only value and to overlook the other values. But that blindness never lasts—in marriage or any other close, long-term relationship (whether at work, in friendship, or with college or apartment roommates). As we've seen, couples who live together before marriage often conceal or downplay their incompatibilities in order to please each other.

When people in a close relationship have conflicting values, they're headed for rocky roads. Suppose you highly value honesty, but your close friend or college roommate thinks it's okay to lie and cheat if not caught. Sooner or later the major conflict, and probably betrayal, will occur. Maybe you'll find money missing from your wallet (with a flimsy excuse given—only after you confront the person: "I just borrowed it and didn't think you'd mind"). Or perhaps you'll discover that the one you trusted has betrayed you by dating your romantic interest behind your back.

"Irreconcilable differences" as reason for divorce doesn't refer to the spouses' disagreeing about whether their meat should be cooked rare, or scorched! Lack of compatible values is probably somewhere at the root of the breakup. For a relationship to be happy and to last, there must be compatible values about what's important, right, and good.

> **Key compatibility factors**
> ★ Values
> ★ Interests
> ★ Personality traits

Activity

1. List three ways TV shows give each of these impressions:
   - Compatibility is important for couples.
   - Love is enough.
2. Explain how, if you were the director, you'd see that TV shows portrayed romantic relationships more realistically.

For discussion

1. What is the difference between your values and your likes or dislikes?
2. Name a basic value you wouldn't be willing to change or compromise. Why is that value so important to you?
3. Why do you think it's so hard to change or compromise one's basic values?
4. Why are value conflicts more likely than other differences to be irreconcilably damaging for close relationships?
5. Have you ever experienced a problem in a relationship that resulted from a conflict of values? Explain.

Many a man in love with a dimple makes the mistake of marrying the whole girl.

ANONYMOUS

What if . . .

. . . after you get married, you find out that your spouse doesn't really share or care much about your interests after all. You also discover that you can't sustain interest in the activities and interests your spouse most enjoys sharing with you. On making those disappointing discoveries, list the positive steps you could take to keep the lack of compatible interests from destroying your marriage.

For discussion

1. Why do you think common interests are more important than compatible personalities to a successful marriage or long-term relationship?

2. What types of interest do you think people most hope to share with their marriage partner? What interests would you want to have in common? Explain.

3. How would you go about discovering someone's real interests and whether those are compatible with what you like and need?

4. How could you tell whether someone genuinely shared your main values and interests or was just trying to please you out of love and a desire to not lose you?

5. What kinds of things do you think dating couples commonly conceal in trying to please each other? What do you think they probably conceal from themselves? Explain.

Love is the glue that cements friendship.

Interests

Interests refer to personal likes and dislikes—for instance, how you enjoy or don't like spending your time, energy, and money. Having compatible interests doesn't mean liking all the same things, but it does mean being comfortable with each other's interests. To preserve their individuality and enrich their relationship, married partners should have some different interests. Trying to share absolutely everything is unrealistic and boring and can be aggravating. One divorcing couple realized that they'd constantly gotten on each other's nerves because they had shared all the same views and interests. So they'd always done everything together.

When romance is new, people often set aside their major interests to focus on or please each other. Only after a while do they resume their other interests. That's why couples considering marriage must allow enough time and opportunity to learn how compatible each other's interests are. Such things seem minor to those in love, but they should be taken seriously before marriage. While dating you might not mind missing your favorite hobby, sports game, or television program for someone's sake, but would you be willing to do so for life?

Suppose one person likes to decorate or renovate the house or to garden—expecting the other person (who could care less about it) to help? If one person's an avid skier while the other hates snow and cold, will the skier leave the spouse at home? Will the non-skier feel left out or resent the time and money spent on skiing? It might pose no problem if the non-skier doesn't mind periodic separations or enjoys sitting by the ski-lodge fire with a few good books.

Before they marry, couples must get past the courting rituals of doing everything just to please each other. They must be themselves and freely express their interests and values. Marriage is a relationship between two *individuals*. To be true to each other, you must each first be true to yourself.

Personality traits

Personality traits are the style or manner in which we express ourselves. Like values and interests, personality traits are a main factor in being compatible. Personality traits that indicate strong beliefs and needs are especially important. Someone who's very possessive, jealous, idealistic, and abrupt must find someone who can compatibly live with those traits—or, better yet, do something about changing those tendencies! Even small annoying traits can become a major source of tension over time.

The average lifespan in our society has been seventy-five years and is increasing. So if you marry someone at age twenty-five, you'll spend at least fifty years either enjoying each other's company or getting on each other's nerves!

For discussion

1. Which types of personality traits do you think are most important to observe—or watch out for—in someone you might think of marrying?

2. Why do you think it generally seems true that long-term relationships are more harmonious when the individuals have personalities that are more alike than different?

3. Why do you think opposite personalities often seem to attract each other—and then later to collide?

4. Why do you think some couples with opposite personalities live together compatibly for a lifetime, while others find their differences intolerable?

5. Are you more attracted to a personality type that is similar to yours or to one that is quite different from yours? Are your closest friends' personality styles more like or more unlike your personality style?

Journal entry

1. What are the main values you need to be able to share with someone to whom you're close?

2. What main interests do you most enjoy sharing with someone?

3. What personality traits do you most like and dislike in someone with whom you're very close?

Review

1. What are the social dimensions of marriage?

2. Why is helping marriages succeed a social concern? What are the key ways to help a marriage succeed?

3. What is meant by a person's values, interests, and personality traits? What does being compatible in each of those areas mean?

4. What factors should a couple consider in assessing that before marriage?

When someone shows you who they are, believe them— the first time.

MAYA ANGELOU

Compatible partners

This questionnaire is based on issues that commonly arise among friends, lovers, and married couples in the key compatibility areas of values, interests, and personality.
To complete the questionnaire, follow the directions your instructor gives you.

Basic values

_____ 1. How important is it to you that you both have a strong belief in God?

_____ 2. Would you want to attend religious services regularly together?

_____ 3. Would you want to marry in a religious ceremony in accordance with your religious tradition?

_____ 4. How important would it be that you both share similar religious convictions?

_____ 5. How important would prayer be in your relationship?

_____ 6. Do you believe practicing one's religion means helping people in practical ways?

_____ 7. Do you believe in treating all persons fairly and equally?

_____ 8. Are your views about social and political issues more conservative than liberal?

_____ 9. How important to you is sexual fidelity?

_____ 10. How strongly do you eventually want a permanent commitment that lasts "until death do us part"?

_____ 11. How important to you is having children someday?

_____ 12. How much compassion do you feel and express when others are sad or in trouble?

_____ 13. How strong and sensitive is your code of ethics (of right and wrong)?

_____ 14. How important is honesty in your daily life?

_____ 15. Do you believe in raising children to uphold basic religious beliefs and values?

Interests

_____ 16. How much of your leisure time do you like to spend watching television?

_____ 17. Do you enjoy camping, hiking, or other outdoor activities?

_____ 18. Do you enjoy loud or lively music more than soft or mellow music?

_____ 19. Do you prefer parties, dancing, and other active social entertainment more than being entertained (for example, going to the movies or a concert, or watching TV)?

_____ 20. Do you prefer being with others rather than spending time by yourself?

_____ 21. Do you enjoy being with friends who are outgoing and perhaps occasionally "rowdy" more than with those who are usually rather quiet and reserved?

_____ 22. In the leisure time you spend together, would you prefer relaxing at home rather than going out somewhere?

_____ 23. Do you enjoy in-depth conversations about serious topics (for example, politics, love, current issues, religion, and so on)?

_____ 24. Are you interested in the creative and artistic aspects of life?

_____ 25. Do you enjoy reading or sharing intellectual pursuits?

_____ 26. How important to you is spending time with relatives?

_____ 27. How important is volunteering your time for charitable causes or social issues?

_____ 28. How comfortable would you be about the other person's avidly pursuing a hobby, sport, or other leisure-time activity in which you had no interest?

_____ 29. Do you prefer movies, games, television programs, or Web-sites that mainly entertain more than those that are more serious and thought provoking?

_____ 30. How much of your leisure time would you want to spend with each other rather than with other people?

Personality traits

_____ 31. How strong willed are you?

_____ 32. Is your personality more introverted than extroverted (for example, more quiet or shy than active and outgoing)?

_____ 33. How independent and self-reliant are you?

_____ 34. How sensitive a person are you in general?

_____ 35. Are you more intense, nervous, or high strung than easygoing, calm, or relaxed?

_____ 36. Are you more lighthearted, fun loving, and playful than serious?

_____ 37. Do you like to plan ahead and know exactly what's coming rather than being more carefree and spontaneous?

_____ 38. Do you patiently persist and persevere until you complete a task rather than becoming impatient, bored, or wanting a change?

_____ 39. Are you more assertive than gentle or passive?

_____ 40. Are you more intuitive than logical or common-sense oriented?

_____ 41. Are you generally more idealistic or optimistic than skeptical or pessimistic?

_____ 42. Are self-discipline and willpower important to you and how you live?

_____ 43. How talkative are you?

_____ 44. How affectionate are you?

_____ 45. Do you tend to express your feelings rather than keeping them inside?

Engaged to marry

Engagement customs and family traditions vary. In our society it's common to exchange rings. Engaged couples usually approach their pastor to formally begin planning their wedding celebration. Some couples ask the priest to celebrate with them the Church's simple blessing ritual for their engagement. Then come the stressful wedding preparations!

The practical marriage preparations often confront couples with some of the realities of being husband and wife. They must agree on where and how they're going to live. Since most couples marry in a religious ceremony, they must discuss what their religious beliefs and practices will mean in their lives together. When disagreements and incompatibilities begin surfacing, so do

serious doubts about spending the rest of their lives together. But once friends and relatives are excited about the wedding, showers and gifts are given, flowers selected, a dress bought, and invitations sent, it seems too late to back out. So couples feel that everyone expects them to go through with the ceremony.

Instead of addressing their serious doubts and problems, couples just cross their fingers and try to forget their misgivings. They tell themselves that the rough spots will iron out after they're married. But that's not the way it works. Couples who disagree often during their engagement more often have trouble in their marriage. Their unsettled issues remain and resurface during the first year of marriage. Even for those couples who live together first, the conflict issues experienced during their engagement cause many couples to separate or divorce shortly after they marry!

Before marrying, it's natural to be a bit apprehensive and wonder, "Am I making the right decision?" Marriage is a complete, permanent commitment. But serious or persistent doubts, worries, and difficulties could be reason for calling off the wedding— yes, even at the very last minute! Engagement isn't final or irreversible. Marriage is the binding, lasting commitment.

Set me as a **seal** upon your heart,
as a seal upon your **arm**;
for **love** is as strong as death,
passion as **fierce** as the grave.
Its flashes are flashes of **fire**, a raging flame.

SONG OF SOLOMON 8:6

The engagement time should provide couples with the opportunity to critically examine their relationship and discuss their suitability for each other. Each person still is and should feel free to end the engagement at any point. Each person is obliged to do so, rather than to marry believing it's probably a mistake. Remember: It's far better to deal with disappointment and emotional hurt before the wedding! To avoid grave last-minute misgivings, it's important to know yourself and each other.

How long two people need in order to make a wise decision about marrying varies with the couple. Those who've known each other at least two years and been engaged at least six months tend to have happier, more successful marriages. They've had enough time to experience the rough spots in the "relationship cycle" (discussed in chapter 6). So they've already seen how they react when the romance cools, and they know their relationship isn't based on attraction or infatuation. They've encountered the faults and differences and know they can live with them. Those couples come to the altar truly accepting each other and ready to promise lasting love and fidelity.

If we could live perfectly what Jesus taught us about loving, we could surmount any difficulty. That's our ideal goal. But as long as we're still learning how to live Jesus' teaching, we're still learning how to love. Love always conquers, but we fail sometimes to love enough.

Project

Choose one.

1. Draw up a compatibility questionnaire that would help you determine a college or apartment roommate's compatibility with you. You may rely on ideas in this text, but your questionnaire should address your specific compatibility needs regarding values, interests, and personality traits.

2. Draw up a list of more detailed questions you think couples should consider about their relationship before becoming engaged or married. Base your list on what Paul says about the specifics of love in 1 Corinthians 13:4–13.

3. Write an advertisement briefly describing yourself and the qualities you're seeking in a college roommate or someone with whom to share an apartment.

4. Write a two-page paper on the insights the various media present—or fail to present— about choosing a compatible marriage partner.

For discussion

1. What engagement customs and traditions are there in your family and religious background? Which one(s) would you like to follow if you marry? Why?

2. If a close friend or relative became engaged, how could you help celebrate the joy without pressuring the person to go through with the wedding?

3. Why do you think many relationships break up during the engagement? How might some of those break-ups be avoided?

4. How would you feel and respond if, a week before your wedding, the other person began expressing serious doubts about marrying you? How could such doubts be discovered sooner?

5. How could you tell whether your last-minute misgivings were normal and insignificant— or indications you should postpone or cancel your wedding?

6. How do you imagine you'd feel if you or your spouse began to feel the intensely romantic feelings lessening? How would you probably react? Explain.

Review

1. What things should couples discuss thoroughly before deciding to marry?

2. What purpose should their engagement period serve?

True **love** doesn't have an **ending.**

Second thoughts

Read the following reality-based situations and respond to the questions. Your instructor will then tell you how things turned out for each couple.

Guy and Sheryl

Guy and Sheryl had been dating about three years and officially engaged for the past three months. The week had been hectic. Their work commitments and the wedding preparations were exhausting them.

Saturday afternoon, Guy decided to relax and watch a basketball game on television. With just seconds to go and the score tied, the doorbell rang.

Guy opened the door. It was Sheryl. Keeping one eye on the game, he kissed her quickly and invited her in. His eyes still glued to the game, he motioned for her to sit down and said, "The game's almost over."

Feeling hurt and rejected, Sheryl told Guy, "You love sports more than you do me." Then she left abruptly, slamming the door.

After the game Guy sat totally bewildered. He thought he showed Sheryl often that he loved her. He couldn't understand why she was so upset. He knew he loved Sheryl. But lately he'd been wondering nervously: "What will married life be like? Am I ready for it?" Now he asked himself: "Is this just a normal misunderstanding—or a sign I should rethink things? If we really love each other, why are we at odds like this?"

1. What's your reaction to Guy's behavior? To Sheryl's? Explain.
2. Why might Guy and Sheryl have responded as they did? Do you think either party overreacted or was insensitive? Explain.
3. If Sheryl, hurt and rejected, asked for your advice, what would you tell her? Explain.
4. Were Guy's doubts usual for someone about to marry, or do you think they indicated more serious problems with the relationship? Explain.
5. If Guy asked you the questions he'd been wondering about, how would you respond and what advice would you give him? Explain.

Kathy and Vic

Two weeks before their wedding, Kathy and Vic had another disagreement. Vic was usually easy to get along with—unless he'd had a few beers, like now.

As the argument escalated, Vic grew angry. Finally, he slapped Kathy, as he'd done once before. Shaken and in tears, Kathy said, "Maybe we should call off the wedding." She feared Vic would hit her again.

Instead, Vic calmed down and said, "I'm sorry—I didn't mean it. I've just got a lot on my mind." Kathy replied, "I need time to think. I'll call and let you know if the wedding's still on." Vic responded, "But everybody's looking forward to it. All the arrangements are made." Then Kathy said, "Well, maybe we should postpone it."

Then Vic broke down and cried. He told Kathy, just like the last time: "I really do love you—I can't live without you. The last thing I ever want is to hurt you. I promise I'll never raise a hand to you again."

Conflicted and fearful, Kathy felt sorry for Vic, but wondered: "What if he doesn't keep his promise this time? Why does he treat me this way if he really loves me? He did seem really sorry. . . ."

Kathy still thought seriously about canceling the wedding. But she knew how that would disappoint her mother, who was so excited and involved in wedding plans. "Every couple has some problems," Kathy thought. "Vic's apology seemed so sincere. As a Christian, shouldn't I forgive—especially the man I love and am engaged to marry?" Confused, Kathy still wasn't sure what she should do. . . .

1. Do you think Kathy's worries were well-founded—or exaggerated? Explain.
2. What's your opinion of Vic's behavior? Do you think he'd probably keep his promise? Explain.
3. If Kathy asked you, how would you advise her?
4. What does Christian forgiveness require of Kathy here? Explain.
5. Should Kathy proceed with the wedding? Explain.

Nicole and Tasos

Over two hundred guests were waiting in the church, and a more than $50,000 wedding reception was prepared for the "happy couple" and their guests. Nicole, the bride, was ready to walk down the aisle. But her fiancé, Tasos, never showed up for their wedding. Instead, without explanation, he took the honeymoon trip to Tahiti by himself. Nicole said later that she was still in love with Tasos and would be willing to give him another chance.[2]

1. Do you think Tasos was wrong in not going through with the wedding? In not showing up in person to at least explain why? In taking the trip to Tahiti anyway?
2. How do you think Nicole probably responded? How would you have responded if you had been jilted at the altar?
3. If Tasos changes his mind, do you think Nicole should give him a second chance?

In summary

The changes facing marriage as an institution often cause people to fear marrying at all. But a marriage generally can succeed if the individuals understand its meaning, find a suitable partner, and are determined to make their marriage work. The origin of marriage is unknown, but humanity's ideal of it has grown throughout Judeo-Christian history. It has developed over time from a non-exclusive, patriarchal property arrangement to an exclusive egalitarian relationship of love.

Marriage is a sacred and permanent commitment of faithful love that originates with God and reflects the covenant God has made with us. The Catholic Church holds that every true marriage is a freely chosen, permanent, sacred covenant. The Church recognizes all true marriages as valid and sacred. To help ensure the success of their marriage, couples need to marry for the right reasons. They must determine their readiness to marry and fulfill the civil and religious requirements for marrying validly and lawfully.

To be truly ready to marry, the couple must also discuss the main issues involved in sharing a life together. They need to be sure they're compatible in the key areas of values, interests, and personality traits. The engagement period should allow couples to address their serious doubts and problems to be sure they're making a wise decision to enter a lasting relationship of love and fidelity.

Key concepts

banns

Church and civil requirements for marrying
   validly and lawfully

compatibility

dowry

engagement

ideals of marriage

Judeo-Christian tradition

key compatibility factors

marriage as a permanent, sacred covenant

preparing to marry

readiness for marriage

reasons people marry

reasons people are afraid to marry

Endnotes

1. From *The Mirages of Marriage* by William J. Lederer and Dr. Don D. Jackson, M.D. Copyright © 1968 by W.W. Norton & Company, Inc. Reprinted by permission of W.W. Norton & Company, Inc.

2. Quotation from "Woman left at altar puts on 'strong face,'" by Larry McShane, The Associated Press (26 November 1997). Information also from that article and other news reports.

CHAPTER 10

THE SACRAMENT OF MARRIAGE

SCRIPTURE

So teach us to count our days
 that we may gain a wise heart. . .
Satisfy us in the morning with your steadfast love,
 so that we may rejoice and be glad all our days.

PSALM 90:12, 14

PRAYER

Loving God,

You created us in love to share your divine life.

We see this high destiny in the love of husband
and wife,

   which bears the imprint of your own divine love.

Love is our origin; love is our constant calling;

   love is our fulfillment in heaven.

The love of man and woman is made holy in the
sacrament of marriage

and becomes the mirror of your everlasting love.

We pray especially for all those who are entering
into marriage today.

May their love for each other grow and endure.

Fill their lives, and ours, with the joy that comes
from loving others as you love us.

We pray in the name of Jesus the Christ. Amen.

SEE THE RITE OF MARRIAGE, PREFACE FOR NUPTIAL MASS, #117.

The history of Christian marriage

We're all influenced by our personal histories. Our childhood experiences still affect how we think, react, and behave. We grow by using what we've learned to shape a better future. Your attitudes about marriage most likely come from your experiences with relatives' happy or unhappy marriages. If you reinforce the positive influences and change your negative perceptions into useful wisdom, you'll more likely build happy relationships in your future. Church and society likewise must learn from the lessons, experiences, and mistakes of previous generations.

In order to understand what the Sacrament of Marriage means for Christians today, you need to understand a few things about its history. (You'll also discover the interesting origins of many popular wedding customs.) As you trace further the origins of today's attitudes and ideas about marriage, you'll see why it took so long before marriage was officially proclaimed a sacrament. And you'll see how people still need to grow in understanding and living marriage's ideal meaning.[1]

Journal entry

Name one positive childhood ideal you were taught that you didn't realize was important until later. Explain one negative experience from your childhood that still influences you.

Jesus' revolutionary view of marriage

During Jesus' time Roman and Jewish marriage ceremonies were mainly family celebrations rather than religious celebrations. Marriage ensured the birth and care of children and a systematic way of transferring property to the next generation. In Roman society, marriage and divorce were simple matters of mutual consent. Divorce and living together outside of marriage were common.

*Although, according to the laws instituted by **Romulus**, a wife could not divorce her husband, no matter how cruel or neglectful he might be, the husband could divorce her if she committed adultery, poisoned her children, or had a duplicate set of his keys made! In the last days of the Roman republic, divorce by either spouse was permitted and annual divorces became the fashion in high society; **Seneca** said that there were women who reckoned their age by the number of husbands they had had.[2]*

During that time young Jewish couples were formally betrothed (promised in marriage) by their parents. The simple family ritual took place sometime before the marriage. On the wedding day the groom and his friends processed with joyful music to the bride's house. There, the bride (whose face was veiled) and her friends joined the groom's procession to the wedding feast. The marriage ceremony was simple, but the celebrating lasted several days. Weddings, though, didn't celebrate love; they celebrated a successful business deal between the two families. Family life was greatly emphasized, and marriage was considered a means for the husband's family line to continue.

The Jews of Jesus' day did expect fidelity of married couples. Their marriage represented God's sacred union with the Jewish people. Also, adultery with or by a married woman seriously violated her husband's property rights. (Rape was also thought to violate, not the woman, but a man's right to own her!) Those caught committing adultery could be stoned to death (as in some cultures today). A husband could divorce his wife just by formally dismissing her. A wife needed her husband's permission to obtain a divorce.

Romulus
legendary founder and first ruler of ancient Rome

Seneca
Roman philosopher and statesperson of about A.D. 65

I give you thanks, O LORD,
with my whole heart . . .
[I] give thanks to your name
for your steadfast love and
your faithfulness. . . .
PSALM 138:1, 2

Jesus preached a revolutionary message about marriage—especially for his day. Even his disciples found it hard to accept. But Jesus' message was so profoundly powerful that, after two thousand years, our civilization accepts it as the ideal. Jesus' teaching on marriage is continuing to change perceptions of marriage throughout the world. What Jesus taught is what most couples now desire of marriage.

Jesus said marriage is a sacred bond of unity between one man and one woman— a bond that should never be broken. In marriage two people become as one. (How that must have aggravated those who thought husbands owned and could do as they pleased with their wives!) Jesus spoke strongly against the common practice of his time whereby women were sometimes divorced for little or no reason. He saw marrying as beginning a loving, faithful union—not as buying a piece of human property.

Jesus spoke of himself as a bridegroom and of his followers as a bride. He said marriage is sacred and mirrors his relationship of loving service with his followers. He performed his first public miracle at a wedding reception, and he compared God's kingdom to a wedding feast. Jesus also emphasized how **fidelity** isn't just being physically faithful to one's spouse, but also being faithful in one's heart. In many ways, he taught that marriage is a sacred union that reveals and expresses God's abiding love for us.

fidelity
loyalty and devotion, being true to

Marriage among the early Christians

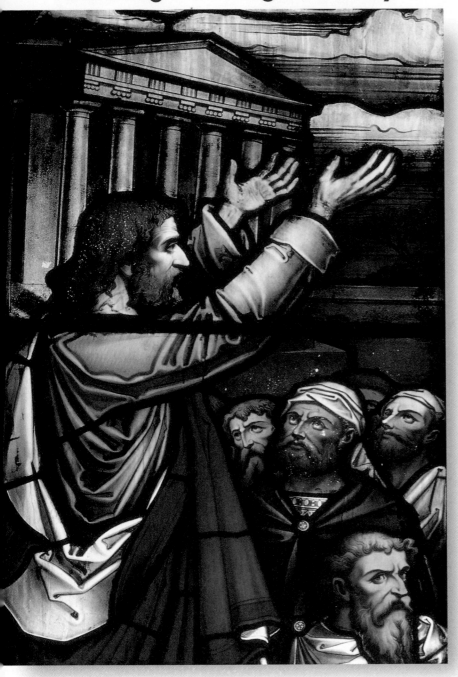

Paul preaching

Pauline privilege

the dissolution of a marriage between two unbaptized persons if one of the partners is later baptized and the unbaptized partner refused to live in peace with the baptized partner; the baptized person is then free to marry another baptized person in the Catholic Church

The earliest Christians expected that the second coming of Jesus and the end of the world would happen soon. Because they didn't focus on continuing the human population, many thought it best to not marry while awaiting Jesus' second coming. In the meantime they began sharing a new view of female-male relationships based on the equality and mutual respect Jesus had preached. Christians' weddings took place in the home, evidently with no specific Christian ritual. People's homes were the first places of Christian worship, and several married couples were active as Church leaders. The home of Priscilla and Aquila, for instance, was a prominent church house. And Scripture describes how that couple risked their lives to share Jesus' message with others.

By the time the Gospels were written, the early Christians began to see that the world wasn't about to end. The Book of Revelation (concerning in part the world's end) described the Church community as a heavenly woman. But Christians soon gave in to social pressures and went back to viewing women as lesser humans than men. Ideas about marriage and family life returned to the surrounding culture's patriarchal attitudes and practices. During times when the early Christians were persecuted for their faith in Jesus, they were instructed to not marry non-Christians. Sometimes couples would be required to seek the permission of the Christian community's leader before marrying—to make sure they were doing so with Christian intentions. But otherwise Christians seemed to marry according to local customs and without a religious ritual.

Like Jesus, his disciple Paul preached that marriage should be a permanent, faithful bond. He did allow remarriage when a non-Christian left his or her spouse who converted to Christianity. The Christian spouse, Paul said, was then free to marry a Christian. (That is now known as the **Pauline privilege**, and the Catholic Church still dissolves marriages under those circumstances.) All early Christian leaders viewed marriage as sacred, but it remained mainly a secular, not a religious, matter.

Marriage views and practices

Romans and Jews of Jesus' time		Jesus' teaching on marriage	Early Christian marriage	Fourth century up to the Middle Ages
• family celebration • way to transmit property and care for children • required mutual consent • divorce and living together common • divorce initiated only by husbands	• betrothal ritual • family celebration • wedding procession • brides veiled • a business deal • male lineage continued • signified God's union with the Jewish people • males' "property right" • divorce the husband's decision only	• a loving, faithful union • is sacred; mirrors Jesus' relationship with his followers • fidelity a matter of heart and body • sacred union expressing God's abiding love	• spouses as equals • weddings at home • no Christian ritual • patriarchal attitudes and practices • ideally, a faithful, sacred, permanent bond • celebrated mainly in a secular matter • divorced converts could marry Christians	• civil regulations to protect women and children • bishops decided civil disputes • patriarchal attitudes, double standards • remarried men (not women) forgiven • kidnapping of brides

By the fourth century, to protect women and children more, civil courts started imposing regulations about divorce and remarriage. When the Germanic tribes conquered Roman territories, Christian bishops, because of their education, were asked to serve as civil judges. As secular and religious attitudes and laws mingled, Church leaders decided disputes about marriage and divorce.

Patriarchal attitudes still prevailed, women were deemed inferior and society upheld a double standard regarding men and women: A man who left his wife and remarried could be sacramentally forgiven—but not so for a women who left her husband. Boys were encouraged to kidnap their young brides—who therefore "married" against their will. Unfortunately, that practice continued in Western civilization for almost a thousand years!

For discussion

1. How did early Christians' view about the future—or the lack of a future—affect their relationships? How do you think teenagers' views about their future affects their relationships today? Explain.

2. When and why did the early Christians return to patriarchal views about male-female relationships? How much do you think social influences affect individuals' views about relationships and marriage today? Explain.

3. Under what circumstances could the exercise of the Pauline privilege affect you in the future?

4. What double standards existed at Jesus' time and during the following centuries about how men and women were viewed and treated? Do you think similar double standards exist in our society? Explain.

5. What lessons about marriage can we learn from the early Christians?

And **when** will there be an end of **marrying**?
I suppose, when there is an end of **living**.

Quintas Tertullian

Marriage in the Middle Ages

By the Middle Ages, Christian couples began asking their local priests to bless their engagement. They then lived together, and after their first child was born, they would have the priest bless their marriage. If the woman didn't become pregnant, a couple might separate. Each partner was free to marry someone else. Children's labor on the farm was essential to a family's survival, so, before marrying, a man had to be sure a woman could bear children. (In those days, people didn't realize that either the man or the woman could be infertile.)

Gradually, couples began inviting their local priests to attend their wedding or to later bless their marriage at church. In some places priests would place a wreath of flowers or a veil over the couple to signify their union. But a religious marriage ceremony wasn't required in the Western Church until the eleventh or twelfth centuries. Although most couples did marry in a public church ceremony, marriages were considered valid if couples simply gave their mutual consent. They could marry publicly at home or privately and in secret. But secret marriages caused major problems, such as bigamy. They also enabled men to dodge their duty of family support by falsely claiming they hadn't really been married! Marriages were still arranged by parents—sometimes shortly after the child's birth—and brides were still bought from their fathers by their husbands.

By the twelfth century, church marriages in the presence of a priest and witnesses became the custom. The nature of marriage as a sacrament came to be somewhat better understood. Marriages could be dissolved only rarely, under circumstances that favored the wealthy. Although Saint Bonaventure said men and women are equal, a double standard still prevailed for men and women in Church and society. Periodic epidemics of fatal sexually transmitted diseases helped scare people into believing that sex and sexual pleasure were sinful even in marriage.

Marriage between Christians and non-Christians was forbidden, by their religions and by civil law. Tragically, these laws were enforced brutally—Jews who became sexually involved with Christians could be mutilated or put to death! In past centuries, Church leaders like St. Augustine had condemned as wrong the idea of unmarried couples living together. Nevertheless, concubinage—living together with an exclusive partner—was rather widely practiced both by **laity** and by clergy during medieval times. The Church disapproved of concubinage arrangements, but they were often recognized as valid marriages. We might compare those relationships to the common-law marriages civil law still recognizes in some places. A man and a woman who live together as husband and wife for a certain period of time may be legally recognized as common-law spouses, even though they've never officially married.

laity

laypersons; members of the Church community who are not ordained ministers

For discussion

1. When and how did each of these practices originate, and how does each affect marriage today?
   - Blessing a couple's engagement or rings
   - Marrying in a religious church service
   - Carrying flowers at weddings
   - Wearing a bridal veil
   - Giving the nuptial blessing at the wedding

2. What happened when medieval society didn't listen to Saint Bonaventure's wisdom about men and women? In what ways do you think individuals, society, and the Church should heed his wisdom today?

3. What similarities or differences do you see between the problems secret marriages caused in medieval times and those resulting from couples' cohabiting today?

4. How did sexually transmitted diseases affect medieval views about sexuality? How do you think the current epidemic of such diseases affects individuals' views and practices today?

Christian marriage in later centuries

Martin Luther

sixteenth-century Catholic monk from Germany who preached religious reform and whose writings and efforts helped establish the Lutheran Church

Council of Trent

major council of the Catholic Church which tried to clarify Church doctrine and establish needed reforms in Catholic liturgy and ethical conduct

sacrament

a visible sign initiated by Jesus' words and actions in order to bring God's presence (grace) to people in a special way

Protestant Reformation

the movement during and following the sixteenth century in which various persons led attempts at Church reform and established distinct Christian denominations

When people like **Martin Luther** started urging change, many aspects of society and the Church needed reform—including the abuses involving secret marriages. The Church's sixteenth-century **Council of Trent** sought to help bring about those reforms. There already had long been a strong tradition—especcially in the ancient Eastern Christian Churches—that marriage was one of the sacraments. That belief came to be expressed even more clearly with the greater introduction of marriage celebrations in church. After the Council of Trent, marriage was more formally proclaimed a **sacrament,** and Church and society outlawed and tried to prevent secret marriages. Banns (proclamations) of forthcoming marriages were to be publicly announced in church three Sundays in a row before the wedding. Catholic couples were required to marry in the presence of two witnesses at a ceremony presided over by a priest.[3]

After the **Protestant Reformation**, Protestant reform groups generally allowed divorce, but were sometimes stricter than Catholics about sex and marriage. Some required males and females to be separated at worship services, and boys and girls to marry in their teens. Some said widowers and widows should remarry right away so they wouldn't be tempted to sin sexually. And some Protestant reformers not only outlawed secret marriages, but said couples living in secret marriages should be drowned!

For several more centuries, Christian Churches continued to have jurisdiction over society's marriage laws and practices. After the American and French Revolutions, church and state were recognized as distinct, and laws and customs were adapted accordingly. Since then, couples have been subject to separate civil and religious regulations on marriage. It wasn't until just a century ago that couples began marrying mainly out of love. Thus it took couples, society, and Church over a thousand years to more fully understand Jesus' teaching about what marriage truly is and means! But given today's divorce rate, we still have a long way to go in living Jesus' message about marriage.

Project

Choose one.

1. Research the origin of wedding customs not discussed in this chapter. Write a two-page paper. Explain whether the customs are still appropriate.

2. Write a two-page paper on wedding customs in your area, especially within your culture and family. Explain the significance of each custom.

Journal entry

How does Jesus' view of marriage compare with your ideal of it? Explain.

For discussion

1. Historically, how have Church and society grown in understanding marriage since early Christian times? What further growth and reforms do you think are needed?

2. What difference does it make in people's attitudes about sex to understand that marriage is sacred?

3. When did civil and religious laws about marriage become distinct? What value for today do you see in each type of regulation?

4. Were you surprised to learn that people only recently began marrying out of love? What else about the history of Christian marriage has surprised you? Explain.

Review

1. What was Jesus' message about marriage, and why was it revolutionary?

2. What is the *Pauline privilege* and how did it originate? Is it available to couples in the Church today? Explain.

3. How did Christians' understanding and practices regarding marriage develop throughout history? How have the attitudes and practices of previous eras affected marriage today?

4. When did marriage come to be more widely spoken of as a sacrament?

5. What is the purpose and origin of announcing the banns of marriage and requiring the presence of a priest (or deacon) and two other witnesses at a Catholic wedding?

"With this ring . . ."

Read about how our wedding ring custom originated and then respond to the questions.

With this ring I thee wed.

In some parts of the ancient world, the groom gave his bride an iron ring to show that she now belonged to him. During the Middle Ages this ring was a sign that the wife's husband had officially bought and paid for her.

The wedding ring did give medieval wives some legal protection. Because each ring was uniquely forged by hand, it proved whom the wife belonged to—and who was obliged to support her. If her husband tried to marry someone else, the wife's ring could support her claim that he was already married to her.

Some version of "with this ring I thee wed" is a standard part of weddings in our society. But today exchanging rings symbolizes the love and fidelity that the couple's wedding vows mean.

Take this **ring** as a **pledge** of my love and **fidelity**.

THE CATHOLIC RITE OF MARRIAGE

For discussion

1. What did the custom of giving a wedding ring signify in Western civilization in early and medieval times? What does it signify today?

2. What do you think the wedding ring signifies for most couples today? How does it symbolize marriage as a sacred covenant?

3. What values—or lack of values—does the wedding ring custom represent in our society today? What views about marriage do you think it signifies?

4. If you marry what custom would you want to follow regarding wedding rings? Are there any other symbolic tokens or gestures unique to your cultural or family background that you'd want to include at your wedding? What would each symbolic token or gesture signify to you?

The sacramental meaning of marriage

Marriage is a sacred covenant. Marriage between two baptized Christians is also a sacrament—as much so as Baptism or Eucharist. Sacraments aren't just rituals that happen inside church. They're to be lived every day. So what does it mean to celebrate and live marriage as a sacrament—from the altar to the groggy attempts at civil conversation over breakfast and the tender caresses in bed at night?

A sacrament is a visible sign Jesus has given us to bring God's loving presence, and support—God's grace—into our lives in a special way. Few feel more blessed by God's love than happily married couples.

Project

Interview three Christian married couples, asking each what their marriage means to them as Christians. Write a two-page paper reporting your findings and your responses.

Marriage between baptized Christians

If you're a baptized Catholic, you may marry someone who isn't a baptized Christian, and do so in a Catholic wedding ceremony. Your marriage will be celebrated by the Church as a sacred, unbreakable covenant, but not as a sacrament. Why?

In the *Sacrament* of Marriage, two baptized Christians celebrate, as do other couples, their sacred union in God's love. They also celebrate something more—their belief in who Jesus is and their belief in trying to live as a couple what Jesus taught and lived. To celebrate and live together what that means, both partners must believe it. That's why marriage can be a sacrament only for two baptized Christians.

The essence of the Sacrament of Marriage is the baptized partners' free, mutual commitment to each other for life. That loving partnership is for their good, and for the children they may have. Thus, in the Church in the West, spouses receive this sacrament from each other, not from the Church's minister. The Church or the priest or deacon doesn't marry a couple; strictly speaking, it's incorrect to say "Father Martinez married us," or "we got married." (In the Eastern Rites of the Catholic Church, the priest is the minister of the sacrament; in the West, it is the couple themselves.)

The priest presides at the wedding and blesses the marriage on behalf of the Catholic community. Frequently a deacon presides at a wedding that does not include the Eucharist, and he may be the witness at weddings that take place at Mass. Where priests and deacons are unavailable, the bishop may designate others to preside. If you're Catholic, you could one day be appointed to preside at a Catholic wedding. But, in the Western Rites, *the couple marry and administer the Sacrament of Marriage to each other*. (So, yes, two baptized Christians permanently marooned on an uninhabited island could probably marry—even sacramentally. In such an exceptional circumstance, the man and woman would be exempt from the usual ceremonial requirements!)

Couples must freely consent to marry. Free mutual consent is the essential element of the marriage sacrament. Living together before marriage may make a couple unable to do that. The same fears or pressures that induce them to live together can negatively color their consent to marry. If they decide "It's time we get married," similar fears and pressures may steer them toward the altar—but prevent a truly free, full commitment.

Many couples don't realize their real reasons for living together or marrying—until they're in the process of divorcing! To truly marry, both persons must really be promising "I do," not just "I'll try."

Married **Christians**, in virtue of the
sacrament of **matrimony**,
signify and share in the mystery of
the **unity** and fruitful love
which exists between **Christ** and his Church;
they help each other to attain to **holiness**
in their married life
and in rearing and **education** of their children;
and they have their own **special** gift
among the **people** of God.

SACRED CONGREGATION OF RITES, "RITES OF MARRIAGE," #1.

For discussion

1. What is your understanding of what marriage is as a sacrament? What do you think living marriage as a sacrament should mean? Explain.

2. Have you ever declined to celebrate something because your heart wasn't in it? How did you feel, or how would you probably feel in that situation? For similar reasons, why can't marriage to someone who's not a baptized Christian be celebrated as a sacrament?

3. If you marry in the future, describe the sacred meaning you'd like your marriage to have.

4. In the Catholic Church in the West, who administers the Sacrament of Marriage to a couple? How does this influence your understanding of marriage as covenant and as sacrament?

5. Presume that the local bishop has appointed you to preside at a wedding between two Catholics. What would you say in your homily about the meaning of the sacramental union the couple is entering? Explain.

6. For couples to enter marriage as a permanent partnership, what is necessary? How might their underlying motives for marrying jeopardize or prevent the couple from doing that?

7. What kind of freedom and maturity would you need before feeling ready to marry someone?

Irreplaceable

The Catholic Church considers the sexual union of husband and wife to be sacred. Therefore,

. . . the acts themselves which are proper to conjugal love and which are exercised in accord with genuine human dignity must be honored with great reverence.

"THE CHURCH IN THE MODERN WORLD," #51.

sexual fidelity
being sexually intimate only with one's spouse

sexual intercourse
the joining of the sex organs of a man and a woman, whereby one partner's sexual organ penetrates the other person's; the act of sexual union in which the male's penis penetrates the female's vagina, and by which new human life is conceived

The act of sexual union between spouses is a sacred aspect of the Sacrament of Marriage. Visible signs symbolize what each of the seven sacraments means. The visible signs of the Sacrament of Marriage are the words of the couple's vows and the lifetime of their loving deeds and affection. Each act of sexual union should renew the couple's pledge of faithful love and their openness to bringing forth new life together. When a couple can't or shouldn't have children, the love they share sexually can be creative in many other ways.

No human can be replaced by another person. In exchanging wedding vows, wife and husband promise each other this: "For as long as you live, no one else will ever take your place in my life." Their sexual union symbolizes and renews their lasting, faithful love. It also expresses the couple's openness to give life to and properly educate and care for children.

Most people ideally want to express their sexuality within a permanent, mutually faithful and loving relationship. Only in a true marriage can there be that complete and lasting mutual commitment. Only in marriage can sexual intercourse and intimacy achieve the ideal meaning individuals want it to have for them. That's why Catholic teaching insists on **sexual fidelity** in marriage and regards sexual intercourse outside of marriage as wrong.

Giving one's body to someone completely, as in **sexual intercourse**, should represent a total gift of oneself—not just a partial or temporary gift that one day might be taken back. Sexual union is meant to represent a permanent and complete personal union. Only in marriage do two people pledge to share that type of open, honest, exclusive, faithful relationship with each other for the rest of their lives.

That love, which married couples share physically and in spirit, makes them one body and one heart. It also opens their hearts to participate in God's action of creating a human life. Thus, sexual union involves sharing one's total person in the dedicated way that can be realized only in the marriage commitment.

Journal entry

1. Which persons are irreplaceable in your life right now?

2. How do you let them know that? How else could you let them know how much you value them?

For discussion

1. What do a couple give, accept, and promise in saying "I do" at their wedding?

2. Why would engaging in sexual intercourse for the wrong reasons pull married couples apart, rather than drawing them closer? What do you think would be some of those wrong reasons?

3. Do you think Christians think of sacraments more as rituals occasionally celebrated in church or as ways of living? Explain.

4. Why doesn't sexual intercourse outside of marriage express the ideal meaning most people want their sexual experience to have?

. . . you have
made the bond of
marriage a holy
mystery,
a symbol of
Christ's love for
his Church.

OPENING PRAYER,
CATHOLIC RITE OF
MARRIAGE

The different meanings of marriage

Just as love often has different meanings for people, so does marriage. People may declare their love for each other and then realize later that they were only infatuated, or individuals may discover that "I do" meant one thing to them and something entirely different to the person they married.

As Catholic law and teaching recognize, **a couple's marriage means what the couple truly pledges that it means when they marry.** We've already discussed what a permanent, lifetime marriage promise means. (The next chapter will discuss more about the practical realities that involves.) When Christians who are not Catholic enter marriage fully believing, pledging, and celebrating their union as sacred, valid, and indissoluble, the Catholic community recognizes those marriage promises as sacred, valid, and indissoluble. When a couple's marriage is celebrated and blessed by their religious community (Catholic or not) as a holy, permanent union, that belief corresponds to the Catholic understanding.

I shall betroth you to myself forever, I shall betroth you in uprightness and justice, and faithful love and tenderness. Yes, I shall betroth you to myself in loyalty . . .

HOSEA 2:21–22A (NJB)

But how does the Catholic Church view it when couples marry intending to enter a merely civil arrangement "unless or until divorce do us part"? The Catholic community recognizes such a marriage as marriage in the legal sense, but it does not recognize it as the permanent covenant or sacrament Catholics mean by marriage. For Church and State, the essence of the marriage union is the couple's mutual intention and consent. Only God and the couple can know whether or not, or in what sense, they are married.

No one—including the Church—can make a couple's marriage mean something less, other, or more than they pledge it to mean when they marry. Only God can know both partners' actual intentions and motives. So only God can know whether the couple's marriage is mainly a conditional legal relationship as sanctioned by civil law or a marriage "truly made in heaven"! But for the Catholic Church to officially celebrate the union as the *sacred, permanent commitment Catholics mean by marriage,* there must be good indication that the couple intends that same meaning.

Couples have reasons for marrying in a religious ceremony or for choosing to not do so. Thus, the Catholic Church generally recognizes that most marriages performed in purely civil ceremonies don't have the same meaning as those celebrated in a religious ceremony signifying lasting love and fidelity. The Catholic Church does acknowledge civil marriages as true and valid marriages according to the civil legal sense in which they were contracted. It acknowledges those spouses' legal status, rights, and obligations regarding each other, their children, and society.

Couples must believe in God before they can intend to unite themselves to each other in God. They must believe marriage is a permanent, sacred covenant before they can make that covenant with each other. They must believe marriage is a sacrament that involves living together what Jesus taught—before they can promise to live their marriage that way. When Catholics marry in a purely civil, secular way outside a religious context, there's lack of evidence that they intend and promise what Catholics believe and celebrate about marriage.

However, it's not up to us to judge negatively couples who marry before a justice of the peace instead of a priest, rabbi, or minister. They are first of all married legally and may also, in some sense, understand their marriages to be sacred and blessed by God. But, remember that, whatever the situation, couples cannot really promise what they don't believe about the permanent and religious dimension of marriage.

Activity

Choose one.

1. Interview at least five adults, asking each what marrying someone means to him or her. Make a collage or computer graphic illustrating the meanings they describe. Be prepared to explain your collage to the class.

2. Make a collage or computer graphic illustrating, or write a two-page paper, on the many meanings of marriage portrayed in today's media (for example, in songs, TV programs, movies, books, and magazines). Be prepared to explain how those meanings support or differ from the Catholic meaning of marriage.

For discussion

1. List at least three different understandings each partner might have when marrying—about what their marriage vows mean. Which of those understandings are complementary? Which ones seem contradictory?

2. What problems arise when spouses understand their vows in contradictory ways?

3. How might people misinterpret Catholic Church teaching about which marriages are valid in the Catholic sense? What misunderstandings could that cause?

4. What is your response to the statement that only God and the couple can know whether or not, or in what sense, they are married?

5. How might a couple claim to fully pledge themselves, but then celebrate or live marriage in a way that contradicts that?

6. Why do you think couples decide for or against marrying in a religious ceremony? What do their choices say about what they're pledging their marriage to mean—and not mean?

Review

1. What is the meaning and essence of marriage as a Christian sacrament? How is the Sacrament of Marriage celebrated?

2. Why can only two baptized Christians celebrate and enter into marriage as a sacrament in the Catholic sense?

3. In the Catholic Church in the West, who marries and administers the Sacrament of Marriage to the couple? Explain.

4. Why does Catholic teaching insist on sexual fidelity in marriage?

5. What should a married couple's sexual union represent about what marriage means? About what the Sacrament of Marriage means? How should sexual union renew the couple's marriage covenant?

6. What different meanings does marriage have in the civil and religious sense? Does the Catholic Church recognize civil marriages as valid? Explain.

I do?

Read the following and respond to the questions.

There's an anecdote told about the groom who when asked at his wedding, "Do you take this woman to be your wife—for richer, and for poorer, for better, and for worse?" replied, "Yes, no, yes, no!"

A groom and bride may go through (or put their families through) great trouble and expense to be able to declare their love at a big formal wedding celebration. Outwardly, they speak words of promise. Yet what they actually share may not be a binding lifelong pledge, but merely a common hope:

If the partners aren't truly pledging lifetime fidelity, they're not really committing themselves without reservation to a lasting marriage. With stars in their eyes and hope in their hearts, they're marrying with their fingers crossed. The escape clause is secretly tucked in back of the mind—"If this doesn't work out, I can always get a divorce." At the first major marital argument, they may fail to see that each difficulty is a chance to grow together and renew their commitment. Instead, they could fear they've made a tragic mistake. They may mentally begin packing their bags and wonder whether they should consult a divorce lawyer.

For discussion

1. What do you think is the difference between exchanging marriage "promises" that are just mutual hopes and making a permanent pledge to each other? Between being normally apprehensive about marrying and being dishonest about one's commitment? Explain.

2. How do you think you could tell whether the person you were marrying truly intended to pledge a permanent commitment? Whether that's what you really intended to pledge? Explain.

3. If you marry, would you prefer that you and your spouse be close friends with others who believe marriage is "until death do us part" or with people who believe in "until divorce do us part"? Why?

4. The person you want to marry gently but firmly insists that you first sign a prenuptial agreement. In it you'd both specify and accept beforehand what property settlement terms would take effect should you divorce. How would you feel about that? Why? Would you sign the agreement if its terms were fair, or would you refuse to sign it? Why?

5. What is the difference between a shared hope and a permanent pledge? Would you want the person you marry to hope, or to pledge, that your marriage will succeed? Explain.

Inter-Church and inter-faith marriage

A married couple's religious beliefs are extremely important to their life together. Our beliefs about God and religion greatly influence what we value and how we behave and relate with others. Compatibility, if not total similarity, in faith and morals, is vital for happiness in marriage. Even couples of the same religious tradition can have such different understandings of what living their faith means that life together becomes extremely difficult.

People often wonder, "What happens when a Catholic wants to marry a non-Catholic with the Catholic Church's blessing? Under what conditions can Catholics marry non-Catholics 'in the Catholic Church'?" In this section we'll address some of the questions about how the Catholic Church views and celebrates such "mixed marriages." Many people in our society do marry someone of another Church or religion. It's even possible that you will, so you should be aware of what implications those differences can have for marriage.

The importance of religious freedom in marriage

religious freedom
the freedom to believe and practice one's religious convictions

A non-Catholic planning to marry a Catholic sometimes fears he or she will be pressured into becoming Catholic. If a non-Catholic friend or relative expressed that fear to you, how would you explain Catholic policy? **The Catholic Church respects and supports each spouse's right to hold and practice his or her religious beliefs freely and without the other spouse's interference.** It opposes any attempt to pressure the non-Catholic party into becoming Catholic. Non-Catholics are always welcome to join the Catholic community. But they're discouraged from deciding to become

Catholic shortly before their wedding merely to please their future spouse. No one should ever be pressured to set aside or abandon his or her faith tradition in order to marry!

Journal entry

1. How important is religious freedom to you personally?
2. What type of interference with your beliefs about religion would you not be willing to tolerate in a spouse?
3. How do you think you could see whether your beliefs about religion would be compatible with someone before marrying the person?

. . . the right to religious freedom has its foundation in the very dignity of the human person. . . .

"DECLARATION ON RELIGIOUS FREEDOM," #2

Why dual-religion marriages are discouraged

Some people choose to become Catholic after marrying a Catholic and having children.

inter-Church
between different Christian denominations

inter-faith
between different faith traditions, such as Jewish and Christian

dispensation
official permission to be released from a certain obligation

For several good, practical reasons, the Catholic Church, other Christian denominations, and non-Christian faiths have long discouraged **inter-Church** and **inter-faith** marriages. Lack of shared religious convictions often results in marital conflicts and in family disapproval or rejection. Married couples' common religious faith helps keep them close despite their problems and life's ups and downs. Without that faith bond, couples may find they don't have enough to hold them together through difficult times.

Couples in inter-faith marriages may feel the lack of being able to share their faith by praying or worshiping together regularly. When couples are dating, they often don't discuss religious issues thoroughly enough. But individuals do tend to get more involved in religious activities after they marry. The person's spouse sometimes resents that increased interest in religion, feeling threatened or alienated by it.

Sometimes a spouse feels—or is—pressured to change to the other's religion. Most major religious groups in our society share with Catholics the strong belief in individuals' religious freedom. Some religious groups, however, don't share that view, and may even be antagonistic toward other religions. Some persons may deem it their sacred duty to "save" their spouse's soul by constantly

criticizing his or her religion. They may badger the spouse to join their religion.

Such stresses can bruise or break a marriage. But couples in love often overlook the differences that become painfully annoying after marriage. That's why the Catholic Church encourages inter-faith and inter-Church couples to know and understand better each other's religious beliefs and practices before they marry. Non-Catholics are invited, where possible, to attend classes or workshops that help familiarize them with Catholic beliefs and practices. Or the couple may be invited to talk with other inter-faith or inter-Church couples about living compatibly in terms of religion.

Basic values are the main compatibility factor. Religious differences can lead to a deep, fundamental divisiveness that cracks a marriage. To marry a person of another faith or another Christian denomination, Catholics obtain a special **dispensation**. They must have good reasons for wanting to marry despite the religious differences. The process of obtaining a dispensation helps the couple thoughtfully examine the religious aspect of their future marriage. They consider the realities they'll face and can see whether they're prepared to live harmoniously with their religious differences. This helps confirm that they both want their marriage to be faithful and permanent.

A main tension in inter-faith and inter-Church marriages is disagreement over the religious upbringing of the children. That's why couples are urged to agree on that before they marry. An important conviction—and obligation—of Catholics is giving their children every opportunity to share their Catholic faith. To protect and support the Catholic spouse's freedom of religion, the Catholic party is required to make this promise before marrying a non-Catholic:

"I reaffirm my faith in Jesus Christ and, with God's help, intend to continue living that faith in the Catholic Church. I promise to do all in my power to share the faith I have received with our children by having them baptized and reared as Catholics."[4]

"To do all in one's power" recognizes the religious convictions of the non-Catholic party and implies that a decision is reached that respects those beliefs. It does not mean an absolute promise at the risk of jeopardizing the marriage.[5]

This promise is explained to the non-Catholic party when preparing for the marriage. But the couple should discuss the matter before they become engaged. If a couple can't agree on such key issues, they should seriously reexamine whether they can have a happy future together.

Catholics who want the Catholic Church to fully bless and celebrate their marriage should consult the parish priest well in advance. About a year ahead of time is recommended—especially when there are special questions or needs. It can take that much time and longer to plan the other aspects of a wedding, such as reserving a reception hall or a caterer. It's certainly not asking too much to give as much time and thought to the even more important aspects of marriage.

"I promise to do all in my power to share the faith I have received with our children."

For discussion

1. What misunderstandings do people sometimes have about the Catholic view of inter-faith and inter-Church marriages? What lack of knowledge or misunderstandings have you had in that regard? Explain.

2. What knowledge and attitudes do you think couples should have about each other's religious beliefs and practices—before becoming engaged?

3. How would you try to be sure you could live compatibly with someone in an inter-faith or inter-Church marriage? What would make you have second thoughts about it, or decide against it? Explain.

4. If you were engaged to someone who pressured you to change to her or his religion, how would you respond? Explain.

Celebrating marriage as a Christian sacrament

In compatible marriages between Christians of different Churches, couples have a common bond of faith in Jesus and what he taught. They can share with each other and their children similar views about right and wrong and how people should treat each other. The spouses are more likely to have similar expectations of how to live together as a family.

Marriage can be considered a Christian sacrament only if it is between two baptized Christians. To intend to sacramentally "unite themselves in Christ," the two persons must have a common belief in, and commitment to, God in Jesus. Baptism signifies that belief. The Catholic Church recognizes the Baptism of non-Catholics as a Christian sacrament when the words and ritual of the Baptism share the Catholic meaning of Baptism.

A non-Catholic Christian seeking to marry a Catholic may be told that he or she must obtain further information about his or her Baptism. Without the necessary information, it may turn out that the couple won't be able to celebrate their marriage as a Christian sacrament. But they would still be able to celebrate it as a sacred covenant in a Catholic wedding ceremony.

The positive side of inter-faith and inter-Church marriages

All couples should share and build on common beliefs that enhance their love and union with each other and with God. It isn't totally essential that spouses share a common religious faith, but each must understand and accept the importance of the other's beliefs. Spouses should feel able to support, rather than just tolerate, each other's religious convictions and practices.

Today, as throughout history, some groups still use religious differences as an excuse to snub or war against each other. Inter-faith and inter-Church couples who harmoniously live their different religions contribute something important to the human community. They show how unity is possible among people who approach God in different ways or call God by different names. They prove that we can all live with mutual respect in ways that enrich rather than threaten each other's faith. Couples of different faiths should discuss how they can pray and serve others together. They should live their faiths harmoniously in ways that encourage human unity.

Christian couples have a common heritage tracing back to a single Church and the same Savior. Jesus said those who follow him must work for world unity and strive to become one in him. Years ago, members of different Christian Churches were taught to fear, scorn, and shun one another. Today the major Christian Churches are working to achieve the unity and reconciliation with one another that Jesus taught. Inter-Church couples play a special role in that ecumenical effort. They witness to how the kind of faith, hope, and love they share every day may one day resolve the differences between their Churches that, for now, still send them in separate directions for Sunday services.

For discussion

1. What aspects of religion do inter-Church couples share? What positive effect should that have on their marriage?
2. Why must both partners be Christian in order to celebrate marriage as a sacrament?
3. How can couples handle religious differences in ways that nourish their love and intimacy?
4. Give examples of groups that use religious differences against other groups.

Review

1. How important does the Catholic Church consider religious freedom prior to and in a couple's marriage?
2. Why are inter-faith marriages discouraged by the Catholic Church and other religions?
3. What common bond do Christians of different Churches have? How should that bond enrich a couple's relationship or marriage?
4. Why can a marriage only between two baptized Christians be a sacrament?
5. Name positive aspects of inter-faith and inter-Church marriages.

The religious dilemma

Read the following true account and respond to the questions.

Maria and Stan had been happily married for several years. They had three children, and everything seemed to be going well . . . until Maria started becoming what her husband felt was a "religious fanatic." Stan had been baptized in a non-Catholic Church when he was young. He believed in God, but hadn't practiced any religion since before he met Maria. Maria was a Catholic whose faith had always meant a great deal to her. Stan had agreed when they married that their children could be raised Catholic. That had never presented a problem and still didn't. Stan supported Maria's effort to serve as a catechist to a religion class that met in their home on Saturdays.

Then Maria got involved with a neighborhood Bible study group; the other members believed that those not "actively practicing" their faith in Jesus wouldn't be "saved." Practicing believers, they said, must try in every way possible to "save" those "straying souls." Maria began pressuring Stan to come to the meetings and to read and study the Bible with her. She began feeling it was wrong that he wasn't a "practicing believer," and she resolved to change him.

"Where **you** go, I will go; where you lodge, I will lodge; your **people** shall be my people, and your **God** my God. Where you die, I will die—there will I be **buried**.

RUTH 1:16b–17a

Stan wasn't interested in going to the group's meetings. And he felt Maria now looked down on him as "less holy" or "less worthy" in God's eyes because he didn't formally express the heartfelt beliefs he tried to live every day.

The issue became a major source of conflict between Stan and Maria. Their marriage was in real trouble, which deeply disturbed Maria. She wanted to do what was right—for her husband, her marriage, and her conscience. Finally, Maria consulted her parish priest about the problem, asking his advice. . . .

For discussion

1. How would you describe Stan and Maria's religious compatibility? Is there anything else that might be at the root of their problem? Explain.

2. What possible problems might you encounter in marrying someone of a different faith or a different Christian denomination? Explain.

3. How could your marriage be enriched by religious differences? Explain, being specific.

4. What particular religious beliefs, attitudes, or practices would you find hard to cope with in your spouse—even if he or she belonged to your Church? Explain.

5. What do you think a couple who are dating seriously should know and discuss about each other's religious convictions and practices? Explain what you'd want to know.

6. How would you respond if you felt excluded by or resented your spouse's involvement in religion? How could you help keep your spouse from feeling that way about your religious participation?

7. How would you advise Maria? If Stan asked your advice, what would you suggest? Explain.

Project

Interview one or two inter-Church or inter-faith married couples about how their religious differences have challenged and enriched their marriage. Ask what advice they'd give to inter-Church or inter-faith couples considering marriage. Write a two-page paper reporting your findings and your responses.

The marriage ceremony

"Getting married in the Church" has more to do with what marriage vows mean than with the church building where the wedding takes place. Some people marry in a church just to please their parents, but most of the 30,000 high school students in one recent survey said "marrying in a church" was important to them. Their reasons weren't superficial. They said a religious ceremony makes the "once-in-a-lifetime" commitment sacred and gives it God's blessing. They felt a church wedding will help them remember the importance of their marriage vows and of relying on God's help when problems arise. Most couples in our society do have a religious wedding ceremony.

To plan a meaningful wedding ceremony, the couple should consider the occasion's real meaning, their own beliefs and hopes, the guests, Church guidelines, and what the person presiding feels comfortable with. Catholic practices about weddings have changed over the years, and some things may change in the future. So the couple should always check with the parish priest or pastoral minister about current Church practice before starting to plan their wedding.

For discussion

1. Why do you think most couples in our society marry in a religious ceremony?
2. What do you think most Catholics mean by "marrying in the Church"? What would your marrying in a religious ceremony mean to you?
3. Why should Catholics check with the parish priest *before* starting to plan their wedding?

Firmly **established** by the Lord, the unity of **marriage** will radiate from the equal personal **dignity** of wife and husband, a **dignity** acknowledged by **mutual** and total love

"THE CHURCH IN THE MODERN WORLD," #49

Marrying in the Church

Couples often wonder what's involved—or allowed—in a Catholic wedding ceremony. To see how much you know about marrying in the Catholic Church, answer the following questions.

1. Who usually presides at the Catholic wedding liturgy? _____

2. Could a Catholic layperson ever preside at a Catholic wedding? _____

3. May couples help plan their wedding ceremony? _____

4. Why are some Catholic weddings celebrated with Mass and others aren't? _____

5. May the couple choose their own prayers and write their own vows? _____

6. Does the couple have to say the words "I do"? _____

7. May the couple include their local cultural customs as part of the wedding liturgy? _____

8. Can secular readings or the couple's favorite secular songs be included in the wedding ritual? _____

9. When one party is not Catholic, is the wedding ritual still the same? _____

10. Can the couple marry in the groom's parish instead of the bride's? _____

11. Can a couple marry in a city and parish other than where they reside so that more of their families and friends can attend the wedding? _____

12. Does the local pastor have to preside at the wedding, or can the couple ask another priest who is a relative or friend to preside at the wedding? _____

13. Where one partner isn't Catholic, can the non-Catholic party's minister or rabbi, for instance, be present at and participate in the Catholic marriage ceremony? _____

14. Can a Catholic ever marry in a non-Catholic ceremony or a place other than a Catholic church? _____

15. Can an inter-Church or inter-faith couple have two wedding ceremonies—one in each of their places of worship? _____

16. May a Catholic ever be married in a civil ceremony? _____

17. May a Catholic be maid/matron of honor or best man at a non-Catholic wedding? _____

18. May a non-Catholic be maid/matron of honor or best man at a Catholic wedding? _____

19. Does the couple have to have a maid of honor or best man at their Catholic wedding? _____

20. How much does having a Catholic wedding cost? _____

What the wedding ritual means

A wedding ceremony, however fancy or simple, is a ritual celebration.[6] Formal words and gestures point to and symbolize the Christian meaning of marriage and the sacred importance of married love. Each aspect of this ritual also highlights the couple's new responsibilities and the special help they'll receive from God.

The bride and groom escorted down the aisle by their parents, the prayers, the songs and readings, the exchange of marriage vows, the blessing and exchanging of rings, the formal pronouncing of the couple as husband and wife, the formal blessing of the couple by the one who presides and by their parents—all help everyone present understand and celebrate the couple's union. Those ritual elements show how the married couple will share in a special way in the mystery of God's love.

The trend in some dioceses today is to encourage couples to celebrate their wedding at one of the parish's regularly scheduled liturgies. This is especially meaningful for a couple who is already involved in that parish and consider the parish community important to their celebration. Those parishioners who attend the liturgy do not expect to attend the reception, unless they have received an invitation.

Sometimes wedding ceremonies aren't as meaningful as they could be. They seem more like concerts of the couple's favorite music or recitals of their favorite poems. But they really aren't celebrations that everyone present can appreciate and participate in. Like any liturgy, the wedding ceremony should express what's really happening in a way that all who are gathered can share and celebrate. It should be prayerful and simple, not a staged extravaganza. The words of the music chosen should be a prayer in which those present can express their faith by singing.

Main elements of a Catholic wedding liturgy

1. **Welcoming of those present**—by the priest (and the couple)

2. **Prayer**—for God's blessing on the bride and groom

3. **Readings**—two or three from Scripture (including one from the Old Testament)

4. **Legal requirement**—some expression that the couple intend and freely consent to marry each other and that there are no impediments to their marriage

5. **Exchange of vows (including blessing and exchange of rings)**—including the intent to marry each other for life

6. **Final prayer and blessing**—the Church's nuptial blessing, or another blessing of the couple by the presiding Church representative (and their parents).

Those attending the ceremony should be able to actively participate, such as by exchanging the sign of peace, singing, or sharing special prayers and blessings for the couple.

A wedding ceremony's elaborateness often over-shadows its meaning. When people fail to see what's most important, the wedding can be just a sign of misplaced priorities. So Catholic guide-lines ask couples to consider these two suggestions when planning their weddings:

1. Try to make the celebra-tion meaningfully simple, instead of emphasizing the materialistic aspects.
2. Make the pre- and post-ceremony celebrations more Christian—for instance, de-emphasize the trimmings and the consuming of alcohol.

The expense and pressures involved in planning a wedding often cause tension for those about to marry and for their families and friends. The average wedding in our society costs almost $20,000! People often go deeply in debt to finance the "dream wedding." Rather than celebrating marriage, many weddings are orchestrated to impress. The frills often overshadow the meaning.

Couples are finding creative ways to make their wedding simpler and more meaningful. Some celebrate joint or separate weddings on the same day, and then have a joint reception for which they share expenses—the hall, the band, and so on. Others find a less formal reception in a yard or park lets everyone have a more relaxed time. Celebrating the wedding more simply can enhance its impressiveness and the couple's dignity. It can sure cut down on the expenses!

For discussion

1. Describe two ways to make a wedding a prayer in which everyone can participate.
2. How do you think concerns about the use of alcohol should influence the planning of wedding festivities?
3. How can wedding plans overshadow the occasion's real meaning? What should a wedding celebrate most of all?
4. List five rules couples should follow to make their wedding a meaningful celebration. Be able to explain your reasons.
5. What cultural customs have you seen at wedding cere-monies you've attended? Are there any you'd like to include at your wedding if you marry?
6. How do you think the events surrounding weddings could be simplified or "Christianized" more–without becoming less enjoyable?
7. If the bishop appointed you to preside at a Catholic wedding–
   • How would you try to help make it meaningful for the couple and their guests?
   • What two main points would you make in your homily? Why?
   • How would you explain to the couple why including their favorite secular love song isn't appropriate during the Church ceremony?

Project

1. Find out the requirements and policies of your parish and diocese regarding wedding ceremonies. Write a two-page paper reporting your findings and your responses.
2. Consult your pastor or pastoral or liturgical minister about ways couples personalize their wed-dings and about dilemmas in planning the ceremony. Write a two-page paper on your find-ings and responses.

Review

1. What are the current Catholic policies and practices regard-ing wedding ceremonies?
2. Why should Catholics check with the parish priest before starting to plan their wedding?
3. What does marrying in the Catholic Church involve in the practical sense?
4. What should the wedding ritual mean? How can it be celebrated in a way that best expresses that meaning?
5. What are the main elements of a Catholic wedding liturgy?
6. In a Catholic ceremony, what must the couple expressly consent to in their wedding vows? Why?

What does this wedding seem to celebrate?

Consider these ways some weddings have been celebrated, and then respond to the questions.

A "show-off **wedding** is an affair on which people spend more money than they can **afford** to impress people they don't care about in an **effort** to transform a religious ceremony into a tasteless, ostentatious **extravaganza**. When it's over, all they have are **sore** feet, a hangover, a nerve-wracking stack of bills, and a lot of criticism from catty guests.

"Ann Landers" column

Anne and Carlo married in a ceremony complete with Cinderella's coach, glass slipper, and the sprinkling of pixie dust over the couple. Fireworks were set off when the couple first kissed after being pronounced wife and husband.

Jay and Lisa married in a drive-through wedding ceremony without even getting out of their car.

Linda and Miguel married on a "roller coaster" at the local amusement park.

Yuko and Sherri married while bungee jumping off the side of a bridge.

Dawne and Lee married in a church wedding, with an elaborate reception afterward that cost over $40,000. Dawne's parents took out a second mortgage on their home to finance the expenses. Dawne knew the cost of the wedding reception and that her parents were of moderate financial means. But they didn't tell her about the second mortgage. They said only, "Don't worry. We'll take care of it. Nothing is too good for our daughter."

For discussion

1. What is your reaction to the ways each couple celebrated their wedding?

2. What values and priorities do you think each of the above weddings reflected? What values and priorities do you think most weddings reflect? Explain.

3. Do you think weddings are often show-off affairs? What do you think is the difference between a show-off wedding and one that celebrates the couple's marriage with appropriate meaning and dignity?

4. If the wedding should represent what the couple's marriage is to mean, what would you say about each of the above weddings in terms of what it represents about the couple's future together? Explain.

5. How many weddings have you attended or helped plan? What did you find most and least meaningful about the ceremony? Why?

6. What do you think keeps wedding ceremonies from being as meaningful as they could be?

In summary

Our current views and practices about marriage are influenced by both personal and historical experience. In Jesus' day weddings were secular family celebrations of an agreement that maintained and continued family life. Divorce was common. Jesus taught, however, that marriage is a sacred, lasting bond of love and fidelity that reflects his loving service of his followers and God's abiding love for us. The earliest Christians respected women and men as equals, but people later reverted to patriarchal attitudes and practices that have influenced society's understanding and practices about marriage ever since.

As the Church further developed its understanding of marriage, it more clearly proclaimed marriage as a permanent sacramental bond. Catholics view marriage as a sacred covenant, and marriage between baptized Christians as also a sacrament. Christian married couples reflect Christ's presence to others by how they live their marriage commitment. In the Catholic Church in the West, the couple marry and administer the Sacrament of Marriage to each other. The official Catholic representative witnesses and blesses their union in the Church's name and may certify its civil status. The essence of any marriage is the couple's mutual consent. The essential element of the Sacrament of Marriage is the couple's free, irrevocable consent to accept each other as partners for life.

Catholic teaching recognizes that a couple's marriage means what they truly pledge when they marry. The Church acknowledges the validity and legal status of all marriages in that sense. To marry in the full Catholic sense, couples must intend to enter a sacred and permanent commitment. The purpose of marriage is to achieve a union that promotes the couple's welfare, and gives life to and properly educates their children. The marital act of sexual union is a sacred aspect of the marriage sacrament, by which the couple renews their marriage commitment. For the Church to officially celebrate a couple's union, there must be good indication that they intend to enter a marriage in the Catholic sense. Catholics may personalize their wedding ritual in ways that appropriately reflect that meaning of marriage.

Key concepts

banns of marriage
Catholic wedding ritual
Christian marriage
common-law marriages
dispensation
fidelity in marriage

inter-faith and inter-Church marriage
Jesus' revolutionary message about marriage
marriage as a sacrament
marrying in the Church
Pauline privilege

religious freedom and marriage
Roman and Jewish marriage practices in Jesus' day
sacrament
sexual fidelity
sexual union between spouses
wedding ceremony

Endnotes

1. Incorporated throughout this chapter are teachings from *Faithful to Each Other Forever: A Catholic Handbook of Pastoral Help for Marriage Preparation*, Bishops' Committee for Pastoral Research and Practices, National Conference of Catholic Bishops, United States Catholic Conference, Inc. (Washington, DC: USCC Office of Publishing and Promotion Services, 1989). See especially pages 18–19.)

2. From "Will the Family Survive the Twentieth Century?" by Joan Bel Geddes, in *Future of the Family*, ed. Clayton C. Barbeau (New York: The Bruce Publishing Company, 1971), 15.

3. See Joseph Martos, *Doors to the Sacred* (New York: Doubleday & Co., 1982), 438.

4. *Apostolic Letter on Mixed Marriages*, no. 7; *Statement on the Implementation of the Apostolic Letter on Mixed Marriages*, National Conference of Catholic Bishops (Washington, D.C.: USCC Office of Publishing and Promotion Services, 1971), as quoted in *Faithful to Each Other Forever: A Catholic Handbook of Pastoral Help for Marriage Preparation*, page 80.

5. From *Decree on Ecumenism*, no. 3, Decisions of the Sacred Congregation for the Doctrine of the Faith (17 May 1966, 18 June 1966, 9 July 1966, 10 December 1966, 12 December 1966, 17 February 1967), as quoted in *Faithful to Each Other Forever*, 80, footnote 94.

6. See *Faithful to Each Other Forever*, 117–118, 120–124.

CHAPTER 11

THE CHALLENGES OF MARRIED LIFE

SCRIPTURE

"But from the beginning of creation, 'God made them male and female.' 'For this reason a man shall leave his father and mother and be joined to his wife, and the two shall become one flesh.' So they are no longer two, but one flesh."

MARK 10:6–8

PRAYER

Lord,

We ask your special blessing on those who are struggling with their relationships

and trying to make their marriages work.

Help all of us to build good relationships that last

and to repair the damage we've done to others.

. . . may we praise you when we're happy

and turn to you in our sorrows. . .

and know that you are with us in our need.

ROMAN TEXT ADAPTED FROM THE NUPTIAL BLESSING,
SEE THE CATHOLIC RITE OF MARRIAGE.

Living the marriage covenant

In these times there seems to be an increasing fear among young people that their marriages won't last. It is important to know that there are ways to improve the chance of having a happy, permanent marriage. While every couple is unique and likewise every marriage, certain things are common to all successful marriages, indeed to all successful relations. Many of the insights that follow apply to both marriage and the single life What others have learned through the joys and sorrows of their relationships might also help you build more loving, lasting relationships.[1]

Adjusting to married life

Don't praise marriage on the third day, but after the third year.

RUSSIAN PROVERB

Wedding preparations are usually so hectic that it's easy to understand why couples need a honeymoon to recover! The honeymoon lets the couple get away together and begin their marriage in a more relaxed way. But it's misleading to assume that the honeymoon is the best time in a couple's life. It's a fallacy that the main task in marriage is to keep things as perfectly happy as on the honeymoon. Rather than making love, many newlyweds fall asleep exhausted on their wedding night. Couples often have less-than-perfect first days of marriage and first sexual experiences.

The lost luggage, the scrambled hotel reservations, and the minor disagreements on the honeymoon aren't superstitious forecasts about the marriage's future. They're just the beginning of many years of learning to live and love together. Having unrealistic expectations about a relationship from the start usually spells trouble. Marriage is a living, growing relationship that requires a lifetime to build together. Newlyweds shouldn't expect their relationship to remain as unchanged as their wedding photos. Making close relationships like marriage work requires mutual effort— and lots of patience and flexibility!

For discussion

1. Why is it false and asking for trouble to expect each of the following?
   - The honeymoon will be the best time in a couple's life.
   - Things should always be as happy and perfect as on the honeymoon.
   - The wedding night will be sexually blissful and fulfilling.
   - "As the honeymoon goes, so goes the marriage."
   - A couple's relationship won't or shouldn't change.
2. What unrealistic expectations do you think people commonly have about their romantic relationships? About marriage?
3. What expectations would you have of marriage? Do you think your expectations are realistic? Explain.

Roles and responsibilities

We'd like to think our era is more enlightened and reasonable than previous ones about respecting the equal dignity of men and women. In many ways it is. But it's only been relatively recently that religious and secular attitudes about gender equality have become more like what Paul encouraged among the early Christians:

> . . . and live in love, as Christ loved us . . .
> Each of you . . . should love his wife as himself,
> and a wife should respect her husband.
>
> EPHESIANS 5:2, 33

In many ways men's rights and capabilities still aren't sufficiently recognized. Historically, though, it's been women who were considered the inferior gender. For example, former male slaves were allowed to vote in our society long before women could. (In other parts of the world, women are still denied that right.) Today the Church and society object to having a double standard of law and morality for women and men. Yet many women are still treated as inferiors—as evidenced by the much higher rate of physical abuse they endure in our society. Catholic teaching addresses what lies at the root of gender inequality:

> Unfortunately the Christian message about the dignity of women is contradicted by that persistent mentality which considers the human being not as a person but as a thing, as an object of trade, at the service of selfish interest and mere pleasure: The first victims of this mentality are women.[2]

The widespread occurrence of rape and the nature of contemporary pornography indicate how often people are treated as property rather than equals. In too many families "there still prevails the phenomenon of 'machismo,' or a wrong superiority of male prerogatives which humiliates women and inhibits the development of healthy family relationships."[3] Legislatures and courts are still struggling to apply family and other civil laws more equally to men and women.

In principle, we're coming closer to recognizing Jesus' values and ideals about human relationships and marriage. In practice, humanity still has a long way to go to fully accept and live them. Understanding the history of gender stereotypes and inequality shows us how the distant past still negatively affects our personal attitudes and behavior. That can help us get rid of the inhuman, unjust, unchristian attitudes which harm men, women, and our relationships.

Scripture insights

Read Ephesians 5:21–33. This passage has been quoted to support the idea that the man should be head of the household and the wife should be subservient to her husband. How does that take out of context and distort what Paul said?

Project

Choose one.

1. Research and write a one-page paper on ways our society needs to address biases against men or women.

2. Ask at least three married couples what they wish they would have realized about their spouse before marriage. Write a two-page paper discussing your findings and responses.

3. Interview at least three married persons about difficulties they experienced in married life—beginning with the honeymoon. Ask how they recommend coping with those adjustments. Write a two-page paper reporting your findings, responses, and recommendations.

4. Interview at least three married couples about roles each spouse assumes and their satisfaction about that. Write a two-page paper reporting your findings and responses. Recommend how teenagers can prepare to assume the roles and responsibilities of marriage.

Journal entry

Complete these statements:

1. The responsibilities I dislike doing most at home are . . .

2. The responsibilities I should assume a fairer share of more at home are . . .

Be prepared to discuss at least one of your responses with the class.

For discussion

1. What changes in laws and policies reflect the equality of men and women? What changes are still needed?

2. What double standards still exist regarding men and women in society?

3. In what ways is the world coming closer to believing in Jesus' values about relationships and marriage?

4. What further changes in attitudes, practices or policies would promote those values at school or at home? In society? In the world?

5. How common do you think the "macho" attitude is in our society?

   • What evidence of that attitude have you encountered personally?

   • How do women sometimes encourage men to be "macho"?

   • What attitudes among women harm men and male-female relationships?

6. How do you respond when someone displays or supports gender-biased attitudes? What should your response be? Explain.

Expectations

Female-male roles used to be fairly well-defined in our society. In most families everyone worked the family farm. As people moved into cities, married women started working almost exclusively in the home—preparing meals, cleaning house, and caring for children. Men took care of things outside the home—providing food and shelter. The high cost of living and women's desire to have a career have changed those roles. Now both spouses most often work outside the home to support the family. They must now share household tasks that only the husband or only the wife used to do.

While many children today are being raised to expect more sharing of household tasks and child-raising, frequently they are still being raised to assume traditional roles. Girls are expected to help cook, sew, and clean house; boys are the ones asked to mow the lawn, take out the garbage, and wash the car. When they marry, they struggle over the differences between how they were raised and what their spouses expect—not to mention what their financial situation requires!

More girls are growing up with a career in mind. But working wives resent being expected to do all the cooking, cleaning, and laundry. Husbands who share the household tasks resent being expected to also do all the yard work and the house and auto maintenance. More men are finding the role of househusband fulfilling. But many husbands expect their wife to have a career, although she'd rather be at home with their young children. In marriage most tasks should be mutual responsibilities. For instance, both persons should establish, stay informed about, and follow a budget plan together no matter who pays the bills. Neither partner should insist on controlling the finances or having broad leeway in spending as a matter of "being trusted."

The problems occur when a couple marries and then finds that they have different expectations about their roles and responsibilities. Studies of high-school students have found that many of you have no intention of assuming the husband-wife roles your spouses will expect of you!

What married lifestyle suits you will depend on your needs and desires and your spouse's—rather than on what's traditional or what everyone else does. Unfortunately, couples in love often don't discuss their expectations about marital roles and responsibilities before they marry. Or each hopes the other's ideas will change! When they don't, spouses get frustrated with their lifestyle and each other.

The Church emphasizes how important it is that couples "be united from the beginning of their love by common interests and shared activities which will intensify their nuptial relationship and insure its unity against disruption because of disappointment in one or another of their hopes."

Human Life on Our Day, 85

The Catholic Church supports the positive impact that sharing roles and responsibilities can have on marriage and family relationships:

Authentic conjugal love presupposes and requires that a man have a profound respect for the equal dignity of his wife: "You are not her master," writes St. Ambrose, "but her husband; she was not given to you to be your slave, but your wife . . . Reciprocate her attentiveness to you and be grateful to her for her love." With his wife a man should live "a very special form of personal friendship." As for the Christian, he is called upon to develop a new attitude of love, manifesting toward his wife a charity that is both gentle and strong like that which Christ has for the church.[4]

Sharing marriage and family responsibilities more equally is a positive development. But don't think that means everything should always be fifty-fifty! At times in every relationship, one of us must give ninety percent to the other's ten. Overall, each person should assume a fair share of the responsibilities. Each partner must recognize and respect the other's needs and reasonable desires. Both must learn to cooperate and compromise graciously, not grudgingly.

Project

Choose one.

1. Interview a young and an older married couple about the expectations and images they had of marriage before they married and those they have now. Write a two-page paper comparing each spouse's expectations and images and describing what insights you gained from your interviews.

2. Interview ten teenagers about their expectations of marriage. Write a two-page paper reporting your findings and commenting on how realistic you think teenagers are in their expectations about marriage.

For discussion

1. What changes in female-male roles do you think are continuing to occur today?

2. Do you think you and your peers are prepared for the roles and responsibilities you'll need to assume in marriage? Why do you think females' and males' expectations about that are often so different?

3. What responsibilities would you be willing or not willing to assume in marriage? Explain.

4. Which responsibilities would you expect your spouse to assume? How would you react if your spouse had a completely different idea about those?

5. How would you respond if someone asked, "Why does the Catholic Church oppose treating women as equals?"

6. What is your response to the attitude St. Ambrose said a husband should have toward his wife? What corresponding attitude do you think a wife should have toward her husband? Explain.

Review

1. In general, what should couples expect in adjusting to married life?

2. How have religious and secular attitudes about gender equality become more like what Paul encouraged among the early Christians?

3. In what ways have people still not accepted Jesus' values and ideals about human relationships and marriage?

4. How does the Catholic Church view sharing roles and responsibilities more fairly in marriage?

5. What must each spouse learn about assuming a "fair share" of the responsibilities? Explain.

If you think **marriage** is a 50–50 **proposition**, you don't know the **half** of it.

"Ann Landers" column

Who's responsible?

With whom could you compatibly share a household? This activity will help you see how realistic your expectations are about sharing future household responsibilities.

On each blank, write what percentage of the responsibility you think each person should assume—for example, 40% / 60%. The percentages you give in each instance should total 100%. Be prepared to discuss your percentages—and be sure they honestly reflect your views!

Household item or decision	% Self / % Roommate	% Self / % Spouse	% Self / % Children
1. Shopping for groceries			
2. Preparing the meals			
3. Setting the table			
4. Doing the dishes			
5. Mending and sewing			
6. Taking care of household maintenance and repairs			
7. Cleaning the house (vacuuming, dusting, and so on)			
8. Working to provide income			
9. Keeping things picked up and orderly at home			
10. Deciding how to furnish or decorate			
11. Deciding whether or not, and where, to move			
12. Making major purchases (appliances, furniture, and so on)			
13. Doing the laundry			
14. Deciding which television programs to watch			
15. Deciding which guests to entertain at home			
16. Buying clothes and other personal items			
17. Managing the finances (bill paying, record keeping . . .)			
18. Changing jobs or careers; pursuing further education			
19. Planning vacations and leisure or social activities			
20. Deciding whether to have pets			
21. Taking care of auto repairs and maintenance			
22. Raising and disciplining the very young children			
23. Raising and disciplining the teenage children			
24. Doing the yard work			
25. Other:			

Living marriage as a sacrament

Marriage is both a unitive and procreative community of love. . . .

"HUMAN SEXUALITY: A CATHOLIC PERSPECTIVE FOR EDUCATION AND LIFELONG LEARNING," 94.

God is present everywhere, all the time. Sacraments may begin with a religious ceremony in church. But they are all ongoing, living ways to receive and share with others God's special gifts and love. Marriage is a sacrament the couple gives each other—not just on their wedding day, but in every unselfishly loving thing they say or do for each other.

Just as God was present on their wedding day, so God is present when spouses lovingly greet each other after a day's work, help with the cooking and the dishes, listen to their children's stories about school, quietly enjoy each other's company, or make love. All those things are holy. Whatever a couple shares in their marriage is sacramental when done with the self-sacrificing love Jesus showed for us. It's all part of two people giving to each other and growing in the Sacrament of Marriage.

Finally, let the spouses themselves, made to the image of the living God and enjoying the authentic dignity of persons, be joined to one another in equal affection, harmony of mind, and the work of mutual sanctification. Thus they will follow Christ who is the principle of life. Thus, too, by the joys and sacrifices of their vocation and through their faithful love, married people will become witnesses of the mystery of that love which the Lord revealed to the world by His dying and His rising up to life again.
"THE CHURCH IN THE MODERN WORLD," #52.

Marriage, then, is both sign and reality of Christ's presence in a couple's every loving thought, word, or action. That's what the Church blesses and celebrates; it's what the Church means by living the Sacrament of Marriage.

Project

Choose one.

1. Interview one or two Christian couples about what their marriage means to them as a sacrament and how they try to live this sacrament in their daily lives together.

2. Write a short poem or a two-page paper, or make a collage, on one of the following themes:
   - The roles and responsibilities of couples today in marriage
   - The images of marriage presented in the Scriptures
   - The images of marriage portrayed by the various media today
   - The biggest adjustments you think you'd have to make if you one day marry
   - How one or more of the Christian couples you know live their marriages as a sacrament

For discussion

1. What do you think it means to live marriage as a Christian sacrament? How do you think Christian couples can best do that in their marriage?

2. Do you think people tend to view their everyday activities as a holy way of living their vocation? Do you view your daily activities that way? Explain.

Being married

The skills involved in building a successful marriage apply to many other relationships. So if you're not thinking about marrying in the future, you can still benefit from the skills all relationships require: care, sacrifice, and faithfulness.

Your current ideas and expectations of relationships have been influenced by society, your religion, and most of all your personal history. Statistically, the happiness of your parents' marriage is very likely to affect how happy your close relationships and marriage are. That does not mean that if your parents' marriage has been wonderful or if it is disastrous, yours will be, too! But we do pattern our relationships on the healthy or troubled ones we've grown up experiencing at home.

You can always improve on and adapt your ideas about and ways of relating to people. First, you must be aware of how you view female-male relationships—and why. Those who've raised you have profoundly influenced the ways you typically respond in close relationships. You must be aware of what those influences are before you can change how they've affected you.

You can't live or "unlive" your parents' ideas about relationships or marriage. You shouldn't even try. Nor should you try to live some fixed image of what a "perfect" relationship is. Each personal relationship is as unique as the persons are! And any relationship must be re-created constantly if it is to grow! Wedding vows are a mutual promise to continually grow and "remarry" each other daily in new and different ways.

According to my friend Jonathan the Jock, it's easier to love a woman more than life itself than to love her enough to turn off the Super Bowl.

JUDITH VIORST

Activity

Make a collage or computer graphic or write song lyrics illustrating what makes a relationship succeed or fail. Be prepared to explain your collage, graphic, or song lyrics to the class.

Journal activity

1. List images and expectations of how men and women relate with each other in marriage. Explain why you have these images and expectations.

2. Put a "+" in front of each positive image or expectation, and a "−" in front of each destructive one.

You will be asked to share and explain one of your images and expectations with the group.

For discussion

1. What is fair to expect of the other person in a romantic relationship? In marriage? What shouldn't people expect, but often do? Explain.

2. Cheryl's mother has been through a bitter divorce. She's constantly critical of men. Guy's father is always telling him that women need to be put in their place. Guy knows his father cheats on Guy's mother. How will their parents' attitudes affect Cheryl's and Guy's relationships with persons of the other gender?

3. How can individuals change their less-than-desirable images and expectations about male-female relationships? Give some realistic examples.

Review

1. How and why is Christian marriage both the sign and reality of Christ's presence?

2. What does it mean to live the Sacrament of Marriage?

3. On what do people pattern their male-female relationships?

4. Why should people avoid having or trying to live a "perfect" image of a relationship?

Images of marriage

Read what one marriage counselor thinks about people's ideal images of marriage. Then respond to the questions.

. . . the honeymoon ends and the marriage begins. It is at this point that I think most divorce happens. We are hung up on honeymoons. My honeymoon was a disaster. I knew next to nothing about tenderness and solicitude . . . I was incapable of dialogue. I wanted to be seen in a certain way. I needed my wife to be a certain way, and obliging girl that she was, she obliged. She seemed to be the kind of person she thought I thought she was, the kind of person she felt I would like. We carried out this double masquerade for about three years . . . It was painful for me to learn that my wife had a mind, a perspective, and feelings of her own different from mine. She was not the girl I married; in fact, she never was. I married my fantasy, and so did she. . . .

My "next" marriage to her began with hope and resolve, as we struggled to find some enjoyment in living and to care for our children. I suspect we were growing in experience, self-sufficiency, and self-esteem.

I don't know how many marriages I have had by now, but I am married at the present time to a different woman of the same name in ways that are suited to our present stage of growth as human beings. . . .

Because we lie so much about our relationships, especially to our children, and because the breadth and depth of authentic experience is not presented in movies, comics, books, or TV, nobody knows what is expected or what is healthy or life-giving or potentially life-giving in marriage. People think that if they get angry or bore one another or fail to respond sexually, that the marriage is finished, that they are out of love . . . The image of the good marriage is perhaps one of its most destructive features. The ideal marriage is a snare, a trap, an image the worship of which destroys life. . . .

Marriage is not an answer, but a search, a process . . . Yesterday's marriage or way of being married is today's trap. The way out of the trap is to resume the dialogue, not to end it . . . Marriage is for growth, for life. It's a place to call home, but like all homes, one must leave it in its present form and then return, and then leave it, and then return.

Kierkegaard refused to marry and thereby defied the nineteenth century. I have refused to divorce, and I defy the twentieth . . . If so few marriages endure, then something is nonviable about that way of being married. I have tried in the twenty-six years of my marriage to be married in the ways designated by tradition, by the mass media, by my friends, by textbooks on marriage, by my wife's image of a good marriage, and none of these ways were for life. None were life-giving, but were rather images, or better, idols. To worship an image of marriage is like any other idolatry, the expenditure of one's own life, time, and vitality to enhance the image. That such a marriage is disastrous is self-evident. When it endures, it becomes a major cause of psychological distress and physical illness.

What do people do who have tried marriage and then gotten out of it? The overwhelming majority remarry and try to live in a way that is more life-giving for the self and others than the first. Frequently, these marriages "fail," as did the first, and I put "fail" in quotes, because I don't think marriages fail; I think people fail marriages."[5]

For discussion

1. What problems does the counselor think being hung up on honeymoons can lead to in marriage?
2. What kind of masquerade did the man and his wife carry on, and how did it hurt their marriage?
3. What does the man believe about the "ideal marriage"? How many times was he married, and what was each "marriage" like? Explain.
4. What trap does the man describe, and how does he recommend getting out of it?

For discussion

1. Do you think couples commonly carry on a kind of masquerade in their relationship? Explain.
2. Do you agree that people lie a lot about their romantic relationships? That the media don't present "the breadth and depth of authentic experience" about human relationships? How do the media often portray human relationships? Give examples.
3. Do you think teenagers view being involved in a special relationship as a process or as an answer to their problems? Explain.
4. What do you think is the difference between having ideals to strive for in a relationship and making one's ideal images of relationship into an idol?
5. Why do most divorced persons remarry? Why do you think second marriages so often fail? Explain.
6. Do you agree that "marriages don't fail; people fail marriages"? Do you think that's also true of other relationships? Explain.

Addressing problems

Couples divorce and other relationships break up for many reasons. A common one is the small complaints that chronically irritate two people about each other until they just can't stand it anymore. Little things pile up until the "last straw" is reached. It's unfortunate when individuals see those things as reasons to end rather than improve the relationship.

This next activity is based on couples' most common gripes about each other. You'll have a chance to examine honestly which complaints apply to you. Then you can make needed changes about yourself before they lead to the heartache of a break-up or divorce: "An ounce of prevention is worth a pound of cure." This activity can also help you think about which quirks in someone else bother the daylights out of you. Maybe you could ignore them temporarily, but you might find them intolerable "until death do you part"!

Love one another, but make not a bond of love:
Let it rather be a moving **sea** between the shores of your souls. . . .
And stand together yet not too **near** together:
For the **pillars** of the temple stand apart,
And the oak tree and the cypress grow not
in **each** other's shadow.

KAHLIL GIBRAN, *THE PROPHET*[6]

An ounce of prevention

Write A–F on each blank to indicate which response best describes you. Your instructor will then tell you how to score and interpret the results. You won't be expected to share your responses.

A — **Never/Not at all**
B — **Rarely/Hardly at all**
C — **Seldom/Not very strongly**
D — **Sometimes/Somewhat, but not strongly**
E — **Often/Somewhat strongly**
F — **Always/Very strongly**

_____ 1. Are you lazy?

_____ 2. Are you critical of others—especially your family and others close to you?

_____ 3. Are you narrow minded?

_____ 4. Are you interested in what affects your family members—even if it doesn't directly affect you?

_____ 5. Do you argue with others frequently?

_____ 6. Do you show your affection enough for those you really care about?

_____ 7. Are you nervous or overly emotional?

_____ 8. Are you easily irritated even by small things?

_____ 9. How honest are you?

_____ 10. Are you impatient?

_____ 11. Do you interfere in matters that are none of your business?

_____ 12. Are you rude to or abrupt with people?

_____ 13. Are you good at managing money without being too loose or tight with it?

_____ 14. Do you discuss disagreements with others calmly and rationally, especially when there are hard feelings between you?

_____ 15. Are you easily influenced by others?

_____ 16. Are you a jealous person?

_____ 17. How sincere are you in what you say and do?

_____ 18. Are you somewhat conceited?

_____ 19. To what extent are you selfish or inconsiderate?

_____ 20. Do you neglect your responsibilities?

_____ 21. Are you loyal and faithful to friends and commitments?

_____ 22. Do you lack ambition?

_____ 23. Do you have any habits that others find annoying?

_____ 24. Do you gossip?

_____ 25. Do you complain a lot?

_____ 26. Do you nag when you want something from someone?

_____ 27. Are you sloppy in your appearance?

_____ 28. Are you easily angered?

_____ 29. Are your feelings easily hurt?

_____ 30. Do you keep your room and belongings reasonably neat, clean, and in good condition?

_____ 31. Do you speak up for what you believe in, without being intimidated?

_____ 32. Do you like conversing with others and listening to what interests them—even the small things?

_____ 33. Would you probably spoil—or be too strict with—your children?

_____ 34. Are you a perfectionist or often frustrated with how others do things because you think you have a better idea?

_____ 35. Do you give your undivided attention to someone who's speaking to you?

_____ **"Prevention" Score**

Dual-career couples

In the vast majority of marriages in our society, both spouses work. In many cases two incomes are necessary to support the household, especially when children are involved. But it's often a struggle to balance work and family obligations. Here's how it typically goes:

- Your boss needs you to work overtime today, but you've also got to pick up your kids at school.
- You're asked to attend an out-of-town business meeting the day your child is playing in an important game you'd promised you wouldn't miss.
- You were planning on a relaxing evening out with your spouse after a hard day's work. But your spouse has to work late, so the plans are cancelled at the last minute and you must cook dinner tonight.
- After a tension-filled day at work, you're exhausted—but tonight your spouse is feeling amorous.
- You've listened to customer complaints all day. When you come home your spouse complains that you haven't been getting your household chores done lately.

Do you get the picture?

Thankfully, more men today are pitching in with household tasks and the care of the children. But dual-career couples are still overloaded, and that strains their relationship. Some couples find that the only solution is for one or both partners to work part-time. More employers are accommodating employees' requests for on-site day-care and after-school programs for young children. They are letting employees work a more flexible schedule. Those things help the couples and boost productivity. There's less tension at work, and there's lower absenteeism and job turnover.

Couples often blame their jobs, though, for problems between them, when the real cause is something else entirely. Perhaps one partner doesn't respect the other's concerns enough. Or the partners don't make enough time for each other. Maybe they need to draw up a plan that will help them manage their time better. What couples definitely need to realize is that they share a common problem. If they work together instead of battling against each other, they can address and fix it.

If I had known what trouble you were bearing what griefs were in the silence of your face, I would have been more gentle, and more caring, and tried to give you gladness for a space.

MARY CAROLYN DAVIES

Journal entry

1. What little things bother you the most about other people?
2. Which of those things shouldn't you let bother you so much?

For discussion

1. What solutions would you propose for each of the dual-career strains listed above? Explain.
2. What do you think would happen in each of those situations if the couple kept battling each other rather than working together to solve the real problem? How might they together successfully address their common problem? Be specific.
3. As an employer how would you try to relieve some of the strains that overload your single and married employees? Explain.

Christian marriage is a sacrament by which man and woman profess to each other solemn vows of love and fidelity, which serve as the outward sign of an interior reality.

HUMAN SEXUALITY: A CATHOLIC PERSPECTIVE FOR EDUCATION AND LIFELONG LEARNING, 94.

Being unfaithful

The vast majority of couples in our society, social researchers say, remain faithful to their spouse for life. But infidelity remains a problem in about one out of four marriages—and in far more relationships outside of marriage! Single persons are not bound to remain in an exclusive relationship with each other. As a single person you shouldn't bind yourself to date someone exclusively while you also still want the freedom to date others. Marriage is the only such exclusive commitment that's permanent.

Being single, you don't have to promise exclusivity in a relationship. But if you do, then you should keep your word until after you both change the agreement, if you do—or until the relationship ends, if it does. People either value fidelity as a priority or they don't. If someone can't honor a temporary promise of fidelity to you, don't believe for a minute that he or she will honor it for a lifetime.

Fidelity is about being loyal and keeping promises. It means you do what you say you're going to do. Our faithfulness to our commitments should reflect God's faithfulness to us. In a marriage or other close relationship, being faithful means not causing the other person needless pain by going back on your word. It means not doing something that will wreck the relationship's foundation. A main way of being unfaithful to someone is to have a sexual or romantic affair with someone else—even if it doesn't involve having intercourse.

Betrayal hurls a spear through the heart of a relationship. Trust is key to any relationship. Once trust is lost it's regained only with great difficulty. It's easier to forgive those who are both truly sorry and trustworthy. You know they'll keep their word to not wrong you again. But when you can't trust someone who apologizes, then what is left of your relationship? When there's a continuing pattern of betrayal, the loss of trust may be irreparable.

Besides sexual and romantic infidelity, there are other ways of being unfaithful to one's spouse. People joke about the golfer who removed his hat and bowed his head on the ninth fairway as his wife's funeral procession passed by. But having a spouse who's married to a hobby or to work instead of to you isn't at all funny. That partner is also being unfaithful to the unity of the marriage covenant, and so is the spouse who no longer makes an effort to help around the house or to be thoughtful and considerate. For that too dents the other partner's trust in the relationship.

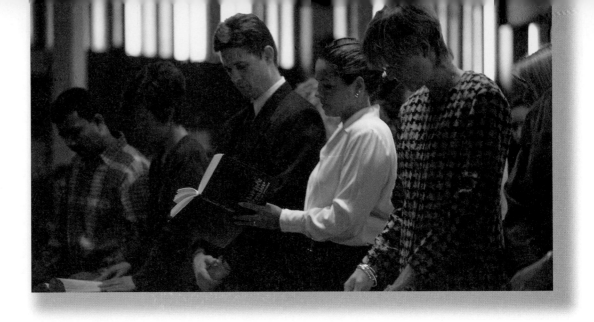

... you, O Lord, are a God **merciful** and gracious ...
abounding in steadfast love and faithfulness.

PSALM 86:15

Being faithful requires being determined to be true to the one you love. It requires the character and unselfishness to sacrifice your preferences to make that happen. That means keeping your priorities straight. If you marry it will mean realizing that your spouse and children are the most important people in your life, and acting accordingly. It will involve putting your loyalty to your family before your desire to further your career. At times you'll have to be willing to give up a purely self-centered pleasure for the greater good of keeping your marriage and family commitments.

Don't use the stress in your life or the problems in your marriage as an excuse for entering into an affair on the side. Instead, as a couple directly address your problems. Renew your mutual determination to make your marriage better than ever. If necessary, seek professional counseling to see you through the rough times. If tempted to give in to your passions in a moment of weakness, stop and think first about what you're risking. Consider the possibility of pregnancy or contracting a sexually transmitted disease. Presume that, most likely, your spouse will suspect or discover the truth. In any case, you will know the truth.

There are some things in life that, once done, cannot be undone. Although they may be forgiven, they cannot be forgotten. In that sense being unfaithful to one's spouse is one of those irrevocable mistakes. So learn the difference between what selfishly seems important at the moment and what is really right and important in the long run. Make it clear to someone who deliberately tempts you that you have no intention of betraying a marriage covenant. Avoid any kind of relationship that would threaten your marriage or someone else's. Don't toy with temptation.

If you're married and tempted to have an affair, ask yourself: "What might happen to our relationship if I do this?" "What will happen when my spouse finds out?" "What would happen if I were betrayed this way—how would I feel?" As a single person, never let yourself get romantically or sexually involved with someone who's married. It's wrong, and it results in more heartache than you'll ever know—unless your spouse someday is unfaithful to you. Romantically flirting with someone who's married is never harmless. Don't fall for the line, "My wife wouldn't mind; we have an open relationship." Or "I'm so miserable—you're the only one who understands me."

Journal entry

Complete these statements:

1. I've been unfaithful to my commitments or broken my word to others by . . .

2. I will try to be more responsible in keeping my promises and commitments by . . .

For discussion

1. How much does fidelity mean to you in a relationship? Why? Why do you think most married couples remain faithful to each other?

2. What would you mean by "being faithful to each other" in your marriage? In an exclusive romantic relationship as a single person? Explain.

3. What reasons do people commonly give for having been unfaithful? Why else do you think people are unfaithful? What is your response to those reasons?

4. How do you think you'd feel and respond if you discovered that your spouse had been unfaithful? Explain.

5. If you were having problems in your marriage and were tempted to be unfaithful, how would you try to handle the situation? Explain.

6. Explain how you would handle this situation, and why: You're single and extremely attracted to someone you work with who's married. You sense that the attraction is mutual. One day the person asks you, "How'd you like to have dinner together sometime this week?" You understand from co-workers that the person is having marital problems.

Honor the commitment others have made to their marriage.

Most relationships between a single and a married person go nowhere. The married person usually feels guilty and torn between relationships, and the single person feels guilty and used. In the end everybody ends up getting hurt—including the married person's spouse and family. If someone has an unhappy marriage, don't try to "rescue" them by making a bad situation much worse. Honor the commitment others have made to their marriage. Encourage them to work out their problems with their spouse. Behave as you'd want someone else to do if you were the other spouse.

extramarital
outside of one's marriage

People engage in **extramarital** affairs for a variety of reasons. More men than women seem to do so purely for sexual pleasure. Women more often give emotional reasons, such as feeling that their husband is no longer affectionate except in bed. Men and women also cite other reasons: They liked the attention and having someone boost their sagging ego. They wanted to prove they're still able to attract someone. Or they found someone who'd listen to or understand them. And the list of excuses goes on . . . .

Seriously violating a marriage covenant breaks more than the wedding vows. It breaks the people involved. Probably the most common big mistake people regret for the rest of their lives is becoming sexually involved outside of marriage. The sad personal consequences, which often enough include an unintended pregnancy or a serious disease, are enormous.

Reviving a troubled relationship

Couples who break up or divorce often look back on what they did or didn't do that broke down rather than strengthened their relationship. Keeping any relationship alive—or reviving it—takes work instead of taking each other for granted. Couples often realize too late that they were too busy to listen to and otherwise show their love for each other. Counselors say that most troubled marriages probably can be saved—if the couple try hard enough and soon enough to revive it. This section will discuss specific ideas that can help.

Make time for and communicate with each other regularly—away from the kids and other energy-consuming concerns. Many long-time couples still "date" each other more formally once a week. When affording a babysitter is a problem, they find another couple with whom they take turns looking after the children. A key way to revive any relationship is to improve the communication between you. (Apply the things you learned in chapter 5!) Yet, many couples spend only an average of about five minutes a day talking with each other.

Build—or rebuild—trust. Without trust you can't recapture loving intimacy. Some people are very trusting by nature while others, having been burned, find it hard to trust. To overcome mistrust takes time, patience, consistency, support, and encouragement. Building trust happens slowly, a step at a time. To encourage another's trust, respect it! Don't thoughtlessly or carelessly make light of the serious matters shared with you. Don't tease in a way that makes someone uncomfortable. And, in an argument, don't use sensitive personal information as a weapon against the person.

Never cause the person to regret having trusted you. Show how much having the other person's trust means to you. Encourage yourself to trust by realizing why it's so important and by anticipating the closeness you'll experience in sharing more of yourself.

Taking the risk of trusting someone is one of the best ways to gain the other person's trust.

Empathize—be able to feel with the other person. That's one of the things that makes us human and draws us close. A computer has been programmed to think so much like a human that even experts can't tell the difference. But only the real person—not the computer—is able to feel. Relationship problems often stem from lack of understanding. To achieve understanding, be more empathetic. Practice putting yourself in the other person's place mentally and emotionally. Imagine how the other person feels. Share the joy, peace, contentment, and satisfaction, as well as the sad feelings. Also appreciate the other person's individuality, enjoying life through the way she or he experiences things.

There is no lonelier person than the one who lives with a spouse with whom he or she cannot communicate.

MARGARET MEAD

Respect each other. A common thread researchers have found in successful marriages is that the spouses respect each other. Their beliefs and convictions are rooted in common values that bond them together in good times and bad.

Be mature enough to respond in ways that build rather than break down intimacy. Instead of letting the little things irritate you, enjoy them. A woman wrote an advice columnist about how she couldn't stand her husband's snoring. That prompted another woman to respond with how she had conquered the same problem: When her husband's snoring kept her awake, she'd lie there thinking how glad she was that the man she loved was alive, healthy, and lying beside her. Rather than just putting up with her husband's snoring, she made it music to her ears. Or find a practical cure for an aggravation—like the band some people wear across the bridge of their nose at night to keep from snoring.

Use your imagination. If your relationship has begun to dull, there are ways to revive the magic. Break out of boring habits and patterns. Find new ways to explore and enjoy both the differences and similarities that exist between you. Delight in the new discoveries you make about each other. There's always more to know about someone and an infinite variety of ways to give and receive love. Recapture your childhood imagination that once made a castle out of a blanket and a box.

Invent creative times rather than relying on the usual.

"Don't let the perfect be the enemy of the good." Suppose you're a perfectionist who's frustrated that the other person doesn't meet your high expectations in every little detail. Try to enjoy the quirks and imperfections that make the other person unique. Think about how your own imperfection—perfectionism— is probably driving the other person crazy! Have more reasonable expectations. Learn to accept minor faults without always trying to make the other person over according to your ideas.

Those who daily rub elbows in a household know these aggravations well: "Did you leave the toilet seat up again?" "Why didn't you tell me we were out of milk when you used the last of it?" "Did you leave the toothpaste top off again this morning?" It takes maturity to keep intimacy blooming amid life's petty irritations! Such aggravations can gradually chip away at love—or explode into major conflicts. Constant bickering is also physically unhealthy. Research has shown that it can increase a spouse's blood pressure to unhealthy levels. To revive a relationship that's sagging under the weight of constant bickering, remind yourself of what's really important—and what isn't! Don't be always whining or making petty disagreements into major crises. Instead of letting someone's minor faults irritate you to death, focus on the person's good qualities that count far more.

See the humanness and humor in minor imperfections. Find the endearing quality about what so uniquely characterizes the person you love. (That's often how affectionate nicknames originate between spouses and among family members.) Notice the things that please you, and appreciate the person's uniqueness. Think about what's so lovable about the one you love. (Practice that by appreciating your friends and family members more now!) Overcome a selfish attitude of wanting everything your way. Many spouses unhappily discover they've married someone who is old enough to sign a wedding license, but who otherwise remained childish. Maturity doesn't come by making it through life, but by learning from life the qualities that add depth and character.

Try a little tenderness. The root of spouses' emotional or sexual difficulties is often a lack of tenderness. Tenderness has to do with expressing love by treating someone in a kind, gentle, sensitive way. Scripture tells us God is warm and tender (see Hosea 11:8). Tenderness involves how one shows affection—in attitudes, words, and actions. Tenderness treats another with care, emotionally as well as physically. Tenderness is knowing when and how much to give or receive, to hold on or let go, to be gentle or firm, to be expressive or hold back. It means being aware of and sensitive to needs, preferences, and what's appropriate and pleasing. Affectionate tenderness isn't just good for your relationship: When a researcher asked a group of men to begin kissing their wives goodbye in the morning and hello at night, the men's blood pressure dropped to a healthier level.

The prophet Hosea knew firsthand the pain of a disastrous marriage. He therefore recognized how important it is for a couple to remain responsive to one another if their love is to endure:

Therefore, I will now allure her, and bring her into the wilderness, and speak tenderly to her.

HOSEA 2:14

Seek counseling as soon as you need it. Don't wait until it's too late to repair the relationship before you finally get counseling together. Some people stubbornly think nobody can tell them anything they don't already know about themselves. So they refuse to seek the counseling that could help save their marriage or relationship. Talking the problem over with a trusted confidante may help you cope better. But it's no substitute for the professional counseling needed for serious problems. If one of you has a problem with the relationship, then you both have a relationship problem. If you're becoming dissatisfied with how things are between you, let the other person know that very clearly. Don't postpone it because you don't want to hurt the other person's feelings. Suddenly dropping the bombshell that "it's over" can be far more hurtful.

What if the other person refuses to change? The one person you can change is you. Instead of just blaming the other person, try looking in the mirror at your faults. It could be that the other person's "faults" are actually responses to yours! Even if that's not the case, you can sometimes break someone else's bad habits simply by changing how you respond. Don't just keep batting blame back and forth. Interrupt the flow of negative energy between you with different, more positive—and perhaps more creative—responses.

Sometimes the only change you can make is learning to adjust to and accept gracefully the minor irritations. Our bodies can turn mental stresses into pain—as in a tension headache, backache, or stiff neck. When we relax and eliminate the mental stress, the pain disappears. Similarly, overlooking or learning to live with the other person's minor faults can get rid of many chronic relationship tensions. For loving someone means accepting the whole less-than-perfect person.

Forgive. If anyone needs to heed Jesus' words about forgiving, it's married couples!

". . . if there is repentance, you must forgive. And if the same person sins against you seven times a day, and turns back to you seven times and says, 'I repent,' you must forgive."

LUKE 17:3–4

The difficulty with marriage is that we fall in love with a personality, but must live with a character.

PETER DE VRIES

Couples need to express their genuine sorrow and ask pardon for ways they wrong each other. They need to forgive each other graciously. Catholics also find strength and renewal in celebrating the Sacrament of Reconciliation often. But forgiveness requires sincere repentance, which involves changing one's behavior. Forgiving doesn't mean putting up with abuse or being someone else's doormat; abuse is destructive to the relationship and the persons. Repeated serious violations of the marriage covenant may mean that there wasn't a true commitment to it from the beginning.

Pray together for God's help. Don't underestimate the power of prayer to strengthen a relationship. Recommitting yourselves to the religious values you share can renew your bond with each other: "For where two or three are gathered in my name, I am there among them" (Matthew 18:20). And sometimes there is nothing left to do but pray— perhaps for the courage to accept what is beyond your power to change or control.

Project

Choose one.

1. Make a list of the types of resources available in your local civic and religious communities to help couples struggling with their relationships. Note resources that are accessible to couples who can't afford to pay for them.

2. Write your list of A through Z "ABCs of Marriage." (For example, S might be "Support each other.") Illustrate your list in some way and be prepared to share it with the class.

For discussion

1. When would you consider seeking professional counseling to help resolve serious problems in a relationship? Explain.

2. If serious difficulties arose in your marriage, which type of religious or civil community would you rather belong to? Explain.

 • One that recognizes divorce as a readily acceptable and available solution

 • One that supports couples' efforts to resolve their problems and make their marriage succeed

3. What support do you think religious and civic communities should offer those having marriage problems? Those who want to enrich their already good marriage?

4. If you were happily married, what kind of support would you want you and your spouse to offer couples preparing for marriage or struggling to save their marriage? Explain.

5. What is your response to the suggestions given in your text for reviving a relationship? Which suggestions would you add for each type of problem? Explain.

6. A wife said: "The first time he's unfaithful, you forgive. The next time, you see a divorce lawyer." What is your response to her comment? Do you think your answer can be reconciled with what Jesus said about forgiving? Explain.

Review

1. How can couples resolve the difficulties that result from being in a dual-career marriage?

2. Why is marital fidelity so important? Why is violating that fidelity wrong? What harm results?

3. What are some of the ways of being unfaithful to one's spouse?

4. What is the best way to respond if tempted to engage in an extramarital affair or an affair with someone else who's married?

5. What are some of the more serious problems that trouble couples' relationships, and how can couples work to overcome those?

The typical tensions

Read about each of the typical tensions below. Then respond to the questions.

Steamed

I usually get home from work before Tom does, so I do most of the cooking. I try to plan a good dinner for us, but he has a habit of not calling to say he'll be late. I work hard at my career too and deserve a little more consideration.

Sick and tired

When I get home from work, I want to leave the office behind. Jan, on the other hand, brings all of the office problems and politics home with her. And she can't just sum it up—no, I've got to hear every little, gory detail. Frankly, I'm tired of hearing about it. Can't we just unwind and enjoy the evening without her work invading our personal lives every night?

Freezing

Kevin just isn't affectionate the way he used to be when we first met. He says he loves me even more than he did then, but I just wish he'd show it more. We don't hold hands; we hardly kiss or touch or hug—except when he wants to hop into bed. Then he wonders why I'm not in the mood.

Housebound

When we first met, Stephanie seemed to be sensitive to my needs. Now all she seems interested in is the house this, the house that. Everything in our spare time revolves around doing something to, in, or around the house. I'm sick of the house. There are more important things in life. We never seem to have time for each other anymore. When I suggest going out for dinner or away for a weekend together, she wants to paint the bedroom or shop for furniture!

The perfectionist's victim

Nothing I do ever seems good enough to Alison. She used to make me feel better about myself than I had ever felt without her. Now she criticizes everything I try to do around the house. If I hang a picture, it's crooked. If I fix lunch for us, I'm at fault because I didn't clean the counters good enough. When I dust or vacuum, she says, "You missed a spot." I'd be willing to do the laundry, but she's afraid I'll shrink her sweaters. I just can't win with her.

Nagged

It's gotten so I hate to come home at night. Kristin does nothing but nag. It's "Do this, do that." It's "You never do anything around the house." She sounds like my mother. I need a break! I just want to put my feet up a while and relax. I wouldn't mind if the house wasn't in perfect order all the time. I wish she'd just chill out.

I married a know-it-all

Anthony just can't take criticism. He's the boss all day at work and thinks he knows everything at home. I'd like to have a little input in our lives, too—like where we go on vacation or how we spend the weekend.

Drowning in debt

I know we're getting pretty deep in debt with our credit card bills, but Drew just won't budget. He insists on handling the finances, and he complains whenever I spend any money. But he doesn't seem to think anything of eating out often for lunch during the week or buying a new tie he doesn't need. He just doesn't seem to understand that we're going broke.

Looking for a little recognition

Luke doesn't seem to understand that my job is important to me, too. But I'm always the one who has to run the errands after work during the week because he's still too tied up at work. When I got a big promotion, all he said was, "Gee, honey, that's nice." But when he closes a deal or gets a raise, it's a major event—"Let's go out to dinner and celebrate." I'd just like a little more recognition for what I contribute to our income—and for doing a good job at the work I love. Just once I'd like for him to ask with real interest how my day went.

Bored silent

Sumiko says, "You talk a blue streak to your friends about sports, but we never talk anymore." But all she wants to talk about is "us." We know each other so well by now—what's there to talk about?

For discussion

1. What seems to be the main tension in each of the above relationships? What do you think might be at the root of the tension?

2. What might each of the complainants do to change the situation for the better?

3. An Eastern philosopher said that marriage in the West starts at a boil and gradually cools. But in the East it starts cool and gradually comes to a boil. What do you think was meant by that? If that is accurate, why do you think it's true? How do you think married couples in our Western society could revive their initial passion for each other?

When marriages crumble

Most people in our society believe marriage should be a permanent commitment of love and fidelity. The extremely high divorce rate makes it clear that some marriages don't sustain those ideals. Approximately one-third of those who marry for the first time end up divorcing. About three-fourths of those who divorce remarry, and about half of those who remarry eventually divorce again. Every year far more marriages crash than cars!

People can do many things to help build a loving, lasting marriage. The Catholic Church today wants couples to believe in marriage and live it as a permanent, sacred, loving commitment. The Church therefore tries to help people achieve a lasting, loving union. Courses like this one are part of that effort, as are the marriage-preparation programs required for engaged couples. In many places civil law is also trying to help married couples stay together. They may be required to seek counseling and show no hope of reconciling before they may file for civil divorce—especially when it affects children.

Catholics who divorce

Couples should do all they can to strengthen their marriage and overcome their problems. But in certain situations, legal separation or divorce may be the best alternative. Someone whose spouse is abusive should not remain in a threatening situation— nor should the couple's children. In such instances one spouse is justified in separating from the other. Where the abusive spouse remains a threat and refuses to seek treatment, the other spouse often must seek a divorce in order to obtain financial support.

Many people (including Catholics) misunderstand or don't know the Catholic Church's position in such situations. Some have remained in an abusive marriage, continuing to be victimized. They thought the Church would consider it wrong to leave their spouse. Catholic teaching does not oppose civil divorce in every situation. The Church stands for human life and dignity. It clearly supports a spouse's efforts to protect her or his well-being and that of the children. A history of consistent abuse may strongly indicate that the abusive spouse wasn't able to consent fully to entering an indissoluble marriage bond.

When their marriage fails, the individuals involved commonly feel like failures. Catholics often feel they've failed God and their Church. So they stop attending the Eucharist and no longer partake in Communion or celebrate the other sacraments. At the time they most need to experience God's love and the Church's support in coping and healing, they feel cut off and shut out. That's both sad and unnecessary.

Divorced Catholics are *not* automatically excommunicated from the Church community! They're generally encouraged to be actively involved in sacramental and other aspects of Church life. They're invited to seek help from the Catholic community to make it through their painful crisis. Many parishes offer support programs for Catholics who are divorcing or divorced.

God never ever abandons anyone! That's precisely what marriage's most sacred dimension, as covenant and as sacrament, is meant to signify. Married couples' life together is to reflect God's faithful, everlasting love for each and all of us. That's why the Church takes so seriously the matter of marriage as a true, permanent bond. Most divorces occur only after individuals have struggled mightily to hold their marriage together. But ending one's marriage doesn't mean also being divorced from God.

Divorced Catholics who remarry

. . . true love makes us capable of taking on the tasks and problems of married and family life and . . . if it does not give us this capacity it cannot be called love.

POPE JOHN PAUL II

Couples enter into a "marriage in the Church" according to what that means religiously—not just legally. So the reasons must involve that same religious meaning in order for the Church to recognize that there was no marriage in the permanent religious sense. Thus the Church limits Catholics' participation in the sacraments—not when they divorce, but when they divorce and remarry without the Church first recognizing that they're free to remarry.

Those Catholics are still part of the Church community. They're welcome to participate in the Eucharistic liturgy (Mass) even though they may not be allowed to participate in Holy Communion. Divorced-remarried Catholics who do receive Communion shouldn't be judged by other parishioners as automatically breaking Church law. The processes by which those Catholics' remarriages may have been officially recognized by the Church are often not widely known in the parish. Divorced-remarried Catholics who have questions about participating in Church life should seek the parish priest's guidance.

Some Catholics have long been divorced and remarried outside the Catholic Church but want to participate fully again in Catholic sacramental life. Many of them have raised children with their current spouse, and breaking up their home would tragically disrupt their families. Recognizing those Catholics' conflict and pain, the Church encourages each parish community to reach out to them with healing compassion. Church representatives are willing to help them examine the possibility of remarrying in the Church. In the meantime those couples are invited to share in Catholic worship, where the whole Church prays with them for strength and guidance.

For discussion

1. What's your reaction to our society's extremely high divorce rate? Explain.

2. Why do you think so many who remarry after divorce end up divorcing again?

3. What steps are Church and civil communities taking to help couples achieve happier, lasting marriages? What further steps would you recommend? Why?

4. How would you respond to the person who says, "What business is it of the Church's if a Catholic divorces or if a divorced Catholic remarries without the Church's permission?"

Divorce and annulment

divorce
a legal declaration that a marriage has ended

declaration of nullity
an annulment declaration, a Church judgment that the marriage was not a true and unbreakable spiritual bond

Fifty years ago, **divorce** was the social exception. Those who did divorce—especially if they remarried—scandalized the community. It was hard to get a divorce from the state, and even more rare to be granted an annulment declaration by Church officials. Throughout history State and Church policies on marriage, divorce, and annulment have varied. Over the centuries humanity's understanding of the nature and meaning of marriage has grown. Thus Church and civil policies and practices have also changed.

In the Catholic Church in the West, the Church minister doesn't marry a couple—they marry each other. So in granting a **declaration of nullity** under certain circumstances today, the Church isn't ending a couple's marriage. It is simply recognizing formally what the couple themselves have already realized—that they made a serious mistake in believing that they were marrying each other for life. An annulment declaration doesn't dissolve a couple's marriage. Catholics believe that genuine marriage covenants should be loving, happy commitments that are lasting and unbreakable:

> *"So they are no longer two, but one flesh. Therefore what God has joined together, let no one separate."*
>
> MATTHEW 19:6

The Church also understands that sometimes individuals thought they were entering into a genuine, lasting marriage in that permanent religious sense, but were mistaken. For instance, perhaps their wedding promises meant one thing to one partner but something else to the other. The annulment declaration is simply an official recognition of that sad reality.

A religious annulment declaration acknowledges that either or both persons did not or could not enter into a marriage covenant that was a true, unbreakable spiritual bond. Thus a Church declaration of nullity means that a person is free to marry again within the Church community. But a religious declaration of nullity has no civil effect. It may be, however, that the same essential elements missing for religious validity were also essential to contract a valid marriage according to civil law. The Church does support the just terms of civil divorce settlements—regarding child custody arrangements, property settlements, and financial support, for instance.

Catholic law describes the essence of marriage as covenant and as sacrament:

> *The essential properties of marriage are unity and indissolubility; in Christian marriage they acquire a distinctive firmness by reason of the sacrament.*[7]

A religious annulment declaration does not deny that the parties were validly married in the civil sense. It doesn't mean that they were never a close, loving couple. It doesn't suggest that they were sinful, guilty, or morally at fault. And it certainly doesn't imply that their children were illegitimate! The religious declaration of nullity declares that the parties did not share a permanent religious marriage bond. In the religious sense, they are therefore not bound by marriage to each other and are free to marry someone else.

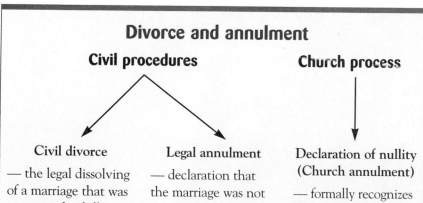

Divorce and annulment

Civil procedures

Church process

Civil divorce
— the legal dissolving of a marriage that was contracted validly according to civil law

Legal annulment
— declaration that the marriage was not contracted according to the basic civil requirements for validity

Declaration of nullity (Church annulment)
— formally recognizes that something prevented the couple from entering a permanent marriage bond in the religious or sacramental sense

Divorced Catholics who've already remarried outside the Church still have the right to apply for an annulment declaration regarding their earlier marriage. On receiving it they may then ask to have their present marriage blessed or validated by the Church.

Unity is an essential element of marriage. The couple's spiritual bond of true union seals their marriage as a permanent covenant. The Church has always upheld the indissolubility of the marriage sacrament. But it also recognizes circumstances that may indicate that the unity essential for contracting marriage as an unbreakable covenant or sacrament was lacking when the couple walked down the aisle.

In such cases the Church is willing to acknowledge what the couple themselves have painfully had to admit: They've certainly been married in some sense. But they have been trying to live a relationship that, from the beginning, wasn't entered into as a lasting marriage covenant as Catholics understand it. Those individuals are granted an annulment declaration which recognizes that fact. The declaration of nullity leaves both parties free to remarry in the Catholic sense and with the Church's full celebration and blessing.

God, grant me the serenity to accept the things I cannot change, the courage to change the things I can change, and the wisdom to know the difference.

REINHOLD NIEBUHR

For discussion

1. How have society's attitudes regarding divorce and divorced persons changed over the last fifty years? How do you think people generally view divorce and divorced persons now? Explain.

2. How would you explain to someone why the Church believes it can't end a permanent sacramental marriage bond that the couple had freely and fully entered into?

3. If the annulment declaration doesn't end or dissolve the couple's marriage, what does it do?

4. Tom's mother is a divorced-remarried Catholic. She divorced her first husband when his alcoholism made him abusive and their life together unbearable. Tom knows his mother is a believing Catholic and would like to have been able to remarry in the Church. What might Tom suggest to his mother? Explain.

A gift not shared

The Catholic Church recognizes the legal validity of civil marriages

Every marriage—whether Catholic or not—is presumed to be valid in some sense. The welfare of individuals, families, and society would be jeopardized if that weren't the case. But the Church recognizes that a couple's marriage can mean only what the couple fully intend for it to mean when they marry. When individuals (whether Catholic or not) marry with the intention of entering a sacred, valid, indissoluble union, then the Church recognizes their marriage to be such.

When couples intend to enter only a civil marriage that they may end any time by divorce, the Church recognizes their marriages as a valid marriage in that civil sense only—but not as the permanent covenant or sacrament Catholics mean by marriage. Remember, the essence of marriage requires the couple's mutual intent and consent. Therefore only the couple's intentions can determine what type of marriage relationship they are entering.

Sometimes, however, individuals don't recognize their real motives for marrying or for marrying each other. They may not realize, for instance, that hoping the marriage will last for life isn't the same as pledging themselves permanently and completely for life. At twenty-five they may think they're mature enough to make a lifetime commitment, but emotional and psychological barriers might prevent them from truly doing so.

To enter into a truly unbreakable marriage bond, each party must have that intention and the proper fully informed consent. In considering annulment petitions, Church representatives consider what symptoms, characteristics, or circumstances may show that, for either party, the full intent to marry in that sense was missing. Perhaps one party was dishonest or too immature to enter fully into a loving communion of life. Or maybe one of the parties wasn't emotionally stable enough for a permanent relationship.

Signs of those things usually surface before marriage, but individuals can be too blinded by love to see them. Or they might not take them seriously enough to postpone or cancel the wedding. Some couples don't recognize until later in their marriage that they never did fully commit themselves to each other. Certainly, there's always room for growth in a marriage, but some couples make a permanent commitment years only after they've married. (Sometimes those couples then decide to have a church wedding or to renew their vows in a church service. That isn't required, however, if their wedding had been in church. Their mutual re-commitment is what's essential.) Too often, though, the necessary commitment is missing from the start and is never achieved—as the couple painfully recognize when filing for divorce.

1. What do you think it means to say that a couple's marriage was a gift in words but not achieved in their life together? Why may that also mean that theirs wasn't a true marriage covenant or sacrament?

2. Describe how a couple might not realize until later in their marriage
   • What their real motives were for marrying
   • That they never fully committed themselves to each other in marriage

3. What do you think is the difference between hoping that one's marriage will last and pledging to each other that it will?

4. Sam wants to know: "Why aren't the 'irreconcilable differences' cited in a couple's divorce proceedings enough for the Church to automatically grant them an annulment declaration?" How would you explain that to him?

5. What do people usually mean by saying that a divorcing couple "just weren't meant for each other"? Is that the same or different from what the Church recognizes in granting an annulment declaration? Explain.

The annulment process can facilitate the healing needed after a marriage has ended.

Society requires certain things before granting couples a civil divorce. Church law also requires that a couple follow certain procedures in seeking an annulment declaration. Civil law considers marriage's legal and social implications: "Irreconcilable differences" may just refer to superficialities—maybe the wife loves cabbage but her husband hates it. The Catholic annulment process, however, focuses on the nature of the marriage relationship. For instance, if one partner values fidelity but the other doesn't, there may be a basic incompatibility of intent. Here, the irreconcilable differences would be a lack of fundamental agreement from the beginning about what marriage means.

If either partner doesn't or can't consent fully to a permanent commitment at the wedding, they can't enter an irrevocable marriage union. Persons may be so emotionally immature or psychologically impaired by alcoholism or other drug addiction, for example, that they can't fulfill the responsibilities of marriage. On the outside the marriage may be celebrated according to civil and Church law. But, although they say "I do" at the altar, something basic is missing.

Marriage is meant to be far more than a civil contract. The marriage vocation is a gift from God that calls for the couple's response in how they live and love. As a covenant, marriage is to be a faithful, lasting communion of life. As a sacrament, marriage is a bond that's unbreakable. When something fundamental has been missing in a marriage from the beginning, the Church recognizes along with the couple that they were never meant for each other.

The annulment process

Divorced Catholics who want to remarry in the Church must first obtain a declaration of nullity (an annulment declaration) through the Catholic process. So must divorced non-Catholics and non-Christians who want to marry a Catholic. If a couple married in a religious ceremony or context, that usually indicates that they entered marriage as a sacred, permanent covenant. It may turn out, however, as discovered through the annulment process, that that was not the case.

Remember: The annulment declaration does not end or dissolve a couple's marriage. It doesn't mean they were never married in any sense. It does officially acknowledge that they hadn't entered into a permanent marriage covenant or sacrament as Catholics understand that in the religious sense.

A divorced non-Christian may alternately seek the special dispensation of the *favor of the faith* (Pauline privilege) in order to marry a Catholic in the Catholic Church. That does dissolve the person's previous non-sacramental marriage. That exception is made because the Church supports religious faith as an even higher value than protecting the permanence of the marriage bond.

The Church has a judicial system consisting of a court, or *tribunal*, in each diocese, as well as higher courts of appeal. The tribunal system's purpose is to protect the Church's integrity and the rights of individual Catholics. It's the diocesan marriage tribunal that considers annulment petitions, helping to determine whether the couple ever intended to marry in the Catholic sense. Unlike civil divorce courts, the marriage tribunal's proceedings and communications about individual cases are kept strictly confidential.

When a couple marries, witnesses must testify to their intent to marry. When seeking an annulment, a person is asked to produce witnesses willing to attest to circumstances that may indicate essential elements were lacking for a permanent marriage bond. The annulment process generally takes several months because of the time needed to obtain and assess that testimony. One party may seek an annulment declaration even if the other spouse opposes it. So there must also be enough time to allow the other spouse to respond.

Granting an annulment declaration has nothing to do with whether the couple's children are legitimate. The Church recognizes that all children are legitimate! Given life by their Creator, they have a right to be here—however they were conceived and whatever their parents' relationship when they were born.

Those entering a second marriage do best if they learn from their earlier mistakes and change any patterns that led to problems.

For the Church to celebrate a marriage as a **sacred permanent commitment**, the couple must also indicate that they have the same intent. When couples ask the Church to accept that theirs was not a marriage in that sense, some evidence is also required. The Church doesn't judge the morality of the couple as persons, nor does the Church judge the morality of their intentions or motives in marrying. The annulment process merely attempts to assess this: When the couple entered into this relationship, did they both intend their marriage to mean the same thing the Church community means by a permanent marriage covenant?

Every marriage has problems from time to time. Even serious problems don't necessarily mean the marriage is on the rocks. Couples should make every reasonable effort to resolve their problems and should willingly seek counseling when needed. For Catholics whose marriages do end in divorce, the annulment process can be enlightening and cleansing. It helps many people discover for the first time the real reasons their marriage didn't last. Those valuable insights bring them the healing and hope they need to put old wounds behind them and build a new, happier future.

For discussion

1. Why don't all serious problems between a couple mean they have reason to seek an annulment declaration? Which kinds of problems do you think might indicate that they do?

2. Marian, a non-Catholic Christian, married Paul, a Catholic, in a Catholic wedding ceremony. After years of unhappiness in their marriage, Paul sought and obtained a divorce and a Catholic annulment declaration. Marian didn't want the divorce, but she was especially outraged about the annulment declaration. She didn't understand "how the Church could say we were never married, and 'bastardize' our seven kids." What does Marian misunderstand? How would you try to explain that to her?

3. A Jewish friend of yours who is divorced wants to marry a Catholic. He has been told that he must obtain a Catholic annulment declaration before the couple may marry in the Church. How would you explain to your friend why the Church considers that necessary?

4. A divorced non-Catholic friend of yours has just found out he must obtain a Catholic annulment declaration in order to marry his Catholic fiancée. He's apprehensive because he doesn't know what the annulment process involves—except that to him it means "dredging up past wounds." Explain what you would say to help inform and reassure your friend.

Review

1. Must or should Catholics remain in an intolerable marriage? What relationship with the Catholic Church do divorced Catholics have? Explain.

2. What is Catholic law and teaching concerning divorce and the indissolubility of marriage? For what reason does the Church sometimes dissolve a marriage?

3. What is a Catholic annulment declaration, and how is it different from a civil divorce or legal annulment?

4. Why does the Catholic Church grant a declaration of nullity, and under what circumstances? What does the Catholic annulment process involve? Why?

5. Why must a Catholic obtain an annulment declaration before remarrying in the Catholic Church?

6. Does being granted a Catholic annulment declaration mean that the children of the marriage are illegitimate? Explain.

7. In what sense does the Catholic Church recognize as valid the marriages of non-Catholics or of Catholics who marry outside the Catholic Church?

Love is the quest,
marriage the conquest,
divorce the inquest.

Relationship portraits— Is something missing?

Read the common relationship portraits below. Consider whether the parties are able to form the intent and fully informed consent needed for entering a **true, permanent marriage covenant or sacrament**. Then respond to the questions.

Bob and Denise

Denise knows that her fiancé Bob adores her. She thinks they're perfect for each other. He always seems to agree with her opinion, and they never argue.

Bob never contradicts Denise and is extremely generous to her. Whenever she mentions that she'd really like to have something, he always finds a way to buy it for her.

Denise considers herself lucky to be marrying a man who loves her so much that he'd do anything for her.

Anna and Bruce

Anna's parents are very wealthy. Her fiancé Bruce grew up in poverty. Both sets of parents are concerned that this difference might cause problems in their future marriage.

Anna is proud of Bruce and thinks he has a promising medical career. Bruce, however, secretly wonders if he'll be able to give Anna the kind of life she's used to. He tells her the next several years will be financially lean, until his practice becomes established. He says Anna will have to hold down a job too until his medical school debts are paid off.

Bruce is bothered that Anna seems to have no concept of money. She loves expensive fashions and always wears the latest styles. She says she wants to look nice for him. But Anna's always behind in paying her bills and spends beyond her means. Bruce knows that Anna relies on her parents to bail her out with the necessary funds. She also goes running to them first whenever she and Bruce have a problem or disagreement.

Karen and Gordon

Karen considers Gordon a "real man" who "knows what he wants and goes after it." Gordon doesn't let anybody push him around. He always lets the other guy "know who's boss." When Karen's worried about something, Gordon always says, "Don't worry, I'll always take care of you." Karen loves and looks up to Gordon and always tries to make a good impression on him by how she dresses and acts.

Jerry and Elena

Jerry wants very much to have lots of kids. Whenever he talks about having children together in the future his fianceé Elena, says "Maybe someday—but let's not think about that right now." Jerry knows Elena comes from an unhappy family background. He suspects she might have been abused as a child. But he figures it's best to leave past experiences behind.

Larry and Chris

Chris and Larry are determined to marry as soon as they both reach legal age. They're in love and determined to make their marriage work. But their parents and friends think they're both too young.

Michael and Crystal

Crystal is flattered that her fiancé Michael considers her sexy. He likes her to wear curve-flattering clothes, but only when she's at home around him. She believes Michael is jealous and possessive because he loves her. What Crystal doesn't like, though, are the jokes he tells and the movies he likes to see in which the woman is always treated as the object of the man's sexual pleasure. After they argued about that once, Michael said he'd stop seeing those kinds of movies and telling those jokes. Crystal suspects he still does those things but just doesn't let her know. She recently found a current magazine he had that depicted naked or skimpily clad women bound up or chained in bondage poses.

Sherry and Kevin

Sherry's a graduate student. Her fiancé Kevin took a job after high school instead of going to college. Since then, Kevin's continued to live at home with his mother while going from one job to another. He doesn't seem able to work in one place very long. He always says his reason for quitting is that his talents aren't appreciated and his bosses are unfair.

Sherry knows Kevin's life hasn't been easy since his father died when Kevin was twelve. She believes that once they're married Kevin's life will be more stable.

She's convinced that sooner or later he'll find a job that will make him happy. In the meantime she thinks she'll be able to support both of them after she receives her degree—a week before their scheduled wedding.

Bill and Beth

Beth told Bill firmly that she'd marry him on one condition—that he give up smoking cigarettes. Bill agreed. A week after he stopped smoking, Beth set the wedding date.

Jolanda and Stan

Stan brags about his ability to "hold his booze." His fiancée Jolanda worries that he drinks too much. She knows Stan's been arrested once for drunk driving. Stan says he doesn't drink hard liquor anymore, just beer. He promises Jolanda he won't drive after he's been drinking. But Stan never told Jolanda that he'd also been arrested another time for possessing cocaine. Even though Stan was guilty, the lawyer had gotten him released on a technicality. Stan still uses cocaine, but doesn't think Jolanda suspects.

Stu and Amy

When Amy couldn't stand any longer the hassles of living at home with her parents, she moved out and into her boyfriend's apartment. After she and Stu lived together several months, Amy was trying to decide whether to marry Stu when she discovered she was pregnant. When she told Stu, he begged her to marry him as soon as possible. Amy finally agreed. She loves Stu and thinks marrying him will be best for the baby. It will help her avoid her parents' wrath and the difficulties of trying to raise the child alone.

For discussion

1. In each relationship portrait
   - What signs are there, if any, that either party might not be able to achieve the unity essential to a true, lasting sacramental marriage bond? Be specific.
   - How might each of those signs indicate that a partner lacks the intent and consent needed to enter into a true, permanent marriage covenant?
2. Why might the signs you've identified be enough reason to seek a Church annulment declaration from a marriage?
3. What attitudes or behaviors might tell you that the person you love isn't ready, able, or truly willing to enter a genuine, lasting marriage covenant with you? Be specific.

Dealing with the difficulties of divorce

Breaking up with someone can be extremely painful. It's far more difficult when it involves the break-up of a marriage, as this letter reveals. It's from a wife to her estranged husband.

Dearest _____,

Somehow leaving notes on the kitchen table to my husband . . . while he works on a relationship with another woman just doesn't seem like proper communication. However, since you'd prefer to stay away from a face-to-face confrontation, I guess this will have to do.

Since we last spoke, I've been mulling over a lot, as I'm sure you have been. . . .

I've tried extremely hard these last few weeks to cope, to be patient, and to understand your requests for time and greater understanding. But I've received little response in return when I've asked anything of you.

I guess I'm just tired of going nowhere on the paths I've tried to explore with you lately. Lover, maybe you are enjoying yourself and can take this indecision, but I can't. Not anymore.

It seems we're marching to "different drummers," and we've each got to follow the music we hear. . . .

_____, I feel it's time to turn the page and end this sad chapter of our lives together. . . .

Perhaps the greatest birthday present I could give you is your freedom and independence to go where you want to go and love whom you want to love.

I'm ready to begin a new life and feel I must. The Lord gave me a rainbow and I've placed my trust in Him. . . .

Unless you feel there's a need to discuss things further, I'll take the necessary action as soon as possible. If you can, please gather your things and make this trip your last. . . .

With the good Lord's blessing, maybe we can still be friends when all this is over and done.

Take care of yourself, _____.

May you find the peace, contentment, and happiness you're so desperately searching for . . . God be with you.

With fond memories and few regrets of a once beautiful marriage.

Whatever brings it about, ending a marriage is always a heartache. A common misconception is that marriages end because the couple don't love each other anymore. But it's precisely the concern for each other that so often makes deciding to end the marriage so difficult. That is indicated in the above letter of a young wife who then obtained a divorce and a Catholic annulment declaration.

Jesus taught that no one should separate a marriage union that God had joined. But he also taught that we should treat others compassionately. For that reason the Catholic Church upholds the ideal of marriage as a binding commitment. It also reaches out to help those coping with the pain of divorce.

> . . . I earnestly call upon pastors and the whole community of the faithful to help the divorced and with solicitous care to make sure that they do not consider themselves as separated from the church, for as baptized persons they can and indeed must share in her life.[8]

Divorce is like a death. Everything said earlier in this text about the painful process people go through when a love relationship ends is certainly true in a marriage break-up. The emotional hurt is often agonizing—for the children involved and for the separating partners. As one twelfth-grade student put it, with tears welling up in her eyes: "This Saturday is the tenth anniversary of the date my father left my mother, and my family is just now really starting to cope with it well."

Our attitudes, feelings, and beliefs about marriage are colored by our personal experiences. That's certainly true of those whose family has been affected by marital conflict or divorce. Before deciding to marry, you must honestly confront your attitudes, feelings, and beliefs—these will affect your happiness in marriage.

Ironically, those who divorce often later marry the same wrong type of person! Even when couples choose the right person, they often divorce because they don't understand how to make it work. When they remarry, many make the same mistakes they made the first time, so their second marriage ends in divorce, too.

That's why it's important to make wise choices about marrying and to do everything possible to make it a loving, lasting union. But once separated, individuals must take steps to cope and heal, both for their sakes and their children's. Before a civil divorce is granted, couples with children are sometimes required to attend classes on dealing with the effects of divorce. Many parishes offer classes and retreats designed to help couples and families cope with the problems of divorce.

What couples should consider before seeking a divorce

1. Parents make mistakes about loving, and they hurt when they lose love. Kids need help realizing that parents aren't born perfect, inseparable, or invulnerable.

2. Children feel they're the ones being divorced. They need to know that their parents still love them and will always love them—no matter what.

3. The spouses should help each other and their children, as far as reasonable, understand the reasons they're divorcing. They should support each other during this difficult time.

4. Family members should be encouraged to talk about what they think, need, and would like regarding their future lifestyle arrangements.

5. The children should never be weapons parents use to cope or "get even."

6. Love is a gift to be given and received freely. Parents and children need to realize that love can't be forced. They shouldn't expect each other to not love a future step-parent or spouse.

Journal entry

1. How has divorce affected your life or the lives of your friends?

2. How has the widespread prevalence of divorce affected your attitude about marriage?

3. What mistakes do you keep making in your relationships with others? Explain.

Project

Choose one.

1. Find out what resources are available in your diocese and parish for individuals and families coping with divorce. Talk with someone involved in ministry to divorced persons about their experiences. Write a two-page paper summarizing what you've learned.

2. Write a poem, song, or two-page paper on coping with the pain of divorce.

3. Talk to at least four divorced men and women who are willing to share with you positive lessons they learned from their first marriage. Write a two-page paper summarizing what you learn.

4. Interview a marriage counselor about the reasons marriages fail. Write a two-page paper on what you learn.

5. Interview two married couples about how they've grown together as a result of problems during their marriage. Write a two-page paper summarizing what you learned.

For discussion

1. What practical problems are connected with divorce? How can family members cope with those problems?

2. What's your response to what couples should consider before seeking a divorce? What advice would you add?

3. Should couples and their families attend preparation classes before being granted a civil divorce? If you were teaching a parish class designed to help couples and families cope with divorce, what would you suggest to them, and why?

4. What advice would you give to help:
   • Someone who's having a hard time coping with being divorced
   • A friend who's having a hard time coping with his or her parents' divorce
   • Younger children understand and cope with their parents' divorce

5. How might a teenager help a parent who's finding it hard to cope with divorce? Explain.

6. Why do you think individuals marry the same type of person they divorced?

7. What main things do you think couples can and should try to do to help keep their marriage together? Explain.

Review

1. What are some of the main difficulties divorce causes? How can individuals and their families best cope with those?

2. How does the Church endeavor to minister to divorced Catholics and their families?

3. What can individuals and couples do to increase the chances that their marriage will last?

In summary

Marriage is a covenant meant to unite the couple in a bond of love for life. Successfully living that covenant involves adjustments that require understanding, effort, flexibility, patience, and mutual support. The partners should respect and treat each other as equals, discuss their expectations, and share fairly in responsibilities. Christian married couples continue giving each other the marriage sacrament. They recreate their marriage daily through the unselfish care, sacrifice, and faithfulness that deepen Christ's presence in their lives. Couples should also have realistic goals and expectations and should prioritize to properly balance work and family obligations. Problems such as infidelity can seriously damage a marriage. If couples address their problems together soon enough, they can usually revive their marriage.

The Catholic community tries to help individuals achieve lasting, loving marriages. But spouses needn't and shouldn't remain in intolerable or abusive marriages. Divorce may be the only way to protect a spouse and children. Divorced Catholics are encouraged to actively participate in and seek support from the Church. Neither God nor the Church abandons them. Ending a marriage is always difficult, but individuals and their children can heal afterward. To help their future relationships succeed, individuals should examine honestly why their marriage failed. They should look to God for the true meaning of all love relationships.

The Church considers unity and indissolubility essential to marriage and considers all valid marriage covenants between baptized persons as sacraments. It presumes that all marriages are valid and mean what a couple fully intends when they marry. Before remarrying in the Church, divorced persons must usually obtain a Catholic annulment declaration. It is granted for reasons based on the Church's religious understanding of marriage. Whatever the status of their parents' relationship, all children are always legitimate.

Key concepts

abusive marriage

annulment

annulment process

declaration of nullity

divorce

dual-career couples

fidelity

infidelity

remarriage

reviving a troubled relationship

roles, responsibilities, and expectations in marriage

Sacrament of Marriage

Endnotes

1. Some of the information and material in this chapter is based directly on the guidelines given in *Faithful to Each Other Forever: A Catholic Handbook of Pastoral Help for Marriage Preparation*, Bishops' Committee for Pastoral Research and Practices, National Conference of Catholic Bishops, United States Catholic Conference, Inc. (Washington, DC: USCC Office of Publishing and Promotion Services, 1989).

2. *On the Family (Familiaris Consortio)*, Apostolic Exhortation of Pope John Paul II (15 December 1981).

3. *On the Family*, 29.

4. *On the Family*, 29.

5. Title and excerpts from "Images of Marriage" by Sidney M. Jourard, PhD, vol. 1, no.3, of the *Journal of Marriage and Family Counseling*, © American Association of Marriage and Family Counselors.

6. From *The Prophet* by Kahlil Gibran. Copyright 1923 by Kahlil Gibran and renewed 1951 by Administrators CTA of Kahlil Gibran Estate and Mary G. Gibran. Reprinted by permission of Alfred A. Knopf, Inc.

7. *The Code of Canon Law*, canons 1055 and 1056.

8. *On the Family*, 45.

CHAPTER 12

FAMILY LIFE

SCRIPTURE

"Let the little children come to
me, and do not stop them; for
it is to such as these that the
kingdom of God belongs."

LUKE 18:16

PRAYER

God, Father, Mother,
Caring Parent who holds me in love,
I thank you for your constant care.
When I am pushed against the cold walls
of misunderstanding and despair,
You gently hold me, warming me
with your blankets of forgiveness.
As a small child trusts in the goodness of its parents,
So I, Lord, want to trust in you.
Teach me to accept the tenderness you offer
And to reach out to others in love.[1]

The importance of family

Who you are has been greatly influenced by your family background. How you think and feel about family life will certainly affect your future decisions about marriage and children. These last few chapters can help you understand your family background better, and more wisely make your choices about family life. First you should know how our present ideas and ideals about family life originated.

The family's history

The development of the family

Early human families

- were probably mainly matriarchal
- perhaps consisting of a woman and her children
- were probably protected by the woman's brother rather than a husband-father

Ancient civilizations

- didn't celebrate marriage with a ritual, but considered marital sex sacred
- needed children to help with survival tasks, and viewed them as a gift of the gods
- performed sacrifices and **fertility** rituals to seek the gods' help in **begetting** children
- thought the man deposited a miniature baby inside the woman, who merely nurtured it until birth
- viewed infertility as a woman's moral fault
- considered male children all-important; often killed baby girls

Ancient Roman families

- were the basic religious and social unit
- were patriarchal, headed by an often-tyrannical father
- separated older children from their mothers
- required mothers to be home all the time

Jesus

- showed respect for the family and his parents
- welcomed children
- portrayed the ideal parent as loving and compassionate
- broadened the idea of family to include *everyone*

The centuries after Jesus

- viewed the Holy Family as the Christian ideal
- continued to see the family as patriarchal

fertility
fruitfulness, ability to produce offspring

begetting
producing offspring

even when they were grown up—and who could be, and frequently were, killed at birth simply because he did not want them.

The Roman wife had no property rights and no rights over her own children. She was expected to stay home all the time, not just some of the time. After her sons reached the age of four or five, they were taken away from her to live in a separate part of the house so that they would escape softening feminine influence. She had nothing to say about their education.[3]

Every effort to make society sensitive to the importance of the family is a great service to humanity.

POPE JOHN PAUL II

In ancient times most children didn't survive into adulthood. So having many children was important to ensure human survival. People often presumed that if a woman couldn't bear children, it was because she had done something morally wrong. A childless woman was disgraced and considered punished by God or the gods. Sons were the key to continuing the population through the husband's family clan. That was true of ancient Israel, as the Old Testament describes. So, as one researcher discovered, unwanted infant girls were sometimes killed or neglected and left to die:

I once saw a copy of an interesting letter from a Roman soldier to his pregnant wife. It is a chatty, affectionate, charming letter, tenderly solicitous of her health, but it ends with a reminder that if the baby is a girl she must not forget to have the midwife kill it.[2]

The ancient Israelites defied the surrounding cultures by strongly condemning such **infanticide**.

In the earlier days of the Roman Empire, the family was the basic religious and social unit. Each family had their own household gods to whom they prayed and looked for protection. However,

The Roman family was far from ideal. The father had a tyrant's power . . . over all other members to a degree that everyone today would consider intolerable. He had literal rights of life and death over his children, whom he could legally have killed for disobedience—

infanticide
murdering of a baby

Jesus challenged that prevailing Roman view of family life. As a youth he showed the normal signs of growing independence. But he showed respect for the family and his parents. As an adult he publicly showed how highly he esteemed his mother. For Jesus, the ideal father wasn't the harsh family dictator, but the tenderly loving and compassionate dad who runs to embrace and forgive his wayward child.

When Jesus' disciples wanted to shoo away the children who gathered around him, he said to let the children come to him. Jesus didn't view children as bothersome, but as signs of the totally open, trusting love of the kingdom of heaven. He also broadened the idea of family to include all people, telling us we're *all* brothers and sisters.

For centuries afterward, Christians upheld the Holy Family—Jesus, Mary, and Joseph—as the Christian ideal. But Christians failed to understand and follow Jesus' teaching and example in their family lifestyle. The father continued to dominate—and often domineer—family life from Roman days until our own.

Scripture insights

Find examples in the Christian Scriptures of how Jesus showed his respect for his own parents.

Project

Do further research on the history of family life. Write a two-page paper explaining what you learn.

Today's families

Home is where the heart is.
PLINY THE ELDER

Family life in our society used to be much different than it is today. Most families were *nuclear families* consisting of two parents and their biological or adoptive children. Until the twentieth century, everyone usually worked together in the family business, most often the family farm. So fathers had a great deal of daily contact with their children. As society became increasingly industrialized, more fathers started working at jobs independent of their family. They became less involved in raising their children—a task that mainly fell to the mother who stayed home to raise the children.

Families in previous generations were also more *extended*. Relatives lived near each other and had close ties. Single adults and grandparents often lived with their relatives. Modern transportation and job relocations have made today's family more mobile. Families often move to a different home every few years. Relatives are geographically scattered, and family get-togethers are rare occasions. In most areas, doors are no longer left open for friends, neighbors, and relatives to just "come on in." Many people live on the same block for years without meeting their neighbors! Today's family tends to be more isolated—an island by itself.

Family life has certainly changed throughout human history! It's still changing. For example, in most two-parent families today, both parents work outside the home. Some changes are good and others aren't ideal. One in four children today grows up in a household with only one parent. Researchers estimate that within the next decade we will have more stepfamilies than nuclear families.

The number of single parents (mostly women) raising children has increased sharply. Over one fourth of today's families with children are headed by a single parent, and that number is increasing. Many are single parents by choice, but most are not. Finally, more couples than in the past choose to not have children. And more other couples are having fewer children and waiting longer to have them.

Our mobile society has resulted in fewer geographically centered families than in the past.

Families today

Nuclear family
a household of parents and their dependent children

Stepfamily
relatives by a parent's remarriage

Blended family
includes both parents' children by their previous marriages

Single-parent family
includes only one parent living in the household

Extended family
a group of relatives, which may include a nuclear family, who live in the same household or near one another

Families now call for more participation and responsibility from each member. Husbands and wives share life's tasks and obligations more as equals. Children's opinions are valued more than in times past when children were to be "seen and not heard." Children's family responsibilities have changed. Most children used to work on the farm or ranch or otherwise helped support the family. (In many countries that's still the norm.) Because of the resulting abuses, child-labor laws were enacted and now restrict how children work. Many children must still work to contribute to their family's income. Others may keep the money they earn.

Changes in family life have brought advantages, but have also raised difficult new questions that you'll need to address in the future: As a single adult, would you want to adopt a child or pursue a career involving children? If you marry, how many children should you and your spouse have, and when? What fertility planning methods are safe, effective, and morally acceptable—and which ones aren't? How do you best prepare for having a child? What makes a good parent? The rest of this chapter will address those and other concerns about family life.

For discussion

1. How do you think the way you think and feel about family life will affect your future decisions regarding marriage and children?

2. Which attitudes and practices regarding family life through out history bother you the most? Appeal to you the most? Explain.

3. With which family structures are you most familiar? Explain.

4. What valuable insights do you think Jesus' views can contribute to improving family life? Explain.

5. In addition to those mentioned, what other questions and problems about family life would you like to discuss?

Catholic teaching on family lifestyles

The positive, healthy changes in family life have helped families grow. Although dramatic, upsetting social changes have affected family life, the family has always been strong and flexible enough to adjust. It has helped children pursue their dreams by handing on to them past lessons and achievements. Some aspects of today's family life make everybody uneasy! But it's no good to just keep living old family lifestyles. Humanity's future depends on today's and tomorrow's families.

Even some of the positive changes have caused more stress in families. But the changes also enable spouses to become real partners. Sharing responsibilities more equally lets family members break away from stiff, confining roles. They can grow as individuals and become closer as a family.

Family no longer means only spouses and their children—there are many other kinds of families. Although its structure has changed, **the family is still society's basic unit.** The stability of the family is especially important in our rapidly changing world. For when the family unit breaks down, so does the foundation of society and government—as the ancient Romans learned the hard way! Perhaps Catholic teaching provides the best definition of what ideally a family is.

> . . . a community of individual persons joined by human love and living a community life that provides for the greatest expression of individualism.[4]

> The family, which is founded and given life by love, is a community of persons. . . . Without love the family is not a community of persons and, in the same way, without love the family cannot live, grow and perfect itself as a community of persons.[5]

The Church supports these positive changes in family life

- Stopping unfair limitations on families
- Freedom to choose one's spouse
- More emphasis on spouses' personal growth and relationship
- Greater concern for children's education
- Women becoming better educated
- The growing recognition that men and women are equal
- Sharing family responsibilities more equally

---

1. How has your experience of your own family affected your ideas about family life?
2. Would you say your attitude about family life is mainly positive or negative?
3. How will you make sure that your past experiences of family life have a positive and not a negative effect on your future?

Activity

Write two or three sentences about what family life means to you. Illustrate those thoughts in a collage or computer graphic. Be prepared to explain your graphic to the class.

For discussion

1. How does Catholic teaching's definition of the ideal family compare with your ideal of what the family should be? Explain.
2. Why is it practical and important to strive for an ideal of family life?
3. How important do you think the family is for our society? For the world? Explain.

Review

1. What has family life been like from ancient times until today?
2. What were Jesus' views about family, and how did they challenge his contemporaries?
3. How do the nature and structures of family life in our society compare with family life in previous generations?
4. How does the Catholic Church define the ideal family? How does it view the modern changes in family life? The importance of family life?
5. Why is the family so important to society? Why is family stability important in a rapidly changing world?

Choosing to have children

caprice
whim, impulse

conceiving
the joining of the male sperm and female egg/ovum, which Catholic teaching views as the moment a new human begins to exist

gestation
pregnancy, in humans—the period of about nine months from conception until birth

Deciding to have children is a sacred, awesome responsibility. It is helping God create life! Yet many people become parents without giving that decision enough thought. Rather than being welcomed joyfully, too many children are resented and unwanted. They're regarded as burdens rather than gifts. At least half of the pregnancies in our society are unplanned! The decision to have or postpone having children must be made responsibly. As Catholic teaching says, "it cannot be the result of mere **caprice** or of superficial judgments concerning relative values as between persons and things, between life and its conveniences" (*Human Life in Our Day*, #20).

Children deserve the best possible beginnings. They're at the mercy of those who care for them—or fail to. **Children have a right to be loved and cared for properly!** The incredibly high rates of child abuse, neglect, poverty, and malnourishment show that too many people are unprepared to assume that grave responsibility.

There is also the increasing problem of people willing to do anything to have children. A 70-year-old father decides to have a child with his much younger wife. A 62-year-old woman undergoes fertility treatments and gives birth. But who considers the children's welfare? By the time the child is your age, his or her parents may well be dead or in a nursing home! That is why Pope John Paul II has denounced the mentality and practice of having children "at all costs," and pointed out that there are moral limits on what parents should do to conceive children. The moral right to have children is not an absolute one.

Why have children

Conceiving and bearing children is awesome and wonderful. But as Catholic teaching points out, it also involves responsibilities that sometimes seem intolerable. Why have children then? Good parents know the answer: **Love.** Spouses share and proclaim their love in and through their children.

Children ought to be conceived and raised by those who want them! One shouldn't have children out of a need to be loved, but out of the desire to give love. Children aren't here to fulfill parents' own unrealized personal dreams. Children are to share in and increase family joy—and realize their own potential. Never decide to have children because of the rewards—or the love—you expect in return. Giving life and sharing love are the great rewards.

Journal entry

What is your attitude at present about having children in your future?

For discussion

1. List as many reasons as you can why married and single persons choose to have children. Keeping in mind what Catholic teaching says about it, which of the reasons are wrong reasons for having children? Right reasons? Explain.

2. Why shouldn't deciding to have or to postpone having children be based on weighing persons against things, or life against conveniences?

3. What is your response to the pope's statement that individuals don't have a right to have children "at any cost"? Explain, using examples.

4. If you decide to have children in the future, what would be your reasons for doing so? Explain.

If you had it to do over. . . ?

Read the results of a survey on having children, and people's reactions to it. Then respond to the questions.

A newspaper columnist conducted a survey asking parents this question, "If you had it to do over again, would you have children?" The results were highly disturbing. Seventy percent of those responding said "No."

One stunned person wrote, "I was shocked when I read that seventy percent of the people who responded to your survey said they were sorry they had children. How in the world do you explain this?"

The columnist replied, "Granted, the negatives have a stronger compulsion to write than the affirmatives; even so, I was amazed by the number of people who wrote to confess that having children was not worth the trouble. . . ."

The negative survey responses "fell roughly into three categories: letters from older parents whose children ignore them, younger people concerned about overpopulation and parents with children who find parenthood interferes with their lifestyles."

"Among those letters, . . . in 'Too Late for Tears,' a mother of two children under eight wrote, 'I was an attractive, fulfilled career woman before I had these kids. Now I'm an exhausted, shrieking, nervous wreck. The children took all the romance out of our marriage. I'm too tired for sex, conversation or anything else.'

"In 'Sad Story. . .,' a seventy-year-old mother of five, wrote, 'Not one of our children has given us any pleasure. God knows we did our best. But we were failures as parents and they are failures as people.'"

The columnist said, "One reason for the disillusionment may be that some people enter parenthood with unrealistic expectations. Everybody loves a cute little baby, but nobody wants a teenager who shoplifts or gets hooked on drugs."

"And then . . . when parents find themselves financially strapped with unexpected bills, are no longer able to take romantic vacations and have to stay up all night with sick kids, they ask themselves, 'Who needed this?'"

"ANN LANDERS" COLUMN[6]

For discussion

1. What problems occur when people become parents without first giving parenting enough thought?

2. Do you agree that many people are unfit to assume the grave responsibility of having and raising children? Explain.

3. What was your initial reaction to the survey results? Explain.

4. What reasons did respondents give for being sorry they'd had children?

5. What conclusions and insights do you draw from the survey results and the respondents' comments?

When teenagers have children

A significant number of all the babies born in our society are born to unwed teenagers. The vast majority of those teenage mothers keep their babies rather than place them for adoption. While a father must share the responsibility for any child he helps bring into the world, most teenage fathers have no intention of marrying the teenage mother and usually leave her to deal with the situation alone.

The majority of unwed teenage mothers end up requiring public assistance and find it an uphill struggle to support themselves and their children. There are also graver risks. Physically, teenage pregnancies are riskier for both mother and baby. For instance, babies born to teenage mothers have one of the highest rates of Down Syndrome.

Unwed pregnant teenagers do seem to be growing wiser in one respect: They often choose to not marry just because they're pregnant, or they postpone marriage and marry later for the right reasons. The highest divorce rate has consistently been among those who marry as teenagers—especially if it's because the young woman is pregnant. Most teenage marriages end in divorce.

Despite all evidence to the contrary, many teenagers still think motherhood is easier than marriage! They think having babies and raising children is sort of like playing with dolls. But caring for real babies is not easy! Real children don't always stop crying or show affection when you want them to. Doctors note that many young mothers say they became abusive because their child wouldn't behave or stop crying.

Most teenage pregnancies are unintended, but many teenage mothers were deliberately careless. A twelve-year-old girl said she wanted to get pregnant as soon as she could "because it would be nice to have a baby of my own. My parents don't love me—we're always fighting and arguing. But I could share a lot of love with a baby, and I could move out of the house and live on my own." Some teenage mothers intend to get pregnant despite what they tell their boyfriends!

It is **easier** for a father to have **children** than for children to **have** a real father.

Pope John XXIII

Project

Interview a teenage parent, or an adult who became a parent as a teenager, about the difficulties of being a parent. Write a two-page paper describing what you learned. Include your reaction.

For discussion

1. Why do so many teenagers in our society (over one million each year) become pregnant?

2. What are the choices for an unwed teenage woman who gives birth? Which are the best alternatives? Explain.

3. What are the risks and consequences of pregnancy for an unwed teenager? How do many of those affect you and others in society?

4. Why is it generally unwise for a teenager to marry because she's pregnant?

5. Why do so many teenage mothers choose to keep and raise their babies rather than place them for adoption?

6. How are young men ignorant or naive about "not getting a girl pregnant"? Are they blamed unfairly? Explain.

7. How does a teenage father usually respond when a young woman becomes pregnant by him? What responsibilities does an unwed teenage father has toward his child and her mother? To society? Explain.

Review

1. Why is deciding to have children a very serious decision, and on what should that decision be based?

2. What does Catholic teaching say about deciding to have children?

3. What basic right do all children have? Why is the right to have children not an absolute one?

4. What are some of the personal and social problems that result from teenage pregnancy?

Teenage parenthood

Read the true account of two teenage mothers' experiences. Then respond to the questions.

At eighteen, Stephanie Palmer welcomed the baby girl she had out of wedlock. But marriage? She wanted to wait until she was more mature.

"Yeah, we have a kid, but marriage is a big responsibility," said Palmer, now twenty and living . . . with her two-year-old daughter, Chastity.

"Everybody knows what it's like dealing with a child, but not everybody can deal with a husband," she said. "I think I'll be a better wife when I get older." . . .

Valerie Rodriguez . . . miscarried when she was seventeen and gave birth to her first baby at eighteen —all the while living with her boyfriend. In an earlier time, a girl in her position might have considered holding a quick wedding.

But while Rodriguez willingly entered into the lifetime commitment of motherhood, she was afraid of that other lifetime commitment—marriage.

"Marriage was just too heavy a responsibility," Rodriguez says.

Now her daughter is fifteen months old, and her boyfriend has moved out.

Isn't being a single mother a heavy responsibility? "I never thought about that," she says . . . .

In some ways, the plight of the unwed teenage mother today is not so different from earlier generations. They feel outside the mainstream of adolescent life—while their friends are double-dating, they are changing diapers.

"After Chastity came along, I knew I had to begin making exceptions," said Palmer . . . "Once you get pregnant you know you have to stop doing the things you used to do . . . I had planned to do other things with my life . . . ."[7]

For discussion

1. What were Stephanie's and Valerie's attitudes about having a child? About marriage? Do you think their attitudes were realistic and responsible? Explain.

2. What problems do unwed teenage mothers face?

3. What responsibilities should an unwed teenage father assume toward his child? Toward his child's mother? Who's affected when such young men don't assume those responsibilities?

4. How far do you think the legal system should go in forcing unwed teenage fathers to assume their responsibilities? Should it make a difference if they didn't intend for the young woman to become pregnant, but she did intend it? Explain.

5. Suggest at least three ways to help decrease the number of pregnancies among unwed teenagers.

Having children

Before they decide to have a child, couples need to consider many things—besides buying baby supplies!

Pregnancy and prenatal care

The mother's and father's physical and mental health is extremely important—not only during pregnancy, but at the time of conception. If, for instance, the mother is deficient in the simple vitamin folic acid when conception occurs, it's much more likely that her baby will be born with serious problems. Yet many women don't begin monitoring their health until after they find out they're pregnant—when the damage has already been done! That's certainly true of unwed teen-agers who didn't intend to get pregnant and don't seek prenatal care because they don't want to believe they're pregnant.

Proper **prenatal care** can make the difference between a healthy baby and one who's born ill, disabled, or dead. A woman should seek medical care as soon as there's even a chance she might become pregnant. (If she's fertile and sexually active, there's always that possibility!) Otherwise, it may be too late to correct or prevent serious problems for her child. That's why being sexually active—whether one is married or single—is a life-and-death responsibility.

A baby can be physically deformed and mentally damaged from drugs *either* parent has been using before conception, or that the mother uses during pregnancy. Male sperm can contain traces of drugs that affect the embryo's delicate formation. The often-permanent effects of fetal alcohol syndrome and other drug addiction are tragically common among newborns. The special care many of those children will require for life is a major social problem and expense. The main damage occurs in the earliest, most critical stages of embryonic and fetal development—before the woman is even aware she's pregnant. Couples are forewarned: "If you drink, don't drive—or risk conceiving a baby!"

The greater the use of alcohol, cocaine, or other such drugs, the greater the risks of harm to the baby. For a pregnant woman, there is no safe amount! A baby deserves the best possible chance to be born normally and healthy. If there's a chance the woman might become pregnant, she should check with her doctor about using any drug. She definitely shouldn't smoke. She's also wise to avoid drugs such as the caffeine found in coffee and soft drinks. She should maintain a nutritious diet.

A woman should consult her doctor as soon as she suspects she's pregnant, so her health and the life within her can be carefully monitored. Women should also seek medical advice about a family history of genetic disease or other problems that could complicate a pregnancy or delivery. For those who can't afford to pay for prenatal medical care and treatment, public assistance is available. Any pregnant woman—whether Catholic or not—can seek guidance and, if necessary, other help from the local Catholic parish and diocese.

A couple's main prayer is that their baby will be born healthy and normal. No one likes to dwell on the negative possibilities. But **miscarriages** are very common—occurring in approximately one out of every four pregnancies. Couples totally unprepared for that possibility can be even more devastated if it happens. No parent can be completely prepared for a miscarriage or having a child with physical or mental abnormalities. Yet complications can and often do happen. So the prospective parents should discuss these issues before deciding to conceive a child: Are we willing and able to cope with a child who has severe problems? How will we support each other and seek the needed help for our child and us if such a misfortune does occur?

prenatal care
healthcare for a woman prior to the birth of her child

miscarriage
the premature expelling from the mother's womb, due to natural causes, of an embryo or fetus that has died or is not developed enough to survive

The pregnant woman's body undergoes many changes to accommodate and nourish the life growing within her. Couples and their children often delight in feeling the baby's movements through the mother's stomach. But being pregnant may also affect a family negatively. Introducing a new member into the family always challenges the other family relationships. For instance, a pregnant woman may feel her changing shape makes her undesirable to her husband. Or she may focus so much on the developing baby that her family feels slighted. The husband or other children may become jealous of the attention paid toward the newcomer.

A significant number of women experience profound depression after their child is born. That doesn't mean they're bad mothers or don't love their children. It may mean that the new mothers need medical treatment for a chemical imbalance due to the dramatic changes that have occurred in their bodies. Knowing and discussing the changes that occur during pregnancy and after birth can help expectant families cope with stresses. When they're well-informed, family members realize that the changes are normal or treatable. But they must still prepare for how adding a new family member will affect and permanently change their lives. Christian couples should remember that bearing and raising children reflects Christ's death and resurrection in which joy triumphs over temporary suffering.

Some of the changes a pregnant woman may experience

- Unexplainable mood swings, due to her body's hormonal changes
- Feeling occasionally or constantly nauseated—especially toward the beginning of the pregnancy
- Feeling extremely tired and lacking energy
- Feeling increasingly uncomfortable while sitting, standing, or lying down (especially toward the end of the approximately nine-month gestation period)

Activity

Design an advertising campaign around one of the issues below. Create and graphically illustrate one sample ad for the campaign. Present your campaign ideas and sample to the class.

- Making teenagers more aware of the concerns associated with teenage pregnancy
- Making people more aware of the possible effects of drug use on a child they may conceive
- Helping women realize the importance of seeking the proper prenatal care promptly

Project

Choose one.

1. Interview a doctor or social worker about the importance of proper prenatal care. Write a two-page paper describing what you learn. Share your findings with the class.

2. Research the birthing options and techniques available in your area. Write a two-page paper reporting your findings and your responses.

3. Interview a foster parent or personnel at an adoption agency about adopting a child or becoming a foster parent. Write a two-page paper reporting your findings and your responses.

For discussion

1. What would you try to be aware of, discuss with your spouse and the doctor, and plan to do before deciding to have a child?

2. How do you think childbearing and child-rearing reflect the deepest rhythms of human existence? The Christian death-resurrection mystery?

3. What do you think would be the most difficult changes you'd have to adjust to if you (if you're a woman) or your spouse (if you're a man) became pregnant? In adding a new child to your family? Explain.

4. If you were informed after school today that there was going to be a new child added to your family, how would you feel about it? How do you think you'd respond? What adjustments would you probably have to make? Explain.

5. How do you think parents can best prepare their other children for the adjustments they'll have to make for a new family member?

Giving birth

It's incredible to think we can actually participate in creating human life! Few experiences are as awe-inspiring as being present at a baby's birth. The couple's ecstatic joy when their child is born testifies to the truths Catholics believe about bearing children:[8]

- Human birth is a kind of miracle.
- Couples help God to create a new human.
- The child comes from, reveals, and enriches the spouses' love.
- Only these two persons could procreate this individual child.
- Christian parents are responsible for sharing their religious values and beliefs with their children.
- Raising children offers unique possibilities for sharing love and experiencing a deep sense of fulfillment.

Many couples use one or more alternative birthing options for delivering their babies. In natural childbirth, the husband may be present and assist his wife in labor and delivery. Many new fathers take pictures of their child's birth. At the appropriate time, the parents can then show their son or daughter "where she or he came from" and better explain the miracle of life. Experiencing their child's birth together helps a couple bond more with each other and with their child. A welcoming environment in the delivery room also helps this bonding.

Labor and delivery are natural processes, not diseases! Hospitals aren't always the ideal place for newborns because of the antibiotic-resistant bacteria they harbor. So some couples opt for a birthing center adjacent to a hospital. Others arrange for a home birth assisted by a midwife. That was common practice in this country a few generations ago—and still is in many parts of the world.

Couples should consider, though, that not having proper medical care available could be

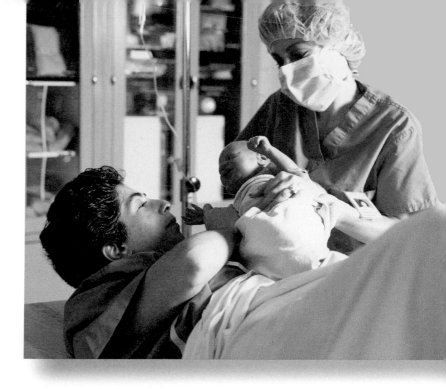

When a woman is in labor, she has pain, because her hour has come. But when her child is born, she no longer remembers the anguish because of the joy of having brought a human being into the world.

JOHN 16:21

dangerous. Difficulties often do occur in childbirth, and assisting at non-emergency home deliveries is illegal in many places. Legislatures continue to debate the pros and cons of this. In some instances midwives are trained and licensed to deliver babies in a hospital or other approved facility, while some legislatures approve them only for home births. Any birthing innovation should recognize both human needs and medical concerns.

Couples should be able to accept willingly and lovingly any child born to them. There may be a good reason, however, to not want the child to be a particular gender—for instance, if the child would almost certainly be born with a serious genetic disease. Such couples should consult their doctor for advice on how to help predetermine their child's gender in a morally acceptable way. However, we're arriving at a time when parents may be able to pre-select all their child's physical characteristics. Such reproductive technologies have profoundly troubling moral implications that we must wrestle with and decide on as a society. Reproductive technology could affect not just the individual couple but the overall genetic makeup of humanity—with possibly disastrous consequences down the road.

There is growing alarm at the increasing number of infertile couples who can't conceive a child without medical intervention, or at all. The widespread epidemic of sexually transmitted diseases is a key cause of male and female infertility. Doctors first try to help infertile couples conceive naturally by teaching them simple fertility awareness techniques. Resorting to fertility drugs to help a woman conceive may increase the likelihood of multiple births—and the risks for mother and child. Many doctors cite the "catastrophes" that sometimes result from multiple births caused by using fertility drugs to conceive. Fertility drugs do raise grave medical and moral concerns. Couples have a right to have children—but not by acting selfishly, irresponsibly, and immorally.

There's obviously a whole lot more to consider about having a child than there's room to discuss here! But you can see why it's so important to be well-informed about the alternatives and possibilities before deciding to have a family. Reliable Internet sites are one good source of free information. It's also important to consult with a good obstetrician who has the right values.

Adoption and foster parenting

Many loving couples want but can't conceive children, and their hope of having a family lies in adopting a child. Thirty years ago, over ninety percent of the unwed teenagers who became pregnant placed their babies for adoption. Today most teen mothers decide to keep their children (although most of them end up on welfare). Largely because of this change, the average waiting period for adoption may be several years in some places. The waiting time may be shortened if a couple is adopting a child from an underdeveloped country or a child with special needs.

Parents should put their child's needs before their own desires. There is so much child abuse. So many children are poorly cared for or not wanted. Whether single or married, someone who can't responsibly love and provide for children should seriously consider placing their child for adoption. It's hard for a woman who's carried a child for nine months to let go of that child. But not everyone should be a parent! Parents shouldn't put their feelings before their baby's welfare. Trying to raise a child when one isn't prepared to do so is very hard. It's often tragic for the child, who ends up being abused or killed. Yet friends and relatives sometimes pressure mothers or fathers into keeping their babies, making them feel selfish for considering adoption. The truly unselfish and loving choice is what's best for the child!

Those who've been adopted generally agree that children should be told from the beginning that they've been adopted. Adoption is a beautiful, loving choice—not a shameful secret! In fact, as daughters and sons of God, we're all adopted!

Project

Interview at least four parents about the role their religious beliefs have played in their family life. Write a two-page paper reporting your findings and giving your responses.

For discussion

1. Have you ever witnessed the birth of a child or an animal? If so, what were your thoughts and feelings about the experience?

2. Explain your response to this comment: "I think letting fathers accompany their wives into the delivery room is a darn good idea. The guy who helped start her pregnancy should have the guts to help her finish it!"

3. Would you want to participate with your spouse in a natural child-birthing process—where the mother remains conscious and the father is present during labor and delivery? Explain.

4. Would you consider having pictures taken of your child's birth? Explain.

5. How do you think the birthing process has been improved for parents and child? Which birthing alternative(s) would you choose—or not choose—for your baby's birth? Explain.

6. In view of Catholic teaching, do you think it's morally acceptable for a couple to keep having more children just to get a child of the gender they want? Explain.

It's natural that adopted children wonder about their birth parents. As one adopted teenager put it, "Sure, I think sometimes about my natural parents—what they must be like, where they are, what circumstances caused them to give me up for adoption. But I love my adoptive parents, and I wouldn't trade them for anyone else—including my birth parents. One thing I can always be sure of is how much they loved and wanted me, given all they went through just to adopt me."

Many couples adopt "special children" who have physical or emotional problems or mental disabilities. Sometimes such children, who would otherwise remain institutionalized for the rest of their lives, are found by couples like the Jensens. George Jensen was a successful architect, and his wife, Mary, was an artist. Money wasn't a problem, nor was having their own children. But they decided to adopt two children. They told the adoption agency they'd be willing to have any child with a curable disease or defect that could be remedied. No matter how expensive or time-consuming the cure, they said they'd willingly pay for it. They were honest about not feeling suited to raise permanently disabled children. But they did offer to give what they felt they could.

Foster parents give a temporary home to displaced children and teenagers whose parents abused them or were unable to care for them. Some couples volunteer to be foster parents for babies and children with AIDS whose parents can't or won't care for them. Not everyone would make a good parent in those special circumstances, but if you could, your life will certainly be enriched. Ideally, every child should be raised with his or her two loving biological parents. But when that's not possible, it's still important to give each child the best possible chance for a good family life.

Where there aren't enough adoptive couples, loving single persons often provide children with a good and loving home. It's a shame that children are sometimes shuffled to a succession of foster homes simply because unenlightened local policies don't allow a qualified, morally upright single person (with a heterosexual orientation or a homosexual orientation) to adopt a child. What's important is giving children the love and care that will enable them to grow and thrive as good persons.

> *The commonest fallacy among women is that simply having children makes one a mother—which is as absurd as believing that having a piano makes one a musician.*
>
> SIDNEY HARRIS

For discussion

1. If a pregnant friend who's single asked your advice about whether to keep her baby or place the child for adoption, what would you tell her? Explain.

2. What would you advise a pregnant married friend who, for good reasons, thought she and her husband wouldn't be good parents to the child she's expecting? Explain.

3. Under what circumstances should a child be placed for adoption? What is the most unselfish, loving choice a parent can make in such situations? Explain.

4. Do you agree that adopted children should be told from the beginning that they've been adopted? Explain.

5. How would you respond to your adopted child's questions about her or his birth parents? Why?

6. What's your response to the Jensens' stipulations about the kind of child they'd be willing to adopt? Explain.

7. Do you think you'd ever consider adopting children or being a foster parent? Explain.

Preparing to be a parent

All children are fragile and precious. As the Church points out, each child has a right to life in its fullest and best sense. Children are entitled to be properly planned for, cared for, and loved. To neglect those responsibilities is one of the most tragic failures to love. Perhaps the biggest, most sacred responsibility you'll ever undertake is bringing new humans into the world and raising them properly.

Married partners' love, as Catholic teaching notes, "is not exhausted by the communion between husband and wife, but is destined to continue, raising up new lives."[9] In deciding to become parents, spouses are, in effect, asking "the Creator to commit to their care the formation of a child."[10] That is why the Church calls raising children the most critically important vocation.

The **procreation** and upbringing of children are among life's most important and difficult tasks. Yet most people are never formally educated in how to be good parents. They learn what it takes only after they've raised their children—when it's too late to do things differently. Those valuable insights should be considered before having children. In the rest of this chapter, you'll have the chance to consider what it means to be a good parent. First complete the following self-test to help you evaluate how good a parent you'd be at this time.

procreation
participation in God's act of creating a new human

. . . parental love is called to become for the children the visible sign of the very love of God. . . .

POPE JOHN PAUL II

Activity

For one week observe how you interact with children—at home, while babysitting, or at work. Note what your attitudes and feelings are when you encounter children. Write a one-page paper describing your responses and your insights from the activity about you perhaps being a parent one day.

Journal entry

Complete these statements:

1. The qualities I have that would help me be a good parent in the future are . . .
2. The qualities I have that would make it hard for me to be a good parent are . . .

Review

1. Before having a baby what should individuals know and do regarding prenatal care, pregnancy, and birth?
2. What kind of help does the Catholic community extend to all pregnant women?
3. Before deciding to have a child, how should couples prepare themselves for the inevitable adjustments and possible complications?
4. What is the Church's teaching on having and raising children?
5. What should couples consider about the moral aspects of having children and of adoption? What general moral limitation is there on a couple's right to have children?

Would you make a good parent?

On the blanks respond with A–F according to how often or strongly the answer yes seems true. You'll then be told how to score and interpret the results. You won't be expected to share your answers or score.

A — Never/Not at all
B — Rarely/Hardly at all
C — Seldom/Not very strongly
D — Sometimes/Somewhat, but not strongly
E — Often/Somewhat strongly
F — Always/Very strongly

_____ 1. Do you tend to take out your problems on your family, friends, or others?

_____ 2. How well do you cope with stress?

_____ 3. Would you prefer that your child be a boy rather than a girl, or vice versa?

_____ 4. How easy is it for you to compromise?

_____ 5. When you're busy or not very interested, do you stop and listen patiently when a friend or family member really wants to tell you something?

_____ 6. If you had to choose between them, would you choose having a career over having children?

_____ 7. Could you accept and cope with a serious disability or birth defect in your child?

_____ 8. Are you afraid that having children might seriously block your happiness in marriage?

_____ 9. Would you have a child if you thought it would strengthen your troubled marriage?

_____ 10. Do you go against your beliefs and let others have their way to avoid unpleasantness?

_____ 11. Do you really want to have children in the future?

_____ 12. How much of your contact with younger children has been positive and enjoyable?

_____ 13. Is it hard for you to cope with minor inconveniences, such as interruptions or changes in your schedule, routine, or plans?

_____ 14. When making a decision, is what other people will think important to you?

_____ 15. Do you think one spouse should have a greater responsibility than the other parent in raising children?

_____ 16. How patient are you?

_____ 17. Do you find it hard to tolerate things being untidy or out of order?

_____ 18. How selfish are you?

_____ 19. In general how easy is it for you to express affection?

_____ 20. How stubborn are you?

_____ 21. How openly supportive are you of other people and their efforts?

_____ 22. Do you get angry or upset over small things?

_____ 23. Do you criticize others for their small faults?

_____ 24. Are you comfortable around young children?

_____ 25. When you do get angry or upset, do you react unfairly?

_____ 26. Do you accept and forgive honest mistakes, even when you've been hurt by them?

_____ 27. When angry or upset with someone you love, do you try to make the person feel bad?

_____ 28. In your family, have you been disciplined fairly?

_____ 29. Has how you've been raised left you feeling hostile, hurt, guilty, angry, helpless, or resentful?

_____ 30. Are you a perfectionist?

_____ 31. Does it bother you to have others depend on you?

_____ 32. Are you annoyed that others differ with you about how a task or job should be done?

_____ 33. Is it hard for you to deal with your emotions, or with the emotions of others?

_____ 34. Do you enjoy and appreciate imaginative or playful activities, such as games?

_____ 35. Do you enjoy trying new things or activities?

_____ 36. How reasonable are you?

_____ 37. How easy is it for you to compromise?

_____ 38. In general, how happy would you say your childhood and adolescent years have been?

_____ 39. Does living in a noisy environment bother you?

_____ 40. Do you have trouble putting others' needs or desires before your own?

_____ **Total score**

Helping children grow

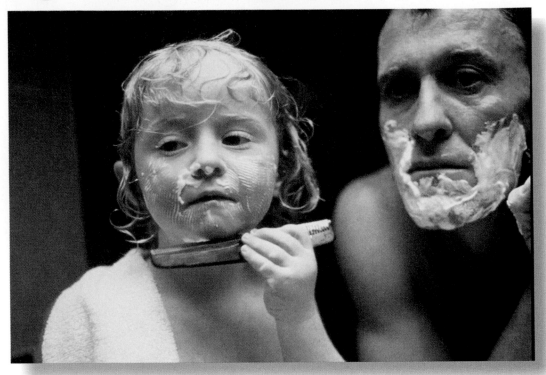

Children have more need of models than of critics.

JOSEPH JOUBERT

Every child should be helped to reach his or her full potential. There are countless theories about the best ways to raise children. But did you ever notice that when people discuss "raising" children, they're most often referring to disciplining? That's sad. Many children's first word is no—the "no" learned from discipline. What if as much effort were put into sharing with children the "yes" of life?

Each child born into a family is uniquely different from all the other children in the family—and in the world. Each child needs to be responded to as an individual and to feel like an individual, rather than as just "one of the Smith clan." Most of all, children need individual love, attention, and affection—and they need it often! They must be assured and reassured of their value and that loving will never stop.

Catholic teaching emphasizes what counselors have often advised: **The best way to be a good parent is to love your spouse—the child's other parent.** That makes children feel secure and happy. It teaches them how to love. Constant bickering, arguing, and selfishness between parents makes children fearful. It also teaches them the wrong values about relationships. To forgive after an occasional argument, however, can teach children how to make peace.[11]

Married and divorced parents should at least avoid speaking negatively to each other and about each other in front of the child. Otherwise, the child learns a distorted view of relationships and persons of the other gender. Children also take it personally, getting the impression that something's wrong with them because one of their parents is "defective." Sometimes children rebel and deliberately try to imitate the other parent's undesirable traits. When it's important to teach a child to not imitate a parent's wrongful behavior, that teaching can be done, but not through criticism of the parent.

Parenting theories range from strict to "anything goes." One parent slams an unruly child into the shopping cart at the store—then slaps him for his "misbehavior"! Another parent just smiles and comments "Kids will be kids" while her daughter is rude and obnoxious to other travelers in an airport waiting area. Neither extreme teaches the child to value himself or herself, others, or life. Moral guidance, reasonable discipline, and freedom help children grow into mature, happy adults.

That balance requires sound, common sense judgment. We can all learn from others' common sense insights. Prospective parents should ask advice from parents they admire—including, perhaps, their own. Good ideas are also available in books or on the Internet—but must be tempered with a parent's own good judgment. Another valuable resource about parenting is the wisdom of the children themselves! Christian parents have the challenging opportunity and duty to share their Christian faith and positive values with their offspring.

Helping children grow throughout the years is a difficult task. Parents can only try to do their best. They can't save their children from every trouble or from making some mistakes of their own. They can guide the children under their care and provide loving support. They must leave the rest and the future in God's hands and their children's.

There are only **two** lasting bequests we can leave our **children**.
One of these is roots; the other, **wings**.

HODDING CARTER

Journal entry

1. What attitudes have you learned in your family about female-male relationships? How do you think that has affected your expectations about relationships and about marriage?

2. What "roots" has your family life given you?

3. What "wings" has your family life given you?

Project

Choose one.

1. Volunteer your services at a local childcare center or elementary school. Write a two-page paper on what you learned about and from the children you observe.

2. Research and write a two-page paper on the stages of child development. Include a paragraph giving your responses to what you learn.

3. Discuss with someone who has raised or known you from infancy the stages you've gone through in your childhood development (for example, in your abilities, behavior, attitudes, personality). Write a two-page paper on what you learn about yourself and about raising children.

4. Ask at least five children, five teenagers, and five adults to complete this sentence: "Kids . . . ." Make a poster or computer graphic illustrating their responses. Be prepared to discuss your project with the class.

5. Write a two-page essay about your thoughts and feelings on being a parent and raising a family someday.

6. Interview at least five parents (you may include your own) about their do's and don'ts for disciplining children. Write a two-page paper on what you learn.

For discussion

1. What positive aspects of life were you taught in childhood? How have those remained part of you?

2. As a parent how could you implement the advice given in your text about raising children? Were there any points with which you disagreed or especially agreed?

3. Give at least three examples you've witnessed of very loose or strict parenting styles. Why is either extreme undesirable?

4. Why do you think it's hard for a parent to maintain a sound balance in raising a child? If you were a parent raising you right now, what do you think you'd find most difficult and most delightful about it? Explain.

5. If you were having problems disciplining your child, where would you seek advice and help?

6. Why shouldn't parents or children expect themselves—or each other—to be perfect?

7. What do you think are reasonable expectations for parents and children to have regarding each other? Explain.

Review

1. What are some of the key ways to be a good parent?

2. What particular responsibility do Christian parents have regarding their children?

3. What factors must parents balance in raising their children?

What's wrong with grownups?

Read the list of complaints voiced by a group of ten-year-old children. Then respond to the questions.[12]

1. Grownups make promises, then they forget all about them, or else they say it wasn't really a promise, just a maybe.

2. Grownups don't do the things they are always telling children to do—like pick up their things, or be neat, or always tell the truth.

3. Grownups won't let their children dress the way they want to—but they never ask a child's opinion about how they should dress. If they're going out to a party, grownups wear just exactly what they want to wear—even if it looks terrible, even if it isn't warm enough.

4. Grownups never really listen to what children have to say. They always decide ahead of time what they're going to answer.

5. Grownups interrupt children all the time and think nothing of it. If a child interrupts a grownup, he gets a scolding or something worse.

6. Grownups make mistakes but they won't admit them. They always pretend that they weren't mistakes at all—or that somebody else made them.

7. Grownups never understand how much children want a certain thing, a certain color, or shape, or size. If it's something they don't admire—even if the children have spent their own money for it—they always say, "I can't imagine what you want with that old thing!"

8. Sometimes grownups punish children unfairly. It isn't right if you've done just some little thing wrong and grownups take away something that means an awful lot to you. Other times you can do something really bad and they say they're going to punish you, but they don't. You never know, and you ought to know.

9. Grownups talk about money too much, and bills, and things like that, so that it scares you. They say money isn't very important, but the way they talk about it, it sounds like the most important thing in the world.

10. Grownups gossip a lot, but if children do the very same thing and say the same words about the same people, the grownups say they're being disrespectful.

11. Grownups pry into children's secrets. They always think it's going to be something bad. They never think it might be a nice surprise.

12. Grownups are always talking about what they did and what they knew when they were ten years old, and it usually sounds as if it couldn't have happened the way they say it. But grownups never try to think what it's like to be ten years old right now.

For discussion

1. What's your response to each of the complaints?

2. Based on your experience, which complaints can you most identify with? What complaints would you add to the list?

3. Do you ever feel annoyed by small children? Do you think you've already forgotten much of what it was like to be a small child? What things do you still remember most about it? Explain.

4. Which of your negative traits or tendencies might give your children reason to complain about you as a parent? Which of your positive traits would give them reason to be proud to have you as a parent? Explain.

5. What did you learn from the children's list of complaints?

In summary

Family life is important not only to the families themselves, but to society, the Church, and humanity. Family life has changed throughout history—from rigid matriarchal or patriarchal structures to more flexible, participatory styles. Jesus supported the integrity of family life and challenged practices that treated family members unjustly. In our society families have become less extended and more isolated and often include a stepparent or are headed by a single parent. The Church defines the family as a group of persons who, joined by love, live a community lifestyle that fosters each member's individuality. It supports changes in family life that enhance family members' dignity and unity.

Having children is a sacred responsibility that participates in God's act of creation. Children should be loved, wanted, and welcomed for the right reasons. Unfortunately, many parents aren't prepared to raise children properly. Having a child is a natural, but not an absolute right, and those who are unable to have children should unselfishly consider the noble options of adoption and foster parenting.

Proper prenatal precautions, care, and preparation are important. Parents-to-be should also discuss how to respond if serious problems arise and should prepare for the adjustments they'll need to make. They should willingly accept and love any child born to them. Children are entitled to be properly prepared for and cared for and to be loved as unique and valuable persons. They should be raised responsibly and never abused. Couples should share their religious faith and positive values with their children. Children thrive best within a happy, wholesome, secure family environment.

Key concepts

adoption

birthing options

blended families

conception

couples' right to have children

extended families

family as basic social unit

family life

foster parenting

miscarriage

nuclear families

pregnancy

prenatal care and prenatal health concerns

procreation

reasons for having or not having children

single parents

stepfamilies

teenage parenthood

Endnotes

1. "Prayer-Starter Responses: You Gently Hold Me," from *Praying* (PO Box 419335, Kansas City, MO 64141).
2. Joan Bel Geddes, "Will the Family Survive the Twentieth Century," in *The Future of the Family*, ed. Clayton C. Barbeau (New York: The Bruce Publishing Company, 1971), 15.
3. Bel Geddes, 14–15.
4. *Human Life in Our Day: Pastoral Letter of the US Bishops* (Washington, DC: National Conference of Catholic Bishops, USCC, 1968, #68.
5. *On the Family, Apostolic Exhortation of Pope John Paul II* (15 December 1981), Part 3, #18.
6. Permission granted by Ann Landers and Creators Syndicate.
7. Scott Kraft, "Many Teen-agers Rate Motherhood an Easier Trip Than Marriage," The Associated Press. Reprinted by permission.
8. See *Faithful to Each Other Forever: A Catholic Handbook of Pastoral Help for Marriage Preparation*, Bishops' Committee for Pastoral Research and Practices, National Conference of Catholic Bishops (Washington, DC: USCC Office of Publishing and Promotion Services, 1989), 38.
9. Pope Paul VI, *Humanae Vitae*.
10. *Human Life in Our Day*, #50.
11. See *Faithful to Each Other Forever*, 108.
12. The ten-year-olds in Mrs. Imogene Frost's class at the Brookside, NJ, Community Sunday School.

CHAPTER 13

RESPONSIBLE FAMILY PLANNING

SCRIPTURE

"I came that they may have
life, and have it abundantly."

JOHN 10:10B

PRAYER

God of life,

You have created us in your image to share your life.

You have made us your partners in creating new human life.

But we are also capable of taking life.

May we realize each day how precious all life is.

Help us care for and protect one another—especially those among us who are helpless.

Give us the wisdom and courage to find alternatives to war and the other forms of violence people do to one another.

Guide us to use wisely and rightly the new technologies of the present and the future.

May we use them to enhance and uphold life, not to demean or destroy it.

Lead us together to everlasting life with you.

Family planning decisions

Humanity owes to the child the best it has to give.

PARAPHRASED
FROM A
UN DECLARATION

Before deciding to marry, couples should discuss and be able to agree on the key aspects of family planning: Do they want to try having a baby right away, or should they wait a year or two—or longer? How many children would they each like to have? What method will they use to help them plan the family they want? The Church makes it clear that "only the husband and wife, through responsible conscience decisions, can and should answer such questions."[1]

When marrying in the Catholic Church, couples promise to accept God's will about having and raising a family. That means trying responsibly to do the best thing for all concerned. Instead, many people make unwise or selfish decisions about having children. They let their emotional needs or pressures from others determine how they'll begin, extend, or limit their family. When they don't consider all that's involved, the results hurt everybody.

Some women, for instance, are dishonest with their husbands. The wife may want to have a baby or have one now rather than later. Or she may want more children, although her husband doesn't. So she gets pregnant, blaming it on error or miscalculation. Or a husband may be uncooperative in helping his wife avoid an unwanted pregnancy. That's not responsible family planning! As Catholic teaching strongly urges, responsible family planning promotes greater reverence for human life, and supports children's well-being and the family's nature and dignity.

Your decisions about having children may be the most important ones you'll ever make. You need to make them wisely, being honest with yourself and your spouse. If you marry, you must decide together as a couple when to begin trying to have children. You must determine how many children you'll have and how far apart you want to space them.

A child should be brought into a loving, healthy, emotionally stable environment. The first child is a major turning point (and often a minor or major crisis) in a couple's relationship. They are no longer just two; they are now a family. Their responsibilities and concerns multiply along with their love and happiness. Husband and wife assume a whole new identity as father and mother. When the second child comes along, the first child likewise assumes a new identity as a big brother or sister. The first-born child is no longer the sole focus of the parents' attention.

There's a whole new person on the scene who needs a lot of time and love. That can seem threatening to either of the spouses or the other children. One spouse may become jealous over the attention the other spouse devotes to the new baby. The newcomer's demands are round-the-clock inconvenient! Couples no longer have the time, freedom, or privacy they did before the baby arrived. Welcoming a child into the family requires sacrifice, maturity—and a lot of adjusting!

Raising a child is also expensive. In earlier times children were a financial asset to their parents. Their help on the farm or ranch was indispensable. Today, it costs a middle-class family about a quarter of a million dollars to raise a child from birth to age eighteen! That doesn't even include the cost of college tuition. There are medical bills that insurance doesn't cover, possibly an unpaid leave of absence from work, then day care, clothing, and so on. And the costs keep rising.

More couples are wisely postponing having children until they can reasonably handle the responsibilities involved. More couples too are sensibly limiting their family's size. But some couples make the mistake of waiting too long to have children. They postpone children until everything else is "perfect" in their lives—which, of course, it never is. Then one day it dawns on them that they're feeling too old to start parenting a young child, and they regret that they didn't start having children sooner. According to Catholic teaching there are legitimate reasons why spouses need to carefully plan the timing and size of their families:

This Council realizes that certain modern conditions often keep couples from arranging their married lives harmoniously, and that they find themselves in circumstances where at least temporarily the size of their families should not be increased.

"Pastoral Constitution on the Church in the Modern World," #48.

The Catholic Church fully supports a couple's using family planning responsibly to properly care for and love their children, who are God's gifts to them. Married partners ultimately have to decide how they can best plan their family—together.

Responsible parenthood, as the Church understands it, places on the properly formed conscience of spouses all the judgments, options, and choices which add up to the awesome decision to give, postpone, or decline life.

U.S. Catholic Bishops, *Human Life in Our Day*, #20.

For discussion

1. What questions about having children would you want to discuss and agree on before deciding to marry someone? Explain.
2. List the main ways you think welcoming a child into the family requires sacrifice, maturity, and adjustment. Which of those would you find the hardest? Explain.
3. How would you respond to someone who asks, "Why is the Catholic Church against family planning?"
4. What is your response to married couples who believe they shouldn't conceive a child at this time, but who are careless about practicing family planning? Explain.

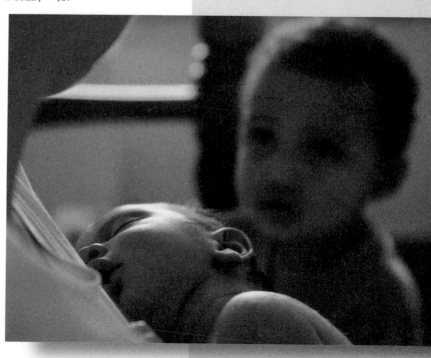

The choice of children

Read this couple's thoughts, feelings, and decisions about children, and then respond to the questions.

Karen . . . is a professor of mathematics. Her husband, Paul, is an artist, . . .and they have been married for three years. They talked about children before getting married.

"We were both very positive," she remembers. "I had wanted children all my life. I was the daughter of a single parent, and it left a longing, an empty place that I fantasized I could fill when I became a parent myself.

". . . the desire for children was so strong it was almost a biological urge. The idea of becoming pregnant was the ultimate sexual turn-on; even my fantasies had to do with pregnancy. And Paul was positive about children, too. It seemed to both of us that it was virtually the only reason for getting married. Then, six months after we were married, Paul changed his mind completely. He wasn't ready, his career was too unsteady, he didn't want a lot of baggage. So I had to make a choice. Was I going to let this be the core issue that would make or break the marriage? Or was I going to let it ride?

"I decided to let it ride, but I was very resentful, very angry. I was being forced to choose between the man I loved and with whom I wanted to live my life and my intense desire for a child. Fortunately . . . I was able to get a lot of the anger out. But you know something? It's still there. It dribbles out—in tears, in anger . . . It even affects my sexual response.

"Friends have said, 'Why don't you just get pregnant?' I'm appalled by that. I think it would be the lowest form of treachery. Someone said that the decision to create life is at least as important a moral decision as the decision to take it, and I believe that. And yet there have been times when I wanted a child so much that I wished it would just happen—that I don't have to make the decision.

"On the surface these days, I'm solid and busy, never bored. And yet there's a sort of echo once in a while. It will hit without warning . . . a hollow feeling. Something unfulfilled. And what's missing is something more fundamental than a baby. It's a feeling of belonging, a kind of growth I'm not experiencing."[2]

For discussion

1. Given how Karen and Paul each feel, what should they have discussed and agreed on before getting married? Explain.

2. Why does Karen want to have a child? What do you think about each of her reasons? Explain.

3. What do Paul's reasons seem to be for not wanting to have a family—at least not at this time? What do you think about each of his reasons? Explain.

4. Do you agree with Karen's belief that "the decision to create life is at least as important a moral decision as the decision to take it"? Explain.

5. Given their present situation, what do you think Karen and Paul should decide right now about having a baby? What advice would you give each of them? Explain.

Catholic teaching on family planning methods

Because procreation is sacred, Catholic teaching urges couples to consider carefully the matter of having and caring for children. The family is the most important unit of society. The Church is concerned that every effort be made to reverence and nourish human life—especially where it's most fragile. Working from that reverence for life, Catholic teaching states that artificial means of birth regulation are unnatural barriers to procreation, to life. But Church guidelines also call for compassion toward couples who don't yet live by that moral norm.

The responsibilities involved in having and raising children are sometimes very difficult. Individuals facing those should rely for support on their faith and hope in God's love. Throughout the tough times and choices, they should keep asking God to help them and continue receiving God's strength and love in the Eucharist. They shouldn't get disheartened if they find it hard to let go of attitudes and practices of family planning that are wrong. Instead, they should keep humbly turning to God's mercy, which is available to them especially in the Sacrament of Reconciliation. Other Catholics should be patient and kind with those couples and should reflect Jesus' message and love toward them. (See *Humanae Vitae*, #25.)

Love is its own reward.

SEE PROVERBS 11:17

Catholic teaching isn't alone in viewing artificial contraceptives as barriers to the natural expression of human sexuality. Many people find them inconvenient, disruptive, awkward, uncomfortable, or unhealthy. That's probably why people have increasingly turned to the natural family planning methods. Many couples now view family planning as the Catholic Church does—as the couple's mutual responsibility. Couples should make and carry out family planning decisions together.

First of all, the Church teaches that it is the couple alone, following their morally responsible conscience judgments, who are to decide those many when and how issues. The bishops at the Second Vatican Council were explicit about this:

"It is the married couple themselves who must in the last analysis arrive at these judgments before God. Married people should realize that in their behavior they may not follow their own fancy but must be ruled by conscience—and conscience ought to be conformed to the law of God in the light of the teaching authority of the Church, which is the authentic interpreter of divine law." ["Pastoral Constitution on the Church," #50.]

We echoed that notion several years later by assigning to the "conscience of spouses all the judgments, options, and choices which add up to the awesome decision to give, postpone or decline life." [Human Life in Our Day, 9.]

culpability
being deserving of blame

The couple's decision of conscience must be morally responsible. Conscience has to do with personal **culpability** for one's decisions and actions. One's conscience may fail to determine that the act in itself is morally wrong. Individuals can act or decide sincerely believing they're doing the morally right thing. But, objectively speaking, their conscience may be incorrect and their conclusion and actions wrong. In that case they're not guilty of a moral wrong because they're following their conscience in good faith, not realizing that it's in error. However, we all have an obligation to overcome an erroneous conscience. Catholic teaching does require that Catholics first consider responsibly and in good faith what the Church teaches on the matter.[3]

A responsible conscience regarding family planning is[4]

1. **Open to life**—has a positive attitude about the wonderful aspects of having and raising children, views children as a most precious gift, and is open to possibly giving life to children

2. **Generous and sacrificing, not selfish**—willingly gives of oneself and sacrifices for one's children, rather than selfishly putting first one's desire for more time, money, things, or freedom

3. **Trusting**—realizes that all decisions are risky since we can't control the future, and strongly trusts God's help in coping with the fears about having and raising children

4. **Wise**—considers the spouses' health, other children in the family, family finances, the spouses' mental and emotional readiness to raise children, and community, national, and world conditions

5. **Humble**—realizes one's role as cooperating with God in creating human life, and recognizes that all life ultimately comes from and remains in God's loving hands

6. **Mutual**—unites spouses in a fully human, unselfish way as friends who prayerfully discuss and agree on the decision

7. **Church-guided**—makes the final decision by following one's conscience, which should be in accord with God's law as authentically interpreted by Church teaching (See "The Church in the Modern World," #51.)

Journal entry

Complete this statement: My idea of responsible family planning is . . .

For discussion

1. Why do many couples prefer using natural family planning methods? What do you know about natural family planning? What are your questions about it?

2. Why is it important that a couple agree on how they will plan their family? What would you do if you and the person you were thinking about marrying disagreed about how you'd plan your family?

3. If you marry in the future, what would your ideal be regarding having children and beginning a family? What would you do if the person you wanted to marry insisted on waiting to discuss the issue until after you marry? Explain.

4. Who should have the main responsibility for family planning? Why do you think that responsibility too often falls to the woman? How can both spouses be irresponsible about family planning?

5. What do you understand by the characteristics of a morally responsible conscience regarding family planning decisions? Explain your response to each characteristic and why you think it's important.

Review

1. What major questions about having a family should couples agree on before they marry?

2. What type of environment should a couple establish before bringing a child into a marriage and family? Explain.

3. Why shouldn't emotional needs or social pressures determine how a couple plans their family? Can a couple wait too long to begin their family? Explain.

4. How does Catholic teaching describe what responsible family planning really means?

5. How does having children multiply a couple's responsibilities, concerns, and opportunities for love and happiness? Be specific.

6. What does Catholic teaching say about the following?
   • Temporarily deciding to not increase the size of one's family
   • Who should make the decision to have, postpone, or decline having children

Family planning and fertility awareness

contraceptive
treatment or device that prevents sperm and ovum from uniting (conception)

embryo
human life in earliest stage of development in uterus, generally the first three months

fetus
human life in later stages of development in uterus, generally from 4th month to birth

ovulation
release of the female ovum from the ovary, making it available for joining with the male sperm

ovum
female cell which, when fertilized, produces offspring

sperm
male cell (spermatozoon) or cells (spermatozoa) which, when united with the female reproductive cell (ovum), results in conception; sometimes incorrectly used as a synonym for the fluid (semen) ejaculated by the male that contains sperm

labor
the muscle contractions that help the body push the fetus through the birth canal during the birth process

A married couple who properly and conscientiously decides to postpone having children, must decide what family planning method to use.[5] Church teaching doesn't (as many people still think) oppose all forms of birth control. It supports the research, education, and promotion of natural family planning methods for couples wishing to postpone or space their children. Catholic teaching does oppose the use of artificial **contraceptives** as being unnatural ways to prevent conception. It strongly opposes any means used to destroy the human **embryo** or **fetus** for the purpose of ending a pregnancy.

Sexual intercourse is and should be a natural, sacred expression of love between spouses. It is also the means of procreation—of actually participating with God in creating new human life. Procreation is one of the two main purposes of human sexuality. Catholic teaching therefore regards artificial means of preventing conception as immoral because they're incompatible with and contrary to that natural procreative meaning and purpose of human sexual union.

There are many methods of controlling conception or preventing birth. More are constantly being developed for men and women. Some couples rely on a combination of methods—depending on their personal and moral views and how important it is that they not risk having children at the time. The methods vary in their effectiveness, health risks, and moral and relational implications for the couple. We'll discuss some of the most commonly used contraceptive methods.

Couples should discuss the matter of family planning intelligently and thoroughly. Catholics should seriously consider all the factors involved in light of Catholic teaching before deciding how they will plan their family.

Family planning methods

To understand how any family planning method works, you must first know how and when conception occurs and how a pregnancy develops. Even though that's been explained to you before, there are probably things you're still fuzzy about or have forgotten. You may also have new questions.

Natural family planning

Ovulation

An **ovum** is released from one (or, less frequently, both) ovaries. Pregnancy is most likely if intercourse occurs during the few days surrounding ovulation.

In the days just before the ovum is released, the uterine lining swells with blood. That prepares the woman's body to nourish a developing fetus if pregnancy occurs.

Menstruation

When conception does not occur, the uterine lining's surplus blood and cells are shed through the vagina. The next fertility cycle then begins. The first day of the menstrual cycle begins on the first day of the menstrual period.

Fertility (menstrual) cycle

of about 28 days (during which the woman's body undergoes changes that prepare for conception and pregnancy)

Conception

If joined with one of the millions of **sperm** the male releases on ejaculating, conception occurs and a new human life begins.

If the fertilized ovum attaches to the uterine lining, it will get the nourishment it needs to develop over the next nine months or so. **Labor** will begin when the woman's body senses that the fetus is ready to be born.

---

ovary

one of two inner female organs that produce reproductive cells (eggs/ova)

Natural family planning (NFP)

a birth control and family planning method that relies on being aware of the time(s) during a woman's fertility cycle that she ovulates and is fertile

The only time in her fertility (menstrual) cycle that a woman can become pregnant is during the (usually) few days before and after she ovulates. **But a woman may ovulate more than once during a single menstrual cycle!** So if she tries to avoid pregnancy by not having intercourse near the time she usually ovulates, she could become pregnant anyway. A woman may also ovulate from both rather than just one **ovary**.

Natural family planning (NFP) relies on being aware of the time(s) during a woman's fertility cycle that she ovulates and is fertile. By knowing exactly when the woman can become pregnant, couples can conceive a child or avoid conception at that time. That frees couples to give themselves to each other sexually in a total way. Natural family planning also poses no physical risks for the couple or the child they might conceive.

Couples interested in practicing NFP should check with their parish or ask their doctor for more information. Dioceses, hospitals, and clinics often sponsor programs that educate couples in how to practice NFP. Couples who use NFP successfully frequently volunteer to train other couples in how to use it. Engaged couples should participate in such training sessions. Simple devices can now help a woman detect the most fertile time(s) in her menstrual cycle. NFP can effectively help couples conceive or avoid conception. But to work successfully, they must practice it faithfully and correctly.

The Church stresses that **family planning is the responsibility of both man and woman!** Natural family planning involves the cooperation of both spouses. But by becoming more aware of and sensitive to each other's body and person, they grow in loving intimacy.

Activity

Find out where in your community, besides from a doctor, a couple could get more information on practicing the NFP birth control method.

For discussion

1. Whose responsibility is practicing family planning—the man's or the woman's? Do you think that's how most teenagers and adults perceive the responsibility? Explain.

2. What is your response to the natural family planning means of birth control? Do you have any further questions about it? Explain.

Examples of the methods Catholic teaching prohibits as morally wrong

Note: The percentage rates given for each contraceptive method indicate how effective that method is on average. They include both the method's effectiveness if used properly and the rate at which individuals' commonly fail to use the method faithfully or correctly.

vagina

the canal or passageway between the uterus and the vulva; receives the penis during intercourse; the birth canal

Barrier methods

Diaphragm

A diaphragm is a flat, rubber-like disk that must be obtained from and fitted by a doctor or health specialist. The woman inserts it into her **vagina**, placing it over her cervix, before each intercourse. A cervical cap is a device that is likewise placed over the cervix and works in a way similar to the diaphragm.

Diaphragms alone: 81–97%   Diaphragms with spermicides: 97%

⇨ Used along with a cream or jelly which is placed around the rim of the diaphragm or in the cap

⇨ Provides a seal over the cervix that prevents pregnancy by keeping the semen (which contains the male's sperm) from passing beyond the woman's cervix and into her uterus

† This method is prohibited as morally wrong, for the reasons explained previously.

Condom ("rubber")

A condom is a tube-like device shaped like a balloon and made of a special type of rubber, synthetic material, or animal skin. Condoms for females are constructed differently from those for males. The two types are not interchangeable.

Condoms alone: 90–97%   Condoms with contraceptive foam: 98%+

⇨ The male condom is placed over the man's erect penis before intercourse. The container end of the female condom is placed inside the woman's vagina before intercourse; its more rigid opening remains outside the vagina.

⇨ Keeps the man's sperm-containing semen from contact with the woman's vagina

⇨ **Disadvantages:** Condoms are not totally effective in preventing conception or disease because they break due to: handling, being worn snugly or with an air pocket at the tip, sexual activity, manufacturing defects, slipping when the penis is withdrawn from the vagina, or being used more than once or when the condom is too old.

⇨ **Benefits:** Condoms are somewhat—but not completely—effective in preventing some sexually transmissible diseases (such as AIDS).

† Condoms are prohibited as a contraceptive method for reasons explained previously. Some bishops and theologians suggest that couples may be permitted—or obliged—to use them to avoid transmitting to a spouse a disease such as herpes or the AIDS virus.

Contraceptive sponge 97%

A contraceptive sponge is a small sponge a woman inserts inside her vagina over the cervix.

⇨ Blocks the sperm from entering into the uterus; also contains one or more chemical ingredients that kill sperm cells

⇨ **Disadvantage:** The sponge can be inserted incorrectly, or be jarred out of place during intercourse. So it's one of the less effective methods of contraception.

† The contraceptive sponge is prohibited as a contraceptive method for reasons explained previously.

Note: In the following charts, the † indicates the teaching of the Catholic Church

Drug and chemical methods

Chemical contraceptives 82–97%

A chemical contraceptive is a substance—such as a foam, cream, jelly, or vaginal **suppository**—that must be inserted into the woman's vagina before sexual intercourse.

Spermicides for female use:

⇨ Their **spermicidal** ingredients help destroy the sperm in the man's **ejaculated semen**.

⇨ **Disadvantages:**

- Don't always form an effective enough barrier to prevent pregnancy
- Sometimes cause infection and discomfort

† Chemicals are prohibited as a contraceptive method for reasons explained previously.

Contraceptive pill or ring 98–99% (pill)

A contraceptive pill is a prescription medicine a woman takes (usually daily) to prevent conception. Male contraceptive pills are also being developed. A vaginal ring is a donut-shaped device inserted in the vagina; like the pill, it releases hormones that can prevent conception. (Its effectiveness rate as a contraceptive has not yet been solidly established.)

⇨ Affects the hormonal balance in the woman's body to imitate pregnancy

⇨ May prevent an actual pregnancy by stopping ovulation altogether

⇨ Or may prevent the fertilized ovum from implanting in the uterine wall, in which case it is an **abortifacient** rather than a contraceptive

⇨ **Advantage:** among the most effective artificial contraceptives, but not 100%

⇨ **Disadvantage:** depending on the pill, may sometimes have harmful side effects ranging from blood clots and strokes to permanent sterility—especially in women who begin using the pill at an early age and continue using it for two years or more

† The pill is prohibited as a contraceptive method for reasons explained previously.

Contraceptive injections, patches, and implants

Under-skin implant: 99+%

A contraceptive implant is a small device inserted under the skin. A contraceptive patch is worn on top of the skin.

⇨ In women, may prevent ovulation, or make the mucus at the opening of the cervix so thick that sperm can't penetrate into the uterus

⇨ Or may act as an abortifacient by preventing the fertilized ovum from implanting in the uterine wall

⇨ In men, disables or destroys sperm for a certain period of time

⇨ **Advantage:** may be effective for a few months to a year or more

⇨ **Possible disadvantage:** Research is continuing on possible harmful side effects, such as an increased risk of cancer.

† These methods are prohibited as contraceptives for reasons explained previously.

---

contraceptive drugs and chemicals
foams, creams, jellies, vaginal suppositories, pills, vaccines, injections, implants

suppositories
small medicated substances that melt when placed inside a body cavity

spermicidal
sperm-killing

ejaculated
discharged; discharged semen through the opening of the male's penis

semen
the fluid containing the male's reproductive cells (sperm/spermatozoa) that is discharged from the male's penis at sexual climax

abortifacient
agent that destroys the embryo or fetus, causing it to abort; morally speaking, those means deliberately intended to destroy the human embryo or fetus in order to terminate a pregnancy

Other methods
Sterilization   99+%

sterilization
process of making incapable of reproduction

contraceptive sterilization
process of deliberately making incapable of reproduction

Surgical or other body-altering means of making a man or woman unable to conceive or procreate a child by the usual means of sexual intercourse. The ability to have sexual intercourse and the man's ability to ejaculate are usually not affected.

† Catholic teaching opposes **contraceptive sterilization** as immoral. Many people, however, become sterile unintentionally—for instance, from the scar tissue of sexually transmissible diseases they've had in the past. Such unintended indirect sterilization, or that which results from accident, illness, or surgery needed for health reasons is not immoral.

Contraceptive surgeries
Hysterectomy: 100%   Tubal ligation (female): 99+%   Vasectomy (male): 99+%

Tubal ligation(female) "tying the tubes"—severs or closes the tubes leading from a woman's ovaries (where the ovum/eggs are stored) to her uterus. The procedure is done by abdominal surgery or entry through the vagina.

⇨ Prevents conception by keeping the male's sperm from fertilizing the female's ovum, or "egg"

Vasectomy (male) is a surgical procedure that cuts or closes off the tubes leading from the man's testicles (where sperm are manufactured and stored) to his penis. The procedure is done through a small incision near the **testicles**. It does not affect sexual arousal nor the ability to achieve an **erection** and ejaculate semen normally.

Hysterectomy (female) removes the uterus and/or ovaries, rendering conception impossible

Oophorectomy (female) removes the ovaries, rendering conception impossible

testicles
pair of ball-shaped male sex glands that hang in a pouch of skin from the groin and in which sperm are manufactured and stored until ejaculated

erection
a response to sexual arousal in which the male's penis becomes rigid and enlarged

⇨ **Advantage/disadvantage:** Some tubal ligations and vasectomies have been reversed. But since reversal isn't always successful, doctors consider both procedures permanent.

⇨ **Disadvantage:** Depending on how the procedures are performed, in rare instances severed tubes have rejoined on their own. That is why tubal ligation and vasectomy have not always been 100% effective in preventing conception.

† All deliberate sterilization for contraceptive reasons is prohibited as morally unacceptable because it defeats one of the main purposes of the sexual union between spouses—the ability to procreate.

Unintended indirect sterilization that results from accidents, illness, or surgery needed for health reasons is not immoral.

Withdrawal   0% – not at all effective

⇨ Withdrawal is an attempt by a man to prevent conception by withdrawing his penis from contact with the woman before he ejaculates his semen near or inside of her vagina.

⇨ **Disadvantage:** The failure rate of withdrawal is extremely high—so high that it's generally not listed as a "birth control" method! Here's why: During heightened sexual arousal—and before ejaculation—the man's penis discharges a few drops of semen. That response is uncontrollable—the man can't keep it from happening. Those few initial drops of semen contain enough sperm to populate a city! Sperm are living, mobile organisms. They can move on their own through the vagina and into the uterus to fertilize an ovum. (That's also why pregnancy occasionally occurs from genital intimacy where the penis contacts only the woman's outer genital area without penetrating her vagina.)

† Catholic teaching opposes deliberately using withdrawal to cancel rather than complete the procreative purpose of sexual intercourse. (Ejaculating outside the vagina is not morally wrong when it is unintentional.)

Project

Select one of the artificial means of birth regulation and find out what its possible negative side effects are. (Possible resources to consult: a pharmacist, current pharmaceutical manual, pharmacy's computerized printout, or reliable healthcare website.) Write a one-page paper reporting your findings and citing your sources. Share them with the class.

For discussion

1. What surprised you the most about the information regarding birth control methods?

2. In addition to the Church's moral reasons for opposing them, what personal reservations or objections would you have about using the barrier, chemical, drug, or sterilization methods to plan your future family? Be specific.

Review

Describe how each of the following works, its success or failure rate—and why it succeeds or fails, the side effects, and so on:

• Barrier methods of birth control

• Chemical methods of birth control

• Birth control drugs

• Sterilization surgeries

Upholding life

The Church wishes to stand for life, promote life, and defend life.
FAITHFUL TO EACH OTHER FOREVER, 39.

Abstinence and continence

abstinence

the practice of not engaging in sexual intercourse

continence

exercising self-restraint periodically by not engaging in sexual intercourse

Catholic teaching holds that unmarried couples should practice complete **abstinence** from sexual intercourse. But it would be unreasonably burdensome to expect all married couples to practice such abstinence whenever they choose to not conceive a child. Spouses' sexual union, as Catholic teaching points out, is an integral part of marriage. It's one of the many important ways married couples express their love.

Continence involves prudently practicing self-restraint at certain times in marriage, such as when it would be unwise to risk pregnancy. All married couples must occasionally practice continence—when one partner is ill or very tired, for instance. The wife may be too uncomfortable to have sex during her menstrual period, a time when her body is also more vulnerable to genital infections. Couples also need to practice continence in connection with natural family planning. They do that by not having sexual intercourse during the few days in each fertility cycle when the woman is most fertile and likely to become pregnant. They then have greater sexual freedom at the other times, not having to worry that pregnancy will occur. They also don't have to remember to take a pill or use other contraceptive devices each time they make love.

All couples must practice sexual continence sometimes—for health reasons, for family planning, or for other reasons. Rather than feeling deprived at those times, couples can find other intimate ways to share their love creatively. They should look for different ways to grow closer—through touch, emotional tenderness, and new insights into how and why they love each other. Couples can find that periodically practicing sexual continence adds more meaning to their relationship and enhances their sex life.

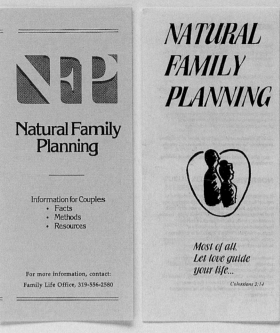

fertility awareness
general term for one or more methods of achieving or preventing contraception that focus on when during the menstrual cycle a woman ovulates and may become pregnant

Fertility awareness methods 75–99%+

⇨ Help prevent (or achieve) pregnancy by telling when during the menstrual cycle the woman ovulates and can become pregnant; also helps determine the best time to become pregnant.

- A woman's menstrual cycle begins on the first day of her menstrual period. It ends on the day before her next period.

- Women generally ovulate at some point in the middle of the menstrual cycle.

- Fertility awareness methods used to avoid pregnancy require practicing abstinence or using other contraceptive means during the fertile period.

† Catholic teaching strongly approves of fertility awareness methods, but disapproves of using artificial contraception in combination with fertility awareness

The calendar rhythm method almost 0%

⇨ Keeps track of the length of past menstrual cycles to try to determine when ovulation will most likely occur in the present menstrual cycle

- Requires total abstinence during and around the time ovulation is expected

⇨ Reasons for this method's high failure rate:

— A woman can ovulate at any time during the menstrual cycle (including during her menstrual period). Stress and anxiety, illness, or even climate change can cause ovulation "out of schedule."

— The length of menstrual periods often varies—especially in teenagers.

Far more accurate natural family planning methods are available, some of which use calendar rhythm's information along with more reliable techniques. Used by itself, calendar rhythm is considered obsolete. Those who rely on it are called "parents"!

⇨ **Side effects:** None that are physically harmful

† Not viewed as morally objectionable, but couples are urged to use more reliable methods of natural family planning either instead of or along with this method

The sympto-thermal method of natural family planning
Effectiveness with training: 99%+   Without training: 75%+

⇨ Uses signs such as body temperature and vaginal mucus changes to quite accurately pinpoint the time of approaching ovulation

- During ovulation, the woman's basal temperature is slightly different on awakening in the morning compared to other times during her cycle. Before getting out of bed each morning, she uses a special, more sensitive thermometer to detect the slight variations in her body temperature.

- The woman consistently checks the nature of her vaginal mucus. (A few days before ovulation, it becomes clearer, instead of a cloudy white. It also takes on a slippery, stretchy consistency—somewhat like that of an egg white.)

- Other body changes help verify the basal temperature readings and vaginal mucus signs: A certain type of pain may accompany ovulation. A detectable change may occur at that time in the woman's cervix or in breast tenderness. Calendar-based calculations compare her bodily signs with when ovulation usually occurs in her fertility cycle.

- Once the temperature or mucus symptoms occur, couples not wanting to conceive must refrain from having sex until four days after the mucus symptoms are gone. Couples trying to conceive a child make sure to have sex during that time.

⇨ **Disadvantages:**

- The necessary symptoms can't be detected accurately during menstruation or certain illnesses, or when vaginal infections are present

- Some amount of continence, abstaining from sexual intercourse, is required.

- While a woman is breast feeding, she may go for months with no basal temperature rise or menstrual bleeding. She can't know when she'll again become fertile. Couples therefore follow this guideline: "When in doubt—abstain."

⇨ **Advantage:** This is the single most effective, healthy, and risk-free method of birth control—but only if it is used properly! Couples need to be instructed in how to use it correctly.

† The Catholic Church encourages couples to use this method, because

- It's effective, healthy, and without harmful physical side effects.

- It treats sex as an expression of love in which the whole person is involved and in control.

- Couples become more aware of and knowledgeable about each other's bodies.

- Intimate communication grows between spouses, and they are encouraged to develop creative ways of expressing their affection non-genitally.

- It fosters a self-discipline and cooperation that enhances the couple's happiness and helps them cope with life's challenges.[6]

For discussion

1. What is abstinence? To whom does it pertain?

2. What is continence? How do you think occasional continence could enhance a married couple's relationship?

3. In your words explain the benefits Catholic teaching gives for natural family planning. What's your response to each of them?

4. How do the natural family planning methods compare in safety, effectiveness, and so on, with the other methods of contraception discussed previously? Explain, being specific.

Abortion

The types of abortion

Spontaneous abortion

⇨ A medical term for the body's expelling, or miscarrying, a fetus at a certain stage of development

⇨ Is due to natural, unintentional causes

† There is no moral guilt involved.

Therapeutic abortion

⇨ Medical procedures directly intended to save the mother's life or eliminate a very serious threat to her health

⇨ Unintentionally and indirectly results in the death of the embryo or fetus

† Catholic teaching holds that, for reasons like that, therapeutic abortion may be morally justifiable and permissible.

Deliberate abortion

⇨ Any procedure that intentionally destroys or results in the destruction of a human embryo or fetus—by chemicals, surgical instruments, or other means

† Catholic teaching condemns all deliberate abortion as the destruction of human life. If there is full knowledge and full consent of the will, abortion is a grave sin. Even supporters of legal abortion strongly oppose viewing it as a means of birth control. Besides abortion's obvious harm to the fetus, there are other moral implications associated with the physical risks and possible psychological effects.

† God is always willing to forgive. Catholic teaching opposes deliberate abortion and actively speaks out against it. At the same time the Church condemns those who use violence, especially murder, to oppose abortion. It also encourages the Church community's many efforts to reach out compassionately to those who've had, helped others obtain, or assisted in such an abortion.

The burden of guilt for such people . . . can be overwhelming. We must proclaim that our God is always "rich in mercy" with a heart open to anyone who repents and wishes to move forward.[7]

Catholic teaching further reminds all of us that we should never be so crushed by our moral failings that we give up hope.

"[H]uman life is **sacred**," and "from its very **inception** it reveals the **creating** hand of God."

POPE JOHN XXIII

Abortifacients

⇨ Are means deliberately intended to destroy the human embryo or fetus in order to end a pregnancy

⇨ Include any pill, device, or drug intended to destroy the fertilized ovum—either directly, or by preventing it from implanting in the uterus

The difference between how contraceptives and abortifacients work:

• Contraceptives prevent conception (the fertilizing of the ovum by the sperm).

• Abortifacients cause the destruction of the fertilized ovum.

† Catholic teaching states, as many other people believe, that human life begins at the moment of conception. It strongly opposes using any abortifacient that is directly intended to end a pregnancy. It also notes that some so-called "contraceptives" may actually be and function as abortifacients.

Intrauterine device (IUD)   98%

⇨ A small device placed in the woman's uterus that prevents fertilization from occurring or that keeps the fertilized ovum from implanting in the uterine wall

⇨ Presumably causes a chronic inflammation of the uterine lining

⇨ If it doesn't prevent conception from occurring, it is an abortifacient rather than a contraceptive. Otherwise it is a contraceptive.

Side effects and disadvantages:

• Not completely effective

• Must be obtained from and inserted by a doctor or health professional

• Has caused life-threatening side effects in many women; many doctors won't insert them

• Has caused serious complications if pregnancy or birth occurs with the IUD still in place

• Insertion or removal of an IUD can be very painful

† The Catholic Church condemns the use of any abortifacient.

Abortion pill   92%

⇨ Induces the woman's body to expel, or abort, the embryo or fetus

⇨ When used after conception or implanting of the fertilized ovum has occurred, it is an abortifacient rather than a contraceptive.

Side effects:

Appears to have few side effects for the woman, but the long-term health risks haven't yet been thoroughly assessed.

† The Catholic Church condemns the use of any abortifacient.

Choose **life** so that you and your **descendents** may live. . . .

DUETERONOMY 30:19

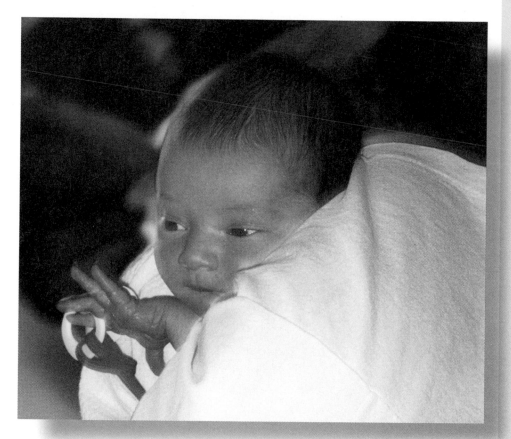

A significant percentage of the pregnancies in our society each year are unintended. The number of abortions performed is staggering and appalling. Even aside from the moral and health implications, you have seen how no form of contraception is completely effective. For single persons, practicing complete abstinence **is** 100 percent effective in preventing pregnancy (and avoiding sexually transmitted diseases). For married persons, being trained in and faithfully practicing the Church-approved sympto-thermal method of natural family planning is a highly effective way to plan for the children they can care for and love.

> . . . *responsible fatherhood and motherhood directly concern the moment in which a man and a woman, uniting themselves in one flesh, can become parents. This is a moment of special value both for their inter-personal relationship and for their service to life. . . . With regard to the question of lawful birth regulation, the [Church] at the present time must take on the task of instilling conviction and offering practical help to those who wish to live out their parenthood in a truly responsible way . . . [for example through] a more precise knowledge of the rhythms of women's fertility.*

> "The Family, Gift and Commitment, Hope for Humanity: Themes for the New Evangelization and the Family in Preparation for the Second World Meeting with the Holy Father," Rio de Janeiro (4–5 October 1997).

To prevent unwanted pregnancies and to plan for their families, men and women need to be better informed about family planning and take their moral responsibilities far more seriously. There is no greater blessing in life than the precious gift of a child. Let us all resolve to help ensure that that gift is properly prepared for and treasured.

Journal

Complete this statement: My view of upholding life by being sexually responsible includes . . .

For discussion

1. What is your response to the attitude that, "If the woman gets pregnant, she can always get an abortion"? Explain.

2. How can you tell whether a birth control method is an abortifacient or a contraceptive?

3. What is your response to the statement that people should be better informed about family planning?

4. How do you think men and women can take their moral responsibilities more seriously in preventing unwanted pregnancies?

Review

1. What are sexual abstinence and continence? Which does Catholic teaching say unmarried persons should practice? Married couples?

2. What is fertility awareness? How does Catholic teaching view it as a means of natural family planning? Explain.

3. Explain how the sympto-thermal NFP method of family planning works. Then explain why calendar rhythm is not at all effective.

4. Explain the different types of abortion and the moral differences between each according to Catholic teaching.

5. What is the difference between a contraceptive and an abortifacient?

6. Explain how each of the artificial or surgical methods of birth control works, their side effects, and whether they're contraceptive or abortifacient.

7. How does the Catholic Church say we are to respond to those who've had, helped others obtain, or assisted in an abortion? Explain why that is the Church community's view.

How would you handle it?

Read the following, and then respond to the questions.

A teenager's view

Whether a couple is mature enough to handle having kids or not depends on the hassles they can take—mentally as well as physically and financially. Surprisingly enough, couples today get married with the idea that their relationship will bloom without difficulty and that they will have a beautiful baby and live happily ever after. Nice try! In fact, one out of every three couples divorce because of relationship problems. When you multiply the problems by one small son or daughter, then you're in deep water. People just don't realize how important it is to sit down with your partner and discuss this matter seriously. Don't let up for one second. Get every little detail on how both of you will handle it—both before you get married and after you get married and before you have kids.

For discussion

1. Do you think this teenager is being realistic, idealistic, and/or pessimistic about planning a family? Explain.

2. With which of the teenager's points do you agree or disagree? Explain.

3. Explain what details about having and raising children you think should be discussed and agreed on in advance by each of the following.

- Couples considering marriage
- The married couple thinking about having their first child
- The married couple thinking about having another child
- Couples deciding what method(s) they'll use to plan their family

Infertility and reproductive technologies

For many couples, spacing children is not a problem. Being unable to have a child is the problem.

Infertility

infertility
the inability to reproduce in the usual, natural way

Infertility is an anguishing major problem for many couples. At least one in twelve couples want but are unable to conceive a child. Infertility can be due to physical factors in the man, the woman, or both. Scar tissue left behind by sexually transmissible diseases commonly results in infertility. Although infertile couples sometimes feel like God is punishing them because they can't conceive children of their own, that is not true! God does not cause our troubles, but helps us rise above them. Jesus' life and death showed us that God is kind and saving—redeeming, not cruel and vengeful!

It's no good for spouses to blame each other for their difficulty in conceiving a child. Catholic teaching compassionately encourages infertile couples to remain strong in their married love. It reminds them that they can share their love in many other ways that bring them and others happiness.

> When **sorrow** so works as to broaden our **life**, . . . then it works toward **salvation** and toward **life**.
>
> HENRY WARD BEECHER

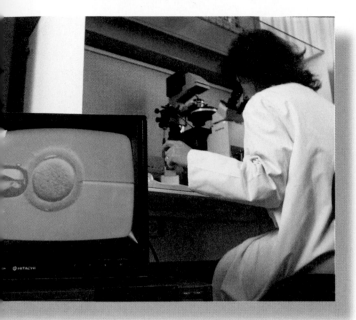

In the Vatican II document, "The Church in the Modern World," the bishops wrote: *Marriage to be sure is not instituted solely for procreation. Rather its very nature as an unbreakable compact between persons, and the welfare of the children [when that is possible], both demand that the mutual love of the spouses, too, be embodied in a rightly ordered manner, that it grow and ripen. Therefore, marriage persists as a whole manner and communion of life, and maintains its value and indissolubility, even when offspring are lacking—despite, rather often, the very intense desire of the couple.*[8]

There are many ways, besides being biological parents, that couples can be fulfilled by sharing themselves and their love with others.

It must not be forgotten . . . that, even when procreation is not possible, conjugal life does not for this reason lose its value. Physical sterility, in fact, can be for spouses the occasion for other important services to the life of the human person, for example, adoption, various forms of educational work, and assistance to other families and to poor or handicapped children. . . .

The social contribution of the family has an original character of its own, one that should be given greater recognition and more decisive encouragement . . . . note must be taken of the ever greater importance in our society of hospitality in all its forms, from opening the door of one's home, and still more of one's heart, to the pleas of one's brothers and sisters, to concrete efforts to ensure that every family has its own home as the natural environment that preserves it and makes it grow. In a special way the Christian family is called upon to listen to the apostle's recommendation. "Practice hospitality" [Rom. 12:13], and therefore, imitating Christ's example and sharing in his love, welcome the brother or sister in need: "Whoever gives to one of these little ones even a cup of cold water because he is a disciple, truly, I say to you, he shall not lose his reward" [Mt. 10:42].[9]

Project

Research one or more of the available reproductive or genetic technologies. Write a two-page paper reporting on your findings and evaluating them in view of Catholic teaching on reproductive technologies. Add your own responses.

For discussion

1. A married friend of yours has just been found to be infertile from having contracted sexually transmitted diseases before marriage. Your friend confides in you about the infertility problem and the feeling that it's probably God's punishment for having been promiscuous. How would you respond, and why?

2. If you and your spouse both wanted children very much but seemed unable to conceive a child—

   • What would you try to do—and not do—to keep your marriage strong?

   • How else would you seek to share your love with others as a couple?

Catholic guidelines on reproductive technologies

genetic
having to do with hereditary characteristics

Scientific research is making startling progress in helping infertile couples have children. Newer techniques help the fertilized ovum implant successfully in the uterus. They may also eliminate certain tragic **genetic** diseases and defects. But many of these techniques and technologies raise profoundly troubling moral questions.

When is and isn't it moral to alter a human embryo's genetic makeup? What types of genetic intervention are morally positive and permissible? Which ones violate human life and dignity? How far should couples go—or be allowed to go—in conceiving a child? Society and our legal system are hotly debating these dilemmas. New technologies are constantly being developed to deal with infertility and genetic problems. Catholics should therefore consult their doctor about their medical alternatives and those in the diocese qualified to help them evaluate the morality of their options. Catholic teaching also offers the guidelines referenced on the next page. Reflect on them carefully—much is at stake for individuals and humanity![10]

> A **child** is not something *owed* to one, but is a *gift*.
>
> CATECHISM OF THE CATHOLIC CHURCH, #2378

Catholic Guidelines

1. Wanting to have a child is a natural human desire, but it is not an absolute right.

2. There is a difference between what couples can do and what they may or should do in order to conceive or obtain a child.

3. Couples may use normal fertility therapy to assist them in having a child. All artificial means to help couples procreate a child must protect the child's life and dignity. They must help conception occur through, rather than outside of, the natural acts of sexual intimacy in marriage which of themselves are designed to result in the procreation of children.

4. Every baby, no matter how conceived, is to be welcomed and cherished as a gift from God.

5. Conception achieves its fullest human meaning when it results from a loving act of sexual union between married partners. This respects both the spouses' and the child's human integrity and dignity. It also protects the connection between love and life, the twin purposes of sexual lovemaking in marriage.

6. Using a third person's body or cells in order to conceive a child goes against the integrity of the spouses and their marriage relationship, their responsibility as parents, and every child's right to be given life within the context of marriage.

7. Artificial techniques that separate conception from the married couple's act of sexual union cut the bond between love and life that should be part of human procreation. That's true even if a process uses the couple's own sperm and ovum, as in artificial insemination or in vitro fertilization.

8. Everyone should support infertile couples who feel like failures, or not good enough, unfulfilled, empty, or incomplete because they're unable to conceive a child. Scientific research on infertility should honor the basic welfare of children and the dignity and meaning of the couple's marriage.

9. Genetic interventions on humans should be aimed at remedying defects and abnormalities. Otherwise they violate the person's "right to bodily integrity" and go against the family's welfare.

Journal entry

Complete this statement: The limits I think should be put on the use of reproductive technologies are . . .

The **family** . . . is truly "the sanctuary of **life**. . . . "

POPE JOHN PAUL II

For discussion

1. Explain whether Catholic teaching views each of the following to be morally positive and permissible, or morally unacceptable:

   • Techniques that aid in conception

   • Human gene-altering technologies

2. What possible problems do you think human gene-altering technologies pose—personally, socially, legally, and morally?

3. How far do you think couples should and shouldn't go in seeking help to conceive a child? In altering their child's genetic makeup before birth?

4. What is your response to each of Catholic teaching's guidelines about reproductive technologies?

5. In view of the Catholic guidelines, what is your response to using artificial insemination to help a woman conceive a child with sperm that had been harvested from her dead husband?

Review

1. What is infertility? What does Catholic teaching say about infertile couples?

2. What is genetic intervention? According to Catholic teaching, when might it be permissible? When is it wrong?

3. Within what context should conception occur?

4. What does Catholic teaching say about family planning, infertility, and reproductive technologies?

5. How can and should couples plan their families responsibly?

Designing kids

In view of Catholic teaching's guidelines on reproductive technologies, explain what you think about each of these ideas:

1. Determining a child's hair, eye, or skin color before birth
2. Letting couples use artificial means to select their child's gender before birth
3. Altering a human embryo's genetic structure so that the child won't be born physically or mentally disabled
4. Surrogate parenthood
5. In vitro fertilization (conception, for example, in a test tube) when it is separate from a married couple's act of sexual intercourse
6. Artificial insemination with a third-party donor's sperm or ovum
7. Artificial insemination with the husband's sperm when it is separate from a married couple's act of sexual intercourse
8. Increasing the chances of having a child of a particular gender by using non-artificial techniques (such as scheduling intercourse to coincide with a certain point in the woman's fertility cycle)
9. A college student's selling his sperm to a sperm bank in order to help pay his tuition expenses
10. A woman's becoming a surrogate mother so that her infertile married sister can have her own biological child

surrogate mother
a woman who bears the child that is conceived from the sperm and ovum of another couple

In summary

Catholic teaching strongly supports responsible family planning and natural family planning methods. Decisions about giving life and about family planning should be made by the properly formed and informed consciences of both spouses. They should seek God's strength in making and living their decisions. Raising children requires sacrifice, maturity, and many adjustments. Family life should be supported and human life reverenced and nourished, particularly where most fragile. Catholic teaching considers artificial means of regulating birth as unnatural barriers to procreation, and strictly prohibits abortifacients that destroy the human embryo in order to end a pregnancy. Church-approved natural family planning (NFP) relies on being aware of the woman's fertility signs and practicing continence during fertile times.

Being infertile makes a couple's marriage no less valuable. They can and should share their love creatively in other ways. Having a child is a natural, but not an absolute, right. The Church supports normal fertility therapies that properly protect life and dignity while helping conception to occur through marital sexual intercourse. It opposes conceiving a child in ways that violate marital unity, spouses' dignity, parents' vocation, or the child's right to be conceived and born within and from marriage. Genetic interventions in human persons should be done only to correct defects and abnormalities. However conceived, every infant is to be accepted and valued as a gift from God.

Key concepts

abortion: spontaneous, therapeutic, or deliberate; abortifacients

abstinence, continence

alcoholism and drug abuse

calendar rhythm

conception

family planning methods: barrier, drug and chemical, natural, fertility awareness; sympto-thermal (NFP)

fertility (menstrual) cycle, infertility

good faith conscience

menstruation

ovary, ovulation, ovum

personal culpability

properly formed conscience

reproductive technologies— Catholic guidelines on

sperm

sterilization: tubal ligation, vasectomy, hyserectomy, oophorectomy

withdrawl

Endnotes

1. *Faithful to Each Other Forever: A Catholic Handbook of Pastoral Help for Marriage Preparation*, Bishops' Committee for Pastoral Research and Practices, National Conference of Catholic Bishops, United States Catholic Conference, Inc. (Washington, DC: USCC Office of Publishing and Promotion Services, 1989), 40.
2. Excerpted from "When It's Too Late to Change Your Mind, Will You Be Sorry You Didn't Have a Child?" by Nancy Eberle; *Glamour Magazine*.
3. Paraphrased from *Faithful to Each Other Forever*, 40.
4. See *Faithful to Each Other Forever*, 40–41.
5. *Faithful to Each Other Forever*, 41.
6. Based on *Faithful to Each Other Forever*, 42 and 44.
7. *Faithful to Each Other Forever*, 133.
8. "Pastoral Constitution on the Church in the Modern World," article 50
9. *On the Family*, Apostolic Exhortation of Pope John Paul II (15 December 1981), #s 14 and 44.
10. Guidelines 1–8 are paraphrased from *Human Sexuality: A Catholic Perspective for Education and Lifelong Learning*.

CHAPTER 14

THE CHALLENGES OF FAMILY LIFE

SCRIPTURE

. . . teach us to count our days
that we may gain a wise heart.

PSALM 90:12

PRAYER

O God, we are one with you. You have made us one with you.

You have taught us that if we are open to one another, you dwell in us.

Help us to preserve this openness and to fight for it with all our hearts. . . .

O God, in accepting one another wholeheartedly, fully, completely, we accept you,

and we thank you, and we adore you, and we love you with our whole being,

because . . . our spirit is rooted in your spirit.

Fill us then with love, and let us be bound together with love as we go our diverse ways,

united in this one spirit which makes you present in the world. . . .

Love has overcome. Love is victorious.

THOMAS MERTON

Troubled families

What's the difference between family troubles and a troubled family? How would you and your family deal with alcoholism, drug abuse, child or spouse abuse, serious illness, or unemployment? How can you best deal with ordinary family problems? When should you seek outside family counseling? In these next sections, we'll discuss some of these important questions about family life.

Every family must deal with problems—even serious ones—from time to time. When their bond of loving community is intact, family members can help each other cope with their individual and common difficulties. But sometimes a family becomes unable to function as a loving community. It becomes a troubled, unhealthy environment.

Where do troubled families come from? Troubled individuals often bring unresolved inner conflicts from their family background into their marriage. That negatively affects their marriage and helps create another troubled family. No family is perfect. But a breakdown of healthy family life is more than an isolated family problem. It's the sign of a troubled family whose members need outside help and support. Children and teenagers in troubled families have a right to seek and receive that help. Those who don't obtain it will probably end up raising their own troubled families.

In this section we'll discuss some of the major family problems that tear so many families apart. Because families hold our society together, the problems that threaten families concern us all.

Three key signs of a troubled family

1. Family members won't admit, even to each other, that they have problems. (Everybody in the family knows there's a serious problem. Outsiders often know or sense it, although they don't say anything about it.)

2. Individual family members focus their energy on coping with the family problems. Parents try to live their lives through their children—or they impose their problems on their children. Family members aren't allowed the freedom to express their true thoughts, feelings, and wants. Individual needs and problems go unmet and unresolved.

3. Family members don't communicate effectively with each other. They often argue with and blame one another or feel obliged to be perfect and agree with each other. Emotional or physical abuse is common in troubled families.

For discussion

1. How would you describe the difference between family troubles and a troubled family?

2. How could you tell if your family were troubled enough that you should seek outside help?

3. When do family problems become social problems that concern us all? What do you think we can do about those problems as individuals and as a society?

Domestic abuse

Abuse in a family seems to be a contradiction in terms. Shouldn't the family be the one place where everyone is safe from abuse of all kinds? Sadly, that is not the case.

Child abuse

child abuse
serious mistreatment of a child—physically, emotionally, psychologically, or spiritually

In our society alone, a child dies from abuse every four hours. **Child abuse** is the leading cause of death in children under age five. Teenagers are often also victims of abuse. Over a million children run away from home each year—many attempting to escape from abusive parents. Half of the children who are severely battered die after being returned to their parents' custody. We must try harder to protect children's health and safety. Too often a parent's custody rights still take precedence over the child's basic wellbeing.

The emotional abuse some parents inflict on their children can be just as cruel as the physical abuse. Words can hit as hard as a fist. Emotional or physical abuse of a child leaves psychological scars that often lead to serious problems when that child is a teenager or an adult.

Why is there so much abuse of helpless, innocent children? Some abusive parents themselves suffer from severe emotional or mental illness. Some children are abused because they are unwanted or are resented as a burden. Probably most abused children are victims of well-intentioned parents who don't know how to control their emotions and tempers when frustrated or angry. Many parents who abuse

their children were themselves abused as children. They handle their children the only way they know—in the same abusive manner their parents responded to them.

Those reasons are no excuse! Catholic teaching makes it clear that nothing excuses intentionally abusing a child. Raising children is difficult and extremely frustrating at times. There are things parents can do to make sure they don't abuse their children.

Five ways to avoid abusing your kids

- Learn to handle your problems and frustrations maturely—not in ways that harm others—especially your children.
- Never discipline while you're angry or upset! If necessary, remove the child to safety. Then wait until you calm down before disciplining the child.
- Take time out. Before you lose control and harm your kids, take the time to calm down. Pray for God's help, and then think rationally about the best way to handle the situation.
- Seek help immediately if you feel strongly tempted to respond to your child abusively. (Call a parent hotline, where someone will understand and advise you.)
- Never, ever shake a baby! The baby's brain will bounce back and forth against the inside of its skull, causing injury or death.

Refusing to admit or do anything about the problem, or blaming it all on the children, results in misery, permanent damage, and often death for the child.

The mother's dilemma

Read the letter a desperate mother wrote asking for a newspaper columnist's advice. Then respond to the questions. When you've finished, your instructor will tell you what the columnist advised.

As I write this, my little boy is lying on the couch under an icebag. His face is as red as a beet and the skin is broken in a few places where I slapped him. When he gets stubborn or has a tantrum, I become so angry I can't control myself. I have hit him like this several times before, even though I know it is wrong.

I read your column every day and have read your advice to look in the phone book under child abuse. I looked and there is nothing in this town. (Population 3,000)

When this boy was born four years ago, I really didn't want him, but my husband was crazy about children and insisted that I have a family. I have always hated this kid, which is a terrible thing for a mother to admit, but it is true. His daddy died two years ago and, thank God, I don't have any others. I am a rotten mother.

Many times I have thought of giving up the boy for adoption. I know there are many couples who would love to have him. He is very smart for his age and dar-ling-looking. But just when I get ready to put my hand on the phone, I tell myself, "Don't do it. Keep him and learn to be a good mother."

I live 1,500 miles away from my own family. I have a good job and work 50 hours a week. Please tell me what to do.

TELLING IT LIKE IT IS . . . ; "ANN LANDERS" COLUMN.[1]

For discussion

1. Why did this mother decide to have this child? Was this a wise choice?

2. Why do you think she continues to abuse her child even though she knows it's wrong?

3. What do you think the chances are that she could "learn to be a good mother"? Where else might she turn for help in her local area?

4. Do you think this mother really hates her child? Explain fully.

5. Given her feelings and attitudes, what obligation does the mother have toward her son? Why do you think she doesn't place her child for adoption?

6. If you were a neighbor and realized what was happening in this situation, how would you try to help the child? How would you try to help the mother?

7. What would you advise the mother to do in this situation? Why?

Incest

Incest is the sexual abuse of children by their parents, siblings, or other relatives. Thousands of children in our society are victims of incest but are afraid to tell anyone about it. Many individuals repress their childhood memories of incest, not allowing them to surface until they're settled in their adult lives and feel less vulnerable.

Incest is an especially vicious form of child abuse. It distorts the wholesome unconditional love a child is entitled to receive. It betrays the loving trust children place in those who should care for them. Sexually abused children and teenagers feel guilty or suicidal. But they're the victims and survivors of incest—not the guilty party! Yet they're often told by the abuser that they are the ones who have caused this to happen. And the abuser further ensures their silence by saying that the incestuous behavior is "our secret" and a way to "show how much we love each other." Incest is always a crime, not a manifestation of love. It shouldn't remain a secret!

Even when individuals are aware that a spouse or family member is sexually abusing their children, they often don't seek help. They fear disrupting the marriage or family, losing financial support, or being embarrassed socially. They too

are often victims—of the other spouse's abuse. Or they're so dependent on the abusive spouse that their own responses enable the abuse to continue.

Believing that family counseling is better than jailing the abuser, many agencies can help while respecting the family's privacy. Nobody should have to tolerate abusive treatment. Incest survivors who receive professional help are more likely to heal. If you ever have good reason to suspect that incest is a problem for you or your family, seek professional help immediately. You and your family will gain far more than you might lose.

Every word and deed of a parent is a fiber woven into the character of a child, which ultimately determines how that child fits into the fabric of society.

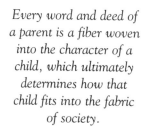

For discussion

1. Why do you think children and teenagers are so often abused? How might you help prevent child abuse?

2. Why do you think mothers are more likely than fathers to physically abuse their children?

3. What is the difference between properly disciplining a child and abusing the child in the name of discipline? Explain and give examples.

4. List ten nonphysical ways parents can abuse their children.

5. What would you do if you seriously suspected someone outside your family of sexually or otherwise abusing a child? If you suspected that was occurring in your family? Explain.

Spouse abuse

Spouse abuse is another family tragedy. A significant percent of all the murders every year in our society are committed by the victim's spouse. Many—probably most—spouse abuse incidents are never reported to authorities. Of those that are, it is estimated that at least thirty million wives a year are battered by their husbands! At least five million of those reported abuse incidents involve serious physical injuries.

Spousal abuse is epidemic. That has prompted one U.S. Surgeon General to say that wives are safer on the streets than in their own homes! Abuse by a husband increases greatly when the wife is pregnant and most vulnerable. Many men are abused by the women they love but are embarrassed to reveal it. Thus, few such incidents are reported.

Many persons (mostly wives) are raped and otherwise sexually abused by their spouses. Catholic teaching strongly condemns such brutal treatment.[2] No one should be used or abused for another's sexual pleasure. Even in marriage, sex is a free, mutual gift. It's not a right to which a spouse is absolutely entitled. Sexual intimacy should deepen spouses' faithful love. No one should ever be forced, pressured, or otherwise used sexually.

Why does abuse occur? Why do people put up with the abuse (as most do) until they, too, sometimes resort to violence? Spouse abuse occurs because people don't learn to handle their conflicts and frustrations maturely and constructively. Deep psychological problems, often rooted in childhood, underlie an abusive personality. Most spouses who report having been abused return to tolerate more abuse. They feel there's no alternative. Some feel completely dependent on the abusive spouse for financial support—especially when children are involved.

Due to the negative messages and abuse they've received, abused spouses often lack self-esteem. They believe they deserve the abuse and shouldn't expect better. Despite the brutal abuse, they don't want to leave the spouse they love, and they fear they won't find anyone better. Many are afraid of what the abusive spouse might do to them if they leave, seek a divorce, or report the abuser.

Spouses raised in a violent family background think it's normal that one spouse hit or beat the other. Spouses commonly think husbands have a right or a duty to "slap their wives around and show them who's boss." A century ago, men were allowed to beat their wives only with an object no thicker than their thumb—hence the expression "rule of thumb"!

No one has the right to abuse another person! Everyone has a right to break free from abusive treatment! When spouse abuse occurs—even just once, both persons need help at once. The abuser always promises tearfully, "I love you, and I'm so sorry. I promise I'll never, ever do that to you again." But once abuse happens, it almost always happens again—despite all the tearful promises.

To so lack emotional control that one becomes violent is extremely serious. Getting help the first time abuse occurs can save a relationship, a marriage, and possibly a life. Postponing counseling to avoid embarrassment or give the person "one more 'last chance'" only makes things worse. Those threatened if they go for help have even more to fear if they don't.

For discussion

1. How do you think you'd respond if your spouse began physically abusing you? Explain.
2. Why do you think spouse abuse is so common?
3. Why do you think women are most often the ones physically abused?
4. In view of Jesus' command to forgive the repentant sinner, why shouldn't spouses continue to forgive and live with an abusive spouse? Explain fully!

Alcoholism and drug abuse

One out of every five people in our society lives with an alcoholic. Alcoholism results in family quarrels, divorce, and violence. (At least one-fourth of all murders in our society each year occur within families, often because of alcoholism or other addictions.) A family member who's addicted to alcohol or other drugs is ill and needs help. The family also needs help to cope with the situation. Based on the statistics, several of your classmates live with a serious family drug problem. Perhaps you do, too.

What's the best way to recover from alcoholism? Experts recommend seeking hospital treatment and then joining a group like Alcoholics Anonymous. Certain medications may help in conjunction with the AA program—which has the best record for helping alcoholics recover. Their excellent programs—Al-Anon and Alateen—offer free help for the alcoholic's family in coping with the problem.

There are many—though not enough—good counseling centers for those with drug-related problems. Don't hesitate to contact them if you or a family member has a drinking or other drug-related problem. You may save a life (or lives). You'll certainly help preserve your mental and emotional balance. Never just suffer in silence. Help is available!

Project

Research one of these topics:
- Dysfunctional families
- Child abuse, spouse abuse, or incest in the family
- How the abuse of alcohol or other drugs affects family life

Write a two-page paper reporting your findings and your responses. Include a list of the resources available in your local area to help families coping with the problem.

Journal entry

Complete this statement:
If I found myself in a troubled family, I would seek help by . . .

For discussion

1. What is your reaction to the widespread alcoholism and other drug abuse in our society? Explain.

2. How would you advise a friend who has an alcoholic parent who refuses to admit the problem and seek treatment?

3. How can you let other teenagers know that they needn't suffer in silence through the nightmare of a family drug addiction?

4. Why do family members have a greater right to seek help than the addictive persons in the family have to keep their addictive, abusive behavior a secret from outsiders?

Review

1. What signs can indicate a troubled family that needs outside help? What results when that help isn't obtained?

2. What does Catholic teaching say about child abuse?

3. How can parents avoid becoming abusive toward their children?

4. Why is incest so wrong, and how can individuals and families best respond to it?

5. What does Catholic teaching say about abuse and the attitudes that encourage it?

6. How common is spousal abuse, and why does it occur?

7. How can individuals and families best respond to problems of spouse abuse, alcoholism, and other drug abuse within the family?

All happy families **resemble** one **another**, every **unhappy** family is unhappy in its **own** way.

LES TOLSTOY

I always thought. . .

Read one mother's true account of emotional abuse and its harmful impact. Then respond to the questions.

I always thought child abuse was what the other people were doing, the drunk who beat his kids, or the gal who tortured the child for wetting the bed. After some self-searching honesty I have found that I was a child abuser in my own way, only the children and I were much luckier than many.

I now firmly believe that child abuse is not only physical, but emotional and spiritual as well. It is a result of being unaware of what our actions are saying.

I can remember when I was about five, the little girl next door had the measles and Dad told me to stay away from her. A day or so later she was in her yard and came up to the fence, so I went over to talk to her (probably thinking the fence would keep the measles, whatever that was, away. Who really knows what a child is thinking?) I was really shocked when my dad grabbed me and beat me until I had welts all over my lower body and legs. The only thing I learned from that was fear and resentment. I spent most of my growing-up years as far away from him as I could. I had a love-hate relationship with him from then on. When I would say the Lord's Prayer—"Our Father"—I'd think to myself, "If God's like this, then who needs Him?" . . .

I remember I had something my aunt wanted to borrow and [I] didn't want to loan it to her. My mother threw such a guilt trip at me, etc., that I felt like a terrible person for a long time after that. The lesson I learned was that if someone treats you nice, you can't say no to them, unless a moral issue was involved.

All these things add up to sick attitudes. They were the only ones I knew and the ones I raised our children with. The sad thing is that they in turn will raise their children with the same attitudes, unless they are willing to find a better way . . . .

To me, child abuse is putting my wants before their needs, putting my friends before them, not listening to their feelings . . . playing God by making decisions for them that they need to make for themselves (even if it's not what I would want for them), and throwing guilt at them. . . .

I've been guilty of pushing the children around when they weren't doing what I wanted them to do (and wondered why they reacted so terribly), smacking a baby on the bottom to get it to lie still when I was changing it.

I realize now there is a better way, and all my actions were saying was that my emotions were controlling me, and the children were paying for it. That's called living with emotions for intelligence. Groups like Parents Anonymous, Emotions Anonymous, and Al-Anon meet all over the country to help us find the answers to overcome the sick attitudes we were taught.

Thanks to these groups I have learned that I don't need to feel guilty over the past, as I did the best I could with the tools I had. I didn't have to change me, just my attitudes. I've found the real me and I'm okay, and I've learned the difference between controlling and guiding. I've also learned that sharing this with you will help me, and I still need all the help I can get.[3]

For discussion

1. How does the mother describe her beliefs about what child abuse is?

2. What examples did she give from her own experience of emotional child abuse? Of physical abuse? Of spiritual abuse?

3. What does she mean by "living with emotions for intelligence"? How did doing that result in her abusing her children?

4. What lessons finally helped the mother overcome the unhealthy attitudes she'd been taught?

Family troubles

QUOTED FROM TELEVISION ADVERTISEMENTS FOR MUTUAL OF NEW YORK INSURANCE COMPANY.

Single, split, and step-parenting

A great number of teenagers in our society have spent part of their childhood living with only one parent. Perhaps you or your friends have, too. As a result of joint-custody divorce arrangements, many children live part-time with each parent. Step-parents often share the responsibility of raising the children. Each situation poses special problems. Catholic teaching recognizes how difficult it is and how many sacrifices are required of those in a one-parent family. So does this widow with three children, who has this advice for single parents:

> I'd say there are several things you have to do when you are left to raise your children alone. First, try to stop feeling sorry for yourself and that things are hopeless. Realize that the children need you more now than ever before. Make yourself get out and talk with people. Ask for their advice and help. And get help from any agency you can find. Most of all, don't give up . . . seek help during the initial period of adjustment and difficulty, develop a plan, consider the children, and, most of all, take good care of yourself.[4]

Divorce and remarriage change the family structure. Parents and children often have trouble coping. Children's loyalties and time become divided. When adults who already each have children marry, unique opportunities and tensions arise in the blended family. Being a step-parent has its own problems. Step-parents must now care for children who often resent their assuming parental authority.

One step-parent who married a man with teenage children offers these helpful insights:

- As a step-parent, understand that you can never replace the child's parent, and you shouldn't try.
- Talk with the children about the feelings and difficulties of being, and having, a step-parent.
- Earn and expect the children's respect and obedience, but don't expect their love. Love is a gift that must be given freely. It requires a relationship built with time and trust.

For discussion

1. What problems might you face in the following situations, and how would you (or do you) handle them?
   - If you had to live with a step-parent when your parent remarried
   - If your family became "blended" when your parent remarried and your stepparent's children came to live with you
   - If you had to move to live with your step-parent and children
   - If your children lived with you and visited the other parent every weekend
   - If your children were split between living part-time with you and part-time with their other parent

2. If you suddenly became a single parent, how would you feel about it? How would you try to cope with the situation?

3. What is your response to the advice the widowed mother with three children gave about the following?
   - Adjusting to becoming a single parent
   - Being a step-parent

Caring for elderly relatives

As more people live longer, caring for an elderly relative is becoming a common family concern. Couples first of all have an obligation to each other and their children: "For this reason a man shall leave his father and mother and be joined to his wife, and the two shall become one flesh." (Mark 10:7–8a). Sometimes families simply can't cope financially or emotionally with another family member. An elderly relative may require constant attention and care or be very hard to live with, creating constant household tension.

Helpless elderly persons are increasingly being abandoned on hospital doorsteps by adult children who feel they can't care for them. That is tragic and unnecessary. When caring for an elderly relative becomes too burdensome, help is available somewhere. Many public and private agencies can help.

incontinent
unable to control a bodily function, such as urination

A main reason adults feel they can't care for an aging parent is that the elderly person has become **incontinent**. A cure is often available for incontinence. Sometimes it's as simple as practicing exercises that strengthen the muscles controlling urination. Such problems should be discussed with the family doctor before they're presumed to be incurable or untreatable.

An elderly parent's illnesses and disabilities can be hard for a caregiver to deal with alone. It's especially important to seek outside support and assistance. All family members should pitch in and do what they can to help. Community programs and volunteer groups can offer practical help and guidance. Adults often feel guilty when it's necessary to place their elderly relative in a care facility. But when caring for an elderly relative is too great a hardship on a family, or when it's in the elderly person's best interests, that may be the best alternative.

Whenever possible, families should open their hearts and homes to their elderly relatives. Living with, giving to, and learning from them can be an enriching experience. How to best care for elderly family members is a question families must consider with love, compassion, generosity, and common sense. Social, employment, and government policies should be designed to help—not hinder—families caring for an elderly relative.

Do not **cast** me off
in the time of old **age**;
do not **forsake** me
when my strength is **spent**.

PSALM 71:9

Project

Choose one.

1. Research the topic of caring for elderly parents or the problem of abuse of the elderly. Write a two-page paper on your findings and your responses. Include a list of resources available in your area to help families caring for elderly members.

2. Research the topic of Alzheimer's disease. Include resources available in your area for helping persons with Alzheimer's and their families and caregivers. Write a two-page paper reporting your findings and your responses.

Report on the results of your project and on your responses to what you learned.

For discussion

1. In each of the following situations, what problems would you face, and how would you handle them?

   • If an elderly relative came to live with your family

   • If you realized that you must put a parent in a care facility

   • If you were an elderly person faced with the choice of entering a care facility or living with one of your children

   • If you had to care for an relative with Alzheimer's disease

   What would you (or do you) find hardest about each situation? Explain.

2. When should and shouldn't couples invite an elderly parent to live with their family? What things would you consider in that situation? Explain.

3. How and where can families get help and support to deal with elderly persons' illnesses and disabilities?

4. Are there elderly relatives in your family who need special care? How do you or would you try to help care for such an individual? Explain.

Serious illness or job loss

Serious illness and unemployment cause hardship and stress for many families. Both situations, especially when prolonged, can change the family's attitudes and lifestyle. Many families do not have great savings to fall back on, so illness and unemployment can result in huge debts, repossessed cars, and even lost homes. The emotional trauma of either situation, especially for the ill person, the primary caregiver, and the unemployed person, can lead to stresses that damage and even destroy individuals, marriages, and other family relationships. And the physical suffering of a serious illness is far more than many people ever expect to experience. When the illness is terminal, the entire fabric of the family changes forever.

Even the most difficult trial can become a path to greater love. At times of illness and unemployment most of all, good communication and loving support are essential. If family members can discuss their feelings together and rally to each other's support, such crises can bring them closer rather than fracturing their family. For this to happen, however, most people have to learn to rely on others for strength and comfort, rather than stoically trying to "go it alone" "with a stiff upper lip."

In true married love it is not so much that two hearts walk side by side through life. Rather the two hearts form one heart. That is why death is not the separation of two hearts, but rather the tearing apart of one heart. It is this that makes the bitterness of grief.

FULTON J. SHEEN

Journal entry

Complete these statements:

1. The most difficult problem my family has had to cope with was . . .

2. How my family copes with problems has affected who I am by . . .

For discussion

1. In each of the following situations, what problems would you face? How would you handle them if you had to cope with each of them? What would you probably find hardest about each of those situations? Explain.

   • Caring for a family member with a serious, long-term illness

   • Unemployment—yours or your spouse's—when you needed the lost financial support to pay the basic bills

2. In addition to those mentioned already, what other major problems do families face? Explain.

3. If faced with a prolonged, difficult family situation, how would you try (or have you tried) to see that it unites rather than damages your family?

Review

1. What does Catholic teaching say about children and one-parent families? What special problems do one-parent families face, and what are positive ways of handling those?

2. What special difficulties can caring for an elderly relative pose? How can family members and others best address those concerns?

3. How can individuals and couples try to see that their family troubles unite rather than damage their family?

Building family unity

Real families don't just happen because people live for years in the same household. Like good marriages, they're built and require work on each member's part. Consider these suggestions, for instance:

To build a happy family

- Work to make your marriage happy.

- Promote an environment where the members understand and respect each other.

- Recognize each family member as a distinct individual. Admire each other's unique gifts and qualities.

- Don't put each other down or compare each other with someone else.

- Treat each family member with respect and as equally important.

- Practice the good communication skills essential to a happy family life.

- Share and work through things together, as a family.

- Share your faith, and pray together. That will help your family realize what it means to be a loving community. It will help the family grow closer during times of joy and sorrow, accomplishment and difficulty.

If we truly want **peace** in the world, let us begin by **loving** one another in our own **families**.

MOTHER TERESA

Before you leave home and launch out on your own, try practicing as many of these suggestions as possible within your family now. Tell family members what you love and admire about them. Make time to enjoy their company and show them your affection. Try to settle or seek help with unresolved problems you may have with a family member. Then you won't carry those problems into your future relationships as burdens or harmful emotional baggage.

The family is the fundamental unit of society and of the Church community. It's where we all learn and develop who we are, and learn how to relate to God and other people. As Catholic teaching says:

The Christian family is an image of God and a sign of the Church. It is the community wherein Christ is most powerfully preached, where Christians first hear the name of God, first learn to pray, and first express their faith. In the words and example of their believing parents, children come to know what faith is and how to live it, what life is and how to honor it. . . .

The family . . . is much more than the sum of its problems. It is . . . the place where the person occurs, where life begins, where fidelity and hope are nourished, where human love reaches its most intense expression.[5]

For discussion

1. Describe five things you think are necessary for healthy, happy family life. Explain your reasons.

2. What problems result when people think theirs will be the perfect family?

3. What happens in human society when families flunk their main responsibilities?

4. What steps do you think we should take as a society to help families become healthier, happier, more loving communities?

5. How do you think you'd need to temper your ideals with the realities of family living before having a family of your own in the future? How else can you prepare yourself to build a happy family of your own some day? Explain.

6. What is meant by saying that the family is the school of deeper humanity?

Review

1. What are good ways families can grow in love and togetherness, and build family unity? Give examples.

2. Why is the family the fundamental unit of society and of the Church community? How is the Christian family an image of God and a sign of the Church?

My advice to parents

Read the advice one teenager says he'd give parents. Then respond to the questions.

I think that, before a family has children, they should make sure that they can afford it and are ready for it emotionally. As far as raising the children goes, I don't think a couple should run out and get a whole different set of books every time the child disobeys. They should look into it carefully and decide exactly how they're going to raise their kids, and then follow through with it. If you keep on switching tactics, then the kids are just likely to become confused, and they won't know what you want them to do.

Love and communication are the most important things in raising kids. If you teach the child to be honest from the earliest age, you'll have fewer problems later. But don't let kids think they can get away with everything just because they're telling the truth. And when you discipline them, make sure they understand why, and don't knock them for stating their own opinions if they think you're being unfair. I think that kids should be heard. So often parents can't stand being challenged by their kids. Often children aren't really challenging them—they just don't understand. And did you ever stop to think that maybe you were being a bit too hard?

I think a child should also have full participation in the family. Making decisions and all. Like if you should move or not. Most parents don't even think of asking their kids beforehand what they think about family decisions. Even little children often come up with some very good points.

For discussion

1. What main points does the teenager make? What is your response to each of them? Explain.

2. What do you think you'd find the most difficult things about being a parent? What do you think would be most rewarding about it? Explain.

3. Which of your qualities and gifts might help you make a good parent? Which of your characteristics would need the most work before you'd be ready to be a good parent?

4. In what ways would you hope to raise your children like you've been raised? How would you want to raise your own children differently than you've been raised? Explain.

In summary

Family members should seek professional help in dealing with serious family problems such as alcoholism or other drug abuse. There is never an excuse for child abuse and neglect or for spouse abuse. Rape and sexual abuse are always wrong. Abuse victims have a right to seek freedom from being treated abusively. Single parenting, step-parenting, caring for an aging relative also pose special challenges for family members. Coping with such situations requires unselfish patience, understanding, good communication, and outside support when needed. Families' problems concern us all, since the family is the basic unit of society and of the Church—as a reflection, sign, and source of Christian faith. Building a unified, happy family requires deliberate effort.

Key concepts

building family unity

caring for elderly relatives

child abuse

domestic abuse

family problems

incest

rape

responsible parenthood

sexual abuse

single parenting, split parenting, step-parenting

spouse abuse

troubled families

Endnotes

1. Permission granted by Ann Landers and Creators Syndicate.

2. See *Human Sexuality: A Catholic Perspective for Education and Lifelong Learning,* United States Catholic Conference (Washington, DC: USCC, 1991), 67.

3. From "But the emotional damage lingers on," by Pat Gardner, *Rocky Mountain News,* Denver, CO (20 June 1979): 61.

4. "One-Parent Families," U.S. Dept. of HEW, Office of Human Development, Publication No. (OHD) 74-44 (Washington, DC: Office of Child Development Children's Bureau, 1974), 2.

5. *Human Life in Our Day: Pastoral Letter of the U.S. Bishops* (Washington, DC: USCC, 1968), #s 89 and 88.

GLOSSARY

abortifacient—agent that destroys the embryo or fetus by or and causing it to abort; morally speaking, those means deliberately intended to destroy the human embryo or fetus in order to terminate a pregnancy

abstinence—the practice of not engaging in sexual intercourse

active listening—giving feedback to indicate that a message has been understood

AIDS—Acquired Immune Deficiency Syndrome, an often fatal illness

anoint—touch or smear with oil as a sign of sacred office or service

archdiocese—district under an archbishop's jurisdiction, usually larger than a diocese

banns—public announcements of an upcoming marriage in church or in the church bulletin

bishop—the third of the Holy Orders; a priest who is given the mission to guide a diocese and the power to ordain

body language—posture, gestures, facial expressions, and other bodily mannerisms that communicate something about the person or the person's attitude

career—long-term employment in one occupation or line of work; profession

chalice—cup which contains the Eucharistic wine used at Mass; special cup used for religious ritiuals.

chastely—in a morally good manner; exercising self-control so that sexuality serves love and fosters personal development

cherish—to hold dear, to love tenderly, to protect and take care of.

child abuse—serious mistreatment of a child—physically, emotionally, psychologically, or spiritually

chrism—oil specially blessed for use in celebrating the sacraments

clergy—those specially ordained to preside at religious rites

clerics—ordained men: deacons, priests, bishops

cohabiting—living together as a couple without being married

commitment—dedication to fulfilling a responsibility or obligation; a promise or pledge to do something

communication blockers—techniques that interfere with communication

communication breakthroughs—techniques that enhance verbal and non-verbal communication

communication skills—specific techniques or abilities that enable people to communicate effectively

communication style—a particular way of sharing information and feelings with another person based on the personality and experiences of the one sharing and the position of the one shared with

compassion—feeling sorry about another's difficulties or suffering

and desiring to help the person; profound sympathy

conceiving—the joining of the male sperm and female egg/ovum, which Catholic teaching views as the moment a new human begins to exist

continence—exercising self-restraint periodically by not engaging in sexual intercourse

contraceptive—treatment or device that prevents the sperm and ovum from uniting (conception)

contraceptive drugs and chemicals— foams, creams, jellies, vaginal suppositories, pills, vaccines, injections, implants

contraceptive sterilization—process of deliberately making incapable of reproduction

copulation—uniting or linking together sexually

Council of Trent—major council of the Catholic Church which tried to clarify Church doctrine and establish needed reforms in Catholic liturgy and ethical conduct

counsels—recommendations or advice

culpability—being deserving of blame

deacon—a person ordained to perform certain priestly functions

deaconesses—women deacons who assisted the apostles and their successors in the early Church in service

declaration of nullity—an annulment declaration, a Church judgment that the marriage was not a true and unbreakable spiritual bond

diaconate—state of being a deacon

diocesan (secular) priest—a priest who represents and works directly for the local bishop

diocese—territory under a bishop's jurisdiction

discernment—the process of using one's reasoning ability and God's guidance, Scripture, Church teaching, and the wisdom of others to make wise and good choices

dispensation—official permission to be released from a certain obligation

divorce—a legal declaration that a marriage has ended

dowry—money, goods, or animals paid to compensate for the loss of the woman's labor from her father's household

egalitarian—characterized by equal rights for every person

ejaculated—discharged; discharged semen through the opening of the male's penis

embryo—a human life in the earliest stage of development in the uterus, generally the first three months

empathy—ability to share in another's thoughts or feelings so that one understands the person better

erection—a response to sexual arousal in which the male's penis becomes rigid and enlarged

evangelical—pertaining to the good news of the gospel

evangelical counsels—vows made in imitation of Jesus as a means of living his gospel message

extramarital—outside of one's marriage

fertility—fruitfulness, ability to produce offspring

fertility awareness—general term for one or more methods of achieving or preventing contraception that focus on when during the menstrual cycle a woman ovulates and may become pregnant

fetus—a human life in the later stages of development in the uterus, generally from the fourth month until birth

fidelity—loyalty and devotion, being true to

gay—homosexual; pertaining to one or more homosexual males

gender identity—one's state or self-awareness of being male or female

genetic—having to do with hereditary characteristics

genitally—having to do with the reproductive and sexual areas of the body

gestation—pregnancy, in humans—the period of about nine months from conception until birth

grace of Holy Orders—God's special spiritual assistance that helps deacons, priests, and bishops fulfill their ministry

gratification—the satisfying of needs or desires, especially for what is pleasurable

hermit—one who lives a solitary life, usually for spiritual or religious reasons

heterosexual—of or characterized by a primary or exclusive sexual attraction toward those of the other gender

homosexual persons—individuals whose primary or exclusive sexual attraction is toward persons of the same gender

incontinent—unable to control a boldily function, such as urination

individuality—total combination of qualities that make each person unique

infanticide—murdering of a baby

infatuation—strong but superficial emotional attraction to someone

infertility—the inability to reproduce in the usual, natural way

integrity—honesty and sincerity

inter-Church—between different Christian denominations

inter-faith—between different faith traditions, such as Jewish and Christian

intimacy—deep loving closeness that usually involves sharing what is most personal and private

Jewish-Christian tradition—The heritage of beliefs and practices dating from the ancient Hebrews to modern-day Jews and Christians

job—work done for pay or other compensation

labor—the muscle contractions that help the body push the fetus through the birth canal during the birth process

laity—persons who are not members of the clergy (such as priests or ministers)

lawfully—according to officially required procedure

lay—pertaining to laypersons (*laity*)—those who are not ordained

layperson—a member of the Church community who is not an ordained priestly minister

lesbian—pertaining to female homosexuality or to one or more homosexual females

lifestyle—the way a person's life is structured according to that person's values and priorities

love at first sight—strong initial romantic or sexual attraction to someone

marital act—sexual intercourse

Martin Luther—sixteenth century Catholic monk from Germany who preached religious reform and whose writings and efforts helped establish the Lutheran Church

materialism—attitude or philosophy about the value and purpose of physical objects

miscarriage—the premature expelling from the mother's womb, due to natural causes, of an embryo or fetus that has died or is not developed enough to survive

narcissism—self-centeredness; conceit; a distorted or exaggerated sense of one's own importance, abilities, appearance, and such

natural family planning (NFP)—a birth control and family planning method that relies on being aware of the time(s) during a woman's fertility cycle that she ovulates and is fertile

occupation—the type of work one does for a living

order priest—an ordained man who takes vows in a religious community

ovary—one of two inner female organs that produce reproductive cells (eggs/ova)

ovulation—release of the female ovum from the ovary, making it available for joining with the male sperm (conception)

ovum—female cell which, when fertilized, produces offspring

pastoral ministry—work of overseeing and serving the local church community

Pauline privilege—the dissolution of a marriage between two unbaptized persons if one of the partners is later baptized and the unbaptized partner refused to live in peace with the baptized partner; the baptized person is then free to marry another baptized person in the Catholic Church

permanent deacons—in the Catholic Church, those ordained to perform certain ministries, while not moving on to ordination to the priesthood; in other Churches, one who assists the minister

persona—the external aspects of one's personality (whether genuine or faked) that one shows to others

prenatal care—healthcare for a woman prior to the birth of her child

priests—those specially appointed or anointed to perform religious rites and to help people communicate with and grow closer to God

procreation—participation in God's act of creating a new human

promiscuous—sexually loose, engaging in sex casually or with many different partners

Protestant Reformation—the movement during and following the sixteenth century in which various persons led attempts at Church reform and established distinct Christian denominations

religious—a layperson, priest, or deacon who is consecrated to serve Jesus and the Catholic Church community by living a sacred commitment to poverty, celibacy, and obedience

rectories—dwellings usually next to the church, where parish priests live

religious congregation, religious community—group of persons, formally recognized by the Catholic Church, who share a vowed communal form of religious life based on the evangelical counsels and their founder's guidelines

religious freedom—the freedom to believe and practice one's religious convictions

repressed—restrained or held back so as to prevent the natural expression of; kept from consciously focusing on painful ideas by forcing them into the unconscious part of one's mind

Romulus—legendry founder and ruler of ancient Rome

sacrament—a visible sign initiated by Jesus' words and actions in order to bring God's presence (grace) to people in a special way

Sacrament of Holy Orders—the Catholic rites by which deacons, priests, and bishops are ordained to perform the rituals and functions of their ministry

self-confidence—belief in one's abilities; self-assurance

self-discipline—using one's will power to control one's thoughts, desires, emotions, or behavior; self-restraint

self-esteem—belief in oneself; self-respect

semen—the fluid containing the male's reproductive cells (sperm/spermatozoa) that is discharged from the male's penis at sexual climax

seminary—a program of study in preparation for ordination to the priesthood; also the campus or institution in which the study takes place

Seneca—Roman philospher and statesperson of about A.D. 65

sexual fidelity—being sexually intimate only with one's spouse

sexual intercourse—the joining of the sex organs of a man and a woman, whereby one partner's sexual organ penetrates the other person's; the act of sexual union in which the male's penis penetrates the female's vagina, and by which new human life is conceived

sexual orientation—one's deeply rooted inborn tendency or ability to experience sexual attraction mainly or exclusively toward those of a certain gender or of both genders

sign of peace—prayerful greeting, such as a kiss or hand shake, shared at Christian services

sperm—male cell (spermatozoon) or cells (spermatozoa) which, when united with the female reproductive cell (ovum), results in the conception of offspring; sometimes incorrectly used as a synonym for the fluid (semen) ejaculated by the male that contains the sperm

sterilization—process of making incapable of reproduction

surrogate mother—a woman who bears the child that is conceived from the sperm and ovum of another couple

terminal—final, extreme

testicles—pair of ball-shaped male sex glands that hang in a pouch of skin from the groin and in which sperm are manufactured and stored until ejaculated

vagina—the canal or passageway between the uterus and the vulva; receives the penis during intercourse; the birth canal

validly—truly, genuinely

vestment—special ceremonial clothing worn when presiding at religious services

virginity—the state of not having had sexual intercourse, or of being "untouched" or "unused"

vow—make a sacred promise to God

vow of poverty—vow taken by religious to live simply, unattached to material things

vulnerable—unprotected, exposed to being hurt

INDEX